SOAR TO SUCCESS

THE READING INTERVENTION PROGRAM

Teacher's Manual

Level 8

Senior Author
J. David Cooper

Authors
Irene Boschken
Janet McWilliams
Lynne Pistochini

HOUGHTON MIFFLIN   BOSTON • MORRIS PLAINS, NJ

California • Colorado • Georgia • Illinois • New Jersey • Texas

Program Reviewers

Mildred F. Bell, Bensley Elementary, Richmond, Virginia; **Susan Bloodworth**, Irmo Middle School, Columbia, South Carolina; **Bob Crain**, Hawkins Middle School, Belfair, Washington; **Candy Cunningham**, Little Lake City School District, Santa Fe Springs, California; **Jessica P. Donaldson**, Pleasant Valley Middle School, Saylorsburg, Pennsylvania; **Sharon K. Gray**, Chapin Middle School, Chapin, South Carolina; **Terri Krueger,** Instructional Services Center, Grandview School District, Grandview, Missouri; **Christie Lehmann**, Schwartzkoff Elementary, Sterling Heights, Michigan; **Donna Nash-Bayley**, Monroe Middle School, Rochester, New York; **Maryann Ouellette**, Literacy Coach, Boston, Massachusetts; **Lori Roelse**, Sheboygan Area School District, Sheboygan, Wisconsin; **Eileen F. Sabbatino**, Gunning Bedford Middle School, Delaware City, Delaware

Printed in the U.S.A.

ISBN: 0-618-06066-9

123456789-B-06 05 04 03 02 01 00

SOAR TO SUCCESS

Contents

Section 1
Overview

• •

 Using the Video
The Staff Development Video corresponds to sections of this manual. View Section 1 of the Staff Development Video at this time.

or

Read this section; then view Section 1. Be sure to use the Viewing Guide (pages R82–R85) as you view the video.

SOAR TO SUCCESS is a small-group reading intervention program. It uses authentic literature, reciprocal teaching, and graphic organizers in fast-paced lessons to help intermediate-grade and middle school students accelerate their reading growth. The program is designed to be used with a group of five to seven students.

This manual will help you to understand and deliver the instruction in this program effectively; to manage the program so that it fits the staffing and classroom organization in your school; and to select, assess, and release students appropriately.

The Staff Development Video, designed to be used interactively with this manual, is an important tool to help teachers learn to use *SOAR TO SUCCESS*. (See Staff Development and Coaching on page T24.)

What Is Reading Intervention?

A reading intervention program is one that prevents or stops reading failure. *SOAR TO SUCCESS* is a reading intervention program for students in grades three and above. As with successful early intervention programs, it is to be used in conjunction with a regular program of classroom instruction in reading and language arts.

Purpose and Goals of *SOAR TO SUCCESS*

SOAR TO SUCCESS was designed to accelerate learning for students who are experiencing difficulty in reading in grades three through eight.

It has been developed to help teachers accomplish two major goals:

1. Accelerate students' reading abilities as quickly as possible.
2. Help students learn to apply and use the comprehension and decoding strategies and skills of an effective reader as they read across the curriculum.

Development of *SOAR TO SUCCESS*

SOAR TO SUCCESS is based on existing reading research and was scientifically tested in classrooms throughout the country.

Research Based The table on page T5 summarizes the key areas of research that were used in developing the *SOAR TO SUCCESS* instructional plan and lessons. This table shows that *SOAR TO SUCCESS* was designed on the basis of existing quality research.

The Research Base for the *SOAR TO SUCCESS* Instructional Model

Area of Research Considered	Major Findings and References

Characteristics of Students Reading Below Level in Grades 3–8	• There is a significant number of students in Grade 3 and above who are reading below level (Mullis, Campbell, & Farstrup, 1993).
	• Students reading below level in Grade 3 and above share some common characteristics (Palincsar & Brown, 1984a; Pikulski, 1991):
	
	    Many know isolated decoding skills but ***do not apply*** them in reading.
	    Many often call words correctly but do not comprehend what they read.
	
	• A major need for students reading below level in Grade 3 and above is to help them accelerate their reading as quickly as possible (Allington & Walmsley, 1995).
	• Students reading below level in Grades 6–8 often develop an attitude or motivation problem (Pikulski, 1991).

Lessons Learned from Early Intervention Programs	• Successful early intervention lessons are systematic, fast-paced, and structured (Hiebert & Taylor, 1994; Pikulski, 1994). A similar pattern of instruction would seem appropriate for upper-grade intervention. • Early intervention programs focus heavily on building fluency (Clay, 1985; Pikulski, 1994). Students in Grade 3 and above need instruction that helps them ***apply decoding skills*** and ***develop effective strategies for constructing meaning.*** • The individual, tutorial intervention programs have been successful (Hiebert & Taylor, 1994; Swartz & Klein, 1997). However, they are very costly and are unable to serve a large number of students (Hiebert, 1994). Therefore, a small-group model would seem more appropriate for upper-grade intervention. • Successful early intervention programs utilize natural-language literature that has been sequenced from simple to complex (Peterson, 1991). Upper-grade students need narrative and expository literature that is motivating and sequenced in difficulty to move them from easy reading to grade-level reading. This is a part of the scaffolded support required to increase below-level readers' reading abilities. • Successful early intervention programs have a strong, on-going staff development program (Hiebert & Taylor, 1994; Pikulski, 1994).
Instructional Strategies	• Graphic organizers have been effective in helping students visually construct meaning (Heimlich & Pittelman, 1986; Pehrsson & Robinson, 1985). • Reciprocal teaching uses four strategies—SUMMARIZE, CLARIFY, QUESTION, and PREDICT. The teacher and students take turns being teacher, modeling the use of the strategies as the text is read in chunks. The research on reciprocal teaching has demonstrated that students using it make large gains in a short amount of time (Carter, 1997; Palincsar, 1984; Palincsar & Brown, 1984a; 1984b; 1986; Rosenshine & Meister, 1994). • Effective instruction in reading needs to be scaffolded, allowing students to gradually increase their abilities to work independently (Collins, Brown, & Newman, 1986; Pearson, 1984; 1985). • The goal of intervention instruction must be to accelerate reading as quickly as possible in order to get students reading successfully on-level or higher (Allington & Walmsley, 1995).

Classroom Proven The basis for *SOAR TO SUCCESS* was an extensive two-year national research study, Project SUCCESS, which was carried out in classrooms in thirteen locations throughout the United States. It proved to be effective in accelerating the reading levels of below-level readers in a small amount of instructional time (see Graph 1, below). Graph 2 shows that students in the research group performed significantly better than control-group students on retelling, answering questions, and comprehension after an average of 76 days of instruction. Graph 3 shows that the research group students performed significantly better in oral reading after the same amount of instructional time. A summary of the research report can be found on page R2 of this manual.

Graph 1. Project SUCCESS 1996–97 National Research Study

Percentage of Students Up to Level in the Project SUCCESS Groups and the Control Groups at the Conclusion of the Instructional Time (Average of 76 Days of Instruction)

Legend: ■ Control ■ Project SUCCESS

Sites* (data values by site):
- Site 1: Control 27, Project SUCCESS 50
- Site 2: Control 10, Project SUCCESS 20
- Site 3: Control 0, Project SUCCESS 77
- Site 4: Control 15, Project SUCCESS 48
- Site 6: Control 36, Project SUCCESS 83
- Site 7: Control 25, Project SUCCESS 67
- Site 8: Control 20, Project SUCCESS 75
- Site 9: Control 5, Project SUCCESS 47
- Site 10: Control 23, Project SUCCESS 64
- Site 11: Control 24, Project SUCCESS 44
- Site 12: Control 9, Project SUCCESS 18
- Site 13: Control 25, Project SUCCESS 86

Sites*

* Site 5 data was not usable.

Evidence of Success in Middle Schools

Between the time of the national research study and the time of the publication of Levels 7 and 8 of *SOAR TO SUCCESS*, Level 6 of *SOAR TO SUCCESS* became available. Middle schools using *SOAR TO SUCCESS* reported substantial gains. See the box following the Summary of Research Report on page R9 in the Teacher's Resource File at the back of this Manual.

Growth of Students in the National Research Study Using Project SUCCESS

Graph 2. Project SUCCESS 1996–97 National Research Study

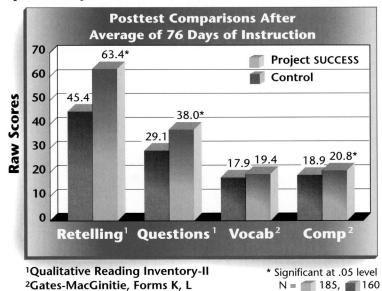

Posttest Comparisons After Average of 76 Days of Instruction

Raw Scores

- Project SUCCESS
- Control

Retelling[1]: 45.4, 63.4*
Questions[1]: 29.1, 38.0*
Vocab[2]: 17.9, 19.4
Comp[2]: 18.9, 20.8*

[1]Qualitative Reading Inventory-II
[2]Gates-MacGinitie, Forms K, L

* Significant at .05 level
N = 185, 160

Graph 2. Research data show that after a short amount of instructional time, low-achieving students make significant gains in retelling, answering questions, and comprehension when they use Project SUCCESS.

Graph 3. Project SUCCESS 1996–97 National Research Study

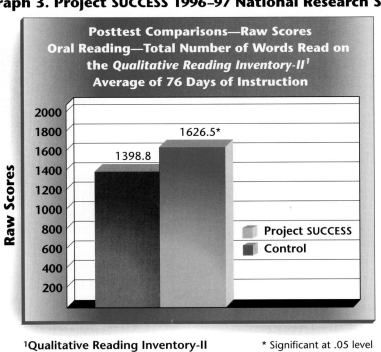

Posttest Comparisons—Raw Scores Oral Reading—Total Number of Words Read on the *Qualitative Reading Inventory-II*[1] Average of 76 Days of Instruction

Raw Scores

1398.8, 1626.5*

- Project SUCCESS
- Control

[1]Qualitative Reading Inventory-II
(Leslie & Caldwell, 1995)

* Significant at .05 level
N = 185, 160

Graph 3. Research-group students performed significantly better in oral reading than the control group after a short amount of instructional time.

Components of

SOAR TO **SUCCESS**

SOAR TO SUCCESS includes the materials you need to accelerate students' reading growth. The program is available in six levels, which are typically used in Grades 3–8. The components of each level are shown on these two pages.

LITERATURE

- A set of 18 authentic books, 7 copies of each, is provided for each level. (See page T12 for complete book list.)

- Books are sequenced from simple to complex as a part of the process of scaffolding instruction. (See pages T10–T11 for Criteria for Selecting and Sequencing Books.)

TEACHER'S MANUAL includes:

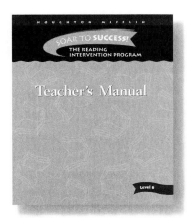

- How to use *SOAR TO SUCCESS* Management and Instruction
- Program Background: Research Base, Classroom Testing, Proven Results
- Assessment: Selection, Placement, and Release
- Lesson Plans for the 18 Trade Books
- Annotated Student Guide and Poster facsimile pages
- Phonics/Decoding Help for Students with Decoding Problems
- Resources and Blackline Masters

STAFF DEVELOPMENT VIDEO

works together with the Teacher's Manual

STUDENT GUIDE includes:

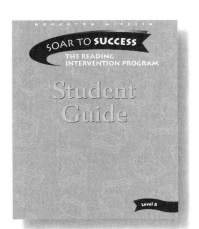

- Graphic Organizers
- Support pages to help students CLARIFY during reading
- Reflecting/Responding pages, including
  —Reflections
  —Homework
- Strategy Prompts
- Reading Logs

POSTERS

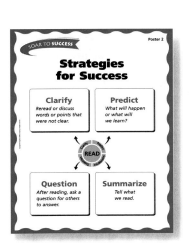

- Strategies
- Graphic Organizers
- Erasable

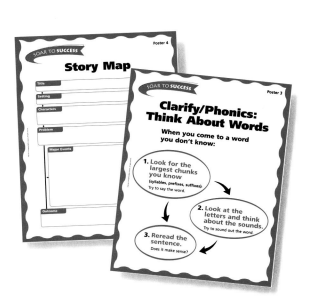

Criteria for Selecting and Sequencing Books

The Lost Expedition
by Barbara Brooks Simons

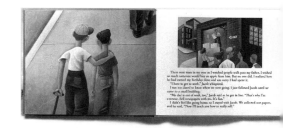

LEVEL 8, BOOK 2

Category I

- Small amount of print per page. (The majority of pages have few sentences.)
- Pictures/illustrations are clear and uncluttered, and directly support the text.
- Text for both fiction and nonfiction is narrative, with a clear, easy-to-follow story line.

Category II

- Still a small amount of print per page, but text may increase to one or two paragraphs on the majority of pages. Short lines of dialogue may increase the amount of text per page.
- Pictures/illustrations still give direct text support; two or three spot vignettes on a page are appropriate.
- Expository nonfiction on highly focused topics with simply stated main ideas and few supporting details. (Often a picture or photograph illustrates each main idea.)
- Short captions (a word, a phrase, or one sentence) may accompany pictures. Simple diagrams with clear labels are appropriate.
- Narrative story lines remain simple.

The Babe and I
by David A. Adler

LEVEL 8, BOOK 4

Category III

- Increased print, with several paragraphs per page. Books themselves become longer.
- Pictures/illustrations are less supportive of text. Captions may increase in length.
- Clear story line, but now multiple characters are appropriate (narrative texts).
- Topics may broaden; main ideas increase in complexity with more supporting details (expository texts).
- Text may contain a secondary element, such as sidebars or speech balloons.
- More inferencing is required by the nature of the text.

Mountains
by Seymour Simon

LEVEL 8, BOOK 7

Category IV

- Text increases to fill the page.

- Story lines become more complex: there may be subplots, mysteries, or multiple problems (narrative texts) that require critical thinking.

- Topics expand to include subtopics, which may be organized by chapter; main ideas increase in complexity and contain more details, requiring readers to organize and analyze information.

- Picture support is less direct; pages may be designed more for visual effect than to help readers with the text. Chapter books may contain spot art, or none at all.

What Are You Figuring Now?
A Story About Benjamin Banneker
by Jeri Ferris

LEVEL 8, BOOK 12

Category V

Note: Level 3 does not include Category V. Books in Category V appear in Levels 4–8.

- Number of chapters increases.

- Size of print decreases as amount of text per page increases.

- Picture support is minimal or nonexistent. Book length may increase to 80–100+ pages.

- Greater inferencing skills are required to follow complex story lines containing multiple characters. Problems, which are multiple, are more sophisticated (narrative texts).

- Increasing amount of new information is presented with more complex text organization. Readers may be required to sift through information and make decisions about how relevant each detail is to the topic at hand.

Sports Lab: How Science Has
Changed Sports
by Robert Sheely

LEVEL 8, BOOK 14

Category VI

- Book may increase in length past 100 pages.

- Size of print may decrease, reflecting the style of on-level literature.

- Pictures as support tools are nonexistent. Photos or illustrations may appear as resources in expository texts.

- Complex story lines require retention of details and application of inferences based on cumulative reading of text. Text may require readers to make judgments about characters and events.

- Expository text organization is increasingly complex and specific. Text may explore issues that arise within certain historical, social or scientific topics. Readers will need to evaluate information to distinguish fact from opinion.

Marisol and Magdalena: The
Sound of Our Sisterhood
by Veronica Chambers

LEVEL 8, BOOK 18

Quality literature for

SOAR TO **SUCCESS**

Level 8

Section 2
The Teaching Plan

The Instructional Plan

Using the Video

The video shows a complete teaching plan in action. View Section 2 of the video before or after reading the Teacher's Manual. Use the Viewing Guide on pages R82–R85 to discuss the instructional plan.

"**T**he instructional plan . . . is fast-paced and uses authentic literature, reciprocal teaching, graphic organizers, and scaffolded support to accelerate students' reading growth."

The instructional plan for *SOAR TO SUCCESS* is a 30-minute to 40-minute daily lesson that is fast-paced and uses authentic literature, reciprocal teaching, graphic organizers, and scaffolded support to accelerate students' reading growth.

The chart on the next page presents the steps of the plan, with a description and rationale for each part. The plan was developed on the basis of quality research and revised in light of findings from the national research study described on pages T4–T7. (For a summary of the research report, see page R2.)

The lesson plans that this Teacher's Manual provides for each book are clearly organized according to the five lesson steps presented in the chart on the following page.

- The Introductory Lesson on pages T69–T74 helps students become familiar with the five steps.

- Lesson plans for Books 1 and 2, on pages 2–31, are presented in detail. Teachers are encouraged to review them for an elaboration of the steps that are presented in the concise lesson-plan charts for the remaining sixteen books.

- Concise lesson-plan charts for Books 3–18 are on pages 32–148.

Teachers and students alike soon become familiar with the uniform, consistent lesson plan, enabling them to focus on accelerating students' reading growth.

The *SOAR TO SUCCESS* Instructional Plan

Component	Description	Rationale
Revisiting (5 minutes)	• Students reread previously read *SOAR TO SUCCESS* books silently to develop fluency. • Teacher works with individual students to take a retelling, conduct an oral reading check, or coach their reading. OR • Teacher and students hold a group conference on independently read books. (See Group Conference, page T17.)	• Builds fluency • Develops comprehension (Samuels, 1979; 1997) • Builds the connection between learning to read and independent reading (Anderson, Wilson, & Fielding, 1988; Center for the Study of Reading, n.d.)
Reviewing (5 minutes)	• Students summarize previous day's reading, using Graphic Organizers. • Students and teacher discuss strategies used and share examples of their use beyond *SOAR TO SUCCESS*.	• Develops comprehension • Keeps students focused on effective comprehension strategies
Rehearsing (5–10 minutes)	• Teacher does a quick text walk, guided preview, cooperative preview, or independent preview of text to be read. (See Previewing, page T18.) • Students may predict, question, or start a K-W-L chart.	• Builds background specifically for the text to be read (Clay, 1979; 1985; 1991) • Sets purpose for reading
Reading and Reciprocal Teaching (10–15 minutes)	• Students silently read a meaningful chunk of text to verify predictions or answer questions. • Following reading, reciprocal teaching is employed, with the students and teacher taking turns assuming the role of the teacher to model these four strategies: –SUMMARIZE –QUESTION –CLARIFY –PREDICT	• Applies strategies and develops comprehension (Pearson, 1984) • Develops students' ability to construct meaning (Palincsar & Brown, 1984a; 1984b; 1985; Palincsar, 1984)
Responding/Reflecting (5 minutes)	• Students do one or more of the following: –Make a written response after discussing their reflections –Complete Graphic Organizers –Reflect on strategies –Discuss and share	• Develops comprehension • Develops use of strategies (Sweet, 1993)

Preparing to Teach the *SOAR TO SUCCESS* Lessons

After you become familiar with the *SOAR TO SUCCESS* program, the following steps will help you prepare for teaching:

Create an Area for SOAR TO SUCCESS Lessons Provide a round, rectangular, or kidney-shaped table where students will work.

- Display these posters and keep them displayed throughout all lessons:
  Poster 1—*SOAR TO SUCCESS* Reading Time
  Poster 2—Strategies for Success
  Poster 3—CLARIFY/PHONICS: Think About Words

- Plan a place to display other posters as they are called for in the lesson plans.

- Keep a supply of pencils and paper in the work area.

Prepare Your Materials Make the following preparations:

- Photocopy and send home the introductory letter, which is discussed on page T67. (The blackline master is on page R92.)

- For each book, photocopy the Home Connection letter (page R93), write the title of the specific book on it, and then photocopy it to send home.

- Strategy Prompts appear in the Student Guide and are referred to in all lesson plans. You may wish to make a set of laminated cards of the individual prompts to keep on the table for students' quick reference during the lessons. You might photocopy each prompt on paper of a different color or paste each onto a card of a different color.

Prepare Yourself to Teach the Lessons Read each book before students read it. Before teaching a lesson, read the lesson plan carefully and think about what your students will need emphasized, particularly in Rehearsing.

Introduce the Program to Students Teach the Introductory Lesson (pages T69–T74), which includes a preview of the materials as well as the lesson steps and the strategies.

Introducing the Student Guide The Introductory Lesson briefly presents the Student Guide. In addition, point out the Strategy Prompts at the back and tell students they will use the prompts when they take turns being the teacher during Reciprocal Teaching for Book 1.

Tell students that they will use the Book Log in the Student Guide to keep a record of books that they read independently outside of *SOAR TO SUCCESS* time. They will bring the log so that they will be ready to discuss the books during Revisiting.

Note—An Option: If you wish to have students remove pages from their Student Guides, provide binders or pocket folders in which students can store their Student Guide pages:
- *Have students decorate the covers.*
- *Store pages in descending order with the current pages (higher numbers) on top.*
- *Include the Book Log.*

Use the Student Guide Pages to Monitor Progress Save all Student Guide pages to use for the students' overall evaluations, portfolios, parent conferences, or administrator conferences.

Teaching the Lessons Effectively

Time Blocks Stick to the time blocks for the instructional plan. Have a clock visible at all times.

Pace Maintain a fast pace. Do not allow students to wander into topics that are tangentially related or unrelated to the topic of the reading. This often happens in the Rehearsing stage of the lesson. If a student gets off the subject, you might say, for example, "That would be interesting to share at our Friday news discussion; right now we need to pay attention to what will help us read this book."

Increasing Student Independence SOAR TO SUCCESS books are organized to foster increased student independence. The lessons at each level are written to scaffold support to help students gain this independence. Within each grade level, the books move across a continuum of modeling that moves from **Strong Teacher Modeling/Support** to **Moderate Teacher Modeling/Support** to **Student Independence**. Achieving the goal of student independence is a critical part of good, fast-paced instruction.

The following guidelines are organized according to specific steps of the lesson plan.

Revisiting

This block of time is used to accomplish several things in the course of a number of lessons. For the teacher, this is a time to do informal assessment. For the student, this is a time to build fluency by rereading familiar books. This is also the time to make the connection between the lessons and independent reading through the Group Conference.

Rereading Have the students select and reread previously read SOAR TO SUCCESS books. They will read them to develop fluency in silent reading, and you can use the opportunity to do informal assessment with one student: to check comprehension by taking a Retelling, or when there is a question about a student's oral reading fluency and decoding strategies, by taking an Oral Reading Check.

In early books, students will reread simply to develop fluency. Beginning with Book 5, in alternate Rereading times, have each student use this opportunity to apply strategies and prepare to model them for the group in the next part of the lesson, Reviewing. Initially you will need to assign each student a strategy to model; starting with Book 12, they can choose their own.

Group Conference Independent reading is an important factor in enabling students to become literate adults. In *SOAR TO SUCCESS* students are encouraged to read independently through the group conference held during Revisiting on alternate days.

The purpose of the group conference is to promote students' responses to and discussion of self-selected books they have read. These activities help students construct meaning, think critically, and monitor their own reading. By being continuously encouraged to think about and react to what they are reading, students develop the metacognitive processes that are important in constructing meaning.

Following are guidelines for holding a group conference:

- Set up a system for having books available for students to read independently.

- Have students bring their Reading Logs and their independent-reading books with them to the *SOAR TO SUCCESS* group.

- Start the group conference by asking the question provided in the lesson plan. Encourage the students to discuss their feelings and understandings about the literature by asking probing questions, such as "Can you tell us more about that?" or "Why did you think that?"

- The question provided is only a starting point; use the students' comments to extend the discussion by encouraging them to connect one book to another and to draw comparisons.

- You may wish to use a very small portion of the conference to share a book you are reading. This helps make you a part of the group rather than simply a facilitator.

Reviewing

This block of time is for students to review strategies, telling how they used them in other class reading, in social studies, science, and math. This discussion helps students connect what they learn in *SOAR TO SUCCESS* with other reading. The Reviewing step is also a time to summarize the section of the book they read in the previous lesson.

Strategies When students are being asked to tell how or when they use certain strategies, keep them focused on the strategies. Use prompts such as the following:

- *That was good, but how (or when) would you actually use that strategy?*

- *You're right; that strategy does help you read better, but how? Does it help you think about the details (or remember big ideas, or figure out words)?*

Rehearsing

When Students Should Have Books in Hand If you are conducting a guided preview, it is usually best for students not to have their books in front of them. Keep students focused by having them look at your book during the preview. Occasionally, a book has features that students should have directly in front of them as you preview. Notes appear in the lesson plans to remind you when students should or should not have their books in front of them.

Previewing Previewing the text sets the scene and provides support for what is to be read. This procedure activates and/or builds background knowledge and provides a context for reading. It thus enables students to read more fluently while constructing meaning. This form of scaffolded instruction begins with heavy teacher support during guided previews and moves students toward independence through cooperative previews and then independent previews.

A **guided preview** is teacher directed and includes strong teacher modeling and support. In a guided preview, the teacher holds the book and quickly "walks" students through the text, calling attention to specific vocabulary, key concepts, or text structure, while providing the context students need prior to reading on their own.

The text structure of expository selections often includes graphic elements critical to students' gaining information from the piece. The teacher needs to show students the features and tell how to use them.

Students interact with the teacher and the text as they predict future events in a narrative text. They tell what they think they will learn from an informational/expository text.

A **cooperative preview** does not involve the teacher directly, as students work in pairs and "walk" themselves and each other through the text, focusing on the same elements as those in a guided preview. The teacher observes the students' interaction with each other and with the text and is available to monitor, provide support, and evaluate students' progress toward independence.

An **independent preview** occurs when the students are able to take themselves through the preview process on their own, setting the scene and the focus for their reading.

How to Conduct a Guided Preview

1. Before teaching the lesson, read the section of text carefully to determine the key concepts and vocabulary that are necessary for student understanding.

2. Use the key vocabulary from the text while quickly "telling" the students the story or highlighting the information they will be learning.

"**A**n effective and efficient guided preview . . . will strongly influence students' success."

3. Hold the book during the guided preview so students can see the illustrations or graphics. This provides a focus for the students and ensures that all are attending to the same section of the text.

4. Read or have students read text-structure elements, such as captions, headings, or pronunciation guides. Point to these graphics as you provide the narrative. Since the group size is small, the teacher's book serves as a "big book."

5. It is important to note that you do not actually read the text to the students, nor is it necessary to give away the ending of a story. However, students may be asked to predict during the preview as they answer questions you pose.

6. Remember that the purpose of the preview is to provide background knowledge and a focus for reading. The pacing is fast, and all student/teacher dialogue must keep to the topic.

7. Keep in mind the importance of an effective and efficient guided preview. It will strongly influence student success in reading and comprehending that section of the book.

8. Note that the guided preview is teacher directed, and students should receive intense modeling and support.

How to Conduct a Cooperative Preview

1. Have pairs of students work together. Pairs may share one copy of the text, or each student may use his or her own book.

2. Ask pairs to preview the text, attending to illustrations and/or graphics that will provide important information before and during their reading. Remind them of text-structure elements such as captions, headings, or pronunciation guides. Suggest that they read these elements together and discuss their connection to the text they will be reading.

3. Remind students that the purpose of the preview is to provide background knowledge and a focus for reading. Their pacing should be fast and all student-to-student interaction and discussion must keep to the topic.

4. Remind students of the importance of focusing on the text in conducting the cooperative preview. The more effectively they focus, the more successful they will be in comprehending the text.

5. After the cooperative preview has been completed, direct students to locate the key vocabulary on given pages, read the text silently, and briefly discuss the meaning.

6. The cooperative preview involves only a moderate amount of teacher support and modeling. Observe and monitor the students' progress and provide instruction and coaching when necessary.

How to Conduct an Independent Preview

1. Remind students of the process they used during the cooperative preview.

2. Explain that during an independent preview they will follow the procedure they used during the cooperative preview but will be expected to do it on their own.

3. Remind students that the more effective and efficient their independent preview is, the more successful they will be in reading and comprehending that section of the book.

4. After the independent preview has been completed, direct students to locate the key vocabulary on given pages, read the text silently, and briefly discuss the meaning.

5. The independent preview is student directed, with no teacher modeling or support. Individual students are expected to apply the strategies and techniques that were modeled and supported during the guided and cooperative previews. However, be available to provide help if students need it.

Reading and Reciprocal Teaching

Observing/Monitoring While students are reading, observe their behaviors to help you assess their progress. The table below presents four behaviors to look for and suggests what these may indicate about each student's reading.

Student Behaviors to Look for During Silent Reading

Behavior	Description	Possible Indications
Tracks with Finger	As the student reads, he/she uses hand or finger to point to each word or to follow each line of print.	• Student is still gaining strength in reading this level of text; support is needed to help him/her follow the text. • Student may need more support with decoding if he/she tends to stop at each word.
Moves Lips While Reading	As the student reads silently, he/she moves lips while reading or mumbles what is being read.	• Student needs continued support in reading this level of text. • Student may need more teacher modeling of silent reading.
Looks at Pictures/ Illustrations	As the student reads, he/she refers to pictures, illustrations, or other text features.	• Student is using all clues to understand the text. • Student may be relying too heavily on picture clues to figure out words.
Finishes Reading Before Others	The student always finishes reading before other students in the group.	• Student is making progress and text is becoming too easy. • Student is hurrying and not really reading. Ask the student to give a summary at the appropriate time to check comprehension. The student may need a stronger rehearsal of the text.

Modeling and Discussion of Strategies Strategies must be modeled and discussed often enough to help students gain independence in their use. Do not overlook this important part of the lessons.

When One Student Finishes When one student finishes before another, have him/her look back to prepare to model the four strategies, SUMMARIZE, CLARIFY, QUESTION, and PREDICT.

Student's Role as Teacher Have each student take the lead as teacher. This means that the student models a strategy; he/she does not just sit and call on others to do the modeling. Emphasize the idea that students take turns being the teacher:

- Remind students before reading that they will be asked to assume the role of teacher by modeling one or more strategies.

- Have several students be the teacher by letting each student model only one of the strategies at a time.

- Don't insist that every student respond after every reading block. Keep the pace of the lessons fast.

Responding/ Reflecting

In middle-school levels of *SOAR TO SUCCESS*, students should be increasingly encouraged to formulate their own responses and contribute them to the group. When the task is to add to a Graphic Organizer, in early books the teacher needs to model and then involve the group in modeling, but soon each student should first add to his or her own Graphic Organizer in the Student Guide, and then use it to contribute to the group poster.

Always discuss students' responses before they write. See the suggestions in Provide Oral Support for Written Work. Encourage students to discuss their specific uses of strategies.

Have the Homework assignment read aloud so that you can be sure students understand it.

Adapting Lessons If Necessary

To provide the consistency that students need and to carefully scaffold instruction, it is important to follow the lesson plans as closely as possible. Adapt lessons only rarely and with care, as recommended in the following suggestions:

Combine Lessons Only If One Was Completed Quickly On rare occasions a group might proceed through a lesson faster than you expected. Therefore, it would be logical to combine that day's lesson with the next one by skipping the next day's Revisiting and Reviewing. However, Revisiting and Reviewing should not be skipped on a regular basis.

Avoid Skipping Parts No part of the instructional plan should be skipped if *SOAR TO SUCCESS* is to achieve its goals as a reading intervention program. This is especially true for the Rehearsing portion of the plan, which prepares students to read successfully.

Complete All Lessons If a lesson is not completed on a given day, pick it up the next day. Do not assign activities for homework. **It is important for the teacher to be present for all parts of a lesson.**

Provide Oral Support for Written Work Here are ways to keep up the pace when writing is suggested:

- If writing to complete Graphic Organizers or to summarize takes up too much time in the lesson, have students provide the information while you do the writing, or have students complete the material orally as a group.

- Reflection questions should always be discussed before students write their responses.

Special Considerations

Special circumstances might occur with the *SOAR TO SUCCESS* students. If any of the following occur, use these guidelines to help you:

Poor Attendance If a student is absent so much that he or she cannot benefit from the carefully scaffolded instruction, *SOAR TO SUCCESS* has no chance to work. It is best to drop that student from the program and give the opportunity to another student who needs it.

Adding New Students If a student is released or moves away, you may have an opening in your *SOAR TO SUCCESS* group. When this occurs, select another student from the *SOAR TO SUCCESS* pool. (See Selecting and Releasing Students on page T37 of this manual.) Start the student at the point where the other students are reading. Explain the process and have the new student move on with the rest of the group. This procedure works until students are beyond Book 9 or 10. It was used effectively in the national research project.

Staff Development and Coaching

Types of Staff Development

Classroom practices and research have shown that effective staff development and coaching help teachers continue to grow and improve in their instruction as they learn new teaching strategies (Showers & Bennett, 1987; Sparks & Hirsh, 1997). Research from a national study supports the importance of both of these elements in helping teachers learn to accelerate the reading of upper-grade students and to use the *SOAR TO SUCCESS* instructional model. (See the summary of the research report in the Teacher's Resource File, page R2 of this manual.)

As you learn to use *SOAR TO SUCCESS,* you have several options to consider in planning your staff development and coaching.

Attend an Intermediate Intervention Institute A two-day, in-depth Intermediate Intervention Institute is available through Houghton Mifflin's Faculty Development Programs at locations throughout the United States. This intensive workshop was developed by the program authors based on their research with Project SUCCESS. For information on the training institute, call 1-888-892-2377, or ask your Houghton Mifflin representative for information.

Using the Video
View Section 3 of the Staff Development Video before or after reading this section of the manual. Use the Viewing Guide on pages R82–R85.

Use the Teacher's Manual and Video Interactively This Teacher's Manual provides the background, instruction, and lessons for teaching *SOAR TO SUCCESS.* You may read the material on your own or work with a group of colleagues to learn the instructional strategies involved in teaching *SOAR TO SUCCESS.* If possible, work with a group of colleagues, as this is the more successful option.

The video interacts with the Teacher's Manual for *SOAR TO SUCCESS.* It is suggested that you use the video along with the Teacher's Manual to learn to teach *SOAR TO SUCCESS.* The video icon placed throughout this manual shows when and how to use the video. We suggest that you view the video initially as you begin to use *SOAR TO SUCCESS,* and then view it in sections throughout your first year of teaching *SOAR TO SUCCESS* for ongoing staff development. The Viewing Guide refers to the sections of the video. (See Teacher's Resource File, pages R82–R85.)

Attend a Houghton Mifflin Workshop A Houghton Mifflin in-service workshop will give you a basic overview of the program. Speak with your Houghton Mifflin representative about scheduling a session.

Hold Monthly Support Meetings Ongoing monthly support meetings should be held within your school, district, or area. Suggestions for these meetings are found on page T28.

Develop a Coaching Plan (See the section below.)

Coaching

Coaching in teaching is the process of helping a teacher internalize a set of instructional strategies through observation and feedback. The research summarized in the table below shows how adding coaching to staff development leads teachers to apply new teaching strategies and concepts.

The process of coaching involves three basic steps:

1. **Observation** The teacher being coached is observed teaching.
2. **Feedback** The observer and the teacher *share* key ideas from the *SOAR TO SUCCESS* lesson.
3. **Follow-up** Another observation is scheduled after the teacher has had time to try the agreed-upon suggestions.

Why Coaching? Training Effectiveness

Training Components	Knowledge Mastery	Skill Acquired	Skill Applied
Presentation of Theory	40–100%	10–20%	5–10%
Theory Plus Demonstration	80–100%	35%	5–10%
Theory, Demonstration, and Practice	80–100%	75%	5–10%
Theory, Demonstration, Practice, Feedback, and Coaching	80–100%	90%	90%

This table, developed by the San Juan (CA) Unified School District, is based on research by Bruce Joyce and Beverly Showers (1981).

Types of Coaching

You will need to develop your coaching plans around your particular teaching situation and the personnel resources available. There are three basic types of coaching to consider:

Peer Coaching This is the type of coaching in which one teacher observes another. This is useful in schools where there are only a few teachers involved in teaching *SOAR TO SUCCESS.*

Outside Coaching An educator other than a teacher serves as the teacher's coach. This person is trained in teaching *SOAR TO SUCCESS* and may also be trained in coaching procedures and techniques.

Self-Coaching When you are in a school situation where you are the only teacher involved in teaching *SOAR TO SUCCESS,* self-coaching may be your only choice. In this case, as you teach a lesson, run an audiocassette player or a videocassette recorder to record your lesson. Afterward, listen to the audio recording or view the video. Compare what you observe with the Staff Development Video.

Procedures for a Coaching Session

Use the following procedures for a coaching session:

Schedule a Time The coach and the teacher to be coached need to talk to schedule a time that is convenient for both.

Determine the Coaching Focus Sometime before the actual coaching session begins, the teacher and coach talk to determine what will be the focus of the coaching session. This focus might be some part of the lesson where the teacher needs more support, a management issue, or one particular student. Keep the focus simple. Do not try to do too much at one time.

Observe and Record The coach uses the coaching form on page R86 to make notes while observing the lesson. (See the sample completed coaching form on the next page.) Throughout the observation, the coach maintains a positive physical demeanor, not acting or reacting in ways that show judgments.

Hold a Follow-up Conference As soon as possible after the coaching session, the coach and teacher hold a short conference.

- The coach begins by noting the effective things observed and then asks the teacher to mention several positive points.

- The coach addresses the agreed-upon focus, and shares thoughts about what was seen.

- The coach asks how the teacher felt about the lesson overall.

- The coach and teacher conclude by agreeing upon the next steps.

 **Coaching Form**

Teacher	P. Trotter		**Coach**	S. Fernandez	
School	Cityview Middle School	**Date** 9/23/00	**Starting/Stopping Time**	10:10 / 10:50	
Book Title	Owl	**Lesson No.** 3	**Level** 8		

Agreed Coaching Focus:

Begin making modeling stronger by showing what qualities make a good model.

Time	Lesson Part	Observations/Questions/Suggestions/Reflections
10:10	**Revisiting** (5 min.) 6 min.	You made sure other students were rereading, and then focused on Joe's Retelling. Good.
10:16	**Reviewing** (5 min.) 6 min.	When Breanna grouped what she learned from the "L" section of the chart into a summary, you praised the use of her own words to summarize, not just reading from the chart. Excellent reinforcement.
10:21	**Rehearsing** (5–10 min.) 10 min.	Good use of the guided preview script to develop vocabulary that tied in with the content they are going to read. You keep the pacing and the focus.
10:29	**Reading/ Reciprocal Teaching** (10–15 min.) 13 min.	Your Clarify/Phonics model was an excellent example of using a prefix and suffix as you chunked and decoded "invisible." Have a student model following your model. You might suggest a word they could use that has a prefix and/or suffix. Students need to group details into key points or main ideas as they summarize. Provide models or point out student models that do this. Use the graphic organizer as a guide.
10:44	**Responding/ Reflecting** (5 min.) 5 min.	

Next Steps:

— In Rehearsing, as you give information, indicate how you got it from the text and graphics.
— If students' predictions seem to come from left field, get them to tell what basis they have for their prediction. Model using the prompt for Predict—"When I predict, I . . ."
— In Reciprocal Teaching, be explicit about what makes a strong model. For example, say, "This section compares things, so my question is How are these things different?"

Monthly Meetings

Monthly meetings are an important part of your ongoing staff development. The chart below presents a list of suggested topics and suggests relevant sections of the Staff Development Video and this Teacher's Manual to use as resources. Monthly meetings may combine several schools or even school districts. The focus of each meeting should be based on teacher needs, which may be determined from coaching or general teacher input. A simple form may be used to survey teachers to determine their needs. See the Teacher's Resource File, page R87.

Suggested Monthly Meeting Topics

Taking a retelling	Review the procedures and then practice as a group. (Teacher's Manual, page T43)
Taking an oral reading check	Tape-record a student as he/she reads, and then practice together. (Teacher's Manual, page T46; Staff Development Video, Section 2)
Observing students during Revisiting and Reading	Discuss things to look for; share procedures for making quick notes. (Teacher's Manual, page T21)
Ongoing assessment	Discuss: What should I look for? Where and how do I record it? (Teacher's Manual, page T41)
Sticking to the tasks and pace of the SOAR TO SUCCESS lessons	Discuss: How do I keep students focused?
What do I do with other students in the classroom during SOAR TO SUCCESS time?	Share suggestions; tell what has worked. (Teacher's Manual, page T33; Staff Development Video, Section 4)
Graphic Organizers	Discuss: How do Graphic Organizers fit in the SOAR TO SUCCESS lessons?
Using strategies in content areas	Discuss: How do I get students to apply strategies in other classes?
Releasing students from SOAR TO SUCCESS	Discuss criteria, procedures, and replacement of students. (Teacher's Manual, page T40)
Reciprocal teaching	Discuss and role-play; use simulation. (Teacher's Manual, pages T56–T63; Staff Development Video, Sections 1 and 2)
Encouraging independent reading	Discuss: What do I do about students who don't want to read independently? How do I ensure that independent reading occurs prior to group conferences?
Group discussions during Revisiting	Discuss: How do I focus group conferences? (Teacher's Manual, pages T17, T39)

Section 4

Organizing and Managing SOAR TO SUCCESS Within a Middle School/Junior High Structure

INTRODUCTION *SOAR TO SUCCESS* is designed as an intervention program to be taught in small groups of five to seven students. This instruction is to be delivered **in addition to balanced literacy instruction.** Middle schools/junior high schools have a variety of organizational patterns and structures. This section provides you with alternative suggestions for organizing an intervention program within your school.

Ways to Use *SOAR TO SUCCESS* There are multiple ways that *SOAR TO SUCCESS* can be used effectively in a middle-school/junior-high-school organizational structure, as shown below.

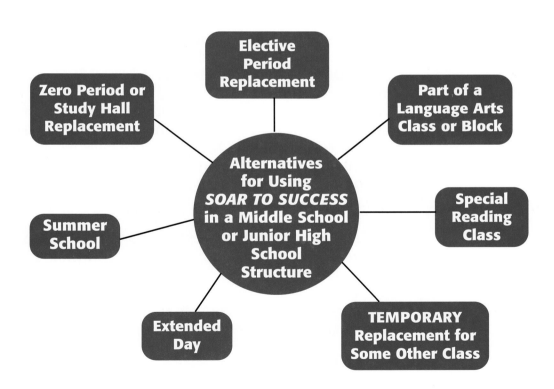

Ways to Use *SOAR TO SUCCESS* in a Middle School/Junior High School Structure

ZERO PERIOD OR STUDY HALL REPLACEMENT This alternative is an easy way to accommodate students' needs without any disruption of their other classes. Students simply attend *SOAR TO SUCCESS* class or a reading class for the period of time needed. When they reach the desired reading level, they return to their zero period or study hall.

ELECTIVE PERIOD REPLACEMENT Instead of taking a normal elective subject, students are assigned to (or given the choice to) attend a *SOAR TO SUCCESS* class or reading class. This class usually lasts for a semester. At the end of the time, each student is evaluated to determine if he or she needs a longer period of time in *SOAR TO SUCCESS*.

PART OF A LANGUAGE ARTS CLASS OR BLOCK When schools have a language arts class or block of 90 minutes or longer, they often take the 40 minutes for *SOAR TO SUCCESS* from within this period of time. Students not in the *SOAR TO SUCCESS* group are involved in other independent reading/literacy activities. This is usually done a minimum of four days per week.

SPECIAL READING CLASS In some middle schools or junior high schools, there is a Reading Class for students who are experiencing difficulty learning to read. This class may involve more than seven students. Therefore, the teacher uses the large-group model described on pages T34–36.

TEMPORARY REPLACEMENT OF SOME OTHER CLASS In some cases where a student's reading ability is far below level, teachers feel it is more beneficial for this student to miss a class such as science, social studies, physical education, or music in order to quickly increase his/her reading ability. *This alternative must be used cautiously!* Parental permission should be obtained for this alternative. It is also suggested that the student be given the option to choose what class he/she misses, if possible.

EXTENDED DAY With this option, *SOAR TO SUCCESS* is taught either before or after school. After school is usually more effective than before school for middle school/junior high students. When setting up this alternative, be sure to consider the number of additional after-school activities in which the students are participating. These can interfere with your reading intervention program.

SUMMER SCHOOL Some districts now have intensive summer school programs. *SOAR TO SUCCESS* works effectively in these situations, especially if you have a long enough day that allows for the teaching of multiple lessons.

Deciding How You Will Use *SOAR TO SUCCESS*

Use the following steps to help you decide how to use *SOAR TO SUCCESS*:

1. Consider your situation. How many students need *SOAR TO SUCCESS*? How many teachers are involved? What scheduling issues or concerns must you consider?
2. Review the alternative suggestions given on page T29.
3. Select the alternative that is best for you or devise an additional one that is more appropriate to your situation.

The remainder of this section provides suggestions for supporting you in using *SOAR TO SUCCESS* in the middle schools or junior high school organizational structure.

Personnel Roles Using *SOAR TO SUCCESS*

If your school or district will have multiple teachers involved in *SOAR TO SUCCESS*, consider using three types of personnel: a site coordinator, teacher(s), and coach(es). The chart below summarizes the roles of each of these individuals.

Personnel Roles for *SOAR TO SUCCESS*

SOAR TO SUCCESS Role	Who Might Have That Role	Responsibilities
Site Coordinator	An educator *trained* in the use of *SOAR TO SUCCESS*	• Coordinate all aspects of *SOAR TO SUCCESS* • Schedule and run support meetings and in-services • Serve as a coach
Teacher	A reading specialist, Title 1 teacher, classroom teacher, or special education teacher *trained* to use *SOAR TO SUCCESS*	• Teach *SOAR TO SUCCESS* groups • May also be a coach
Coach	An educator *trained* in the use of *SOAR TO SUCCESS*	• Coach teachers • May also teach *SOAR TO SUCCESS groups*

Managing *SOAR TO SUCCESS* in a Language Arts Class or Block

If you have a language arts class or block of 90 minutes or more, you might consider using *SOAR TO SUCCESS* as part of that class for students who are reading below level. The following four steps should help you develop a plan for managing your block:

1. Develop a daily schedule.
2. Identify independent activities other students will do while you teach your *SOAR TO SUCCESS* group.
3. Discuss routines and the daily schedule with students.
4. Try your plan and revise as needed.

1. Develop a Daily Schedule The first step to successfully using *SOAR TO SUCCESS* as an intervention program within your language arts block is developing a workable daily schedule. This schedule must provide time for the reading, writing, literature, spelling, and grammar you must teach *plus* a block of 40 minutes for your *SOAR TO SUCCESS* group and independent activities for other students.

2. Identify Independent Activities for Other Students to Do When you are teaching your *SOAR TO SUCCESS* group, you need worthwhile, independent activities for the other students. The table on page T33 presents a list of suggested alternatives. This table concludes with blank spaces for you to add ideas of your own.

3. Develop and Discuss Routines with Students To make your management smooth and efficient, you need to develop predictable routines with students.

- First, post the daily schedule you decide to use.

- Explain that you will teach the *SOAR TO SUCCESS* group while other students are doing independent activities.

- Show students the independent or small-group activities that you plan to use, on a transparency or chart. Point out that the activities on this chart will be changed daily (or weekly). Note that these activities will provide students with needed independent practice and application of many reading and language skills. Tell students that they will need to time and pace themselves so that they can accomplish what they need to do during this 40-minute block.

- Designate one or two student monitors. These are individuals to whom other students may go for help during their independent work time while you are teaching *SOAR TO SUCCESS*. Change these monitors as your choices for independent activities change.

- Tell students how you will make yourself available; for example, tell them that you will check in with other students while *SOAR TO SUCCESS* students are in their Silent Reading time.

- Explain that you will review the results of the independent activities to ensure that the time has been spent productively.

- Develop with students a set of guidelines for behavior during independent work time. These guidelines should be reviewed and revised as needed.

What Other Students Do During *SOAR TO SUCCESS* Time

Activity*	Suggestions/Comments
Independent Reading	Some time can be devoted to independent reading. The amount of time should be adjusted to student interests and needs. (See the discussion of Independent Reading on page T34.)
Response Activities	Have students complete a response activity for materials they are reading independently. Post a chart with suggestions, such as writing an opinion of the book, a character description, a time line of events, etc.
Newspaper Activities	Students can read student newspapers or local newspapers. Specific activities can be assigned using these materials.
Independent Writing	Students can complete independent writing activities.
Practice of Strategies and Skills	Strategies and skills can be practiced through reading and writing activities. For example, students needing to expand vocabulary can make a word map or word web using vocabulary from books they have read or textbooks they are using in other classes. Alternatively, students can write a summary of something they have read, focusing on particular aspects of grammar they have studied.
Computer Time	Provide computer activities to reinforce comprehension—writing, spelling, or grammar skills.

Other Ideas

Activity*	Suggestions/Comments

* Several of these activities can take place at one time.

4. Try Your Plan and Revise as Needed Occasionally review your plan and discuss with students how things are going. Make revisions as needed. This may require such things as:

- Discussing the monitors' roles

- Talking about what it means to work independently

- Modeling routines that are causing students difficulties

- Adding more categories of activities

- Revising or adding new guidelines for behavior

Independent Reading for *SOAR TO SUCCESS* Students

- Use the bibliography of high-interest, easy-reading books on pages R12–R13 to provide appropriate books for *SOAR TO SUCCESS* students.

- Have *SOAR TO SUCCESS* students keep a record of their independent reading by using the Book Log in the Student Guide.

- Some teachers create a library that they keep in their work area for *SOAR TO SUCCESS* students. Students check out books to take home or to other classes for independent reading. Books might include titles from the bibliography on pages R12–R13; copies might come from the school library, public library, or the teacher's own collection. This little library would also be useful in a summer-school program.

Using a Large-Group Intervention Model for *SOAR TO SUCCESS*

The very positive results obtained in the *SOAR TO SUCCESS* research occurred with groups of five to seven students (see pages T6-T7). However, many middle school/junior high school situations present teachers with 20 or more below-level readers in a single class. While the gains made in small-group (five to seven students) instructional situations cannot be equaled in larger group situations, we present a model for larger groups that has met with some success. See the diagram below. The following points should help you implement this plan, if necessary. Keep in mind, the larger the instructional group, the less gain you are likely to get.

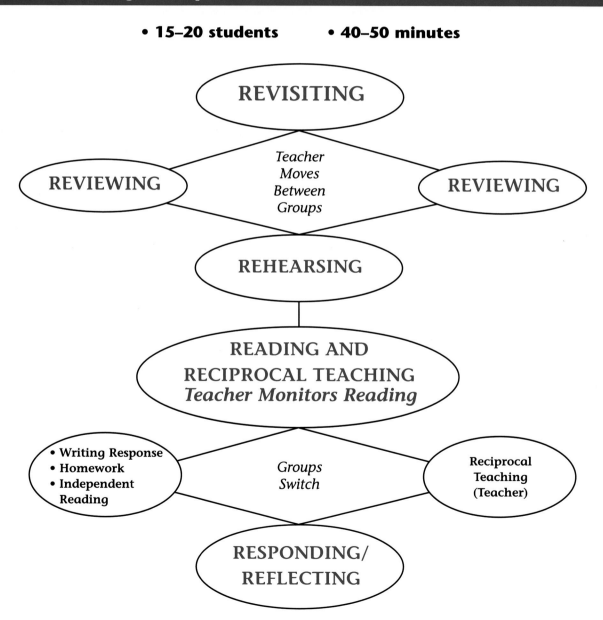

A Large–Group Intervention Model for Middle School

- **15–20 students**   - **40–50 minutes**

REVISITING

REVIEWING   *Teacher Moves Between Groups*   **REVIEWING**

REHEARSING

READING AND RECIPROCAL TEACHING
Teacher Monitors Reading

- Writing Response
- Homework
- Independent Reading

Groups Switch

Reciprocal Teaching (Teacher)

RESPONDING/ REFLECTING

Revisiting This portion of the lesson is done by the whole group at one time. On days when Group Discussions are held, the group can be divided into two smaller groups. The teacher can move back and forth between the two groups to listen to the discussion after giving the same prompt to both groups.

Reviewing Divide the group into two smaller groups. Move back and forth between the groups to monitor activities.

Rehearsing This portion of the lesson is done by the whole group under the teacher's direction.

Reading and Reciprocal Teaching

- Everyone reads silently at the same time.

- After reading, the teacher starts one group on their written response in the Student Guide. Students may begin work on their Homework assignment and do independent reading.

- The second group does Reciprocal Teaching with the teacher.

- Next, the two groups switch activities.

- On the following day, the teacher starts with the group that did written work first on the preceding day. Continue to alternate this pattern daily.

Responding/Reflecting This portion of the lesson is done with the whole group.

Section 5
Selecting and Releasing Students

When planning a reading intervention program, you want to select students who will profit the most from the intervention in the shortest amount of time. The ultimate goal of any intervention program is to get students out of the intervention so that they can fully benefit from their other subject-area instruction. This section presents guidelines and procedures for selecting students, determining how to assess progress, and releasing students from the *SOAR TO SUCCESS* program.

Selecting Students

The diagram on page T38 summarizes the procedures for selecting students for *SOAR TO SUCCESS*.

1. **Use assessment instruments.**

   • Examine existing standardized achievement test data to find students who are reading considerably below level. Consider for intervention students whose scores in Reading Comprehension and/or Vocabulary

     —are at the 40th percentile or lower or
     —do not meet district cut-off score.

   • Administer the Timed Fluency Test to students who fall below the cut-off score for the standardized achievement test. See pages R162–R164 for the Timed Fluency Test.

     —For students with good fluency (scoring at Expected Progress), *SOAR TO SUCCESS* is appropriate without additional phonics/decoding or fluency support.
     —For students with poor fluency (scoring Below Expected Progress), administer the *Houghton Mifflin Phonics/Decoding Screening Test*. Identify levels of phonics/decoding and fluency intervention according to the guidelines in the chart on page R156, which are summarized below:

   A. **Student decodes well** (scoring 80% on the Phonics/Decoding Screening Test)
      but has poor fluency (scoring Below Expected Progress on the Timed Fluency Test):

      Start student in *SOAR TO SUCCESS*. Replace Group Conferences with extra rereading of previously read *SOAR TO SUCCESS* books for fluency.

Selecting Students for *SOAR TO SUCCESS*

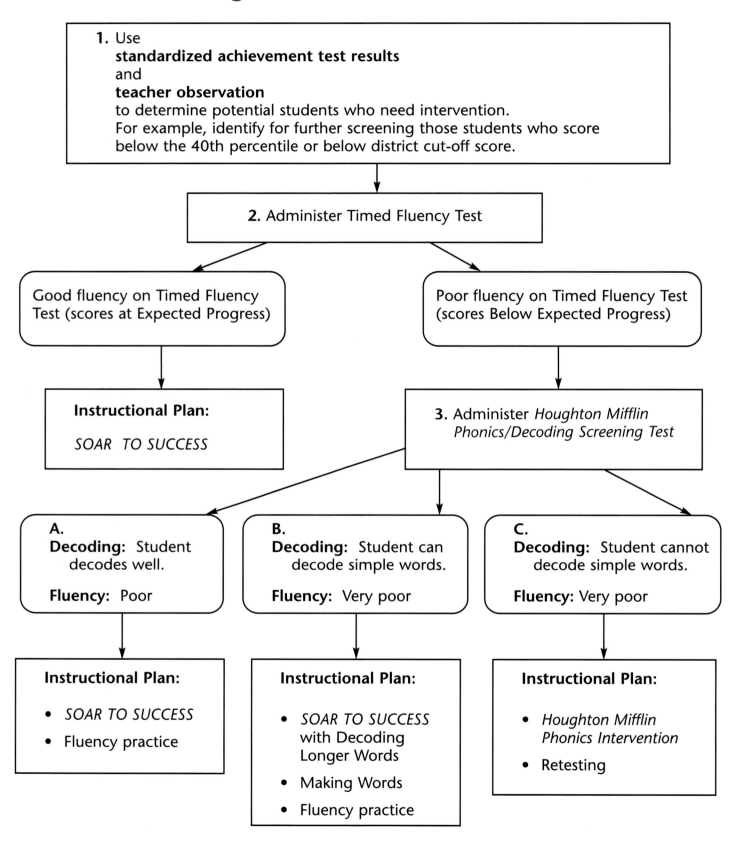

1. Use
standardized achievement test results
and
teacher observation
to determine potential students who need intervention.
For example, identify for further screening those students who score
below the 40th percentile or below district cut-off score.

2. Administer Timed Fluency Test

Good fluency on Timed Fluency Test (scores at Expected Progress)

Poor fluency on Timed Fluency Test (scores Below Expected Progress)

Instructional Plan:

SOAR TO SUCCESS

3. Administer *Houghton Mifflin Phonics/Decoding Screening Test*

A.
Decoding: Student decodes well.

Fluency: Poor

B.
Decoding: Student can decode simple words.

Fluency: Very poor

C.
Decoding: Student cannot decode simple words.

Fluency: Very poor

Instructional Plan:

- *SOAR TO SUCCESS*
- Fluency practice

Instructional Plan:

- *SOAR TO SUCCESS* with Decoding Longer Words
- Making Words
- Fluency practice

Instructional Plan:

- *Houghton Mifflin Phonics Intervention*
- Retesting

B. Student can decode simple words

—scores 80% on Phonics/Decoding Screening Test through Task F, including pseudowords, but
—below 80% on Multisyllabic Words (Tasks G and H)
or
—80% on Phonics/Decoding Screening Test through Task C
—below 80% on some other task, typically long vowels and diphthongs (Tasks D and F) and
—below 80% on Multisyllabic Words (Tasks G and H)
but has very poor fluency (scores Seriously Below Expected Progress on the Timed Fluency Test):

Start student in *SOAR TO SUCCESS*; use Decoding Longer Words and Making Words lessons; provide frequent teacher and student modeling of CLARIFY/PHONICS.

C. Student can't decode simple words

—scores below 80% on Phonics/Decoding Screening Test **and has very poor fluency** (scores Seriously Below Expected Progress on Timed Fluency Test):

Begin with Houghton Mifflin Phonics Intervention; begin *SOAR TO SUCCESS* when student is able to score 80% on the phonics tasks in the *Houghton Mifflin Phonics/Decoding Screening Test* and has improved to score at least Below Expected Progress on the Timed Fluency Test.

2. **Use other criteria.**

   • Look for signs of potential for improvement. Consider:

     —listening scores considerably higher than reading scores
     —math computation scores higher than problem-solving scores

   • Include students who are learning English as a second language if they have reached an Intermediate Fluency level of English (last of the four stages of development identified by Krashen and Terrell, 1983). These students have passed beyond the Speech Emergent level (in which they used incomplete sentences and nonstandard forms). At the Intermediate Fluency level, students are still building receptive vocabulary, but their answers are more extended than the short phrases or short sentences used by students who are still in the Speech Emergent level.

   • Include students who have been identified for special education services if they meet the criteria for *SOAR TO SUCCESS*.

3. **Select students who have the greatest need and show the greatest potential for improvement.** *SOAR TO SUCCESS* groups should be no larger than seven students per group. In some cases, you may want to use the large-group model (see page T35).

Testing Students

Do some type of formal assessment of your *SOAR TO SUCCESS* students during the program to determine progress. The *SOAR TO SUCCESS* Informal Reading Inventory (page R95) is designed to help you determine student progress in your intervention program. For district purposes, use a standardized test for overall evaluation of *SOAR TO SUCCESS* students. If possible, use the tests already given in the district. ***Avoid adding more testing.***

Releasing Students

To determine when a student has reached the point where he or she is reading on-level or higher and should be released from *SOAR TO SUCCESS,* follow these procedures:

1. Observe the student in the *SOAR* group. Does the student

   - summarize thoroughly?

   - finish before others?

   - always have correct answers?

   - show signs that the books are becoming too easy?

2. Confer with the subject-area teachers to determine the student's classroom performance. Is the student

   - showing improvement in reading the grade-level materials?

   - demonstrating improved comprehension?

   - doing written work in response to reading that demonstrates effective comprehension?

3. Verify the student's reading of classroom (on-level) materials, using the following procedures:

   - Select two or three pages from the text being read in class.

   - Have the student read the text silently.

   - Have the student retell what was read. Retelling score should be 75% or higher.

   - Have the student read the text orally. Word Call should be 90% or higher.

   - Have the student write a response to what was read.

If items 1, 2, and 3 all indicate that the student should be released, complete steps 4, 5, and 6.

4. Retest with the *SOAR TO SUCCESS* Informal Reading Inventory or any other measure you are using to determine student growth.

5. Retest with a standardized test at the appropriate time in the year, if such a test is being used.

6. Record the data on the Student Record of Progress found in the Teacher's Resource File, page R90.

Section 6
Assessment

• •

SOAR TO SUCCESS provides the resources to determine overall student progress over time and to measure ongoing student growth throughout the instructional program. The table below summarizes the four resources available to help you build a strong assessment program. Directions and guidelines for using each of these resources are presented in the following sections.

Assessment Resources for *SOAR TO SUCCESS*

Resource	How to Use/Administer	Value/Uses
Timed Fluency Test	• Individually administered	• Determines speed and accuracy of student's oral reading.
Phonics/Decoding Screening Test	• Individually and group administered	• Determines the level of student's phonic/decoding knowledge • Provides analysis/diagnosis of student's specific skill knowledge
***SOAR TO SUCCESS* Informal Reading Inventory**	• Individually administered • Give Form A as a pretest and Form B as a posttest. • Give Form C if additional evaluation is needed.	• Shows student progress over time
Retellings • **Informal during Revisiting** • **Formal during Revisiting or at other times**	• Individually administered • Student silently reads passages. • Individually administered • Student silently reads passages.	• Shows student comprehension in specific books • Shows student comprehension in specific books • Allows comparison of student performance on same passages
Oral Reading Checks	• Individually administered • Student reads passages aloud.	• Shows use of phonics, structure, and overall decoding skills • Checks fluency
***SOAR TO SUCCESS* Record of Progress**	• Individually kept for each student	• A record of books completed by each student • A record of student performance

Using the *SOAR TO SUCCESS* Informal Reading Inventory

The *SOAR TO SUCCESS* Informal Reading Inventory (IRI) is an instrument that allows you to determine student progress in the program. There are three forms of the test:

Form A is usually given as a pretest at the beginning of the program, and Form B is given as a posttest when a student completes the program or is released from the program. Form C consists of extra passages that can be used for additional evaluation, if needed. The table below lists the components of the Informal Reading Inventory.

Using Other Informal Reading Inventories Your school or district may provide a different informal reading inventory. If so, you can use that inventory with *SOAR TO SUCCESS*.

There are also many published informal reading inventories that you can use to determine student progress. Following are a few of the more widely used inventories:

- Burns, P. C., & Roe, B. D. (1999). *Informal Reading Inventory* (4th ed.). Boston: Houghton Mifflin, Grades 1–12.

- Shanker, J. L., & Ekwall, E. E. (2000). *Ekwall/Shanker Reading Inventory* (4th ed.). Boston: Allyn & Bacon, Grades 1–9.

- Johns, J. J. (1997). *Basic Reading Inventory* (7th ed.). Dubuque, IA: Kendall/Hunt, Grades 1–12.

- Leslie, L., & Caldwell, J. (1995). *Qualitative Reading Inventory-, II.* New York: HarperCollins, Grades 1–Jr. High.

- Swearingen, R., & Allen, D. (2000). *Classroom Assessment of Reading Processes* (2nd ed.). Boston: Houghton Mifflin.

Informal Reading Inventory Components

Component	Purpose	Where Located
Administering, Scoring, and Interpreting the Informal Reading Inventory	Guidelines for using the IRI	Pages R94–R100, R152–R153
Student Passages	Provides passages for student to read	Protocols and Student Passages, pages R101–R151
Teacher Protocol Sheets for Student Passages	Presents a record sheet for the teacher	Protocols and Student Passages, pages R101–R151

Using Retellings

Ongoing assessment of each student's reading takes place during the **Revisiting** block of the *SOAR TO SUCCESS* instructional plan. On days when students are rereading previously read books, the teacher takes either an informal retelling or an oral reading check. The retelling assesses comprehension; the oral reading checks assess decoding and fluency. Retelling is used as ongoing assessment; the oral reading check is used *only when there are questions or concerns about how a student is decoding*. There are two types of retelling that you may use: informal and formal.

Taking an Informal Retelling

This is a quick, informal assessment of comprehension.

Use previously read *SOAR TO SUCCESS* books.

Have the student select (or you select) the part of the book he/she wants to reread.

Have the student read the text silently. Tell the student that he/she is going to retell it after reading.

After reading, ask the student to retell the text in his/her own words. Make a tally mark for each correct point the student gives. In an acceptable response, the student is able to retell a majority of the key points covered in the section read.

Keep a record of the student's responses on the Student Log Sheet for Revisiting shown on page T49. Record date and type of assessment, as shown on page T49. Typical descriptions of responses might include:

- satisfactory

- all events in order

- scattered responses

- missed one major point

In the sample Student Log Sheet on page T49, the teacher took a retelling from Shawn F. on September 15, and Shawn's score was Acceptable. This sheet is also used to note when an Oral Reading Check (ORC) is taken. On September 25, an ORC was taken on Olivia A., and her score was Acceptable. (See page T46, Taking an Oral Reading Check.) A blank copy of the Student Log Sheet for Revisiting is found in the Teacher's Resource File, page R27.

## Book 3

Retelling Protocol for *Owl*

• •

Name *Shawn F.*   **Date** *9/22*

Directions to the Teacher: Do not tell the student the title of the book. Ask the student to reread pages 12 through 21 silently and be ready to retell the key points in his or her own words. Ask the student to close the book before retelling. As the student retells the information, number the key items in the space provided. The order of the retelling does not affect the score. **Do not prompt** until the student has told all that he or she can recall from the rereading.

If the student leaves out key points, prompt by using the statements/questions provided. You may reword or adjust prompts to suit your situation. Complete the scoring and observation guide.

Directions to the Student: "You have read this book before. Reread pages 12–21 silently now. When you are finished, I want you to retell the key points in your own words."

Retelling Response Summary		Scoring Guide		
	Number Correct		**Unprompted**	**Prompted + Unprompted**
Unprompted	*2*			
Prompted	*4*	Acceptable	5–7	(5–7)
Unprompted + Prompted	*6*	Unacceptable	(0–4)	0–4

Observation Guide

(Check items that apply)

	Retelling smooth and connected; reflected a good summary
✓	Retelling disorganized
	Required no prompting
	Gave only the important ideas
✓	Gave important ideas plus details
	Told unnecessary details
	Could not tell without prompting
	Showed signs of misreading words (Example: Kept saying "owltees" instead of "owlets")

His misreading of "tiniest" as "tinniest" interfered with comprehension.

| | Other |

Unprompted Retelling (Number in order given.)	Key Points	Prompts (Use after unprompted retelling, if needed.)	Prompted Retelling (Check items correctly given.)
_1_	1. Mother and father owls spend most of their time catching food for their large families.	1. What do mother and father owls do most of the time?	
	2. Baby owlets are born with soft, fluffy white feathers that gradually turn darker.	2. How do baby owlets change?	✓
	3. Owls live all over the world—from rain forests to snowfields to deserts. (**Note**: Details of specific habitats are not required.)	3. Where do owls live?	✓
_2_	4. Barn owls live in barns and many other places.	4. Where do barn owls live?	
	5. The great horned owl and the long-eared owl are big owls that have tufts of feathers that look like horns or ears.	5. What can you tell me about some big owls?	✓
	6. Elf owls are the smallest owls; they live in Mexico and the Southwest. (**Note**: Students need mention only one of these locations.)	6. What are the smallest owls, and where do they live?	
	7. Saw-whet and pygmy owls are also very small. (**Note**: Students need mention only one of these owls by name.)	7. What are some other small owls?	✓

Taking a Formal Retelling

Protocols for a formal retelling are found in the Teacher's Resource File, pages R28–R63. This procedure may be used during **Revisiting** or at times outside the lesson plan.

Introduce the book as indicated on each retelling protocol and follow the guidelines for scoring. Here are some important points to keep in mind as you use the retelling procedure:

- It is not necessary to have students do a retelling on each book.

- Teacher observations during retelling are very important.

  — Noting the order in which students give ideas helps you see how the student organizes his/her thinking.
  — Students' answers may show that their miscues are affecting their comprehension. For example, a student reads *net* for *nest*. This may show a problem with decoding that affects comprehension and shows that the student has not focused on the need for a word to make sense.

- A retelling is just one measure of a student's comprehension. Actual reading performance in instructional materials and independent reading materials should also be considered.

An annotated example of a formal retelling is provided on the next two pages. Note that you should circle a score range in each column (*Unprompted* and *Prompted + Unprompted*) so that you can compare them for instructional purposes.

Taking an Oral Reading Check

The Oral Reading Check (ORC) is used only when you are concerned about a student's fluency. Students may be able to recognize many words but it may take them so long to do it that the process has negative effects on their comprehension. There is no precise rate at which students should read; the decision about a student's rate should be made on an individual basis (Lipson & Wixson, 1997). As you take an ORC, you should note how long it takes a student to read the passage. If a student reads along and automatically figures out the words, his/her fluency is appropriate. If it takes the student a long time to read the passage, more rereading and work in decoding may be needed to improve fluency.

Procedures for Taking an Oral Reading Check

Protocols for taking an Oral Reading Check using a preselected passage from each book in this level are found on pages R64–R81. Make a copy of the protocol you choose to use.

Taking an Oral Reading Check

Say:

Please read aloud this text for me. As you read, I will mark what you say. We will look at what I mark later.

Have the student read the text aloud.

As the student reads, make notes about his/her reading, using the coding system presented in the table. (Note: If you have a coding system of your own, it is not necessary to change to the one presented here.) Page T48 presents a marked passage to illustrate taking an Oral Reading Check.

Mark (and count) each miscue, even consistent repeats of a misreading.

Code for Marking an Oral Reading Check

Behavior	Coding	
Word Read Correctly	✓	If you are using a blank sheet, put a check mark for each word read correctly.
Misreading	*grows* ~~growls~~	Write what student said above word to have been read.
Omission	(horse)	Circle the word omitted.
Self-correction	*SC* *grows* ~~growls~~	Write **SC** above or beside a self-correction. Self-corrections *are not* counted as errors.
Teacher Tells a Word	*T* popcorn	Write **T** above a word you must tell a student.

Scoring and Interpreting an Oral Reading Check

After the student's reading, count the total number of words the student read correctly. (Self-corrections are not counted as wrong.)

When you use the Oral Reading Check Protocols provided for each book, use the scoring guide below the passage. Calculations will not be necessary.

Using the *SOAR TO SUCCESS* Student Record of Progress

Keeping an accurate record of student progress is important in using *SOAR TO SUCCESS*. A Student Record of Progress can be found in the Teacher's Resource File, pages R90–R91. The example on pages T50–T51 illustrates how to complete this form.

Oral Reading Check

Name *Olivia A.*   **Date** *9/19*

A Beauty of a Plan
Book #1, pages 2–4 (96 words)

It was four o'clock on a sunny Wednesday afternoon. But there were (still) students hard at work at
Mead
~~Meadow~~ Middle School.

Mr. Flores ran the shop ~~classes.~~ *class* Some days he let students stay late to work on their ~~projects.~~ *program*

Sheila Ross and Michael DeWitt put the ~~finishing~~ *finish. SC* touches on their cabinet. *T   T*

"Wow!" Michael said. "This is our best work yet!"

Sheila and Michael ~~cleaned~~ *clean SC* up and got ~~ready~~ *reading SC* to go.

"Mr. Flores," said Sheila, "we're finished!"

Mr. Flores checked their work. "~~Looking~~ *Looks* good!" he said. "I can't wait to see the ~~plans~~ *plan* for your

next project!"

Scoring Guide   *13* — *3* = *10*
                  Number of Miscues   Self-corrections   Miscues Counted

                  ✓ Acceptable: 0–10 miscues
                  _____ Unacceptable: 11+ miscues

Observations _____ fluent oral reading (See TM, page T48 for criteria.)
                  _____ good self-correction strategies
                  _____ needs to use phonics (_____)
                  ✓ needs to use structural elements (*endings*)
                  _____ overuses context

Comments *She self-corrected after read on a little, showing she was looking for*
              meaning. Then she did look at endings.

Student Log Sheet for REVISITING

Student Name	Date / Assessment / Text Used	Date / Assessment / Text Used	Date / Assessment / Text Used	Date / Assessment / Text Used	Date / Assessment / Text Used	Date / Assessment / Text Used	Date / Assessment / Text Used
1. Olivia A.	9/19 ORC Acceptable A Beauty of a Plan	9/27 Retell Acceptable The Lost Expedition					
2. Shawn F.	9/15 Retell Acceptable A Beauty of a Plan	9/22 Retell Acceptable Owl					
3. Mateo J.	9/18 ORC Unacceptable A Beauty of a Plan	9/26 Retell Unacceptable The Lost Expedition					
4. Tanya L.	9/14 Retell Acceptable A Beauty of a Plan	9/25 ORC Acceptable Owl					
5. Chris O.	9/20 ORC Unacceptable The Lost Expedition	9/28 Retell Acceptable (prompt) Owl					
6. May Y.	9/21 Retell Acceptable (prompt) The Lost Expedition						
7.							

Student Record of Progress

Name *Mateo J.*   **Level** *8*

Date Program Started *10-8-2000*   **Date Released** *2-1-2001*

Explanation of Release:

Completed level satisfactorily. See Comments.

Informal Reading Inventory

Date	Score	Comments
9-5-2000	*Lev. 1 Instr.*	*Compreh. Lev. 2, 75%; Lev. 3, 70%; Frustration in Level 4*
2-1-2001	*Lev. 3 Instr.*	*Confirms he is ready to release*

Retellings

Book Title	Book No.	Category	Performance/Comments
The Lost Expedition	*2*	*I*	*Unacceptable*
Journey Home	*5*	*III*	*Unacceptable (prompted). Disconnected*
Cal Ripken, Jr.	*6*	*III*	*Acceptable (prompted)*
Tunnels, Tracks, and Trains	*10*	*IV*	*Acceptable. Well-organized*
Sports Lab	*14*	*V*	*Acceptable (prompted)*
El Duque	*17*	*VI*	*Acceptable (unprompted!)*

Oral Reading Checks

Book Title	Book No.	Category	Performance/Comments
A Beauty of a Plan	1	I	Unacceptable (84%)
The Babe and I	4	II	Unacceptable (88%)
Mountains	7	III	Acceptable (92%)
An Even Break	16	V	Acceptable (93%)

Books Completed

Book Title	Category	Date Completed	Performance/Comments
A Beauty of a Plan	I	10-30	Needs modeling of CLARIFY/PHONICS
The Lost Expedition	I	11-5	Beginning to participate
Owl	II	11-12	Still needs CLARIFY/PHONICS modeling
The Babe and I	II	11-19	Modeled a key QUESTION
Journey Home	II	11-24	
Cal Ripken, Jr.	III	12-4	Enjoys this selection
Mountains	III	12-11	Using CLARIFY/PHONICS better
Jesse Jackson	III	12-18	
Lakota Hoop Dancer	III	1-8	
Tunnels, Tracks, and Trains	III	1-15	
Gloria Estefan	IV	1-22	Reads increasingly fluently
Benjamin Banneker	IV	1-29	
Lightning	IV	2-5	Likes science, now that he can read it
Sports Lab	IV	2-12	
Lisa Leslie	V	2-26	Modeled QUESTION well
An Even Break	V	3-5	Good PREDICT model
El Duque	VI	3-12	
Marisol and Magdalena	VI	3-19	Interested; modeled SUMMARIZE well

Comments: *He scarcely applied phonics at first, but we modeled CLARIFY/PHONICS often, and he's using it now. His other teachers see him using strategies in other subjects, reading just about on level, and showing interest in independent reading.*

Reciprocal Teaching and Graphic Organizers

SOAR TO SUCCESS lessons incorporate two important teaching strategies: reciprocal teaching and graphic organizers. Both teaching strategies help students accelerate their reading progress and develop independence in the process of constructing meaning. Years of research on reciprocal teaching have demonstrated that this strategy helps students make large gains in a short amount of time (Carter, 1997; Palincsar, 1984; Palincsar & Brown, 1984a; 1984b; 1986; Rosenshine & Meister, 1994). Graphic organizers have been shown to be effective in helping students construct meaning visually (Heimlich & Pittleman, 1986; Pehrsson & Robinson, 1985).

Reciprocal Teaching

"Years of research on reciprocal teaching have demonstrated that students make large gains in a short amount of time. . . . Graphic organizers have been shown to be effective in helping students construct meaning visually."

Purpose Reciprocal teaching is an instructional strategy designed to help students construct meaning and apply reading skills and strategies to all of their reading.

Description Reciprocal teaching is an interactive dialogue between the teacher and students that is held in place of a teacher-led discussion. The teacher and students **take turns being the teacher** and modeling four strategies after reading a chunk of text.

As students become more proficient at using the four strategies, the teacher drops back and allows the students to assume more independence in modeling the strategies.

The Four Strategies Used with Reciprocal Teaching There are four strategies used with reciprocal teaching, which research has shown to be important in helping students develop effective comprehension. These strategies are **SUMMARIZE**, **QUESTION**, **CLARIFY**, and **PREDICT**. The table on page T53 defines each of the strategies. The strategies may be used in any order.

The Four Strategies Used with Reciprocal Teaching

Summarize	Question
• Student retells in his or her own words the key points of what was read.	• Student poses a question about the content of the text to be answered by others.

Clarify	Predict
• Student tells the process he or she used to clear up confusing parts or unknown words in the text—by rereading, looking at illustrations, analyzing unknown words, etc.	• Student predicts what is likely to happen or to be learned next.

Learning to Use Reciprocal Teaching in Your Instruction

Reciprocal teaching is an effective, easy-to-use instructional strategy. It is a core strategy in the *SOAR TO SUCCESS* lessons. But it is also a strategy you will want to use in other lessons—for reading, science, social studies, and other content areas.

Key Points in Reciprocal Teaching These key points will help you learn to use reciprocal teaching:

- The texts used with reciprocal teaching are divided into meaningful chunks. This is one way to scaffold support for the lessons. (The *SOAR TO SUCCESS* lessons do this for you.)

- The four strategies—**SUMMARIZE, CLARIFY, QUESTION,** and **PREDICT**—are used over and over in any order. **Not all strategies are used after each reading.**

- The strategies are always displayed on a poster for students.

- The students silently read the first chunk of text.

- After reading, the teacher and students **take turns being teacher.** This means that the teacher or a student first models a strategy. An example of a sequence of reciprocal teaching after reading follows.

  Teacher: Laura, please model SUMMARIZE for us.

  Laura: Two boys find a dog on the beach. They name him Strider and decide to share taking care of him.

  Teacher: Mel, how about you giving a summary.

  Mel: Two boys named Leigh and Barry found a stray dog on the beach. They decided they will both own him and care for him. They named him Strider.

Teacher:	Who has a question to ask?
Michael:	What have the boys decided to do about Strider?
Gloria:	They have decided to keep him, and both will take care of him.
Eduardo:	Where will Strider live?
Brenda:	He'll stay nights with Leigh, and during school, he can stay in Larry's yard, which has a fence.
Teacher:	I want to model CLARIFY for us. I wasn't sure what *joint custody* meant on page 16, but I read on and learned they will split the cost and each will have him part of the time. They are really sharing him. So *joint custody* must mean sharing. Does anyone else have something to CLARIFY? (A student models CLARIFY.)
Teacher:	Who will model PREDICT?
Jimmy:	Leigh's landlady sounds mean, so I predict that she won't let Leigh keep Strider in the house.
Teacher:	Leigh's mom thinks it's okay, so I predict Barry's parents will let him keep Strider. (The lesson continues.)

- **The pattern after reading:** In most lessons, you should model all four strategies or have students model all four strategies. After silent reading, follow a pattern of checking predictions or answering questions. You or the students should then model Summarize; the other strategies should be modeled in any order.

- **Scaffolding modeling:** Early in the program, you will model a strategy first and then have students model. But soon begin to have students model first, with you providing models as needed. Later in the program, the students should be doing most of the modeling, but you should still provide models as needed.

The *SOAR TO SUCCESS* lessons give you many examples of good models for each of the four strategies. However, you will often need to create your own models to meet the individual needs of students.

Criteria for Models

Summarize	Question
A good **Summary** • gives only the key points related to the story line or main ideas • is told in your own words	A good **Question** • may be answered directly from the text • may require making inferences • may require evaluation • may involve all of the above
Clarify	**Predict**
A good **Clarification** • tells how you went about clearing up a problem you had with your reading • may focus on an idea, a word meaning, or a word pronunciation	A good **Prediction** • uses information from the text • uses information you already know • is logical based on the above

Teaching Students to Use Reciprocal Teaching

The following steps are an effective way to introduce reciprocal teaching to your students.

Prepare

Display *SOAR TO SUCCESS* Poster 2, which presents the four strategies used in reciprocal teaching. Keep this poster (and Posters 1 and 3) displayed during all lessons.

Prepare a set of prompt cards for each strategy. (See Strategy Prompts at the end of the Student Guide.) These are cards that give the students the words to say as they learn to use each strategy. Print the prompts on cards of different colors. Keep them on your teaching table. When a student begins to model a strategy, have him or her use the card to start the model. As students become accustomed to modeling, remove the cards.

Teach

Use the Introductory Lesson for *SOAR TO SUCCESS* found on page T69.

Do not expect students to master the strategies at this point.

Refine

Continue using the strategies throughout the lessons. Take turns with the students being teacher. Provide as much teacher modeling as needed.

A Simulation of Modeling the Reciprocal Teaching Strategies

This simulation of modeling is provided to help you check your own understanding of the strategies so that you can model them effectively. These strategy models are based on the book *Island of the Blue Dolphins* by Scott O'Dell. Don't be concerned that you are not reading the text from the book. Focus on whether you recognize each strategy.

Read each of the models. Decide whether it is QUESTION, SUMMARIZE, CLARIFY, or PREDICT. If possible, compare and discuss the models with a colleague before you check your answers. Answers are found at the end of the section, on page T59.

1. A young girl is left alone on an island and must learn to survive. Her only friends are animals who live on or around the island.

   In model 1 the strategy is _____.

2. The girl is going to sail in a canoe to find her people.

   In model 2 the strategy is _____.

3. On page 47 the girl builds a strong fence around her new home. Why does she need to build a fence?

   In model 3 the strategy is _____.

4. On page 61 I come to the word a-n-c-e-s-t-o-r-s. I couldn't say it. First I looked for a chunk I knew. I recognized t-o-r-s; it says *tors*. I knew *an* was the first sound in *answer; est* is a sound I also know. I said *ankestors*. It didn't make sense. Then I said *ancestors*. I reread the sentence. It makes sense.

   In model 4 the strategy is _____.

5. Why is the girl afraid of the wild dogs?

   In model 5 the strategy is _____.

6. The girl feels very tired as she tries to return to the island in her canoe. A swarm of dolphins comes and swims around the canoe. They help her reach the island safely.

   In model 6 the strategy is _____.

7. I read the word *weapons* on page 50. I didn't know what it meant. I reread the sentence and I know that the girl needs to protect herself. A weapon must be something she can use to protect herself from the wild dogs.

   In model 7 the strategy is _____.

8. What are some of the weapons that the girl makes?

   In model 8 the strategy is _____.

9. The girl will fight with the leader of the wild dogs.

   In model 9 the strategy is _____.

10. The girl waits for the ship to return all summer. Once, she sees a whale and thinks it is a ship. The girl gives up hope after the first winter storm.

    In model 10 the strategy is _____.

11. Why does the girl go to the cave where the wild dogs live?

    In model 11 the strategy is _____.

Graphic Organizers

Students having difficulty learning to read are helped in constructing meaning by using more concrete, hands-on types of activities. Graphic organizers provide this type of support.

Description

• A graphic organizer is a visual diagram of the ideas presented in a text. Page T58 shows samples of some different types of graphic organizers.

Visual Ways to Help Students Construct Meaning

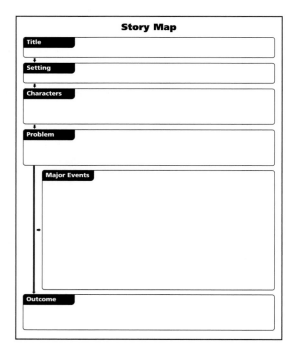

Story Map

Title

Setting

Characters

Problem

Major Events

Outcome

K-W-L Chart

Title

What I **K**now	What I **W**ant to Find Out	What I **L**earned

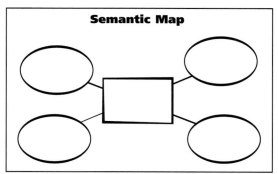

Semantic Map

Main Ideas and Details

Title _____

1. Main Idea _____
   a. Detail _____
   b. _____
   c. _____
   d. _____
2. _____
   a. _____
   b. _____
   b. _____
   b. _____
3. _____
   a. _____
   b. _____
   c. _____
   d. _____
4. _____
   a. _____
   b. _____
   c. _____
   d. _____

Event Map

Title

Event 1

Event 2

Event 3

Event 4

Event 5

Event 6

Event 7

Event 8

Using Graphic Organizers with *SOAR TO SUCCESS*

- For each book in *SOAR TO SUCCESS,* a graphic organizer is provided to use with the lessons. These organizers are used to help students develop their ability to comprehend.

- Students having difficulty reading often take a long time to express their ideas in writing. Therefore, in the *SOAR TO SUCCESS* lessons the writing moves from student dictation to the teacher to more independent writing by individual students. Initially, students work as a group with the teacher to complete a graphic organizer on a poster. Later, as they become more familiar with each type of graphic organizer, they may start a graphic organizer as a group but then complete it on their own in their Student Guides, using the poster as a reference.

Answers for Reciprocal Teaching

1. Summarize
2. Predict
3. Question
4. Clarify
5. Question
6. Summarize
7. Clarify
8. Question
9. Predict
10. Summarize
11. Question

Helping Students with Decoding Problems

Some struggling readers in upper elementary (3–5) and middle school (6–8) grades have specialized needs in terms of learning to decode words. This section of the *SOAR TO SUCCESS* manual provides guidelines to help you develop a plan to meet the needs of these students.

These guidelines amplify and extend the recommendations made in Section 5 under Selecting Students (page T37). They assume that the Timed Fluency Test has been administered as part of the screening process.

Decoding Needs of Struggling Older Readers

There are four basic decoding problems that may pose difficulties for struggling older readers. Each of these problems is described in the table on the next page with suggestions for intervention.

Assessing Students' Phonics/Decoding Needs

Assessment of students' phonics/decoding needs should take place as a part of the student selection process (see page T37).

- Determine students' general decoding abilities by doing such things as:
  Have students take the Timed Fluency Test.
  Have students orally read from materials used in their reading, language arts, or other classes.
  Have students orally read a preprimer-primer passage. Acceptable performance is 90% accuracy or higher.

- For students who have insufficient phonics/decoding abilities, administer the *Houghton Mifflin Phonics/Decoding Screening Test*.

Using the *HOUGHTON MIFFLIN PHONICS/DECODING SCREENING TEST*

- Description
  The *Houghton Mifflin Phonics/Decoding Screening Test* consists of a series of individually administered tasks designed to help you determine the specific type of phonics/decoding instruction students need.

- Components
  The components of the *Houghton Mifflin Phonics/Decoding Screening Test* are in the Resource File, pages R162–R175.

Problem	Description	Intervention Using *SOAR TO SUCCESS*
Does not apply known skills to unknown words	• Student knows phonics/decoding skills. • Student does not independently use phonics/decoding when encountering an unknown word in reading.	• Model CLARIFY/PHONICS during *SOAR TO SUCCESS* lessons. Use Decoding Longer Words lessons.
Can decode simple words but is unable to decode longer words	• Student has difficulty decoding words of three or more syllables.	• Use Decoding Longer Words and Making Words lessons. • Have student model CLARIFY/PHONICS lessons with longer words during *SOAR TO SUCCESS* lessons.

Lacks basic phonics/decoding skills	• Student is unable to orally read a pre-primer/primer passage with 90+% accuracy.
	or
	• Student could not decode simple words on the *Houghton Mifflin Phonics/Decoding Screening Test*.
		• Use the results of the *Houghton Mifflin Phonics/Decoding Screening Test* to determine specific needs.
		• Use *Houghton Mifflin Phonics Intervention* until student achieves goals set.
		• Place in *SOAR TO SUCCESS* after student achieves goals of *Houghton Mifflin Phonics Intervention*.
		  – Place heavy emphasis on CLARIFY/PHONICS during *SOAR TO SUCCESS* lessons.
		  – Use Decoding Longer Words and Making Words lessons.

Lacks fluency: Scored Below Expected Progress or Seriously Below Expected Progress on the Timed Fluency Test	• Has poor oral reading fluency but other test scores have not shown poor decoding skills.	• Examine results of the *Houghton Mifflin Phonics/Decoding Screening Test* for specific weaknesses. • Increase rereading for fluency during Revisiting; provide additional rereading for fluency outside *SOAR TO SUCCESS* time (see Bibliography, page R12).

Unable to decode words because of oral language difficulties	• Student lacks sufficient oral language to use phonics/decoding appropriately. This may be a native-language speaker or a second-language learner.	• Provide oral language development through
		  – Read Alouds
		  – Listening Experiences
		  – Discussion Experiences
		• Administer the *Houghton Mifflin Phonics/Decoding Screening Test* after student has developed a good oral language base. (For students acquiring English, this should be the Intermediate Fluency Level.)
		• Use *Houghton Mifflin Phonics Intervention* as needed.
		• Place in appropriate level of *SOAR TO SUCCESS* **after** students achieve goals of oral language development and *Houghton Mifflin Phonics Intervention*.

Components of the *HOUGHTON MIFFLIN PHONICS/DECODING SCREENING TEST*

Component	Description
• Teacher's Manual for Administering, Scoring, and Analyzing the *Houghton Mifflin Phonics/Decoding Screening Test* (R162–R175)	• Provides all instructions needed for using the test
• Student Materials (R176–R179)	• Students perform tasks and read from pages. • Pages should be photocopied and mounted inside a manila folder or on card stock.
• *Houghton Mifflin Phonics/Decoding Screening Test* Protocol and Analysis Sheets (R170–R175)	• Teacher marks student responses to phonics/decoding tasks. • One set of Protocol and Analysis Sheets must be photocopied for each student being tested.

• **Who Takes the** *Houghton Mifflin Phonics/Decoding Screening Test?*
Any student having serious difficulties with phonics/decoding and/or who has scored Below Expected Progress on the Timed Fluency Test should be given the test.

• **Procedures for Administering, Scoring, and Analyzing the** *Houghton Mifflin Phonics/Decoding Screening Test*
Specific instructions for using the test are found in the Resource File, pages R165–R175.

Providing Decoding Support by Focusing on CLARIFY/PHONICS— Think About Words

Always keep the **CLARIFY/PHONICS—Think About Words** strategy, Poster 3, on display in your *SOAR TO SUCCESS* work area. Remind students to use it as they read.

Model **CLARIFY/PHONICS—Think About Words** frequently, focusing on the use of different decoding skills:

Example: Teacher Model—Focus on Phonics

> When I came to the word *h-a-p-p-y,* I didn't know it. I looked at the patterns of consonants and vowels to identify chunks. I could see *h-a-p-p.* I knew *y* had a long *e* sound. I blended them together—*happy*—and reread the sentence. It made sense.

Example: Teacher Model—Focus on Word Parts

I came to the word *u-n-t-i-e* and didn't know it. I saw the word parts *un* and *tie*. I knew them and could put them together to say the word *untie*. I reread it in the sentence and it made sense.

Have students take turns modeling **CLARIFY/PHONICS—Think About Words** often.

Stress Rereading for Fluency in Revisiting

When you take an Oral Reading Check during Revisiting, look for students' strengths and needs in specific decoding skills and strategies.

During Revisiting, do more rereading of previously read books to build fluency. If the lesson plan suggests a group conference, change this activity to rereading of previously read books so that students will reread familiar text to build fluency. This will give you an opportunity to check and coach.

Confer with Other Teachers

Talk with the students' other teachers about how you are approaching the students' decoding needs. Share with the teachers your posters of strategies for decoding and ways of modeling them. *The students must use the same approach to figuring out words in all classes.*

Lessons for Extra Support in Decoding

Two procedures are provided for students in *SOAR TO SUCCESS* who need extra support with decoding: Decoding Longer Words lessons and Making Words lessons. These lessons are given **outside the time allotted for *SOAR TO SUCCESS* lessons.** These lessons are provided as part of the Optional Day Lesson Plans (see Teacher's Resource File, page R180).

The Decoding Longer Words lessons teach students key skills needed to pronounce unknown words by dividing them into chunks or syllables to help sound them out. Remember, breaking words into chunks or syllables for pronunciation does not always match dictionary respellings. For pronunciation, students need only to approximate the sound chunks or syllables and check against their oral language.

Procedure for Making Words

A Making Words activity is provided for each book as part of the Optional Day Lesson Plans (see Teacher's Resource File, page R180) with a suggested target word from the book and words to build from it. Each Making Words activity provides an encoding opportunity related to the Decoding Longer Words skill.

Description
An active, hands-on manipulative teaching strategy to help children learn to use letter/sound relationships and word patterns

For Whom
Any students needing support in learning to use letter/sound relationships to decode words and spell

Time
10–15 minutes

Materials
You may make your own letter cards or purchase them from Houghton Mifflin Company (Letter Cards and 7 Plastic Trays, ordering code: 1-34621). If you make your own letter cards, it helps to make the consonant cards one color, the vowel cards another color, and the letter y a third color. Print the lowercase letter on one side, the capital letter on the other. Letter trays can be made from file folders or other heavy stock folded to create a long groove to stand the letters in.

Occasionally an activity calls for you to make a card for a prefix or a suffix. This is to provide an encoding application to reinforce the skill in the Decoding Longer Words lesson.

Before you conduct each activity, prepare an index card for each word that will be made so that you can have students sort the word cards according to patterns after they have finished making words. You may use the same cards when students add words to a Word Wall.

Procedure

1. Select a target word from a book students have read. Make a list of words you want students to make, progressing from two-letter words to the word you want to complete the lesson:

   important (target word, from *Arctic Tundra*)

   an
   ant
   art
   tart
   part
   port
   import
   important

2. Give each student a set of letters for the target word and a tray.

3. Ask students to make the word *an*. Use it in a sentence.

4. Then make the word yourself. After most students have made it in their trays, show your word to them; have them check their word and show it to you.

5. Ask: What one letter would you add to *an* to make *ant*?

6. You and the students each make the word *ant* in your own trays. Show your word to students; have them check their word and show it to you.

7. Continue the lesson, building the words you want to have made:

   • Change a letter to make *art.*

   • Add a letter to make *tart.*

   • Change a letter to make *part.*

- Change a letter to make *port*.

- Add the prefix *im* to make *import*. *We import oil from other countries.*

- Now use all your letters to make a word from the book, *important (Arctic Tundra, page 15).*

8. Throughout the lesson, help students see various patterns in the word building. At the end have students sort the words, which you have put on index cards. Have them find and arrange together:

  - Words that rhyme (*art, tart, part*)

  - Words with *port* as a base (*port, import, important*)

  - Words with two or more chunks (*import, important*)

9. Add to a Word Wall the target word and/or any others selected by students.

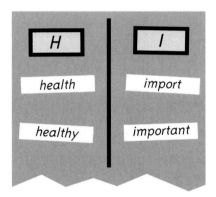

10. Locate the final word in the book in which it appears to help students build the connection between what they are learning about words and their reading.

Home-School Connections

Communication with students' families is an important part of all good literacy programs. This is especially important for a good intervention program.

The suggestions that follow and the materials provided in the Teacher's Resource File can help you establish and maintain home contact. Families lead busy lives, and it is not always easy for teachers to communicate directly with parents to encourage their support of their child's participation in *SOAR TO SUCCESS.* Certain changes in family life in recent years can make contact with parents difficult. Families who have immigrated recently may not yet speak or read English. Many parents' jobs make lack of time another serious obstacle to their involvement. Still, family participation in a child's education is as important as ever.

Introducing the Program to Students' Families

Communicate with parents to tell them about the opportunity their child has in becoming a part of the *SOAR TO SUCCESS* group. Contact with parents can be made by telephone, through a conference, or through the Introductory Family Letter found in the Teacher's Resource File, page R92.

Stress that this is a program that will help their child accelerate his or her reading and, hopefully, bring him or her up to level. Tell parents that in order to benefit from *SOAR TO SUCCESS* it is important for their child to

- have the family's support and interest in the child's reading.
- attend school regularly.
- stay in the same school.

If for any reason you feel a student is not going to have regular attendance or stay in the school, consider another student for the program (unless you have extra space).

Make the following points with parents:

- After completing each book, the student will bring home a letter and will tell about the strategies that he or she is using in *SOAR TO SUCCESS,* so the family can share in the child's progress and praise the successes.

- The *SOAR TO SUCCESS* program teaches reading strategies, or ways that students can read effectively to get more out of their reading. Suggest that parents encourage their child to tell them about the strategies and to model, or demonstrate, how they can use them in reading a newspaper or magazine article or other information at home.

- Some pages in the Student Guide are graphic organizers that students complete in class to help them summarize the book, so they will be able to tell their families about the book they are reading.

- Other pages in the Student Guide give Strategy Prompts, which students use during their lessons. Students can use those to explain the strategies to their families.

- There is some homework for each book, and parents should make sure there is a quiet place and time for the student to do it. Tell them that sometimes the assignment will involve some brief research, so it will help if the student can go to a school library or a community library. (Adjust your recommendation according to the school schedule and facilities and to what is available in the community.)

Consistent communication will help families understand what the child is participating in. Make sure that all teachers and other school personnel who communicate with the family are aware that the student is in *SOAR TO SUCCESS* and support it.

Maintaining Contact with Students' Families

After students complete each *SOAR TO SUCCESS* book, use one or both of the following options to share students' successes and progress with families:

- Send home the *SOAR TO SUCCESS* book for a student to share and discuss. Use Home Connection Letter #1, found in the Teacher's Resource File, page R93.

- Send home the Student Guide pages with the graphic organizer and the student's responses to the book. Use Home Connection Letter #2, found in the Teacher's Resource File, page R94.

Use Homework assignments as a way of encouraging families to be involved in students' reading progress.

Encourage parents to discuss any questions or suggestions they have about their child's reading progress, and make any needed conference arrangements as convenient as possible for the parents.

Section 10
Introductory Lesson for Levels 7–8

Note: Keep this introduction to five minutes in order to devote at least minimum times to the five parts of the Introductory Lesson.

Complete this lesson before you begin the first book. On the day before this lesson, ask students to bring a book they are reading on their own, which they will need for the group conference.

TIME: 40 minutes

Materials:

- Books students are reading independently
- Single copies of books from the *SOAR TO SUCCESS* level
- Introductory Poster, Posters #1–5, this Introductory Lesson
- Single copy of Student Guide from the level you are teaching
- Paper and pencils

Introducing *SOAR TO SUCCESS*

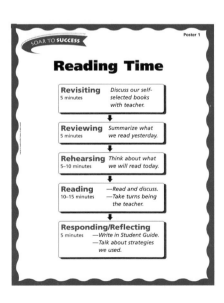

- Display Poster #1.
- Tell students that *SOAR TO SUCCESS* time is designed to help them move ahead quickly in their reading skills and in their understanding of what they read.
- Show students the materials they will be using and briefly explain the function of each.

  — 18 books

  — posters

  — selected Reflections, Strategy Notes, and graphic organizers from the Student Guide

- Using Poster 1, briefly preview each of the blocks in the daily instructional plan and tell students that the lessons will move at a fast pace each day. Tell students that now you will do each of the parts of the lesson with them.

Introducing Revisiting

Note: Remember that Revisiting should be limited to five minutes.

Explain that each day during the five-minute Revisiting time, students will be either

- rereading previously read *SOAR TO SUCCESS* books

OR

- having a group conference about books they are reading independently (see page T17).

Rereading

Explain that on the days when students reread, they will select a *SOAR TO SUCCESS* book that they have read previously and they will reread it, so they can practice the four reading strategies that you will teach them in today's lesson.

Group Conference

Tell students that during *SOAR TO SUCCESS* lessons they will read only *SOAR TO SUCCESS* books, but during other times in the day they will need to read other books they have chosen to read on their own. During each Group Conference in Revisiting, they will tell about such a book that they are reading independently.

Tell students that for each day, they should bring in what they are reading independently. They will keep a log of their independent reading. (See the log on page R26 and Student Guide page 91.) Remind students that you asked them to bring in any books they are reading independently, and ask them to take them out now.

Modeling a Group Conference

As you model the Group Conference, keep it within the five-minute Revisiting time block.

- Explain that for each Group Conference, you will give students one or two prompts to focus their discussion. Ask volunteers to suggest what kinds of topics they might discuss. Emphasize that students do not need to have finished a book in order to discuss it.

- Hold a Group Conference using the following prompts:

  — Is your book informational or does it tell a story?

  — Who or what is your book about?

Introducing Reviewing

Note: Remember to limit the time for Reviewing to five minutes.

- Point out the Reviewing block on Poster 1. Ask students what *reviewing* means. Explain that this is a time each day when students will discuss the four Reciprocal Teaching reading strategies that you will teach them today and/or they will summarize what they read the previous day.

- Display Posters 4 and 5. Tell students that these diagrams are graphic organizers and ask if anyone has seen either of them before. (Students may have used graphic organizers in the past, but possibly not consistently or effectively.) Explain that Poster 4 is a graphic organizer called a Story Map. Poster 5 is called a K-W-L Chart. They will be using these and other graphic organizers to organize the important information as they read a book, and they will use them to summarize during Reviewing.

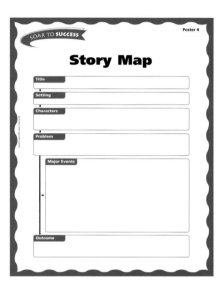

Introducing Rehearsing

Note: Remember to limit the time for Rehearsing to five to ten minutes.

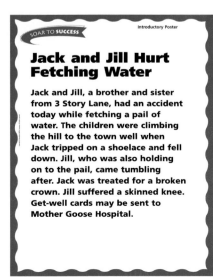

- Tell students that each day during Rehearsing you will preview the day's text before they read it. Explain that you will show them the illustrations, talk about what is happening on each page, and point out key vocabulary words. This preview will help them read and understand more easily.

Modeling Rehearsing

Introduce the Poster Display the Introductory Poster and tell students that they are going to read something that they are familiar with—the story of Jack and Jill. Ask students if they know this story and have volunteers recall what they remember from the rhyme. Point out the title and say that this is like a newspaper headline because here the story is told as a newspaper article.

Guided Preview Say: This story is about a brother and sister, Jack and Jill, who went to fetch a pail of water and had an **accident**. (Point to *accident*.)

Introducing Reading and Reciprocal Teaching

Note: Remember to limit the time for Reading and Reciprocal Teaching to ten to fifteen minutes.

Display Posters 2 and 3. Explain that during the Reading part of the lesson, the students and you will be using Reciprocal Teaching—a procedure in which students take the role of teacher. (See pages T56–T63.)

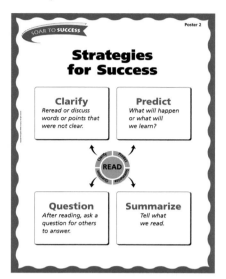

Point to Poster 2 and explain that during Reciprocal Teaching, students will use these four strategies. Tell them that Poster 3 tells more about one of the four strategies—how to Clarify and use phonics to figure out a word they don't know. As they use the strategies, they will take turns modeling each one. When they model, **they will be demonstrating the use of a strategy from their reading.**

- Tell them that these posters will be displayed at all times during the *SOAR TO SUCCESS* lesson to help them learn and use the four strategies.

- Have students read silently the story "Jack and Jill Hurt Fetching Water" from the Introductory Poster. Then read the story aloud while students follow along.

- Explain that you will model using each of the four strategies with the story about Jack and Jill. You will model one strategy and then ask some of them to model the same strategy. When they model the strategy, they are taking the role of the teacher. First, the teacher—or a student taking the role of the teacher—models a strategy; then a student models it. Then someone models another strategy, and so on. Taking turns this way is the procedure for Reciprocal Teaching, which they will do every day in *SOAR TO SUCCESS*.

You may need to model a strategy more than once in this introductory lesson.

Teacher Models and Students Model

SUMMARIZE: When I **SUMMARIZE**, I tell in my own words the important things about the story—the characters, the setting, and the important things that have happened. *Jack and Jill went to get some water and they had an accident.*

Some students model **SUMMARIZE**.

CLARIFY/PHONICS: When I come to a word I don't know, first I use chunks I know. To figure out this word (point to *fetching*), I looked at the beginning, middle, and ending sounds. I knew the sounds for *f* and *ch*, and also the *-ing* ending. The part *f-e-t* looked like *bet* with the /f/ sound. I blended them together to pronounce *fetching*. Then I reread the sentence. It must be a word that means "getting."

CLARIFY: When I need to **CLARIFY** something I don't understand, I reread the text, or look at a picture that might help. *How did Jill get hurt too?* I reread the part that says she was also holding on to the pail. So Jack must have pulled her along as he fell.

Some students model **CLARIFY**.

QUESTION: When I **QUESTION**, I ask something that could be answered as I read, or after I've read. *What were Jack and Jill doing when they got hurt?*

Some students model **QUESTION**.

PREDICT: When I **PREDICT,** I use clues from what I've already read or previewed. If we had more to read, I would predict that Jill will get out of the hospital before Jack does.

Some students model **PREDICT**.

Introducing Responding/Reflecting

Note: Remember to limit the time for Responding/Reflecting to five minutes.

- Explain that during this block of time, students will either

  — talk and write about how they are using the strategies

  OR

  — write and discuss something they have just read about.

  They may also update their graphic organizers.

They will use their Student Guide pages during this time. In addition to the Reflection that they will write during the lesson, the Student Guide page will include a homework assignment.

- Distribute paper and pencils and have students respond briefly to this prompt: *List the four strategies.*

- Tell students that today the homework assignment is to tell their family about the four strategies they are going to use in *SOAR TO SUCCESS*. If you have not already sent the Introductory Family Letter (page R92), do that after you summarize the Introductory Lesson.

Summarizing the Introductory Lesson

- Use Poster 1 to briefly review the five lesson blocks, asking students to tell what you do in each one.

- Refer to Poster 2. Have students recall the four strategies and tell what you do when you use them.

- Tell students that these posters will remain up throughout *SOAR TO SUCCESS* time to remind them of the lesson blocks and times. Each day when they begin the group, they should know that they need to get right to work.

- Answer students' questions.

Lesson Plans

A Beauty of a Plan

by Angela Shelf Medearis

Illustrations by Eric Velasquez

*S*ummary: Sheila enjoys shop class and wants to become an architect. Grandma says she must drop shop class if she can't find a practical use for the things she learns there. Sheila and the rest of her class design and install a new interior for Grandma's beauty salon.

Materials

Lesson 1	Lesson 2	Lesson 3	Lesson 4
• Independent Reading books	• Independent Reading books	• Independent Reading books	• Independent Reading books
• *A Beauty of a Plan* pp. 2–5	• *A Beauty of a Plan* pp. 6–13	• *A Beauty of a Plan* pp. 14–23	• *A Beauty of a Plan* pp. 24–32
• Posters 2, 3, 4	• Posters 2, 3, 4	• Posters 2, 3, 4	• Posters 2, 3, 4
• Student Guide (SG) pp. 5–7	• Student Guide (SG) pp. 5–7	• Student Guide (SG) pp. 5–6, 8	• Student Guide (SG) pp. 5–6, 8
• Strategy Prompts, SG pp. 89–91	• Strategy Prompts, SG pp. 89–91	• Strategy Prompts, SG pp. 89–91	• Strategy Prompts, SG pp. 89–91
• Markers	• Markers	• Markers	• Markers
			• Home Connection letter

Scaffolding

Strong Teacher Support	Moderate Teacher Support	Student Independence
For Book 1 (Category I), strong teacher support is provided through modeling and previewing. However, students should be encouraged to practice using strategies frequently.		

Help with Phonics and Decoding Longer Words: For students who need explicit instruction, see the Optional Lesson on page R182 of the Teacher's Resource File in this manual.

Lesson Overview

	Lesson 1	Lesson 2	Lesson 3	Lesson 4
Revisiting (5 minutes)	• Group Conference: Independent Reading	• Group Conference: Independent Reading	• Group Conference: Independent Reading	• Group Conference: Independent Reading
Reviewing (5 minutes)	• Review Reciprocal Teaching Strategies (Posters 2, 3)	• Review Reciprocal Teaching Strategies (Posters 2, 3) • Teacher Models SUMMARIZE	• Review Reciprocal Teaching Strategies (Posters 2, 3) • Students Summarize	• Review Reciprocal Teaching Strategies (Posters 2, 3) • Students Summarize
Rehearsing (5–10 minutes)	• Introduce the Book • Teacher Models PREDICT • Students Predict • Guided Preview, pp. 2–5 Key Vocabulary: *projects*	• Students Predict • Guided Preview, pp. 6–13 Key Vocabulary: *salon, designing, semester, architect*	• Students Predict • Guided Preview, pp. 14–23 Key Vocabulary: *measurements, partitions, opportunity, plywood, install*	• Students Predict • Guided Preview, pp. 24–32 Key Vocabulary: *vacation, exhibit*
Reading and Reciprocal Teaching (10–15 minutes)	• Silent Reading/Group Read-Aloud • Check Predictions • Teacher Models SUMMARIZE, QUESTION, CLARIFY/ PHONICS, PREDICT • Students Model Strategies	• Silent Reading/Group Read-Aloud • Check Predictions • Teacher Models SUMMARIZE, QUESTION, CLARIFY/ PHONICS, PREDICT • Students Model Strategies	• Silent Reading/Group Read-Aloud • Check Predictions • Teacher Models SUMMARIZE, CLARIFY, QUESTION, CLARIFY/ PHONICS, PREDICT • Students Model Strategies	• Silent Reading/Group Read-Aloud • Check Predictions • Teacher Models SUMMARIZE, CLARIFY, QUESTION • Students Model Strategies
Responding/ Reflecting (5 minutes)	• Story Map (Poster 4, SG p. 5) • Reflection #1 (SG p. 7) • Strategies Discussion (Posters 2, 3) • Homework 1	• Story Map (Poster 4, SG p. 5) • Reflection #2 (SG p. 7) • Strategies Discussion (Posters 2, 3) • Homework 2	• Story Map (Poster 4, SG p. 5) • Reflection #3 (SG p. 8) • Strategies Discussion (Posters 2, 3) • Homework 3	• Story Map (Poster 4, SG p. 5) • Reflection #4 (SG p. 8) • Homework 4 • Home Connection letter

A Beauty of a Plan *by Angela Shelf Medearis*

Illustrations by Eric Velazquez

Lesson 1

Revisiting
(5 minutes)

Group Conference Briefly discuss with students the books they have been reading independently. **Prompts:** *Who or what is your book about? Tell about your favorite part so far.*

....

Note: For this first book, the Revisiting activity each day will be a Group Conference, a discussion of independently read books outside of this program. (See pages T17 and T34 for guidelines on group conferences and independent reading.)

For subsequent books, in alternating lessons, have students select and reread previously read SOAR TO SUCCESS books. Beginning with Book 3, while most students reread silently to develop fluency, the teacher works with one student, coaching or taking a retelling or Oral Reading Check. (See pages T43–T49 for information on these options.)

Starting with Book 5, in alternate lessons in which students reread books they have selected, they should develop a model of a strategy that they will share in Reviewing. Assign each student a strategy. As students approach independence (Book 12), each student selects a strategy to model. Suggestions in the Lesson Plans for specific books reflect this sequence.

....

Reviewing
(5 minutes)

POSTER

Posters 2, 3

Review Reciprocal Teaching Strategies Display Posters 2 and 3 and review each strategy with students. Remind students that they took turns using the strategies during the introductory lesson. Call on volunteers to tell how they used each strategy. Tell students that they will take turns using these strategies again to help them read *A Beauty of a Plan*.

Rehearsing
(5–10 minutes)

Introduce the Book Show the book cover and read its title, author, and illustrator. Use the following model to predict what the book is about, based on the title and cover art.

Teacher Model/*Predict* *When I PREDICT, I use what I have read or clues from the pictures to help me figure out what I will learn or what will happen in the book. The book title and the cover help me predict that the girl in the story is creative and likes to draw.*

Students Predict Have students predict what will happen in the book based on the title and the cover. List their predictions for later use. Explain that they will verify, or check, their predictions after reading.

Key Vocabulary

projects

Guided Preview/Vocabulary pp. 2–5 Use the preview points. Tell students you are using words that will help them read the story by themselves. Tell them not to be concerned if they have difficulty with the pronunciation of proper names in this book, but to keep reading. Emphasize the key vocabulary word (boldfaced) and point to it as you speak. Do not teach the word in isolation.

▶ *pages 2–3 The students in Mr. Flores's shop class are working on their **projects** (p. 2). Sheila and Michael are finishing their project.*

▶ *pages 4–5 Now Sheila has to decide what their next project will be. What do you think they might do?*

*Note: **After** introducing and previewing the book, hand out a copy to each student.*

Reading and Reciprocal Teaching
(10–15 minutes)

Posters 2, 3   **SG p. 6**

Purpose Setting/*Predict* Remind students of the predictions they made about what would happen in *A Beauty of a Plan*. Students will check their predictions after they read.

Silent Reading or Group Read-Aloud Students read pages 2–5 silently or, for this first book, read aloud as a group. Remind them that after they read, you and they will model using strategies and take turns being the teacher. Model for students how to use **Strategy Notes** (SG p. 6) to jot down strategies they use when reading this section and to use those notes when they model strategies. They can jot down a QUESTION, a word or a point they need to CLARIFY or were able to CLARIFY, what they PREDICT, and notes to help them SUMMARIZE.

Reciprocal Teaching (after reading)

Check Predictions Call on students to reread the predictions you listed during Rehearsing. Were their predictions verified so far in the book?

Teacher and Students Model Using Strategies Call students' attention to strategies listed on Posters 2 and 3. Remind students of the way they used and shared strategies during the introductory lesson.

After you model each strategy, call on students to take turns modeling it. Remind students to use their Strategy Notes (SG p. 6) to help them model.

Teacher Models (each to be followed by student modeling)

SUMMARIZE *When I SUMMARIZE, I tell in my own words the important things I have read–the characters, the setting, and the important events that have happened. The characters are Sheila, Michael, and Mr. Flores. The setting is Meadow Middle School. Michael and Sheila have finished building a project in shop class. Now Sheila must pick a new project for them to work on.*

Have some students model SUMMARIZE.

QUESTION *When I QUESTION, I ask something that can be answered as I read or after I finish reading. What did Michael design for the project he and Sheila just completed?*

Have some students model QUESTION.

CLARIFY/PHONICS *When I come to a word I can't say, I look for chunks I know. To figure out this word* (point to the word **cabinet** on page 3)*, I divide it into the chunks* **c-a-b***,* **i***, and* **n-e-t***. I can sound out the first chunk,* **cab***. The second chunk is a single vowel,* **i***. I'm not sure yet how to pronounce it. The last chunk is* **net***. I try the long and short sounds for* **i** *until I get the word* **cab/i/net***. I reread the sentence, and it makes sense.*

Have some students model CLARIFY/PHONICS.

PREDICT *When I PREDICT, I use the pictures or what I have read to tell what will happen next or what I will learn. I predict that Sheila will carefully plan the new project.*

Have some students model PREDICT.

Responding/ Reflecting

(5 minutes)

Poster 4   **SG pp. 5, 7**

Story Map Display Story Map Poster 4 and explain that a Story Map can help students remember the important elements of the story–characters, setting, and important events in order. Have students tell what they know so far about the setting, the characters, and the events in *A Beauty of a Plan*.

Model adding information to the **Setting** and **Characters** boxes on the Story Map Poster. Remind students to save their Story Maps (SG p. 5) for the next lesson.

Respond Discuss Reflection #1 on SG p. 7 with students, and then have them write and share their own responses: *What would you pick as a project for shop class? Why would you choose that project?*

Strategies Discussion Students briefly discuss how using the strategies helped them read the first section of *A Beauty of a Plan.* **Prompt:** *How did PREDICT help you as you read?*

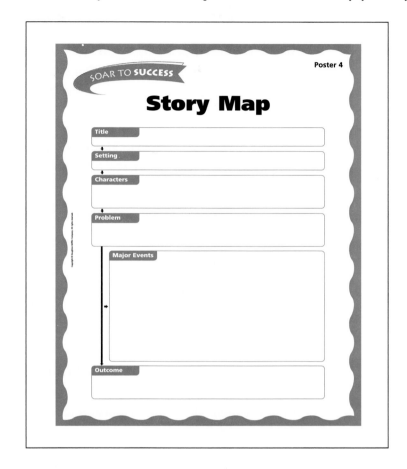

Homework Assign Homework 1 (SG p. 7). Ask students to think about and write a brief response to a new question before your next meeting: *What makes something a good project for a shop class?* Students should write their responses on a separate sheet of paper.

Lesson 2

Revisiting
(5 minutes)

Group Conference Briefly discuss with students the books they have been reading independently. **Prompt:** *Tell about an interesting character or fact in your book.* Remind students to keep up their book logs and to bring them to Group Conference for reference.

Reviewing
(5 minutes)

Posters 2, 3   **SG p. 5**

Review Reciprocal Teaching Strategies Display Posters 2 and 3 and review each strategy with students. For each strategy, ask a volunteer to tell quickly how it is useful.

Teacher Models Summarize Help students use the Story Map (SG p. 5) to summarize what has happened so far in the story.

Rehearsing
(5–10 minutes)

Students Predict Have students predict what will happen in this section, based on the pages they have already read. List their predictions for later use. Explain that they will verify, or check, their predictions after reading.

Teacher Model/*Predict* If needed, use the following model to help students: *When I PREDICT, I use the pictures or what I have read to help me figure out what I will learn or what will happen next in the book. After reading pages 2–5, I predict that in this part Sheila will pick a project.*

---

*K*ey *V*ocabulary

*salon, designing,
semester, architect*

---

*Note: **After** previewing
the book, hand out a copy
to each student.*

Guided Preview/Vocabulary pp. 6–13 Use the following preview points, emphasizing boldfaced vocabulary as words that will help students as they read. Continue to point to words as you speak. Do not list or teach the words in isolation.

▶ ***pages 6–7*** *Sheila leaves school and rushes to her grandmother's beauty **salon**. (p. 6)*

▶ ***pages 8–9*** *Sheila tells Grandma she loves **designing** (p. 8) and building things. Grandma sends her upstairs to do her chores. When she gets upstairs, Sheila finds a snack that Grandma left out for her. What does that tell you about Grandma's feelings toward Sheila?*

▶ ***pages 10–11*** *Grandma asks Sheila to drop shop class next **semester** (p. 10), or term. Do you think Sheila wants to drop shop class?*

▶ ***pages 12–13*** *Sheila wants to be an **architect** (p. 12) when she grows up. Grandma says she'll earn her living in the beauty salon, and shop class won't help there.*

Reading and Reciprocal Teaching

(10–15 minutes)

Posters 2, 3   SG p. 6

Purpose Setting/*Predict* Remind students of the predictions they made about what would happen in this section of *A Beauty of a Plan.* Students will check their predictions after they read.

Silent Reading or Group Read-Aloud Students read pages 10–15 silently or read aloud as a group. Remind them that after they read, you and they will model using strategies and take turns being the teacher. Encourage students to use Strategy Notes (SG p. 6) to jot down strategies they use when reading this section and to use those notes when they model strategies. They can jot down a QUESTION, a word or a point they need to CLARIFY or were able to CLARIFY, what they PREDICT, and notes to help them SUMMARIZE.

Reciprocal Teaching (after reading)

Check Predictions Call on students to reread the predictions you listed during Rehearsing and discuss which predictions were verified.

Teacher and Students Model Using Strategies Call students' attention to the strategies listed on Posters 2 and 3. Remind students of the way they used and modeled strategies during the introductory lesson and the first lesson of *A Beauty of a Plan,* using the Strategy Prompts. After you model each strategy, call on students to take turns modeling it. Remind students to use their Strategy Notes (SG p. 6) to help them model.

Teacher Models (each to be followed by student modeling)

SUMMARIZE *When I SUMMARIZE, I tell in my own words the important things I have read. Grandma wants Sheila to drop shop class. She says it won't teach Sheila anything they can use around the beauty salon. They make a bet. Sheila has three weeks to find a way to use her shop knowledge at the beauty salon. If she does, Grandma will sweep for a month. But if she doesn't, Sheila will have to sweep and drop shop class.*

Have some students model SUMMARIZE.

QUESTION *When I QUESTION, I ask something that can be answered as I read or after I finish reading. What does Sheila want to be in the future?*

Have some students model QUESTION.

CLARIFY/PHONICS *When I come to words I can't say, I look for chunks I know. In this word* (point to the word **nursing** on page 11), *I recognize the ending **-i-n-g**. The word begins with **n**, and I know the **u-r** says /**ur**/. I blend it together: **n/ur/s/ing**. I recognize that word, and it makes sense.*

Have some students model CLARIFY/PHONICS.

PREDICT *When I predict, I use the pictures or what I have read to tell what will happen next or what I will learn. I PREDICT that Sheila will win the bet with Grandma.*

Have some students model PREDICT.

Responding/ Reflecting

(5 minutes)

Poster 4   **SG pp. 5, 7**

Story Map Model adding information to the **Problem** and **Major Events** boxes on the Story Map Poster. Ask students to update their Story Maps (SG p. 5). Then, as a group, update the Story Map on Poster 4.

Respond Discuss Reflection #2 on SG p. 7 with students, and then have them write and share their own responses: *Why does Grandma want Sheila to drop shop class?*

Strategies Discussion Students briefly discuss how using the strategies helped them read this section of *A Beauty of a Plan.* **Prompt:** *Who used CLARIFY? How did CLARIFY help you?*

Homework Assign Homework 2 (SG p. 7). Ask students to think about and complete the assignment before your next meeting: *Imagine that you are Sheila. What would you do to help at the beauty salon?* Students should write their responses on a separate sheet of paper.

Lesson 3

Revisiting
(5 minutes)

Group Conference Students discuss the books they have been reading independently. **Prompt:** *Does your book have illustrations in it? If it does, do they make your book more interesting? What illustrations would you add to your book?* Remind students to keep up their book logs and to bring them to Group Conference for reference.

Reviewing
(5 minutes)

Posters 2, 3   SG p. 5

Review Reciprocal Teaching Strategies Display Posters 2 and 3 and ask students to tell when and how they used each strategy when reading *SOAR TO SUCCESS* books and in other reading. Use the Story Map (SG p. 5) to summarize what has happened so far in the story.

Rehearsing
(5–10 minutes)

Students Predict Have students predict what will happen in this section, based on the pages they have already read. List their predictions for later use. Explain that they will verify, or check, their predictions after reading.

Teacher Model/*Predict* If needed, use the following model to help students: *When I PREDICT, I use the pictures or what I have read to help me figure out what I will learn or what will happen next in the book. After reading pages 6–13, I predict that this part will show Sheila figuring out how to win the bet.*

$\mathcal{K}$ey $\mathcal{V}$ocabulary

measurements, partitions, opportunity, plywood, install

Guided Preview/Vocabulary pp. 14–23 Use the following preview points, emphasizing boldfaced vocabulary as words that will help students as they read. Continue to point to words as you speak. Do not list or teach the words in isolation.

▶ *pages 14–15 Sheila takes **measurements** of the salon. What do you think she's going to do?*

▶ *pages 16–17 Sheila shows her plan to Michael. She wants to build storage cabinets and **partitions** (p. 17)–small walls that separate one area from another.*

▶ *pages 18–19 Michael tells Mr. Flores about the plan. He thinks it's a great **opportunity** for a class project.*

▶ *pages 20–21 Other students agree to help. Sheila's Uncle Al brings supplies like paint and **plywood** (p. 21).*

*Note: **After** previewing the book, hand out a copy to each student.*

▶ *pages 22–23 Sheila tells the others they will **install** the new stuff on Monday– Grandma will be away from the shop all day. Why is it important for Grandma to be away?*

Reading and Reciprocal Teaching

(10–15 minutes)

Posters 2, 3   SG p. 6

Purpose Setting/*Predict* Remind students of the predictions they made about what would happen in this section of *A Beauty of a Plan.* Students will check their predictions after they read.

Silent Reading or Group Read-Aloud Students read pages 16–23 silently or read aloud as a group. Remind them that after they read, you and they will model using strategies and take turns being the teacher. Encourage students to use Strategy Notes (SG p. 6) to jot down strategies they use when reading this section and to use those notes when they model strategies. They can jot down a QUESTION, a word or a point they need to CLARIFY or were able to CLARIFY, what they PREDICT, and notes to help them SUMMARIZE.

Reciprocal Teaching (after reading)

Check Predictions Call on students to reread the predictions you listed during Rehearsing and discuss which predictions were verified.

Teacher and Students Model Using Strategies Call students' attention to strategies listed on Posters 2 and 3. Remind students of the way they used and modeled strategies during the introductory lesson and previous lessons of *A Beauty of a Plan*, using the Strategy Prompts. After you model each strategy, call on students to take turns modeling it. Remind students to use their Strategy Notes (SG p. 6) to help them model.

Teacher Models (each to be followed by student modeling)

SUMMARIZE *When I SUMMARIZE, I tell in my own words the important things I have read. Sheila creates a new design for the beauty salon. She, Michael, and several other students spend three weeks building things like benches and storage cabinets. Sheila's Uncle Al, a carpenter, helps. They plan to install everything on a Monday, when Grandma will be away from the shop all day.*

Have some students model SUMMARIZE.

CLARIFY *When I don't understand an idea, I reread, read ahead, or look at the picture to figure it out. Then I reread the sentence to see if it makes sense. On page 16, I read the sentence where Sheila says,* **I'm going to need a good cabinetmaker**. *I've never seen the word* **cabinetmaker** *before. I see that it's a compound word, made up of two parts:* **cabinet** *and* **maker**. *Then I reread the paragraph. Sheila is asking Michael for help building things for the beauty salon. A* **cabinetmaker** *must be someone who makes cabinets.*

Have some students model CLARIFY.

QUESTION *When I QUESTION, I ask something that can be answered as I read or after I finish reading. How does Uncle Al help Sheila?*

Have some students model QUESTION.

CLARIFY/PHONICS *When I come to a word I can't say, I look for chunks I know. In this word* (point to the word **carpentry** on page 16), *I recognize* **car** *at the beginning,* **pen** *in the middle, and* **try** *at the end. But when I blend the chunks, I get* /**car**/**pen**/**trī**/, *and that doesn't sound right. Then I try* /**car**/**pen**/**tree**/. *I recognize that word, and it makes sense when I reread the sentence.*

Have some students model CLARIFY/PHONICS.

PREDICT *When I PREDICT, I use the pictures or what I have read to tell what will happen next or what I will learn. I predict that Grandma will like the improvements in the beauty salon.*

Have some students model PREDICT.

Responding/ Reflecting

(5 minutes)

Poster 4   **SG pp. 5, 8**

Story Map Ask students to add to the **Major Events** box on their Story Maps (SG p. 5). Then, as a group, update the Story Map on Poster 4.

Respond Discuss Reflection #3 on SG p. 8 with students, and then have them write and share their own responses: *How does Mr. Flores help Sheila's project?*

Strategies Discussion Students briefly discuss how using the strategies helped them read this section of *A Beauty of a Plan*. **Prompt:** *Who used SUMMARIZE? How did it help you?*

Homework Assign Homework 3 (SG p. 8). Ask students to think about and complete the assignment before your next meeting: *Imagine that you are one of Sheila's classmates, and that you have an aunt who is a carpenter. Write a note to your aunt asking for help on the project.* Students should write their responses on a separate sheet of paper.

Lesson 4

Revisiting
(5 minutes)

Group Conference Students discuss the books they have been reading independently. **Prompt:** *Would you recommend this book to someone else? Why or why not?* Remind students to keep up their book logs and to bring them to Group Conference for reference.

Reviewing
(5 minutes)

Posters 2, 3   **SG p. 5**

Review Reciprocal Teaching Strategies Display Posters 2 and 3 and for each strategy, ask a volunteer to tell briefly how it is useful in classroom reading. Use the Story Map (SG p. 5) to summarize what has happened so far in the story.

Rehearsing
(5–10 minutes)

Students Predict Have students predict what will happen in this section, based on the pages they have already read. List their predictions for later use. Explain that they will verify, or check, their predictions after reading.

Key Vocabulary

vacation, exhibit

....

Note: **After** previewing the book, hand out a copy to each student.

....

Guided Preview/Vocabulary pp. 24–32 Use the preview points. Emphasize the key vocabulary words (boldfaced), and point to them as you speak. Do not list or teach the words in isolation.

▶ *pages 24–25 On Monday, Grandma doesn't go out. Since the girls are on **vacation** from school, she wants to spend time with them.*

▶ *pages 26–27 Jackie takes Grandma to see an **exhibit** at the museum.*

▶ *pages 28–29 The students spend the whole day working.*

▶ *pages 30–31 Sheila looks sad. What do you think that means?*

Reading and Reciprocal Teaching
(10–15 minutes)

Posters 2, 3   **SG p. 6**

Purpose Setting/*Predict* Remind students of the predictions they made about what would happen in this section. Students will check predictions after they read.

Silent Reading or Group Read-Aloud Students read pages 24–32 silently or read aloud as a group. Remind them that after they read, you and they will model using strategies and take turns being the teacher. Encourage students to use Strategy Notes (SG p. 6) to jot down strategies they use when reading this section and to use those notes when they model strategies.

Reciprocal Teaching (after reading)

Check Predictions Call on students to reread the predictions you listed during Rehearsing and discuss which predictions were verified.

Teacher and Students Model Using Strategies Display Posters 2 and 3. Call on students to take turns modeling the strategies, using their Strategy Notes (SG p. 6).

Teacher Models (each to be followed by student modeling)

SUMMARIZE *When I SUMMARIZE, I tell in my own words the important things I have read. On Monday, Jackie takes Grandma to a museum. Sheila and her classmates complete all their work. When Grandma comes home, she just goes upstairs. But she comes back downstairs with a broom, thanks Sheila, and then begins to sweep.*

Have some students model SUMMARIZE.

CLARIFY *When I don't understand an idea, I reread, read ahead, or look at the picture to figure it out. I reread the sentence to see if it makes sense. On page 24, Sheila says, "Won't Aunt May worry if you're late?" I wonder who Aunt May is. I flip back to page 22. Sheila says, "The salon is closed on Mondays. Grandma always leaves at 8 o'clock to visit my aunt for the day." That must be who Aunt May is.*

Have some students model CLARIFY.

QUESTION *When I QUESTION, I ask something that can be answered as I read or after I finish reading. Why does Jackie take Grandma to the museum?*

Have some students model QUESTION.

Responding/ Reflecting

(5 minutes)

Poster 4   **SG pp. 5, 8**

Story Map Ask students to tell you what events to add to the Events box and what outcome to add to the Outcome box on the Story Map on Poster 4. Then have them complete their own Story Maps (SG p. 5).

Respond Discuss Reflection #4 on SG p. 8 with students, and then have them write and share their own responses: *Why didn't Grandma say anything when she first saw the salon?*

Homework Assign Homework 4 (SG p. 8). Ask students to think about and complete the assignment before your next meeting: *Is there a business in your neighborhood that could use the kind of help Sheila gave? Write a short paragraph telling what that business needs.* Students should write their responses on a separate sheet of paper.

Home Connection Students take home *A Beauty of a Plan* and the Home Connection letter.

....

Note: An Optional Lesson for each book is provided in a section beginning on page R180 at the back of the Teacher's Manual. It includes:

* *Summarizing the Book, a review activity that will build students' ability to summarize.*

* *Decoding Longer Words, a lesson in word-analysis skill and using the decoding strategy to apply it; with blackline masters for practice and application.*

* *Making Words, an active, hands-on manipulative teaching strategy to help students use letter/sound relationships and word patterns.*

....

A Beauty of a Plan

Name _____

Students use this page to jot down notes or questions as they read. It should not be used for assessment. Sample notes are shown.

Strategy Notes

Clarify

Students stay late to work? p. 2

"extra credit" p. 20

Predict

Sheila's plan for the beauty salon will be the next shop project she does with Michael. p. 14

Sheila will find a way to get Grandma out of the house. p. 24

Question

Does Jackie go to school with Sheila? p. 6

Summarize

Pages 24–26: Grandma is still home at 8:30. Jackie asks why she's not going to Aunt May's. She says that, since school is closed for vacation, she'd rather spend time with Sheila and Jackie. Jackie tells Grandma she wants to go to a museum. She takes Grandma out, leaving Sheila home to finish the project.

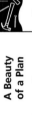

A Beauty of a Plan

Name _____

Sample responses are shown.

Story Map

Title

A Beauty of a Plan

↓

Setting

Meadow Middle School, Grandma's beauty salon, Sheila's home above the salon

↓

Characters

Sheila, Michael, Mr. Flores, Grandma, Jackie

↓

Problem

Sheila has three weeks to use her designing and building skills to improve the beauty salon or she'll have to drop shop class.

Major Events   (May vary)

1. Sheila and Michael finish their shop project. Now Sheila has to pick a new project.
2. Grandma asks Sheila to drop shop class.
3. Grandma and Sheila make a bet that Sheila can't use what she learned in shop class to improve the beauty salon.
4. Sheila takes measurements and draws up plans.
5. Mr. Flores agrees to give students extra credit if they work on Sheila's project.
6. Everything is built and set to be installed.
7. Grandma doesn't want to leave, but Jackie takes her to a museum.
8. The students finish their work.
9. Grandma sees the work and silently goes upstairs.

↓

Outcome

Grandma comes back down with a broom, compliments Sheila on her work, and begins to sweep the floor—which shows that she lost the bet.

A Beauty of a Plan

Name _____

Students use this page to think about their reading and to prepare for discussion. It should not be used for assessment. Sample responses are shown.

REFLECTION 3
How does Mr. Flores help Sheila's project?

He agrees to give extra credit to students in the shop class who help Sheila with her project.

HOMEWORK 3
Imagine that you are one of Sheila's classmates, and that you have an aunt who is a carpenter. Write a note to your aunt asking for help on the project.

REFLECTION 4
Why didn't Grandma say anything when she first saw the salon?

Grandma went upstairs to get the broom and start sweeping so Sheila would know who won the bet.

HOMEWORK 4
Is there a business in your neighborhood that could use the kind of help Sheila gave? Write a short paragraph telling what that business needs.

8   Level 8, Book 1, *A Beauty of a Plan*

A Beauty of a Plan

Name _____

Students use this page to think about their reading and to prepare for discussion. It should not be used for assessment. Sample responses are shown.

REFLECTION 1
What would you pick as a project for shop class?

For my project, I would build something for my dog, like a doghouse.

HOMEWORK 1
Write a short list telling what makes something a good project for a shop class.

REFLECTION 2
Why does Grandma want Sheila to drop shop class?

She doesn't think it has any practical use. She thinks Sheila will have to work in the beauty salon to earn money, and shop class can't help there.

HOMEWORK 2
Imagine that you are Sheila. Write a short paragraph explaining what you would do to help at the beauty salon.

Level 8, Book 1, *A Beauty of a Plan*   7

The Lost Expedition

by Barbara Brooks Simons

with Expedition Photos by Frank Hurley and Illustrations by Laurence Schwinger

*S*ummary: In 1914, the explorer Ernest Shackleton and 27 men began an expedition to Antarctica. This book tells of the two years they were stranded on the ice, and of the amazing efforts Shackleton made to rescue his men.

Materials

Lesson 1	Lesson 2	Lesson 3
• Previously read book	• Independent reading books	• Previously read book
• *The Lost Expedition* pp. 2–11	• *The Lost Expedition* pp. 12–21	• *The Lost Expedition* pp. 22–32
• Posters 2, 3, 4	• Posters 2, 3, 4	• Posters 2, 3, 4
• Student Guide (SG) pp. 9–11	• Student Guide (SG) pp. 9–11	• Student Guide (SG) pp. 9–10, 12
• Strategy Prompts, SG pp. 89–91	• Strategy Prompts, SG pp. 89–91	• Strategy Prompts, SG pp. 89–91
• Markers	• Markers	• Markers
		• Home Connection letter

Note: It is not necessary for students to know or be held responsible for all the facts presented in the book. The purpose of these lessons is to help students learn strategies for comprehending informational text.

Scaffolding

Strong Teacher Support	Moderate Teacher Support	Student Independence
For Book 2 (Category I), strong teacher support is provided through modeling and previewing. However, students should be encouraged to practice using strategies frequently. Student modeling should occur after each teacher model.		

Help with Phonics and Decoding Longer Words: For students who need explicit instruction, see the Optional Lesson on page R183 of the Teacher's Resource File in this manual.

Lesson Overview

	Lesson 1	Lesson 2	Lesson 3
Revisiting (5 minutes)	• Previously read book	• Group Conference: Independent Reading	• Previously read book
Reviewing (5 minutes)	• Review Reciprocal Teaching Strategies (Posters 2, 3)	• Review Reciprocal Teaching Strategies (Posters 2, 3) • Students Summarize	• Review Reciprocal Teaching Strategies (Posters 2, 3) • Students Summarize
Rehearsing (5–10 minutes)	• Introduce the Book • Teacher Models PREDICT • Students Predict • Guided Preview pp. 2–11 Key Vocabulary: *floes, leads, adapted, challenges*	• Students Predict • Guided Preview pp. 12–21 Key Vocabulary: *currents, abandon, salvage, obstacles*	• Students Predict • Guided Preview pp. 22–32 Key Vocabulary: *desolate, navigational, glaciers, attempts*
Reading and Reciprocal Teaching (10–15 minutes)	• Silent Reading • Check Predictions • Teacher Models SUMMARIZE, CLARIFY/PHONICS, QUESTION, PREDICT • Students Model Strategies	• Silent Reading • Check Predictions • Teacher Models SUMMARIZE, CLARIFY/PHONICS, CLARIFY, QUESTION, PREDICT • Students Model Strategies	• Silent Reading • Check Predictions • Teacher Models SUMMARIZE, CLARIFY, QUESTION • Students Model Strategies
Responding/ Reflecting (5 minutes)	• Story Map (Poster 4, SG p. 32) • Reflection #1 (SG p. 34) • Strategies Discussion (Posters 2, 3) • Homework 1	• Story Map (Poster 4, SG p. 32) • Reflection #2 (SG p. 34) • Homework 2	• Story Map (Poster 4, SG p. 32) • Reflection #3 (SG p. 35) • Strategies Discussion (Posters 2, 3) • Homework 3 • Home Connection letter

The Lost Expedition *by Barbara Brooks Simons*

Lesson 1

Revisiting
(5 minutes)

Students reread previously read *SOAR TO SUCCESS* book. Have students reread silently for fluency.

....

Note: For this second book, the Revisiting activity each day will be either a Group Conference to discuss independently read books outside of this program or a rereading of Book 1 to develop fluency. (See pages T17 and T34 for guidelines on group conferences and independent reading.)

For subsequent books, in alternate lessons, have students select and reread previously read SOAR TO SUCCESS books. Beginning with Book 3, while most students reread silently to develop fluency, the teacher works with one student, coaching or taking a retelling or Oral Reading Check. (See pages T43–T49 for information on these options.)

Starting with Book 5, in alternate lessons in which students reread books they have selected, they should develop a model of a strategy that they will share in Reviewing. Assign each student a strategy prior to reading. As students approach independence (Book 12), each student selects a strategy to model. Suggestions in the Lesson Plans for specific books reflect this sequence.

....

Reviewing
(5 minutes)

Posters 2, 3

Review Reciprocal Teaching Strategies Display Posters 2 and 3 and review each strategy with students. Tell students that they will take turns using these strategies again to help them read *The Lost Expedition.*

Rehearsing
(5–10 minutes)

Introduce the Book Show the book cover and read its title and the names of the author, photographer, and illustrator. Point to the photograph of the ship on the cover. Guide students to discuss the ship and the surrounding ice. Then show students the map on the back cover. Point out that it shows Antarctica, the icy continent at the southern tip of the world. Ask for suggestions about where the ship might be located and why. Use the following model to predict what the book is about, based on the title and cover photograph.

Teacher Model/*Predict* *When I PREDICT, I use the pictures or what I have read to tell what will happen next or what I will learn. The book title and the covers help me predict that* The Lost Expedition *is about a sailing ship that gets lost in Antarctica, a faraway place covered with ice.*

Students Predict Have students predict what will happen in the book based on the title and the cover. List their predictions for later use. Explain that they will verify, or check, their predictions after reading.

$\mathcal{K}$ey $\mathcal{V}$ocabulary

floes, leads, adapted, challenges

Guided Preview/Vocabulary pp. 2–11 Use the preview points. Tell students you are using words that will help them read the story by themselves. Tell them not to be concerned if they have difficulty with the pronunciation of proper names in this book, but to keep reading. Emphasize key vocabulary words (boldfaced) and point to them as you speak. Do not list or teach the words in isolation.

▶ ***pages 2–3*** *Antarctica is so cold that the sea around the continent freezes into **floes**, huge sheets of floating ice. In the early 1900s, Ernest Shackleton was one of the first people to explore Antarctica. Why do you think people hadn't done this before?*

▶ ***pages 4–5*** *In 1914, Shackleton chose a crew to join him on an expedition to cross the entire Antarctic continent. They left England on a ship called the* Endurance.

▶ ***pages 6–7*** *As the* Endurance *neared the Antarctic continent, it was surrounded by ice. It had to be steered through **leads**, narrow pathways through the ice.*

▶ ***pages 8–9*** *Soon the ship was stuck in the ice. The crew would have to stay there for months until the ice melted. They **adapted**, or became used to, life on the ice.*

▶ ***pages 10–11*** *The men faced many **challenges**. What sorts of things were they doing to pass the time?*

Note: **After** *introducing and previewing the book, hand out a copy to each student.*

Reading and Reciprocal Teaching

(10–15 minutes)

Posters 2, 3   **SG p. 10**

Purpose Setting/*Predict* Remind students of the predictions they made about what would happen in *The Lost Expedition.* Students will check predictions after they read.

Silent Reading Students read pages 2–11 silently. Remind them that after they read, you and they will model using strategies and take turns being the teacher. Encourage students to use **Strategy Notes** (SG p. 10) to jot down strategies they use when reading this section and to use those notes when they model strategies. They can jot down a QUESTION, a word or a point they need to CLARIFY or were able to CLARIFY, what they PREDICT, and notes to help them SUMMARIZE.

Reciprocal Teaching (after reading)

Check Predictions Call on students to reread the predictions you listed during Rehearsing. Were their predictions verified so far in the book?

Teacher and Students Model Using Strategies Call students' attention to strategies listed on Posters 2 and 3. Remind students of the way they used and modeled strategies with *A Beauty of a Plan,* using the Strategy Prompts.

After you model each strategy, call on students to take turns modeling it. Remind students to use their Strategy Notes (SG p. 10) to help them model.

Teacher Models (each to be followed by student modeling)

SUMMARIZE *When I SUMMARIZE, I tell in my own words the important things I have read—the characters, the setting, and the important events that have happened. The characters are Ernest Shackleton, Captain Frank Worsley, and the crew of the* Endurance. *The setting is Antarctica. Shackleton wanted to be the first explorer to cross Antarctica on foot. However, the ship got trapped in the ice, and the men spent months waiting for the spring thaw.*

Have some students model SUMMARIZE.

CLARIFY/PHONICS *When I come to a word I can't say, I look for chunks I know. To figure out this word* (point to the word **immediately** on page 7), *I divide it into chunks. I know what the ending* **-l-y** *sounds like. Then I separate the chunks* **i-m-**, **m-e-d**, **i**, *and* **a-t-e**. *The first chunk is* **im**. *I don't know if the* **e** *in* **m-e-d** *is short or long. When I blend the chunks using a short* **e**, *it doesn't sound quite right, so I try the long* **e** *sound. I try* **/im/meed/**; *then I recognize what the word should be—***im/med/i/ate/ly**. *I reread, and it makes sense in the sentence: "Almost immediately, the ship was surrounded by ice."*

Have some students model CLARIFY/PHONICS.

QUESTION *When I QUESTION, I ask something that can be answered as I read or after I finish reading. What did the men do to keep busy?*

Have some students model QUESTION.

PREDICT *When I PREDICT, I use the pictures or what I have read to tell what will happen next or what I will learn. I PREDICT that the men of the* Endurance *will face additional problems and challenges.*

Have some students model PREDICT.

Responding/ Reflecting
(5 minutes)

Story Map Display Story Map Poster 4 and explain that it can help students remember the important elements of the story—characters, setting, and important events in order. Have students tell what they know so far about the setting, the characters, and the events.

Poster 4   **SG pp. 9, 11**

Model adding information to the **Setting** and **Characters** boxes on the Story Map poster. Model adding to the **Problem** box; for example: *The* Endurance *and its crew get trapped in the ice.* Remind students to save their Story Maps (SG p. 9) for the next lesson.

Respond Discuss Reflection #1 on SG p. 11 with students, and then have them write and share their own responses: *If the crew had managed to free the ship from the ice, what do you think they would have done?*

Strategies Discussion Students briefly discuss how using the strategies helped them read the first section of *The Lost Expedition.* **Prompt:** *Who used SUMMARIZE? How did it help you?*

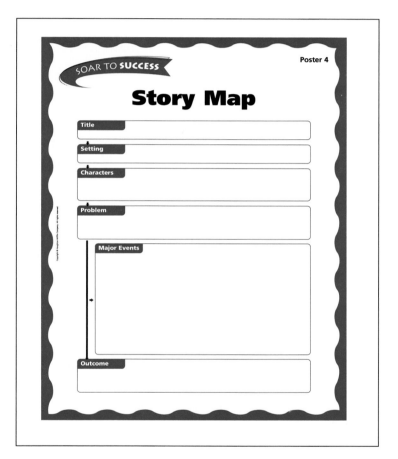

Homework Assign Homework 1 (SG p. 11). Ask students to think about and write a brief response to a new question before your next meeting: *What sorts of things would you do to pass the time if you were on the* Endurance *stranded on the ice?* Students should write their responses on a separate sheet of paper.

Lesson 2

Revisiting
(5 minutes)

Group Conference Students discuss the books they have been reading independently. **Prompts:** *Who or what is your book about? Tell about your favorite part so far.* Remind students to keep up their book logs and to bring them to Group Conference.

Reviewing
(5 minutes)

Posters 2, 3   **SG p. 9**

Review Reciprocal Teaching Strategies Display Posters 2 and 3 and ask students to tell when and how they used each strategy when reading *SOAR TO SUCCESS* books and in other reading. Use the Story Map (SG p. 9) to summarize what has happened so far in the story.

Rehearsing
(5–10 minutes)

Students Predict Have students predict what will happen in this section, based on the pages they have already read. List their predictions for later use. Explain that they will verify, or check, their predictions after reading.

Teacher Model/*Predict* If needed, use the following model to help students: *When I PREDICT, I use the pictures or what I have read to tell what will happen next or what I will learn. After reading pages 2–11, I predict that the men of the* Endurance *will have a difficult time getting back to land.*

Key Vocabulary

currents, abandon, salvage, obstacles

Guided Preview/Vocabulary pp. 12–21 Use the following preview points, emphasizing boldfaced vocabulary as words that will help students as they read. Continue to point to words as you speak. Do not list or teach the words in isolation.

▶ *pages 12–13* *The weather started to get warmer in October, but strong ocean* **currents** *and winds pressed the ice against the ship. What do you think Shackleton was writing about in his diary?*

▶ *pages 14–15* *The ice started crushing the* Endurance. *The men had to* **abandon** *the ship and set up camp on the ice. They had to* **salvage** *what they could from the ship, especially its lifeboats. Why did they save the lifeboats?*

▶ *pages 16–17* *Shackleton and his men dragged the boats across the ice floes, heading toward the open sea.*

▶ *pages 18–19* *The men faced many* **obstacles** *as they crossed the ice. At last, the ice began to break up. What dangers did that pose?*

▶ *pages 20–21* *As the ice broke up, the men continued their journey in the lifeboats. They had 60 miles to travel to the nearest island.*

---

*Note: **After** previewing the book, hand out a copy to each student.*

Reading and Reciprocal Teaching

(10–15 minutes)

SG p. 10   Posters 2, 3

Purpose Setting/*Predict* Remind students of the predictions they made about what would happen in this section of *The Lost Expedition.* Students will check predictions after they read.

Silent Reading Students read pages 12–21 silently. Remind them that after they read, you and they will model using strategies and take turns being the teacher. Encourage students to use Strategy Notes (SG p. 10) to jot down strategies they use when reading this section and to use those notes when they model strategies. They can jot down a QUESTION, a word or a point they need to CLARIFY or were able to CLARIFY, what they PREDICT, and notes to help them SUMMARIZE.

Reciprocal Teaching (after reading)

Check Predictions Call on students to reread the predictions you listed during Rehearsing and discuss which predictions were verified.

Teacher and Students Model Using Strategies Call students' attention to the strategies listed on Posters 2 and 3. Remind them of the way they used and modeled strategies during *A Beauty of a Plan* and the first lesson of *The Lost Expedition*, using the Strategy Prompts. After you model each strategy, call on students to take turns modeling it. Remind students to use their Strategy Notes (SG p. 10) to help them model.

Teacher Models (each to be followed by student modeling)

SUMMARIZE *When I SUMMARIZE, I tell in my own words the important things I have read: The weather got warmer, but powerful currents and winds pressed huge masses of ice against the ship, crushing it. Before the ship sank, Shackleton and his men took supplies and lifeboats from the ship. They then walked across miles of frozen ice and sailed through icy water in lifeboats to find land.*

Have some students model SUMMARIZE.

CLARIFY/PHONICS *When I come to a word I can't say, I look for chunks I know. To figure out this word* (point to the word **determined** in line 1 on page 16)*, I break it into chunks. I recognize the chunks* **term** *and* **in***. I know how to pronounce the ending* **-e-d***. When I blend the first chunk,* **d-e***, with the other chunks, I get the word* **de/term/in/ed***. Shackleton was determined–that makes sense.*

Have some students model CLARIFY/PHONICS.

CLARIFY *When I don't understand an idea, I reread, read ahead, or look at pictures to figure it out. Then I reread the sentence to see if it makes sense. On page 17, I am not sure what an* **ice field** *is. When I reread page 16, I realize that most of the sea is covered by huge areas of ice. That must be what an ice field is–a huge area of ice.*

QUESTION *When I QUESTION, I ask something that can be answered as I read or after I finish reading. I'll ask: Why couldn't the men save everything from the* Endurance?

Have some students model QUESTION.

PREDICT *When I PREDICT, I use the pictures or what I have read to tell what will happen next or what I will learn. Because the photos from the expedition still exist, I PREDICT that the men from the* Endurance *will reach land safely.*

Have some students model PREDICT.

Responding/ Reflecting

(5 minutes)

Poster 4   **SG pp. 9, 11**

Story Map Ask students to add to their Story Maps (SG p. 9). Then, as a group, add any new information to the Story Map poster.

Respond Discuss Reflection #2 on SG p. 11 with students, and then have them write and share their own responses: *For how many months did the men walk across the ice? How did you reach your answer?*

Homework Assign Homework 2 (SG p. 11). Ask students to think about and complete the assignment before your next meeting: *If you were to join an exploring expedition, what special personal possessions would you take with you? Why? Write a short list.* Students should write their responses on a separate sheet of paper.

Lesson 3

Revisiting
(5 minutes)

Students reread previously read *SOAR TO SUCCESS* books. Have students reread silently for fluency.

Reviewing
(5 minutes)

Posters 2, 3   **SG p. 9**

Review Reciprocal Teaching Strategies Display Posters 2 and 3, and for each strategy ask a volunteer to tell quickly how it is useful in classroom reading. Use the Story Map (SG p. 9) to summarize what has happened so far in the story.

Rehearsing
(5–10 minutes)

Students Predict Have students predict what will happen in this section, based on the pages they have already read. List their predictions for later use. Explain that they will verify, or check, their predictions after reading.

𝒦ey 𝒱ocabulary
desolate, navigational, glaciers, attempts

Guided Preview/Vocabulary pp. 22–32 Use the preview points. Emphasize the key vocabulary words (boldfaced) and point to them as you speak. Do not list or teach the words in isolation.

▶ *pages 22–23 The entire crew finally reached a **desolate** island. Shackleton realized they couldn't survive there very long. Why?*

▶ *pages 24–25 Shackleton and Worsley left with four other men on one of the lifeboats. Worsley's **navigational** skills kept them on course for South Georgia Island. How hard would it be to sail 800 miles across the open sea?*

▶ *pages 26–27 Shackleton's lifeboat finally reached South Georgia, but the whaling station was miles away, across mountains and **glaciers**.*

▶ *pages 28–29 Shackleton and two men set off to cross the mountains, and finally reached the whaling station. How difficult would it be to make this trek after their previous hardships?*

▶ *pages 30–31 The three men on the other side of South Georgia were rescued. Then Shackleton made several **attempts** to return to his stranded men.*

▶ *page 32 After four months, Shackleton finally rescued his men.*

....
*Note: **After** previewing the book, hand out a copy to each student.*
....

Reading and Reciprocal Teaching

(10–15 minutes)

Posters 2, 3   SG p. 10

Purpose Setting/*Predict* Remind students of the predictions they made about what would happen in this section of *The Lost Expedition.* Students will check predictions after they read.

Silent Reading Students read pages 22–32 silently. Remind them that after they read, you and they will model using strategies and take turns being the teacher. Encourage students to use Strategy Notes (SG p. 10) to jot down strategies they use when reading this section and to use those notes when they model strategies.

Reciprocal Teaching (after reading)

Check Predictions Students reread the predictions you listed during Rehearsing and discuss which predictions were verified.

Teacher and Students Model Using Strategies Display Posters 2 and 3. Remind students of the way they used and modeled strategies in previous lessons, using the Strategy Prompts. After you model each strategy, call on students to take turns modeling it. Remind students to use their Strategy Notes (SG p. 10) to help them model.

Teacher Models (each to be followed by student modeling)

SUMMARIZE *When I SUMMARIZE, I tell in my own words the important things I have read. The men finally reached a desolate island; but Shackleton, Worsley, and four others set sail to get help at the whaling station 800 miles away. After four months, Shackleton managed to return to rescue his men on Elephant Island.*

Have some students model SUMMARIZE.

CLARIFY *When I don't understand an idea, I reread, read ahead, or look at pictures to figure it out. Then I reread the sentence to see if it makes sense. On page 28, I didn't understand what **blinding snow** meant, but then I saw the picture that showed the men climbing a glacier. In the picture, the snow is falling so hard that they cannot see where they are going.*

Have some students model CLARIFY.

QUESTION *When I QUESTION, I ask something that can be answered as I read or after I finish reading. How did the men survive the winter on Elephant Island after Shackleton left for help?*

Have some students model QUESTION.

Responding/ Reflecting

(5 minutes)

Poster 4

SG pp. 9, 12

Story Map Ask students to tell you what events to add to the Events box and what outcome to add to the Outcome box on the Story Map (SG p. 9).

Respond Discuss Reflection #3 on SG p. 12 with students, and then have them write and share their own responses: *Circle a strategy that helped you to read* The Lost Expedition. *How did this strategy help you?* Encourage students to use their own words.

Strategies Discussion Students briefly discuss how using the strategies helped them read this section of *The Lost Expedition*. **Prompt:** *Who used CLARIFY? How did CLARIFY help you?*

Homework Assign Homework 3 (SG p. 12). Ask students to think about and complete the assignment before your next meeting: *Write a paragraph explaining why you think the author called this book* The Lost Expedition. Students should write their responses on a separate sheet of paper.

Home Connection Students take home *The Lost Expedition* and the Home Connection letter.

....

Note: An Optional Day lesson plan for each book is provided in a section beginning on page R180 at the back of the Teacher's Manual. It includes:

• *Summarizing the book, a review activity that will build students' ability to summarize*

• *Decoding Longer Words, a lesson in a word-analysis skill and using the decoding strategy to apply it; with blackline masters for practice and application*

• *Making Words, an active hands-on manipulative teaching strategy to help students use letter/sound relationships and word patterns*

....

Lost Expedition

Name _____

Strategy Notes

Students use this page to jot down notes or questions as they read. Sample notes are shown. It should not be used for assessment.

Clarify

In Antarctica, summertime comes in December. p. 6

ached? p. 21

Predict

I predict the ice will melt and the men will use the lifeboats. pp. 16–17

Question

Why would the men need the lifeboats? p. 14

Why did it take Shackleton four months to get back to his crew? p. 30

Summarize

Pages 12–15: As the weather warmed, the ice around the *Endurance* pressed against the sides of the ship. The ship was crushed. Shackleton ordered his men to leave the ship, taking some supplies and the lifeboats. The men set up camp on the ice. One month later, the *Endurance* sank into the water.

Lost Expedition

Name _____

Story Map

Sample responses are shown.

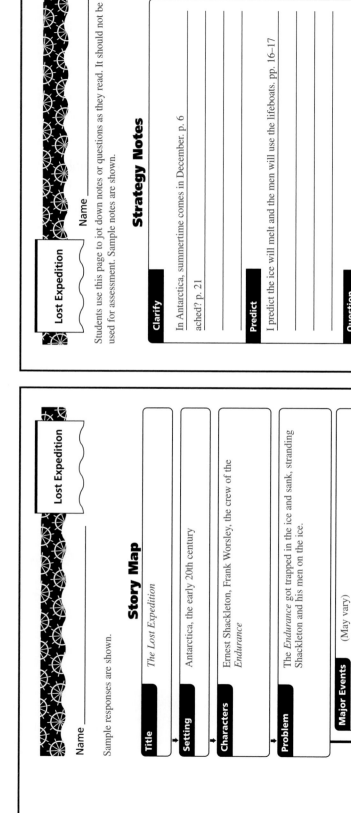

Title

The Lost Expedition

Setting

Antarctica, the early 20th century

Characters

Ernest Shackleton, Frank Worsley, the crew of the *Endurance*

Problem

The *Endurance* got trapped in the ice and sank, stranding Shackleton and his men on the ice.

Major Events   (May vary)

1. Shackleton wanted to be the first man to cross the Antarctic continent on foot. He and his crew boarded the *Endurance*.
2. Shackleton waited on South Georgia for warmer weather, then set sail in December. The *Endurance* got stuck in the ice and could not be freed.
3. The crew built warmer living quarters and waited for the spring thaw.
4. Strong currents and winds pressed ice against the ship, crushing it.
5. Before the ship sank, the men salvaged supplies and possessions.
6. Shackleton and his men dragged the lifeboats across the ice and set sail through cold waters.
7. The crew made it safely to Elephant Island.
8. Shackleton and a small group sailed to South Georgia for help.
9. Shackleton tried for four months to rescue his other men.

Outcome

Shackleton rescued his stranded crew.

Lost Expedition

Name _____

Students use this page to think about their reading and prepare for discussion. It should not be used for assessment. Sample responses are shown.

REFLECTION 3

Circle the strategy you used most to read *The Lost Expedition*.

Strategy Box	
Predict	Question
Summarize	(Clarify)

Name one place where you used this strategy or modeled it for someone else. Write the page number(s).

I used Clarify on p. 13.

How did this strategy help you?

When Shackleton wrote that his task now was to reach land, I wasn't sure what he meant. Then I reread the page before, and realized that the ice was not land, and that without the ship they could not continue the expedition. He wanted to turn back.

HOMEWORK 3

Write a paragraph explaining why you think the author called this book *The Lost Expedition*.

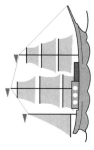

12 Level 8, Book 2, *Lost Expedition*

Lost Expedition

Name _____

Students use this page to think about their reading and to prepare for discussion. It should not be used for assessment. Sample responses are shown.

REFLECTION 1

If the crew had managed to free the ship from the ice, what do you think they would have done?

They probably would have tried to sail back to the island of South Georgia, away from the Antarctic continent. The ice would be worse the closer they were to Antarctica.

HOMEWORK 1

What sorts of things would you do to pass the time if you were on the *Endurance* stranded on the ice? Write a short paragraph answering this question.

REFLECTION 2

For how many months did the men walk across the ice? How did you reach your answer?

They walked across the ice for about three and a half months. On page 17, it says they started in late December, and on page 18 it says the ice floe broke up in early April.

HOMEWORK 2

If you were to join an exploring expedition, what special personal possessions would you take with you? Why? Write a short list.

Level 8, Book 2, *Lost Expedition* 11

Owl

by Rebecca Stefoff

*S*ummary: This book describes the characteristics, behavior, and habitats of owls all over the world. The text is accompanied by photographs showing these nocturnal birds hunting and nesting in the wild.

Note: It is not necessary for students to know or be held responsible for all the facts presented in the book. The purpose of these lessons is to help students learn strategies for comprehending informational text.

Materials

Lesson 1	Lesson 2	Lesson 3
• Previously read books	• Independent reading books	• Previously read books
• *Owl* pp. 6–11	• *Owl* pp. 12–19	• *Owl* pp. 20–27
• Posters 2, 3, 5	• Posters 2, 3, 5	• Posters 2, 3, 5
• Student Guide (SG) pp. 13–15	• Student Guide (SG) pp. 13–15	• Student Guide (SG) pp. 13–14, 16
• Strategy Prompts, SG pp. 89–91	• Strategy Prompts, SG pp. 89–91	• Strategy Prompts, SG pp. 89–91
• Markers	• Markers	• Markers
		• Home Connection letter

Scaffolding

Strong Teacher Support	Moderate Teacher Support	Student Independence
For Book 3 (Category II), strong teacher support is provided through modeling and previewing. However, students should be encouraged to practice using strategies frequently.		

Help with Phonics and Decoding Longer Words: For students who need explicit instruction, see the Optional Lesson on page R184 of the Teacher's Resource File in this manual.

Lesson Overview

	Lesson 1	Lesson 2	Lesson 3
Revisiting (5 minutes)	• Peviously read books: Retelling/Oral Reading Check	• Group Conference: Independent Reading	• Previously read books: Retelling/Oral Reading Check
Reviewing (5 minutes)	• Review Reciprocal Teaching Strategies (Posters 2, 3)	• Students Discuss Strategies • Students Summarize	• Students Discuss Strategies • Students Summarize
Rehearsing (5–10 minutes)	• Introduce the Book • K-W-L (Poster 5, SG p. 13) • Guided Preview, pp. 6–11 Key Vocabulary: *glides, prey* • K-W-L/Question (Poster 5, SG p. 13)	• Guided Preview, pp. 12–19 Key Vocabulary: *owlets, snowfield, tufts* • K-W-L/Question (Poster 5, SG p. 13)	• Guided Preview, pp. 20–27 Key Vocabulary: *saw-whet, pygmy, invisible, burrows* • K-W-L/Question (Poster 5, SG p. 13)
Reading and Reciprocal Teaching (10–15 minutes)	• Silent Reading • Check Questions • Teacher Models SUMMARIZE, QUESTION • Students Model Strategies	• Silent Reading • Check Questions • Teacher Models SUMMARIZE, PREDICT • Students Model Strategies	• Silent Reading • Check Questions • Teacher Models CLARIFY/PHONICS • Students Model Strategies
Responding/ Reflecting (5 minutes)	• K-W-L (Poster 5, SG p. 13) • Reflection #1 (SG p. 15) • Strategies Discussion (Posters 2, 3) • Homework 1	• K-W-L (Poster 5, SG p. 13) • Reflection #2 (SG p. 15) • Strategies Discussion (Posters 2, 3) • Homework 2	• K-W-L (Poster 5, SG p. 13) • Reflection #3 (SG p. 16) • Homework 3 • Home Connection letter

Owl	Lesson 1	Lesson 2
Revisiting (5 minutes)	▸ **Students reread previously read SOAR TO SUCCESS books.** • Have students reread silently for fluency. • Have one student read silently and retell a section of a book. Note comprehension. (Use passages and protocols for Retelling, TM pp. R32–R33, or Oral Reading Check, TM p. R66.)	▸ **Group Conference** Students discuss independent reading. **Prompt:** *Describe an interesting event or unusual fact from your book.* Remind students to keep up their book logs and to bring them to Group Conference for reference.
Reviewing (5 minutes)	▸ **Students review Reciprocal Teaching strategies.** (Posters 2, 3) Students discuss strategies used with *The Lost Expedition* and other classroom reading.	▸ **Students discuss** strategies they have used with other classroom reading. ▸ **Students Summarize** Students use the book and their K-W-L Charts (SG p. 13) to summarize pp. 6–11.
Rehearsing (5–10 minutes) *Note: After the Guided Preview in Lessons 1 and 2, hand out books.*	▸ **Introduce the Book** Show the cover, title, and author's name. Ask students what kinds of things they might learn from this book. ▸ **K-W-L** Introduce K-W-L Posters. Explain that K-W-L is a way to organize and explain facts. Ask students what they know about owls. Help them fill in the **K** column on their K-W-L Charts (SG p. 13). ▸ **Guided Preview/Vocabulary** pp. 6–11. *pp. 6–9* The owl has its wings spread as it **glides** (p. 7) through the air. What time of day is it? *pp. 10–11* The owl's big eyes help it hunt for food on the ground. The owl catches its **prey** (p. 11). ▸ **K-W-L/Question** Students write questions about owls under **W** on their K-W-L Charts (SG p. 13).	▸ **Guided Preview/Vocabulary** pp. 12–19. *pp. 12–13* Parents care for their **owlets** (p. 12). How do the baby owls differ from the adult owls? *pp. 14–15* Owls can even live in a place as cold as a **snowfield** (p. 15). Where else might owls live? *pp. 16–17* Not all barn owls live in barns, but they all have heart-shaped faces. *pp. 18–19* These owls have **tufts** (p. 19) of feathers on their heads that look like ears or horns. ▸ **K-W-L/Question** Help students add questions to the **W** column on their K-W-L Charts (SG p. 13).
Reading and Reciprocal Teaching (10–15 minutes) *Note: After students check their questions, model Summarize, then have students model it. Model the other strategies (in any order), having students use their Strategy Notes to model each one after you. Samples are provided.*	▸ Refer to Posters 2 and 3. Remind students to use these strategies as they read. ▸ **Purpose-setting** Students read to answer their **W** questions. ▸ **Silent Reading** pp. 6–11. Remind students to use SG p. 14 to help them model strategies. ▸ **After reading, students check** to see which of their **W** questions were answered. ***Teacher Models*** • **SUMMARIZE** *An owl spends its day in hiding, but comes out at night to feed on mice and other animals. It sits on tree branches to eat. Sometimes it drops fur or bones while it is eating.* • **QUESTION** *Where do owls go during the day?*	▸ **Purpose-setting** Students read to answer their **W** questions. ▸ **Silent Reading** pp. 12–19. Remind students to use SG p. 14 to help them model strategies. ▸ **After reading, students check** to see which of their **W** questions were answered. ***Teacher Models*** • **SUMMARIZE** *Baby owls must be fed and cared for by their parents. Owls teach the owlets how to use their claws and beaks. Owls live all over the world, in snowy places as well as deserts. You can identify different owls by the shapes of their heads and feathers.* • **PREDICT** *I predict that the next section will tell more about specific kinds of owls.*
Responding/ Reflecting (5 minutes) *Note: Assign the lesson homework (SG p. 15) at the end of each lesson.*	▸ **K-W-L** Students add to their K-W-L Charts (SG p. 13). ▸ **Respond** Students discuss, complete, and share Reflection #1 on SG p. 15: *What makes owls good hunters?* ▸ **Strategies Discussion** (Posters 2, 3) **Prompt:** *When did you use CLARIFY? How did CLARIFY help you?*	▸ **K-W-L** Students add to their K-W-L Charts (SG p. 13). ▸ **Respond** Students discuss, complete, and share Reflection #2 on SG p. 15: *How can you tell owls apart?* ▸ **Strategies Discussion** (Posters 2, 3) **Prompt:** *When did you use PREDICT? How did PREDICT help you?*

Owl	Lesson 3
Revisiting (5 minutes)	▶ **Students reread previously read *SOAR TO SUCCESS* books.** • Have students reread silently for fluency. • Have one student read silently and retell a section of a book. Note comprehension. (Use passages and protocols for Retellings, TM pp. R32–R33 or Oral Reading Check, TM p. R66.)
Reviewing (5 minutes)	▶ **Students discuss** strategies they have used with other classroom reading. ▶ **Students Summarize** Students use the book and their K-W-L Charts (SG p. 13) to summarize pp. 12–19.
Rehearsing (5–10 minutes) *Note: **After** the Guided Preview in Lesson 3, hand out books.*	▶ **Guided Preview/Vocabulary** pp. 20–27. *pp. 20–21* These are elf, **saw-whet,** and **pygmy** owls. How do these owls differ from the owls we saw before? *pp. 22–23* The snowy owl is almost **invisible** because its white feathers blend in with the white snow. *pp. 24–27* These owls live in **burrows** (p. 24), which are holes in the ground. ▶ **K-W-L/Question** Help students add questions to the **W** column on their K-W-L Charts (SG p. 13).
Reading and Reciprocal Teaching (10–15 minutes) *Note: After students check their predictions, model Summarize, then have students model it. Model the other strategies (in any order), having students use their Strategy Notes to model each one after you. Samples are provided.*	▶ Refer to Posters 2 and 3. Remind students to use these strategies as they read. ▶ **Purpose-setting** Students read to answer their **W** questions. ▶ **Silent Reading** pp. 20–27. Remind students to use SG p. 14 to help them model strategies. ▶ **After reading, students check** to see which of their **W** questions were answered. ***Teacher Model*** • **CLARIFY/PHONICS** *To figure out this word* (point to **prairie** on p. 25), *I divide it into chunks. I know the chunk **air** in the middle, and **i-e** sounds like /**ee**/. When I blend **p-r** with those chunks, I get the word **pr/air/ie**. I check the dictionary and find that it means a large area of level or rolling land with grass but no trees or very few trees.*
Responding/ Reflecting (5 minutes) *Note: Assign the lesson homework (SG p. 16) at the end of the lesson.*	▶ **K-W-L** Students add to their K-W-L Charts (SG p. 13). ▶ **Respond** Students discuss, complete, and share Reflection #3 on SG p. 16: *How do the places where owls live help them avoid danger?* ▶ **Home Connection** Students take home *Owl* and the Home Connection letter.

Name _____

Owl

Students use this page to jot down notes or questions as they read. It should not be used for assessment. Sample notes are shown.

Strategy Notes

Clarify

Why does the snowy owl lay its eggs on the ground? p. 23

flicker p. 27

Predict

Page 21 From the photos, I think I'll learn about some very small owls.

Question

Where do owls go during the day? p. 8

Do barn owls always live in barns? p. 16

Summarize

Pages 15–17: Owls live all over the world, in freezing places and in tropical places. They live in the city and in the country.

Name _____

Sample responses are shown.

K-W-L Chart

Title	*Owl*	
What I Know	**What I Want to Find Out**	**What I Learned**
Owls are birds.	**Pages 6–11**	**Page 10**
Owls can fly.	What do owls eat?	Owls eat insects, birds, fish, and mice.
Owls have big eyes.	**Pages 12–19**	**Page 12**
	How many babies does a mother owl usually have?	Most owls raise four to six young each year.
	Where do owls live?	**Page 15**
		Owls live everywhere. There are owls near the North Pole and in the rainforest.
	What is the biggest owl?	**Page 19**
		The great horned owl is 22 inches tall.
	Pages 20–27	**Page 21**
	What is the tiniest owl?	The elf owl is less than six inches long.
	Where do owls go when the sun rises?	**Page 27**
		The owl returns to its nest. It waits for another sunset to fly again.

Owl

Name _____

Students use this page to think about their reading and to prepare for discussion. It should not be used for assessment. Sample responses are shown.

REFLECTION 3

How do the places where owls live help them avoid danger?

Holes in a cactus hide the smallest owls from animals that might hunt them.

Northern lands covered with snow make the snowy owl almost invisible.

HOMEWORK 3

Do research to find the names of two species of owl not covered in this book. Write two facts about each kind of owl.

16 Level 8, Book 3, *Owl*

Owl

Name _____

Students use this page to think about their reading and to prepare for discussion. It should not be used for assessment. Sample responses are shown.

REFLECTION 1

What makes owls good hunters?

Owls are good hunters because they don't make noise when they fly.

They can also see in the dark. They have sharp claws and beaks to help them

attack.

HOMEWORK 1

What other flying creatures come out to play or hunt at night? Write a short list of those you know about.

REFLECTION 2

How can you tell owls apart?

You can look at owls to tell them apart. Different owls have different colored

feathers and markings.

HOMEWORK 2

What are some common birds you have seen flying around your neighborhood? Write about one of them, and give your ideas about how the environment supports that bird.

Level 8, Book 3, *Owl* 15

The Babe & I

by David A. Adler

Illustrated by Terry Widener

*S*ummary: A young boy helps his family make ends meet during the Great Depression. He and his friend find a way to sell a lot of newspapers and, in the process, the boy gets to meet Babe Ruth.

Materials

Lesson 1	Lesson 2	Lesson 3
• Previously read books	• Independent reading books	• Previously read books
• *The Babe & I* pp. 4–15	• *The Babe & I* pp. 16–23	• *The Babe & I* pp. 24–32
• Posters 2, 3, 4	• Posters 2, 3, 4	• Posters 2, 3, 4
• Student Guide (SG) pp. 17–19	• Student Guide (SG) pp. 17–19	• Student Guide (SG) pp. 17–18, 20
• Strategy prompts, SG pp. 89–91	• Strategy prompts, SG pp. 89–91	• Strategy prompts, SG pp. 89–91
• Markers	• Markers	• Markers
		• Home Connection letter

Scaffolding

Strong Teacher Support	Moderate Teacher Support	Student Independence
	For Book 4 (Category II), continue to coach and model as you encourage students to practice using strategies independently.	

Help with Phonics and Decoding Longer Words: For students who need explicit instruction, see the Optional Lesson on page R185 of the Teacher's Resource File in this manual.

Lesson Overview

	Lesson 1	Lesson 2	Lesson 3
Revisiting (5 minutes)	• Previously read books: Retelling/Oral Reading Check	• Group Conference: Independent Reading	• Previously read books: Retelling/Oral Reading Check
Reviewing (5 minutes)	• Review Reciprocal Teaching Strategies (Posters 2, 3)	• Students Discuss Strategies • Students Summarize	• Students Discuss Strategies • Students Summarize
Rehearsing (5–10 minutes)	• Introduce the Book • Students Predict • Guided Preview, pp. 4–15 Key Vocabulary: *Depression, wrinkled, shabby, newsie*	• Students Predict • Guided Preview, pp. 16–23 Key Vocabulary: *elevated, carriage, unemployed*	• Students Predict • Guided Preview, pp. 24–32 Key Vocabulary: *quietly, recognize, uniform*
Reading and Reciprocal Teaching (10–15 minutes)	• Silent Reading • Check Predictions • Students Model Strategies • Teacher Models CLARIFY/PHONICS	• Silent Reading • Check Predictions • Students Model Strategies • Teacher Models SUMMARIZE, PREDICT	• Silent Reading • Check Predictions • Students Model Strategies • Teacher Models SUMMARIZE, QUESTION
Responding/ Reflecting (5 minutes)	• Story Map (Poster 4, SG p. 17) • Reflection #1 (SG p. 19) • Strategies Discussion (Posters 2, 3) • Homework 1	• Story Map (Poster 4, SG p. 17) • Reflection #2 (SG p. 19) • Strategies Discussion (Posters 2, 3) • Homework 2	• Story Map (Poster 4, SG p. 17) • Reflection #3 (SG p. 20) • Homework 3 • Home Connection letter

The Babe & I	Lesson 1	Lesson 2
Revisiting (5 minutes)	▶ **Students reread previously read SOAR TO SUCCESS books.** • Have students reread silently for fluency. • Have one student read silently and retell a section of a book. Note comprehension. (Use passages and protocols for Retellings, TM pp. R34–R35, or Oral Reading Check, TM p. R67).	▶ **Group Conference** Students discuss independent reading. **Prompt:** *What questions would you like to ask the author of the book you are now reading?* Remind students to keep up their book logs and to bring them to Group Conference for reference.
Reviewing (5 minutes)	▶ **Students review Reciprocal Teaching strategies.** (Posters 2, 3) Students discuss strategies used with *Owl* and other classroom reading.	▶ **Students discuss** strategies they have used with other classroom reading. ▶ **Students Summarize** Students use the book and their Story Maps (SG p. 17) to summarize pp. 4–15.
Rehearsing (5–10 minutes) *Note: **After** the Guided Preview in Lessons 1 and 2, hand out books*	▶ **Introduce the Book** Show the cover, title, and author's name. Explain that the boy in the story helped support his family during the Depression. ▶ **Students Predict** Ask students what they think the book will be about. Record their predictions. ▶ **Guided Preview/Vocabulary** pp. 4–15. *pp. 4–7* The boy telling this story was upset because he didn't get a bike for his birthday. He lived during the **Depression** (p. 5), when millions of people were out of work and didn't have much money. *pp. 8–9* The boy and his friend passed a woman in **wrinkled** (p. 9) and **shabby** (p. 9) clothes. *pp. 10–11* The boy discovered that his father also sold apples. How might this have made him feel? *pp. 12–15* The boy's friend got him a job as a **newsie** (p. 13), selling newspapers.	▶ **Students Predict** Based on pages 4–15, students predict what might happen in the next section. Record their predictions. ▶ **Guided Preview/Vocabulary** pp. 16–23. *pp. 16–17* The boys walked to an **elevated** (p. 16) train station. People were rushing to Yankee Stadium. *pp. 18–19* The boy made twenty-five cents for the family money jar. *pp. 20–21* The boy could have sold more papers if he had a way to carry more of them, so he rented a baby **carriage** (p. 21) from his neighbor. *pp. 22–23* The boy and his Dad disagree about whether selling apples is a job. Do you think that the father is **unemployed** (p. 23)?
Reading and Reciprocal Teaching (10–15 minutes) *Note: After students check their predictions, they model Summarize, with you modeling if needed. Then they model all other strategies in any order, using their Strategy Notes. Model for them as needed. Samples are provided.*	▶ Refer to Posters 2 and 3. Remind students to use these strategies as they read. ▶ **Purpose-setting** Students read to check their predictions. ▶ **Silent Reading** pp. 4–15. Remind students to use SG p. 18 to help them model strategies. ▶ **After reading, students check** to see if their predictions were verified. ***Teacher Models*** • **CLARIFY/PHONICS** To *figure out this word* (point to **reminded** on page 9)*, I divide it into chunks. I know the prefix **re-**, and I recognize the word **mind**. When I put those together and add the ending **-e-d**, I get **re/mind/ed**. In the dictionary, I read that **remind** means cause to remember.*	▶ Refer to Posters 2 and 3. Remind students to use these strategies as they read. ▶ **Purpose-setting** Students read to check their predictions. ▶ **Silent Reading** pp. 16–23. Remind students to use SG p. 18 to help them model strategies. ▶ **After reading, students check** to see if their predictions were verified. ***Teacher Models*** • **SUMMARIZE** *The two boys sold newspapers at Yankee Stadium to fans who wanted to read about Babe Ruth. The boy put the money he earned in the money jar. He rented a carriage so he could carry more papers.* • **PREDICT** *I predict that the boy will sell a lot of newspapers.*
Responding/ Reflecting (5 minutes) *Note: Assign the lesson homework (SG p. 19) at the end of each lesson.*	▶ **Story Map** Review the parts of a story. Have students fill in **Setting** on their Story Maps (SG p. 17). ▶ **Respond** Students discuss, complete, and share Reflection #1 on SG p. 19: *Why did the father pretend that he had a job?* ▶ **Strategies Discussion** (Posters 2, 3) **Prompt:** *When did you use CLARIFY? How did CLARIFY help you?*	▶ **Story Map** Have students update their Story Maps (SG p. 17). ▶ **Respond** Students discuss, complete, and share Reflection #2 on SG p. 19, using the information on pages 18–21 of *The Babe & I.* ▶ **Strategies Discussion** (Posters 2, 3) **Prompt:** *When did you PREDICT? How did PREDICT help you?*

The Babe & I	Lesson 3

Revisiting
(5 minutes)

► **Students reread previously read *SOAR TO SUCCESS* books.**
- Have students reread silently for fluency.
- Have one student read silently and retell a section of a book. Note comprehension. (Use passages and protocols for Retellings, TM pp. R34–R35, or Oral Reading Check, TM p. R67).

Reviewing
(5 minutes)

► **Students discuss** strategies they have used with other classroom reading.
► **Students Summarize.** Students use the book and their Story Maps (SG p. 17) to summarize pp. 16–23.

Rehearsing
(5–10 minutes)

*Note: **After** the Guided Preview in Lesson 3, hand out books.*

► **Students Predict** Based on pages 16–23, students predict what might happen in the final section. Record their predictions.
► **Guided Preview/Vocabulary** pp. 24–32.

pp. 24–25 The boy and his father told each other their secrets about work, and walked **quietly** (p. 25) along the street.

pp. 26–29 A stranger gave the boy five dollars for a newspaper. The boy didn't **recognize** (p. 27) Babe Ruth out of his **uniform** (p. 27)**.** The boy used the money for two tickets to the game. What would you have done?

pp. 30–32 The Yankees were the best team in baseball in 1932. In what ways are the boy and his father a team?

Reading and Reciprocal Teaching
(10–15 minutes)

Note: After students check their predictions, they model Summarize, with you modeling if needed. Then they model all other strategies in any order, using their Strategy Notes. Model for them as needed. Samples are provided.

► Refer to Posters 2 and 3. Remind students to use these strategies as they read.
► **Purpose-setting** Students read to check their predictions.
► **Silent Reading** pp. 24–32. Remind students to use SG p. 18 to help them model strategies.
► **After reading, students check** to see if their predictions were verified.

Teacher Models
- **SUMMARIZE** *The boy and his father share their secrets. The next day, Babe Ruth gives the boy five dollars for a paper, and the boy buys tickets to the game.*
- **QUESTION** *Why did Babe give the boy so much money?*

Responding/Reflecting
(5 minutes)

Note: Assign the lesson homework (SG p. 20) at the end of the lesson.

► **Story Map** Have students fill in the Outcome box on their Story Maps (SG p. 17).
► **Respond** Students discuss, complete, and share Reflection #3 on SG p. 20: *Circle the section you liked best. How did the strategies help you?*
► **Home Connection** Students take home *The Babe & I* and the Home Connection letter.

The Babe & I

Name _____

Students use this page to jot down notes or questions as they read. Sample notes are shown. It should not be used for assessment.

Strategy Notes

Clarify

During the Great Depression, millions of people had no jobs. p. 5

newsies p. 13

Tears were rolling down Dad's cheeks. p. 25

Predict

Jacob will help his friend make money. pp.12–13

Question

Why didn't people want to read the paper? p. 14

Summarize

Pages 24–25: The boy's father knows that his son has been selling newspapers, and realizes that his son knows he has been selling apples to make money. They seem to understand each other.

18 Level 8, Book 4, *The Babe & I*

The Babe & I

Name _____

Sample responses are shown.

Story Map

Title

The Babe & I

Setting

New York City, 1932, during the Great Depression

Characters

Young boy, Jacob, the boy's mother and father, Babe Ruth

Problem

The boy's family needs to make money during the Depression.

Major Events   (May vary)

1. The boy wants a bicycle for his birthday, but he gets a dime.
2. The boy's father leaves for work. The boy sees him selling apples on the street.
3. Jacob tells the boy he can make money by getting a job with him selling newspapers.
4. Jacob says they should sell papers at Yankee Stadium.
5. The boy makes money for his family, but his mother asks him to keep his job a secret.
6. The boy rents a carriage from his neighbor so he can sell more papers and make more money.
7. Eventually, the father learns that his son is selling papers.
8. The boy keeps his father's secret about selling apples.
9. Babe Ruth buys a newspaper and gives the boy five dollars.
10. The boy and Jacob go to a baseball game to watch Babe.

Outcome

The boy realizes that he and his father work together as a team, just as Babe and the Yankees work as a team.

Level 8, Book 4, *The Babe & I* 17

The Babe & I

Name _____

Students use this page to think about their reading and prepare for discussion. It should not be used for assessment. Sample responses are shown.

REFLECTION 3

Circle the section you liked best in *The Babe & I*.

PAGES 4–15	PAGES 16–23	PAGES 24–32
The boy becomes a newsie during the Great Depression.	The boy makes extra money for his family.	The boy meets Babe Ruth and sees a Yankees game. *(circled)*

How did one or more of the four strategies help you read that section?

Predict

Predict helped me to know that Babe would play the game.

Question

Question helped me understand why Babe Ruth would give the boy a huge tip.

Clarify

_____

Summarize

_____

HOMEWORK 3

Imagine that you are a newspaper reporter who talks to the two boys about the way they sell papers. Write a short newspaper article about their method.

20 Level 8, Book 4, *The Babe & I*

The Babe & I

Name _____

Students use this page to think about their reading and prepare for discussion. It should not be used for assessment. Sample responses are shown.

REFLECTION 1

Why did the father pretend that he had a job?

The boy's father is ashamed. He wants his family to think he can make enough money for them. He is embarrassed about selling apples.

HOMEWORK 1

Do research to find out more about Babe Ruth. Write his final record for home runs and one other interesting fact about him.

REFLECTION 2

Using the information on pages 18–21, figure out how much the boy would make if he sold 100 papers.

Each paper sold for 2¢. The boys paid 1¢ for each paper sold. So 100 papers would cost $1.00, and sell for $2.00. The boy also had to pay 10¢ for the carriage. So he would make 90¢.

HOMEWORK 2

Mrs. Johnson agreed to rent her carriage to the boy for ten cents each afternoon. Write a paragraph explaining why this was a good deal for her and for the boy.

Level 8, Book 4, *The Babe & I* **19**

Journey Home

by Lawrence McKay, Jr.

Illustrated by Dom & Keunhee Lee

*S*ummary: Mai and her mother go to Vietnam to search for her mother's birth family. They discover that home can be a place all around them and inside them at the same time.

Materials

Lesson 1	Lesson 2	Lesson 3
• Previously read books	• Independent reading books	• Previously read books
• *Journey Home* pp. 2–11	• *Journey Home* pp. 12–21	• *Journey Home* pp. 22–32
• Posters 2, 3, 4	• Posters 2, 3, 4	• Posters 2, 3, 4
• Student Guide (SG) pp. 21–23	• Student Guide (SG) pp. 21–23	• Student Guide (SG) pp. 21–22, 24
• Strategy Prompts, SG pp. 89–91	• Strategy Prompts, SG pp. 89–91	• Strategy Prompts, SG pp. 89–91
• Markers	• Markers	• Markers
		• Home Connection letter

Scaffolding

Strong Teacher Support	Moderate Teacher Support	Student Independence
	For Book 5 (Category III), continue to coach and model as you encourage students to practice using strategies independently.	

Help with Phonics and Decoding Longer Words: For students who need explicit instruction, see the Optional Lesson on page R186 of the Teacher's Resource File in this manual.

Lesson Overview

	Lesson 1	Lesson 2	Lesson 3
Revisiting (5 minutes)	• Previously read books	• Group Conference: Independent Reading	• Previously read books: Retelling/Oral Reading Check
Reviewing (5 minutes)	• Review Reciprocal Teaching Strategies (Posters 2, 3)	• Students Discuss Strategies • Students Summarize	• Students Discuss Strategies • Students Summarize
Rehearsing (5–10 minutes)	• Introduce the Book • Students Predict • Guided Preview, pp. 2–11 Key Vocabulary: *orphanage, adopted, celebrated, language*	• Students Predict • Guided Preview, pp. 12–21 Key Vocabulary: *cyclo, photograph, statue, pier*	• Students Predict • Cooperative Preview, pp. 22–32 Key Vocabulary: *countryside, rubble, pagoda*
Reading and Reciprocal Teaching (10–15 minutes)	• Silent Reading • Check Predictions • Students Model Strategies • Teacher Models SUMMARIZE, CLARIFY	• Silent Reading • Check Predictions • Students Model Strategies • Teacher Models SUMMARIZE, CLARIFY/PHONICS	• Silent Reading • Check Predictions • Students Model Strategies • Teacher Models QUESTION, CLARIFY/PHONICS
Responding/ Reflecting (5 minutes)	• Story Map (Poster 4, SG p. 21) • Reflection #1 (SG p. 23) • Strategies Discussion (Posters 2, 3) • Homework 1	• Story Map (Poster 4, SG p. 21) • Reflection #2 (SG p. 23) • Homework 2	• Story Map (Poster 4, SG p. 21) • Reflection #3 (SG p. 24) • Homework 3 • Home Connection letter

Journey Home	Lesson 1	Lesson 2
Revisiting (5 minutes)	▶ **Students reread previously read *SOAR TO SUCCESS* books.** • Have students reread silently for fluency; assign each a different strategy to model in Reviewing.	▶ **Group Conference** Students discuss independent reading. **Prompt:** *Why did you choose to read your book? Are you enjoying the book? Why?* Remind students to keep up their book logs and to bring them to Group Conference for reference.
Reviewing (5 minutes)	▶ **Students review Reciprocal Teaching strategies.** (Posters 2, 3) Students discuss strategies used with *The Babe & I* and other classroom reading, and model strategies they used in Revisiting.	▶ **Students discuss** strategies they have used with other classroom reading. ▶ **Students Summarize** Students use the book and their Story Maps (SG p. 21) to summarize pp. 2–11.
Rehearsing (5–10 minutes) *Note: **After** the Guided Preview in Lessons 1 and 2, hand out books.* *Note: To keep the emphasis on comprehension, students should not be held responsible for proper names in the book.*	▶ **Introduce the Book** Show the cover, title, and author's name. Explain that this story is told by a girl visiting Vietnam with her mother, searching for her mother's birth family. ▶ **Students Predict** Ask students what they think might happen in the story. Record their predictions. ▶ **Guided Preview/Vocabulary** pp. 2–11 *pp. 3–5* Mai's mother, Lin, was left at an **orphanage** (p. 3) during the Vietnam War. She was **adopted** (p. 5) and brought to America. All she had was this kite. She went back to search for her birth family. *pp. 6–7* Mai **celebrated** her tenth birthday, and felt old enough to go to Vietnam, too. *pp. 8–9* Mai and her mother go to Vietnam together. Lin is studying the Vietnamese **language**. Why? *pp. 10–11* Mai is in Saigon, a city in Vietnam.	▶ **Students Predict** Based on pages 2–11, students predict what might happen in the next section. Record their predictions. ▶ **Guided Preview/Vocabulary** pp. 12–21 *pp. 12–13* Lin and Mai take a **cyclo**, or bike taxi, through Saigon to the People's Hall of Records. *pp. 14–15* Lin shows the man at the Hall of Records a **photograph** of herself as a baby at the orphanage. What do you think they are hoping to find? *pp. 16–17* The next day, Lin and Mai go into the country. They pass a **statue** of Kuan Yin and make a wish. What do you think Lin and Mai wish for? *pp. 18–21* They go to orphanages and visit the waterfront. They see a stall with kites near the **pier** (p. 20). Why do you think they are excited?
Reading and Reciprocal Teaching (10–15 minutes) *Note: After students check their predictions, they model Summarize, with you modeling if needed. Then they model all other strategies in any order, using their Strategy Notes. Model for them as needed. Samples are provided.*	▶ Refer to Posters 2 and 3. Remind students to use these strategies as they read. ▶ **Purpose-setting** Students read to check their predictions. ▶ **Silent Reading** pp. 2–11. Remind students to use SG p. 22 to help them model strategies. ▶ **After reading, students check** to see if their predictions were verified. ***Teacher Models*** • **SUMMARIZE** *Mai's mother, Lin, was given up for adoption when she was a baby during the Vietnam War. Now, she and her daughter are traveling back to Vietnam to find her birth parents.* • **CLARIFY** *This sentence on page 5* (point to **Her past is like a puzzle**) *must mean that Lin's past is something to be solved, like a mystery.*	▶ **Purpose-setting** Students read to check their predictions. ▶ **Silent Reading** pp. 12–21. Remind students to use SG p. 22 to help them model strategies. ▶ **After reading, students check** to see if their predictions were verified. ***Teacher Models*** • **SUMMARIZE** *Lin and Mai go to the Hall of Records to check birth records. They visit orphanages, showing Lin's baby picture to the nuns. Finally, a waterfront merchant recognizes the kite in Lin's picture.* • **CLARIFY/PHONICS** *I don't recognize this word* (point to **translates** on page 21). *I see the prefix* **trans-** *and the chunk* **lates**. *When I blend them, I get* **trans/lates**. *It makes sense.*
Responding/ Reflecting (5 minutes) *Note: Assign the lesson homework (SG p. 23) at the end of each lesson.*	▶ **Story Map** (Poster 7) Review the parts of a story. Have students fill in **Setting** on their Story Maps. ▶ **Respond** Students discuss, complete, and share Reflection #1 on SG p. 23: *Why does the kite have special meaning for both Lin and Mai?* ▶ **Strategies Discussion** (Posters 2, 3) **Prompt:** *When did you use SUMMARIZE? How did it help you?*	▶ **Story Map** Have students update their Story Maps (SG p. 21). ▶ **Respond** Students discuss, complete, and share Reflection #2 on SG p. 23: *Circle one strategy that helped you. Explain how you used this strategy.*

Journey Home	**Lesson 3**

Revisiting
(5 minutes)

▶ **Students reread previously read SOAR TO SUCCESS books.**

- Have students reread silently for fluency.
- Have one student read silently and retell a section of a book. Note comprehension. (Use passages and protocols for Retellings, TM pp. R36–R37, or Oral Reading Check, TM p. R68.)

Reviewing
(5 minutes)

▶ **Students discuss** strategies they have used with other classroom reading.

▶ **Students Summarize** Students use the book and their Story Maps (SG p. 21) to summarize pp. 12–21.

Rehearsing
(5–10 minutes)

Note: To keep the emphasis on comprehension, students should not be held responsible for proper names in the book.

▶ **Students Predict** Based on pages 12–21, students predict what might happen in the final section. Record their predictions.

▶ **Cooperative Preview/Vocabulary** Have partners preview pages 22–32, noting the illustrations. If needed, coach as follows:

pp. 22–25 As they drive in the **countryside** (p. 22), they get directions to the kite-maker's village.

pp. 26–29 The kite-maker had found Lin in the **rubble** (p. 29), or ruins, after her parents died. Why do you think he took her to the orphanage?

pp. 30–32 The kite-maker takes Lin and Mai to the **pagoda** that holds Lin's parents ashes.

After the preview, have students locate each word boldfaced above, read aloud the sentence, and briefly discuss the meaning.

Reading and Reciprocal Teaching
(10–15 minutes)

Note: After students check their predictions, they model Summarize, with you modeling if needed. Then they model all other strategies in any order, using their Strategy Notes. Model for them as needed. Samples are provided.

▶ **Purpose-setting** Students read to check their predictions.

▶ **Silent Reading** pp. 22–32. Remind students to use SG p. 22 to help them model strategies.

▶ **After reading, students check** to see if their predictions were verified.

Teacher Models

- **QUESTION** *Why did the kite-maker leave Lin at an orphanage when she was a baby?*
- **CLARIFY/PHONICS** *I don't recognize this word* (point to **oxen** on page 22). *I try breaking it into chunks:* **ox** *and* **en**. *I know an ox is an animal. The picture (p. 23) shows a cart pulled by an ox. Then I reread:* **carts pulled by oxen**. *Maybe* **oxen** *is the plural of* **ox**. *I check by looking* **ox** *up in the dictionary, and I find out I'm right.*

Responding/ Reflecting
(5 minutes)

Note: Assign the lesson homework (SG p. 24) at the end of the lesson.

▶ **Story Map** Have students fill in the Outcome box on their Story Maps (SG p. 21).

▶ **Respond** Students discuss, complete, and share Reflection #3 on SG p. 24: *Pretend you are in Mai's place. How would you feel traveling so far away?*

▶ **Home Connection** Students take home *Journey Home* and the Home Connection letter.

Journey Home

Name _____

Strategy Notes

Students use this page to jot down notes or questions as they read. It should not be used for assessment. Sample notes are shown.

Clarify

Hall of Records? p. 15

craters? p. 22

Predict

If Lin finds the kite-maker, she will find out about her birth family. p. 20

Question

Why is Mai different at home? p. 12

How did Lin survive the bombing? p. 29

Summarize

Pages 12–15: Lin and Mai visit the People's Hall of Records to try to find information about Lin's birth parents, but they have no luck. Mai knows how sad Lin is, because Mai has never seen her father either.

Journey Home

Name _____

Story Map

Sample responses are shown.

Title

Journey Home

Setting

America and Vietnam

Characters

Mai, her mother Lin, Kuan Yin, Tran Quang Tai (the kite-maker)

Problem

Mai's mother, Lin, is a Vietnamese orphan who was raised in America. She wants to find out about her birth parents in Vietnam.

Major Events   (May vary)

1. Mai and her mother, Lin, pack to go to Vietnam, where Lin hopes to find her birth family.
2. Mai wants to bring her mother's special kite, but Lin says no.
3. Mai and Lin travel together to Saigon, Vietnam.
4. They visit the People's Hall of Records, looking for a photo that looks like Lin as a child.
5. They go to the countryside and make a wish to Kuan Yin.
6. Mai and Lin visit many orphanages and then go to the waterfront.
7. A merchant recognizes the kite in the picture and gives them the name of the kite-maker.
8. They go to the country and find the kite-maker, who recognizes Lin's photo and tells her her Vietnamese name, and that he rescued Lin when her parents were killed in the war.

Outcome

Lin has found out about her parents, her name, and who she is.

Journey Home

Name _____

Students use this page to think about their reading and to prepare for discussion. It should not be used for assessment. Sample responses are shown.

REFLECTION 3

Pretend you are in Mai's place. How would you feel traveling so far away?

I would feel scared being in a strange place. But I would want to find my mother's birth parents. I would definitely keep looking for clues and keep trying to find my grandparents. I would want to understand the history of where my family came from.

HOMEWORK 3

Write a short letter to Lin congratulating her on the discovery of her name.

Journey Home

Name _____

Students use this page to think about their reading and to prepare for discussion. It should not be used for assessment. Sample responses are shown.

REFLECTION 1

Why does the kite have special meaning for Lin and Mai?

The kite was the only possession Lin had from Vietnam when she came to America. It is the one connection Mai and Lin have to the place where Lin was born.

HOMEWORK 1

Do research to find out more about Vietnam. List three places or things Lin and Mai might see while they are there.

REFLECTION 2

Circle one strategy that has helped you read *Journey Home* so far.

Strategy Box			
Predict	Summarize	Clarify	Question

Explain how you used this strategy.

Question helped me to understand why Lin and Mai were going to different parts of Vietnam. It helped me to understand why they would travel so far and ask so many people for help.

HOMEWORK 2

Lin and Mai are looking for a kite-maker. Pick an adult friend or relative, and write a brief description of the job he or she does for a living.

Cal Ripken, Jr.: Play Ball!

by Cal Ripken, Jr., and Mike Bryan

*S*ummary: In 1995, Cal Ripken, Jr., a highly respected player for the Baltimore Orioles, broke the record for playing the most consecutive games. This is his biography.

Note: It is not necessary for students to know or be held responsible for all the facts presented in the book. The purpose of these lessons is to help students learn strategies for comprehending informational text.

Materials

Lesson 1	Lesson 2	Lesson 3	Lesson 4
• Previously read books	• Independent reading books	• Previously read books	• Independent reading books
• *Cal Ripken, Jr.: Play Ball!* pp. 4–14	• *Cal Ripken, Jr.: Play Ball!* pp. 15–25	• *Cal Ripken, Jr.: Play Ball!* pp. 26–35	• *Cal Ripken, Jr.: Play Ball!* pp. 36–48
• Posters 2, 3, 8	• Posters 2, 3, 8	• Posters 2, 3, 8	• Posters 2, 3, 8
• Student Guide (SG) pp. 25–27	• Student Guide (SG) pp. 25–27	• Student Guide (SG) pp. 25–26, 28	• Student Guide (SG) pp. 25–26, 28
• Strategy Prompts, SG pp. 89–91	• Strategy Prompts, SG pp. 89–91	• Strategy Prompts, SG pp. 89–91	• Strategy Prompts, SG pp. 89–91
• Markers	• Markers	• Markers	• Markers
			• Home Connection letter

Scaffolding

Strong Teacher Support	Moderate Teacher Support	Student Independence
	For Book 6 (Category III), continue to coach and model as you encourage students to practice using strategies independently.	

Help with Phonics and Decoding Longer Words: For students who need explicit instruction, see the Optional Lesson on page R187 of the Teacher's Resource File in this manual.

Lesson Overview

	Lesson 1	Lesson 2	Lesson 3	Lesson 4
Revisiting (5 minutes)	• Previously read books: Retelling	• Group Conference: Independent Reading	• Previously read books: Retelling	• Group Conference: Independent Reading
Reviewing (5 minutes)	• Review Reciprocal Teaching Strategies (Posters 2, 3)	• Students Discuss Strategies • Students Summarize	• Students Discuss Strategies • Students Summarize	• Students Discuss Strategies • Students Summarize
Rehearsing (5–10 minutes)	• Introduce the Book • Students Predict • Guided Preview, pp. 4–14 Key Vocabulary: *lineup, consecutive, minor leagues, competitive*	• Students Predict • Guided Preview, pp. 15–25 Key Vocabulary: *draft, innings, slump*	• Students Predict • Cooperative Preview, pp. 26–35 Key Vocabulary: *identity, concentrate, batting average, groove*	• Students Predict • Cooperative Preview, pp. 36–48 Key Vocabulary: *salute, dugout, ceremony*
Reading and Reciprocal Teaching (10–15 minutes)	• Silent Reading • Check Predictions • Students Model Strategies • Teacher Models SUMMARIZE, PREDICT	• Silent Reading • Check Predictions • Students Model Strategies • Teacher Models SUMMARIZE, CLARIFY/PHONICS	• Silent Reading • Check Predictions • Students Model Strategies • Teacher Models SUMMARIZE, QUESTION	• Silent Reading • Check Predictions • Students Model Strategies • Teacher Models CLARIFY/PHONICS
Responding/ Reflecting (5 minutes)	• Event Map (Poster 8, SG p. 25) • Reflection #1 (SG p. 27) • Strategies Discussion (Posters 2, 3) • Homework 1	• Event Map (Poster 8, SG p. 25) • Reflection #2 (SG p. 27) • Strategies Discussion (Posters 2, 3) • Homework 2	• Event Map (Poster 8, SG p. 25) • Reflection #3 (SG p. 28) • Strategies Discussion (Posters 2, 3) • Homework 3	• Event Map (Poster 8, SG p. 25) • Reflection #4 (SG p. 28) • Homework 4 • Home Connection letter

Cal Ripken, Jr.: Play Ball!	Lesson 1	Lesson 2
Revisiting (5 minutes) *Note: Do an Oral Reading Check only when you are concerned about a student's decoding or fluency*	▶ **Students reread previously read *SOAR TO SUCCESS* books.** • Have students reread silently for fluency; assign each a different strategy to model in Reviewing. • Have one student read silently and retell a section of a book. Note comprehension. (Use passages and protocols for Retellings, TM pp. R38–R39.)	▶ **Group Conference** Students discuss independent reading. **Prompt:** *What book are you reading? Why did you choose it?* Remind students to keep up their book logs and to bring them to Group Conference for reference.
Reviewing (5 minutes)	▶ **Students review Reciprocal Teaching strategies.** (Posters 2, 3) Students discuss strategies used with *Journey Home* and other classroom reading, and model strategies they used in Revisiting.	▶ **Students discuss** strategies they have used with other classroom reading. ▶ **Students Summarize** Students use the book and their Event Maps (SG p. 25) to summarize pp. 4–14.
Rehearsing (5–10 minutes) *Note: After the Guided Preview in Lessons 1 and 2, hand out books.*	▶ **Introduce the Book** Show the cover, title, and author's name. ▶ **Students Predict** Ask students what they think the book will be about. Record their predictions. ▶ **Guided Preview/Vocabulary** pp. 4–14. *pp. 4–7* Cal Ripken decided that when he got into the Oriole **lineup** (p. 6), he would play well and play every day. He ended up breaking the record for playing the most **consecutive** (p. 6) games. *pp. 8–10* As children, the Ripkens traveled with their dad, who was in the **minor leagues** (p. 8). *pp. 11–14* Cal was **competitive** (p. 11) and sometimes cheated. He learned you have to play by the rules.	▶ **Students Predict** Based on pages 4–14, students predict what might happen in the next section. Record their predictions. ▶ **Guided Preview/Vocabulary** pp. 15–25. *pp. 15–18* Cal's father took a job near home with the Orioles. He helped Cal, who was playing high school baseball. After high school, Cal was picked in the baseball **draft** (p. 18). How do you think Cal felt? *pp. 19–22* You can tell from the title, "The Minors," that Cal started in the minor leagues. He played in the longest game in history—33 **innings**! (p. 20) *pp. 23–25* In the major leagues, Cal started out in a batting **slump** (p. 25). But he ended up being named Rookie of the Year. What do you think that honor means?
Reading and Reciprocal Teaching (10–15 minutes) *Note: After students check their predictions, they model Summarize, with you modeling if needed. Then they model all other strategies in any order, using their Strategy Notes. Model for them as needed. Samples are provided.*	▶ Refer to Posters 2 and 3. Remind students to use these strategies as they read. ▶ **Purpose-setting** Students read to check their predictions. ▶ **Silent Reading** pp. 4–14. Remind students to use SG p. 26 to help them model strategies. ▶ **After reading, students check** to see if their predictions were verified. ***Teacher Models*** • **SUMMARIZE** *Cal's father was a manager and player for the Orioles. The family often traveled with the team, which was hard on the children. Cal and his brothers and sister played a lot of sports, especially baseball.* • **PREDICT** *From the chapter title, I know I'll learn about a baseball family.*	▶ **Purpose-setting** Students read to check their predictions. ▶ **Silent Reading** pp. 15–25. Remind students to use SG p. 26 to help them model strategies. ▶ **After reading, students check** to see if their predictions were verified. ***Teacher Models*** • **SUMMARIZE** *Cal's dad helped him practice. Cal played in the minor leagues to develop his skills and then was called up to the majors. Eventually he was named Rookie of the Year.* • **CLARIFY/PHONICS** *To figure out this word* (point to **doubleheader** on page 25), *I break it into familiar word chunks, **double** and **head**. Then I add the ending **-e-r**. I blend the chunks together and get **double/head/er**.*
Responding/Reflecting (5 minutes) *Note: Assign the lesson homework (SG p. 27) at the end of each lesson.*	▶ **Event Map** Display Poster 8. Help students fill in events 1 and 2 on their own Event Maps (SG p. 25). ▶ **Respond** Students discuss, complete, and share Reflection #1 on SG p. 27: *How are you like Cal? How are you different?* ▶ **Strategies Discussion** (Posters 2, 3) **Prompt:** *When did you use QUESTION? How did it help you?*	▶ **Event Map** Using Event Map Poster 8, help students update their own Event Maps (SG p. 25). ▶ **Respond** Students discuss, complete, and share Reflection #2 on SG p. 27: *How do you feel about what Cal has accomplished with his baseball skills?* ▶ **Strategies Discussion** (Posters 2, 3) Ask students how strategies have helped them so far.

Cal Ripken, Jr.: Play Ball!

	Lesson 3	Lesson 4
Revisiting (5 minutes) *Note: Do an Oral Reading Check only when you are concerned about a student's decoding or fluency.*	▶ **Students reread previously read *SOAR TO SUCCESS* books.** • Have students reread silently for fluency. • Have one student read silently and retell a section of a book. Note comprehension. (Use passages and protocols for Retellings, TM pp. R38–R39.)	▶ **Group Conference** Students discuss independent reading. **Prompt:** *Tell about an exciting event or an interesting fact from your book.* Remind students to keep up their book logs and to bring them to Group Conference for reference.
Reviewing (5 minutes)	▶ **Students discuss** strategies they have used with other classroom reading. ▶ **Students Summarize** Students use the book and their Event Maps (SG p. 25) to summarize pp. 15–25.	▶ **Students discuss** strategies they have used with other classroom reading. ▶ **Students Summarize** Students use the book and their Event Maps (SG p. 25) to summarize pp. 26–35.
Rehearsing (5–10 minutes)	▶ **Students Predict** Based on pages 15–25, students predict what might happen next. Record predictions. ▶ **Cooperative Preview/Vocabulary** Have partners preview pages 26–35, noting chapter titles and photos. If needed, coach as follows: *pp. 26–29* Cal wanted his children to have a regular childhood and their own **identity**. *pp. 30–33* Cal tried to **concentrate** on one game at a time. By 1991, he led the league with a **batting average** of .348. *pp. 34–35* Cal was in a **groove** (p. 34) as he played his best and everything worked for him. Do you think this will continue throughout his career? After the preview, have students find each word boldfaced above, read aloud the sentence, and briefly discuss the meaning.	▶ **Students Predict** Based on pages 26–35, students predict what might happen in the final section. Record their predictions. ▶ **Cooperative Preview/Vocabulary** Have partners preview pages 36–48, noting chapter titles and photos. If needed, coach as follows: *pp. 36–40* There was a **salute** (p. 36) to Cal at his 2,000th game. A year later, he tied Gehrig's record. *pp. 41–45* The next night, Cal broke the record. He came out of the **dugout** (p. 42) for the crowd's applause. Afterward, there was a **ceremony** (p. 43). *pp. 46–48* One night, three years later, Cal chose not to play. Do you think he did the right thing? After the preview, have students find each word boldfaced above, read aloud the sentence, and briefly discuss the meaning.
Reading and Reciprocal Teaching (10–15 minutes) *Note: After students check their predictions, they model Summarize, with you modeling if needed. Then they model all other strategies in any order, using their Strategy Notes. Model for them as needed. Samples are provided.*	▶ **Purpose-setting** Students read to check their predictions. ▶ **Silent Reading** pp. 26–35. Remind students to use SG p. 26 to help them model strategies. ▶ **After reading, students check** to see if their predictions were verified. *Teacher Models* • **SUMMARIZE** *Cal was very successful playing for the Orioles. He also got married and started a family. At one point, Cal, his father, and his brother Billy all worked for the Orioles. Cal's record of consecutive games continued to grow.* • **QUESTION** *Why does Cal want to spend as much time as possible with Rachel and Ryan?*	▶ **Purpose-setting** Students read to check their predictions. ▶ **Silent Reading** pp. 36–48. Remind students to use SG p. 26 to help them model strategies. ▶ **After reading, students check** to see if their predictions were verified. *Teacher Models* • **CLARIFY/PHONICS** *I'm not sure how to pronounce this word* (point to **attention** on page 38). *I know the chunks **at** and **ten**. The chunk **t-i-o-n** comes at the end of the word and sounds like /**shun**/. At first I don't recognize the word, but when I stress **ten** instead of **at**, and I put the chunks together and get **at/ten/tion**, the word makes sense in the sentence.*
Responding/ Reflecting (5 minutes) *Note: Assign the lesson homework (SG p. 28) at the end of each lesson.*	▶ **Event Map** Using Event Map Poster 8, help students update their own Event Maps (SG p. 25). ▶ **Respond** Students discuss, complete, and share Reflection #3 on SG p. 28: *Tell how Cal won the home run hitting contest.* ▶ **Strategies Discussion** (Posters 2, 3) **Prompt:** *When did you use CLARIFY? How did CLARIFY help you?*	▶ **Event Map** Have students complete their Event Maps (SG p. 25). ▶ **Respond** Students discuss, complete, and share Reflection #4 on SG p. 28: *Circle a strategy that helped you. Tell how you used this strategy.* ▶ **Home Connection** Students take home *Cal Ripken, Jr.: Play Ball!* and the Home Connection letter.

Cal Ripken, Jr.: Play Ball!

Name _____

Strategy Notes

Students use this page to jot down notes or questions as they read. It should not be used for assessment. Sample notes are shown.

Clarify

The Orioles had minor league teams all over the country. p. 8

baseball scouts p. 17

The ball field exploded. p. 39

Predict

Cal and his brother will rebuild the Orioles team. p. 28

Question

How many years did Cal stay in the Orioles starting lineup, playing every game? p. 25

Summarize

Pages 15–18: When Cal played high school baseball, his father helped him to improve his game. Cal also enjoyed challenging math problems. He liked all kinds of challenges. Soon, baseball scouts started coming to games to look for good players. Cal was drafted by the Baltimore Orioles.

26   Level 8, Book 6, *Cal Ripken, Jr.: Play Ball!*

Cal Ripken, Jr.: Play Ball!

Name _____

Sample responses are shown.

Event Map

Title

Cal Ripken, Jr.: Play Ball!

Event 1

Cal grows up in a family of athletes with a father who is a professional baseball coach.

Event 2

Cal is picked by the Orioles in the baseball draft and is a success in the minor leagues.

Event 3

In his first couple of seasons in the major leagues, Cal is named Rookie of the Year and Most Valuable Player.

Event 4

Cal gets married and has a son and daughter.

Event 5

Cal wins the home run hitting contest the night before the All Star game.

Event 6

Cal ties Lou Gehrig's record for most consecutive games played.

Event 7

Cal breaks the record and is nicknamed the "Iron Man" of baseball.

Event 8

On September 20, 1998, Cal takes himself out of the lineup after 2,632 consecutive games.

Level 8, Book 6, *Cal Ripken, Jr.: Play Ball!*   25

Cal Ripken, Jr.: Play Ball!

Name

Students use this page to think about their reading and to prepare for discussion. It should not be used for assessment. Sample responses are shown.

REFLECTION 3

Describe what Cal did at the home run hitting contest. Why was it special?

He hit 12 home runs on 22 swings. He was the first shortstop in history to do that.

HOMEWORK 3

Pretend you have won an award for Most Valuable Student. Keeping Cal Ripken, Jr.'s positive attitude in mind, write your award acceptance speech.

REFLECTION 4

Circle a strategy that helped you to read Cal Ripken, Jr.: Play Ball!

Strategy Box

Predict (Summarize) Clarify Question

Explain how you used this strategy.

Summarize helped me to understand the steps it took for Cal to go from the minor leagues to the major leagues. I see how much hard work it took for him to break all those records.

HOMEWORK 4

Do research to find out more about Lou Gehrig, the man whose record Cal Ripken broke. Write two interesting facts about him.

28 Level 8, Book 6, *Cal Ripken, Jr.: Play Ball!*

Cal Ripken, Jr.: Play Ball!

Name

Students use this page to think about their reading and to prepare for discussion. It should not be used for assessment. Sample responses are shown.

REFLECTION 1

How are you like Cal? How are you different?

Cal and I both like to play sports. Like Cal, I never give up and always keep trying my hardest until I learn how to do something well. Cal cheated in games when he was young, and I don't do that.

HOMEWORK 1

Write about the records you would like to break when you get older.

REFLECTION 2

How do you feel about what Cal has accomplished with his baseball skills so far? Why do you feel the way you do?

I like the way Cal has kept trying his hardest. In high school he was not the best hitter, but he kept practicing. Even when he reached the majors he got into a slump, but he came out of that, too. He never gave up. I admire that.

HOMEWORK 2

Write a newspaper article about Cal Ripken's rookie season in the big leagues.

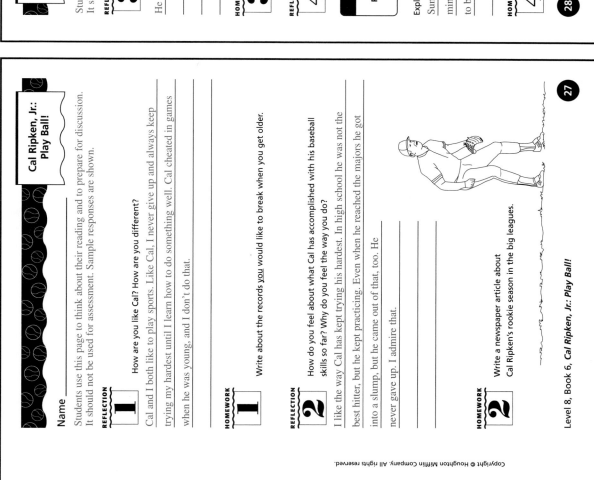

27

Level 8, Book 6, *Cal Ripken, Jr.: Play Ball!*

Mountains

by Seymour Simon

Summary: *Mountains* explains how mountains are formed and how they affect weather, vegetation, animals, and humans.

Note: It is not necessary for students to know or be held responsible for all the facts presented in the book. The purpose of these lessons is to help students learn strategies for comprehending informational text.

Materials

Lesson 1	Lesson 2	Lesson 3
• Previously read books	• Independent reading books	• Previously read books
• *Mountains* pp. 4–13	• *Mountains* pp. 14–21	• *Mountains* pp. 22–32
• Posters 2, 3, 6	• Posters 2, 3, 6	• Posters 2, 3, 6
• Student Guide (SG) p. 29–31	• Student Guide (SG) p. 29–31	• Student Guide (SG) p. 29–30, 32
• Strategy Prompts, SG pp. 89–91	• Strategy Prompts, SG pp. 89–91	• Strategy Prompts, SG pp. 89–91
• Markers	• Markers	• Markers
		• Home Connection letter

Scaffolding

Strong Teacher Support	Moderate Teacher Support	Student Independence
	For Book 7 (Category III), continue to coach and model as you encourage students to practice using strategies independently.	

Help with Phonics and Decoding Longer Words: For students who need explicit instruction, see the Optional Lesson on page R188 of the Teacher's Resource File in this manual.

Lesson Overview

	Lesson 1	Lesson 2	Lesson 3
Revisiting (5 minutes)	• Previously read books: Retelling	• Group Conference: Independent Reading	• Previously read books: Retelling
Reviewing (5 minutes)	• Review Reciprocal Teaching Strategies (Posters 2, 3)	• Students Discuss Strategies • Students Summarize	• Students Discuss Strategies • Students Summarize
Rehearsing (5–10 minutes)	• Introduce the Book • Semantic Map (Poster 6, SG p. 29) • Guided Preview, pp. 4–13 Key Vocabulary: *altitude, solitary, satellite, plates*	• Guided Preview, pp. 14–21 Key Vocabulary: *fault, magma* • Semantic Map/ Question	• Cooperative Preview, pp. 22–32 Key Vocabulary: *erosion, habitats, terraces* • Semantic Map/ Question
Reading and Reciprocal Teaching (10–15 minutes)	• Silent Reading • Check Information • Students Model Strategies • Teacher Models SUMMARIZE, PREDICT	• Silent Reading • Check Information • Students Model Strategies • Teacher Models CLARIFY/PHONICS	• Silent Reading • Check Information • Students Model Strategies • Teacher Models SUMMARIZE, QUESTION
Responding/ Reflecting (5 minutes)	• Semantic Map (Poster 6, SG p. 29) • Reflection #1 (SG p. 31) • Strategies Discussion (Posters 2, 3) • Homework 1	• Semantic Map (Poster 6, SG p. 29) • Reflection #2 (SG p. 31) • Strategies Discussion (Posters 2, 3) • Homework 2	• Semantic Map (Poster 6, SG p. 29) • Reflection #3 (SG p. 32) • Homework 3 • Home Connection letter

Mountains	Lesson 1	Lesson 2
Revisiting (5 minutes) *Note: Do an Oral Reading Check only when you are concerned about a student's decoding or fluency.*	▶ **Students reread previously read SOAR TO SUCCESS books.** • Have students reread silently for fluency; assign each a different strategy to model in Reviewing. • Have one student read silently and retell a section of a book. Note comprehension. (Use passages and protocols for Retellings, TM pp. R40–R41.)	▶ **Group Conference** Students discuss independent reading. **Prompt:** *Show and discuss the illustrations in the book you are reading. If your books has no illustrations, discuss why the author didn't include them.* Remind students to keep up their book logs and to bring them to Group Conference for reference.
Reviewing (5 minutes)	▶ **Students review Reciprocal Teaching strategies.** (Posters 2, 3) Students discuss strategies used with *Cal Ripken* and other classroom reading, and model strategies they used in Revisiting.	▶ **Students discuss** strategies they have used with other classroom reading. ▶ **Students Summarize** Students use the book and their Semantic Maps (SG p. 29) to summarize pp. 4–13.
Rehearsing (5–10 minutes) *Note: After the Guided Preview in Lessons 1 and 2, hand out books.*	▶ **Introduce the Book** Show the cover, title, and author's name. ▶ **Semantic Map** Display Poster 6. Explain to students that this is a good way to organize information about a topic. Ask what kinds of information students think they will learn about mountains. Record their responses. ▶ **Guided Preview/Vocabulary** pp. 4–13. *pp. 4–9* Mountains can vary in height. The air temperature drops about 3° F for every increase in **altitude** (p. 8) of 1,000 feet. *pp. 10–11* Most mountains are not **solitary** peaks. This **satellite** photo shows part of the Himalayas. *pp. 12–13* Most mountain ranges are formed when huge **plates** (p. 12) of the earth's crust push and pull against each other.	▶ **Guided Preview/ Vocabulary** pp. 14–21. *pp. 14–15* When two **plates** push against each other, the rock can be forced upward, forming mountains. *pp. 16–17* Other mountains form when rock on one side of a **fault** moves away from the rock on the other side. The diagram shows the separated rock strata. *pp. 18–21* Volcanoes and dome mountains are both formed by **magma** (p. 18). These diagrams show the different ways they form. The Adirondacks are dome mountains, and so is this mountain in Yosemite National Park. ▶ **Semantic Map/Question** Ask what kinds of information students think they will learn next. Record their responses.
Reading and Reciprocal Teaching (10–15 minutes) *Note: After students review the information, they model Summarize, with you modeling if needed. Then they model all other strategies in any order, using their Strategy Notes. Model for them as needed. Samples are provided.*	▶ Refer to Posters 2 and 3. Remind students to use these strategies as they read. ▶ **Purpose-setting** Students read to find information about mountains for their Semantic Maps. ▶ **Silent Reading** pp. 4–13. Remind students to use SG p. 30 to help them model strategies. ▶ **After reading, students decide** what new information is important for their Maps. *Teacher Models* • **SUMMARIZE** *Over millions of years, mountains are born, change, and disappear into the earth. The tallest mountains are covered with snow year round. Most mountains are part of a mountain range.* • **PREDICT** *I predict that we will learn how mountains change their shape and size.*	▶ **Purpose-setting** Students read to add information to their Semantic Maps. ▶ **Silent Reading** pp. 14–21. Remind students to use SG p. 30 to help them model strategies. ▶ **After reading, students decide** what new information is important for their Maps. *Teacher Models* • **CLARIFY/PHONICS** *In this word* (point to **eruption** on page 18), *I see the* **-t-i-o-n** *ending,* /**shun**/. *In* **e-r-u-p,** *I see a single consonant between vowels, so I break before the* **r** *and stress* **r-u-p,** *making it sound like* **up.** *I blend the chunks;* **e/rup/tion** *makes sense. I don't understand the word, so I look in a dictionary. I find that* **eruption** *means a "bursting forth."*
Responding/ Reflecting (5 minutes) *Note: Assign the lesson homework (SG p. 31) at the end of each lesson.*	▶ **Semantic Map** Ask students how high and how long the mountain ranges in this book are. Then have them add to their Semantic Maps (SG p. 29). ▶ **Respond** Students discuss, complete, and share Reflection #1 on SG p. 31. ▶ **Strategies Discussion** (Posters 2, 3) **Prompt:** *When did you use CLARIFY? How did CLARIFY help you?*	▶ **Semantic Map** Students add to their Semantic Maps (SG p. 29). ▶ **Respond** Students discuss, complete, and share Reflection #2 on SG p. 31: *How are folded mountains formed? Compare to fault-block mountains.* ▶ **Strategies Discussion** (Posters 2, 3) Ask students how strategies have helped them so far.

Mountains	Lesson 3

Revisiting
(5 minutes)

Note: Do an Oral Reading Check only when you are concerned about a student's decoding or fluency.

▶ **Students reread previously read *SOAR TO SUCCESS* books.**
- Have students reread silently for fluency.
- Have one student read silently and retell a section of a book. Note comprehension. (Use passages and protocols for Retellings, TM pp. R40–R41.)

Reviewing
(5 minutes)

▶ **Students discuss** strategies they have used with other classroom reading.
▶ **Students Summarize** Students use the book and their Semantic Maps (SG p. 29) to summarize pp. 14–21.

Rehearsing
(5–10 minutes)

▶ **Cooperative Preview/Vocabulary** Have partners preview pages 22–32, noting the photos. If needed, coach as follows:

pp. 22–25 Mountains are worn down by **erosion** from the weather and by glaciers. They are also changed by the expansion and contraction of rocks.

pp. 26–29 Mountains effect the weather around them. **Habitats** on the mountain change with altitude.

pp. 30–32 People make **terraces** in order to grow crops on steep mountains.

After the preview, have students find each word boldfaced above, read aloud the sentence, and briefly discuss the meaning.
▶ **Semantic Map/Question** Ask what kinds of information students think they will learn next. Record their responses.

Reading and Reciprocal Teaching
(10–15 minutes)

Note: After students review the information, they model Summarize, with you modeling if needed. Then they model all other strategies in any order, using their Strategy Notes. Model for them as needed. Samples are provided.

▶ Refer to posters 2 and 3. Remind students to use these strategies as they read.
▶ **Purpose-setting** Students read to add information to their Semantic Maps.
▶ **Silent Reading** pp. 22–32. Remind students to use SG p. 30 to help them model strategies.
▶ **After reading, students decide** what new information is important for their Maps.

Teacher Models
- **SUMMARIZE** *As time passes, all mountains begin to erode and change. Mountains have an effect on weather and climate. Trees, animals, and humans all adapt to the mountain environment.*
- **QUESTION** *What is the timberline?*

Responding/ Reflecting
(5 minutes)

Note: Assign the lesson homework (SG p. 32) at the end of the lesson.

▶ **Semantic Map** Have students complete their Semantic Maps (SG p. 29).
▶ **Respond** Students discuss, complete, and share Reflection #3 on SG p. 32: *Circle a strategy that helped you. Explain how you used this strategy.*
▶ **Home Connection** Students take home *Mountains* and the Home Connection letter.

Mountains

Name _____

Students use this page to jot down notes or questions as they read. It should not be used for assessment. Sample notes are shown.

Strategy Notes

Clarify

Compared to the Himalayas, the Appalachians are foothills. p. 9

Most great mountain chains are folded mountains. p. 14

mountain goats feeding on sheer slopes p. 28

Predict

When magma wells up inside the Earth, it will cause the crust to crack and a

volcano to form. p. 16

Question

How many plates make up the Earth's crust? p. 12

What happens if magma can't break through the crust and form

a volcano? p. 20

Summarize

Pages 18–21: Some mountains are formed by erupting volcanoes. Magma pushes up through the Earth's crust. The lava and cinders that harden make a volcanic mountain. Sometimes when magma pushes up, it doesn't come to the surface. It pushes the ground up into a round, hardened dome shape.

Mountains

Name _____

Sample responses are shown.

Semantic Map

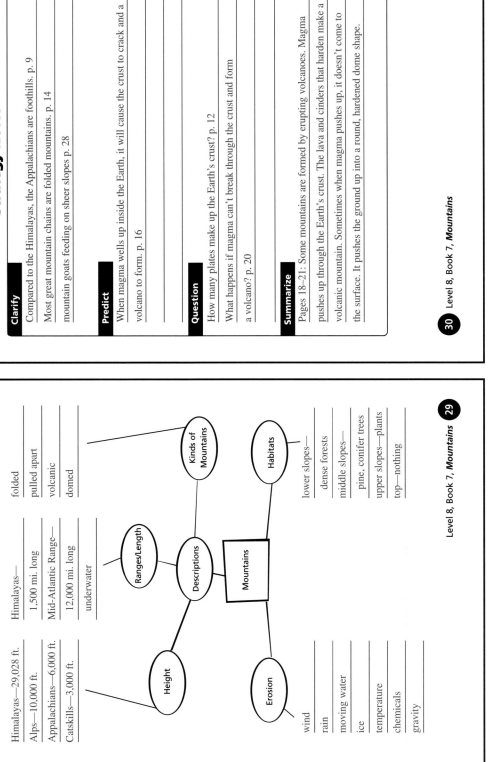

Himalayas—
1,500 mi. long
Mid-Atlantic Range—
12,000 mi. long
underwater

Himalayas—29,028 ft.
Alps—10,000 ft.
Appalachians—6,000 ft.
Catskills—3,000 ft.

folded
pulled apart
volcanic
domed

lower slopes—
dense forests
middle slopes—
pine, conifer trees
upper slopes—plants
top—nothing

wind
rain
moving water
ice
temperature
chemicals
gravity

Kinds of Mountains

Habitats

Ranges/Length

Descriptions

Mountains

Height

Erosion

Mountains

Name

Students use this page to think about their reading and to prepare for discussion. It should not be used for assessment. Sample responses are shown.

REFLECTION 3

Circle a strategy that helped you to read *Mountains*.

Strategy Box		
Predict	Summarize	Clarify	(Question)

Explain how you used this strategy.

I used this strategy on page 30. I asked myself the question, "How do people live and farm at the tops of very high mountains?" Then I found the answer on that page.

HOMEWORK 3

Do some research to find out about a famous mountain climber. Tell the name of the climber and the mountain he or she climbed. Write two interesting facts about the person's experience.

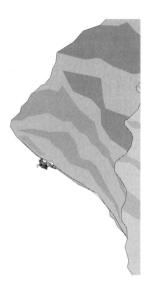

32 Level 8, Book 7, *Mountains*

Mountains

Name

Students use this page to think about their reading and to prepare for discussion. It should not be used for assessment. Sample responses are shown.

REFLECTION 1

When snow on mountains melts, how does it affect life below?

When snow melts, the water forms rivers that flow down onto the land around the foothills. People there can plant crops and benefit from the melted snow.

HOMEWORK 1

Examine the information and photographs of the Himalayas, the Andes, and the Appalachians. Write a paragraph telling how these mountains are alike and how they are different.

REFLECTION 2

How are folded mountains formed? Compare this to fault-block mountains.

Folded mountains form when plates in the Earth's crust press together and buckle upward. Fault-block mountains are formed when plates pull apart and break.

HOMEWORK 2

Write a summary that explains how magma can cause mountains to form.

Level 8, Book 7, *Mountains* 31

Jesse Jackson: I Am Somebody!

by Charnan Simon

Summary: This book tells the story of Jesse Jackson's life–from young African-American activist to acclaimed community and world leader.

Note: It is not necessary for students to know or be held responsible for all the facts presented in the book. The purpose of these lessons is to help students learn strategies for comprehending informational text.

Materials

Lesson 1	Lesson 2	Lesson 3
• Previously read books	• Independent reading books	• Previously read books
• *Jesse Jackson: I Am Somebody!* pp. 6–14	• *Jesse Jackson: I Am Somebody!* pp. 15–29	• *Jesse Jackson: I Am Somebody!* pp. 30–42
• Posters 2, 3, 8	• Posters 2, 3, 8	• Posters 2, 3, 8
• Student Guide (SG) pp. 33–35	• Student Guide (SG) pp. 33–35	• Student Guide (SG) pp. 33–34, 36
• Strategy Prompts, SG pp. 89–91	• Strategy Prompts, SG pp. 89–91	• Strategy Prompts, SG pp. 89–91
• Markers	• Markers	• Markers
		• Home Connection letter

Scaffolding

Strong Teacher Support	Moderate Teacher Support	Student Independence
	For Book 6 (Category III), continue to coach and model as you encourage students to practice using strategies independently.	

Help with Phonics and Decoding Longer Words: For students who need explicit instruction, see the Optional Lesson on page R189 of the Teacher's Resource File in this manual.

Lesson Overview

	Lesson 1	Lesson 2	Lesson 3
Revisiting (5 minutes)	• Previously read books: Retelling	• Group Conference: Independent Reading	• Previously read books: Retelling
Reviewing (5 minutes)	• Review Reciprocal Teaching Strategies (Posters 2, 3)	• Students Discuss Strategies • Students Summarize	• Students Discuss Strategies • Students Summarize
Rehearsing (5–10 minutes)	• Introduce the Book • Students Predict • Guided Preview, pp. 6–14 Key Vocabulary: *civil rights, segregation, unwritten*	• Students Predict • Cooperative Preview, pp. 15–29 Key Vocabulary: *protest, theological seminary, discrimination, boycott, nonviolent*	• Students Predict • Cooperative Preview, pp. 30–48 Key Vocabulary: *humanity, coalition, apartheid*
Reading and Reciprocal Teaching (10–15 minutes)	• Silent Reading • Check Prediction • Students Model Strategies • Teacher Models SUMMARIZE, CLARIFY/PHONICS	• Silent Reading • Check Predictions • Students Model Strategies • Teacher Models SUMMARIZE, QUESTION	• Silent Reading • Check Predictions • Students Model Strategies • Teacher Models SUMMARIZE, CLARIFY
Responding/ Reflecting (5 minutes)	• Event Map (Poster 8, SG p. 33) • Reflection #1 (SG p. 35) • Strategies Discussion (Posters 2, 3) • Homework 1	• Event Map (Poster 8, SG p. 33) • Reflection #2 (SG p. 35) • Strategies Discussion (Posters 2, 3) • Homework 2	• Event Map (Poster 8, SG p. 33) • Reflection #3 (SG p. 36) • Homework 3 • Home Connection letter

Jesse Jackson	Lesson 1	Lesson 2
Revisiting (5 minutes) *Note: Do an Oral Reading Check only when you are concerned about a student's decoding or fluency.*	▶ **Students reread previously read SOAR TO SUCCESS books.** • Have students reread silently for fluency; assign each a different strategy to model in Reviewing. • Have one student read silently and retell a section of a book. Note comprehension. (Use passages and protocols for Retellings, TM pp. R42–R43.)	▶ **Group Conference** Students discuss independent reading. **Prompt:** *Summarize what has happened in your book so far.* Remind students to keep up their book logs and to bring them to Group Conference for reference.
Reviewing (5 minutes)	▶ **Students review Reciprocal Teaching strategies.** (Posters 2, 3) Students discuss strategies used with *Mountains* and other classroom reading, and model strategies they used in Revisiting.	▶ **Students discuss** strategies they have used with other classroom reading. ▶ **Students Summarize** Students use the book and their Event Maps (SG p. 33) to summarize pp. 6–14.
Rehearsing (5–10 minutes) *Note: After the Guided Preview in Lesson 1, hand out books.*	▶ **Introduce the Book** Show the cover, title page, and author's name. Point out the timeline and index at the back of the book. ▶ **Students Predict** Ask students what they think the book will be about. Record their predictions. ▶ **Guided Preview/Vocabulary** pp. 6–14. Read the chapter titles with students. *pp. 6–9* We have laws to protect our **civil rights** (p. 7). Some of these laws exist because of people like Jackson. *pp. 10–11* Jackson grew up in South Carolina where they practiced **segregation** (p. 11). Read the boxed section information and CLARIFY segregation. *pp. 12–14* Jackson attended the University of Illinois. The North didn't have written segregation laws, but there were **unwritten** (p. 13) laws.	▶ **Students Predict** Based on pages 6–14, students predict what might happen in the next section. Record their predictions. ▶ **Cooperative Preview/Vocabulary** Have partners preview pp. 15–29, noting chapter titles, photos, captions, and boxes. If needed, coach as follows: *pp. 15–21* Jackson helped stage a **protest** (p. 17) at a lunch counter that wouldn't serve blacks. He went to a **theological seminary** (p. 19), became a minister, and continued to fight **discrimination** (p. 19). *pp. 22–27* Jackson staged a **boycott** (p. 25) in Chicago. *pp. 28–29* After Dr. King was killed, many people rioted. Jackson called for a **nonviolent** (p. 28) reaction. After the preview, have students find each word boldfaced above, read aloud the sentence, and briefly discuss the meaning.
Reading and Reciprocal Teaching (10–15 minutes) *Note: After students check their predictions, they model Summarize, with you modeling if needed. Then they model all other strategies in any order, using their Strategy Notes. Model for them as needed. Samples are provided.*	▶ Refer to Posters 2 and 3. Remind students to use these strategies as they read. ▶ **Purpose-setting** Students read to check predictions. ▶ **Silent Reading** pp. 6–14. Remind students to use SG p. 34 to help them model strategies. ▶ **After reading, students check** to see if their predictions were verified. ***Teacher Models*** • **SUMMARIZE** *Jesse Jackson has spent his life fighting for the civil rights of all Americans. Growing up, he encountered segregation.* • **CLARIFY/PHONICS** *I don't know this word* (point to **democracy** on page 7). *I break the word into the chunks* **d-e**, **m-o-c**, **r-a**, *and* **c-y**. *I know the* **c-y** *is pronounced /**see**/, and when I blend the chunks together I get* **de/moc/ra/cy**. *It makes sense.*	▶ **Purpose-setting** Students read to check their predictions. ▶ **Silent Reading** pp. 15–29. Remind students to use SG p. 34 to help them model strategies. ▶ **After reading, students check** to see if their predictions were verified. ***Teacher Models*** • **SUMMARIZE** *At college, Jackson participated in many peaceful protests. Then he became a minister who fought for civil rights. He worked with Martin Luther King, Jr. in the Southern Christian Leadership Council. He staged boycotts in Chicago. When Dr. King was assassinated, he called for nonviolence.* • **QUESTION** *What was Operation Breadbasket?*
Responding/ Reflecting (5 minutes) *Note: Assign the lesson homework (SG p. 35) at the end of each lesson.*	▶ **Event Map** Display Poster 8. Help students fill in events 1 and 2 on their own Event Maps (SG p. 33). ▶ **Respond** Students discuss, complete, and share Reflection #1 on SG p. 35: *What would you have done at the University of Illinois if you were Jackson? Why?* ▶ **Strategies Discussion** (Posters 2, 3) **Prompt:** *When did you use CLARIFY? How did CLARIFY help you?*	▶ **Event Map** Using Event Map Poster 8, help students update their own Event Maps (SG p. 33). ▶ **Respond** Students discuss, complete, and share Reflection #2 on SG p. 35: *Tell how you felt about the march from Selma.* ▶ **Strategies Discussion** (Posters 2, 3) Ask students how strategies have helped them so far.

Jesse Jackson	**Lesson 3**
Revisiting (5 minutes) *Note: Do an Oral Reading Check only when you are concerned about a student's decoding or fluency.*	▶ **Students reread previously read *SOAR TO SUCCESS* books.** • Have students reread silently for fluency. • Have one student read silently and retell a section of a book. Note comprehension. (Use passages and protocols for Retellings, TM pp. R42–R43.)
Reviewing (5 minutes)	▶ **Students discuss** strategies they have used with other classroom reading. ▶ **Students Summarize** Students use the book and their Event Maps (SG p. 33) to summarize pp. 15–29.
Rehearsing (5–10 minutes)	▶ **Students Predict** Based on pages 15–29, students predict what might happen in the final section. Record their predictions. ▶ **Cooperative Preview/Vocabulary** Have partners preview pp. 30–42, noting chapter titles, photos, captions, and boxes. If needed, coach as follows: *pp. 30–33* Jackson started PUSH, a group formed to serve **humanity** (p. 30). Then he started a group for *young* black Americans called PUSH-Excel. *pp. 34–37* In 1984, Jackson ran for President. He called his supporters the *Rainbow* **Coalition** (p. 36). *pp. 38–42* Jackson fought injustices like **apartheid** (p. 38). He ran again for President in 1988. After the preview, have students find each word boldfaced above, read aloud the sentence, and briefly discuss the meaning.
Reading and Reciprocal Teaching (10–15 minutes) *Note: After students check their predictions, they model Summarize, with you modeling if needed. Then they model all other strategies in any order, using their Strategy Notes. Model for them as needed. Samples are provided.*	▶ **Purpose-setting** Students read to check their predictions. ▶ **Silent Reading** pp. 30–42. Remind students to use SG p. 34 to help them model strategies. ▶ **After reading, students check** to see if their predictions were verified. ***Teacher Models*** • **SUMMARIZE** *Jackson encouraged young black students to excel and he campaigned for black politicians. He also entered politics and ran for president twice. He continues to fight for fairness and justice in America and around the world.* • **CLARIFY** *I am not too sure what **America's forgotten people** means on page 40. When I reread the pages, I see that it means people whose rights and opportunities have been forgotten or ignored.*
Responding/ Reflecting (5 minutes) *Note: Assign the lesson homework (SG p. 36) at the end of the lesson.*	▶ **Event Map** Have students complete their Event Maps (SG p. 33). ▶ **Respond** Students discuss, complete, and share Reflection #3 on SG p. 36: *Circle one strategy that helped you. Explain how you used this strategy.* ▶ **Home Connection** Students take home *Jesse Jackson* and the Home Connection letter.

Jesse Jackson

Name _____

Students use this page to jot down notes or questions as they read. It should not be used for assessment. Sample notes are shown.

Strategy Notes

Clarify

Grandmother Tibby wanted Jackson to be somebody. p. 10

watch-ins and wade-ins p. 18

Students signed contracts p. 33

Predict

Jackson will become a student activist. p. 17

Question

Why wasn't Jackson allowed to be the quarterback for the football team? p. 13

What did Jackson do for the Greensboro civil rights movement? p. 18

Summarize

Pages 40–41: In 1988, Jackson ran for president for the second time, hoping that the Rainbow Coalition would speak for America's forgotten people. He won 7 million votes, but did not get the nomination. People said America was not ready for an African-American president.

34 Level 8, Book 8, *Jesse Jackson: I Am Somebody!*

Jesse Jackson

Name _____

Sample responses are shown.

Event Map

Title
Jesse Jackson: I Am Somebody!

Event 1
Jackson is born in South Carolina, where many laws forced blacks and whites to live separately.

Event 2
Jackson goes to the University of Illinois, where he is unable to be a football quarterback because he is black.

Event 3
He transfers to a mostly black college in North Carolina and becomes a student activist.

Event 4
Jackson becomes a minister and joins the SCLC, which was led by Dr. Martin Luther King, Jr.

Event 5
Jackson organizes a group from Chicago to march in Alabama to support black voting rights, starts Operation Breadbasket, then stages boycotts.

Event 6
When Dr. King is shot, Jackson calls for nonviolence. He starts groups called PUSH and PUSH-Excel.

Event 7
Jackson establishes the Rainbow Coalition and runs for president.

Event 8
Jackson fights for the rights of people around the world.

Level 8, Book 8, *Jesse Jackson: I Am Somebody!* **33**

Jesse Jackson

Name _____

Students use this page to think about their reading and to prepare for discussion. It should not be used for assessment. Sample responses are shown.

REFLECTION 3

Circle one strategy that helped you read Jesse Jackson.

Strategy Box		
Predict	Summarize	Clarify
		(Question)

Explain how you used this strategy.

Question helped me to understand what motivated Jesse Jackson to fight for civil rights across the United States and all over the world.

HOMEWORK 3

Pretend you are promoting Jackson's PUSH-Excel program. Write a short speech that you will deliver to students on his behalf.

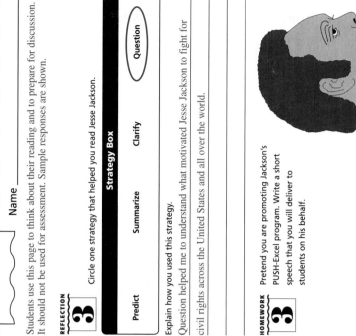

36 Level 8, Book 8, *Jesse Jackson: I Am Somebody!*

Jesse Jackson

Name _____

Students use this page to think about their reading and to prepare for discussion. It should not be used for assessment. Sample responses are shown.

REFLECTION 1

What would you have done at the University of Illinois if you were Jackson? Why?

I would have stayed and tried to change things because I believe in getting involved.

HOMEWORK 1

Write about something you would like to speak up about and why it is important to you.

REFLECTION 2

Tell how you felt about the march from Selma, Alabama, to Montgomery, Alabama, and why. The march was both inspiring and frightening. I was glad that it brought together whites and blacks, who had not joined together as a group before.

HOMEWORK 2

Decide what you would like to learn about the march from Selma, Alabama, to Montgomery, Alabama. Write down your question and some key words you can use to look for the information.

35 Level 8, Book 8, *Jesse Jackson: I Am Somebody!*

Lakota Hoop Dancer

by Jacqueline Left Hand Bull and Suzanne Haldane

Summary: Kevin Locke is a Hunkpapa Indian. This book follows his activities as he prepares for and performs the traditional Lakota hoop dance.

Note: It is not necessary for students to know or be held responsible for all the facts presented in the book. The purpose of these lessons is to help students learn strategies for comprehending informational text.

Materials

Lesson 1	Lesson 2	Lesson 3	Lesson 4
• Previously read books	• Independent reading books	• Previously read books	• Independent reading books
• *Lakota Hoop Dancer* pp. 4–9	• *Lakota Hoop Dancer* pp. 10–15	• *Lakota Hoop Dancer* pp. 16–23	• *Lakota Hoop Dancer* pp. 24–31
• Posters 2, 3, 9	• Posters 2, 3, 9	• Posters 2, 3, 9	• Posters 2, 3, 9
• Student Guide (SG) pp. 37–39	• Student Guide (SG) pp. 37–39	• Student Guide (SG) pp. 37–38, 40	• Student Guide (SG) pp. 37–38, 40
• Strategy Prompts, SG pp. 89–91	• Strategy Prompts, SG pp. 89–91	• Strategy Prompts, SG pp. 89–91	• Strategy Prompts, SG pp. 89–91
• Markers	• Markers	• Markers	• Markers
			• Home Connection letter

Scaffolding

Strong Teacher Support	Moderate Teacher Support	Student Independence
	For Book 9 (Category IV), continue to coach and model as you encourage students to practice using strategies independently.	

Help with Phonics and Decoding Longer Words: For students who need explicit instruction, see the Optional Lesson on page R190 of the Teacher's Resource File in this manual.

Lesson Overview

	Lesson 1	Lesson 2	Lesson 3	Lesson 4
Revisiting (5 minutes)	• Previously read books: Retelling	• Group Conference: Independent Reading	• Previously read books: Retelling	• Group Conference: Independent Reading
Reviewing (5 minutes)	• Review Reciprocal Teaching Strategies (Posters 2, 3)	• Students Discuss Strategies • Students Summarize	• Students Discuss Strategies • Students Summarize	• Students Discuss Strategies • Students Summarize
Rehearsing (5–10 minutes)	• Introduce the Book • Students Predict • Guided Preview, pp. 4–9 Key Vocabulary: *traditional, reservation, ancestral, junction*	• Students Predict • Cooperative Preview, pp. 10–15 Key Vocabulary: *culture, nurtured, powwows, signifies*	• Students Predict • Cooperative Preview, pp. 16–23 Key Vocabulary: *rattan, pliable, regalia, geometric, extinct*	• Students Predict • Independent Preview, pp. 24–31 Key Vocabulary: *continuity, rhythmic, deftly, ignorance, interlinked, sphere*
Reading and Reciprocal Teaching (10–15 minutes)	• Silent Reading • Check predictions • Students Model Strategies • Teacher Models CLARIFY	• Silent Reading • Check predictions • Students Model Strategies • Teacher Models SUMMARIZE, CLARIFY/PHONICS	• Silent Reading • Check predictions • Students Model Strategies • Teacher Models SUMMARIZE	• Silent Reading • Check predictions • Students Model Strategies • Teacher Models SUMMARIZE, QUESTION
Responding/ Reflecting (5 minutes)	• Main Ideas and Details (Poster 9, SG p. 37) • Reflection #1 (SG p. 39) • Strategies Discussion (Posters 2, 3) • Homework 1	• Main Ideas and Details (Poster 9, SG p. 37) • Reflection #2 (SG p. 39) • Strategies Discussion (Posters 2, 3) • Homework 2	• Main Ideas and Details (Poster 9, SG p. 37) • Reflection #3 (SG p. 40) • Strategies Discussion (Posters 2, 3) • Homework 3	• Main Ideas and Details (Poster 9, SG p. 37) • Reflection #4 (SG p. 40) • Homework 4 • Home Connection letter

Lakota Hoop Dancer	Lesson 1	Lesson 2
Revisiting (5 minutes) *Note: Do an Oral Reading Check only when you are concerned about a student's decoding or fluency.*	▶ **Students reread previously read *SOAR TO SUCCESS* books.** • Have students reread silently for fluency; assign each a different strategy to model in Reviewing. • Have one student read silently and retell a section of a book. Note comprehension. (Use passages and protocols for Retellings, TM pp. R44–R45.)	▶ **Group Conference** Students discuss independent reading. **Prompt**: *Who is the author of your book? Do you want to read more books by this author? Why or why not?* Remind students to keep up their book logs and to bring them to Group Conference for reference.
Reviewing (5 minutes)	▶ **Students review Reciprocal Teaching strategies.** (Posters 2, 3) Students discuss strategies used with *Jesse Jackson* and other classroom reading, and model strategies they used in Revisiting.	▶ **Students discuss** strategies they have used with other classroom reading. ▶ **Students Summarize** Students use the book and their Main Ideas and Details Charts to summarize.
Rehearsing (5–10 minutes) *Note: **After** the Guided Preview in Lesson 1, hand out books.*	▶ **Introduce the Book** Show the cover, dedication, title page, and authors' names. Show the glossary, which includes pronunciations for Lakota words. ▶ **Students Predict** Ask students what they think the book will be about. Record their predictions. ▶ **Guided Preview/Vocabulary** pp. 4–9. Locate South Dakota on a map. *pp. 4–7* Kevin Locke, whose Indian name is Tokeya Inajin, is a Lakota hoop dancer who performs this **traditional** (p. 5) dance around the world. He lives on an American Indian **reservation** (p. 7) in South Dakota, his **ancestral** (p. 7) home–where his people have lived for generations. *pp. 8–9* Kevin's family lives at the **junction** (p. 9) of two rivers. Kevin believes he is a joiner of two cultures. What do you think he means?	▶ **Students Predict** Based on pages 4–9, students predict what they might learn in the next section. Record their predictions. ▶ **Cooperative Preview/Vocabulary** Have partners preview pages 10–15, noting chapter titles and photos. If needed, coach as follows: *pp. 10–11* Kevin wants to preserve his heritage and **culture** (p. 10). As a child, his uncles **nurtured** (p. 10) his love of Lakota traditions. *pp. 12–13* Indians gather at **powwows** (p. 12) to dance, have fun, compete, and watch ceremonies. *pp. 14–15* The hoop **signifies** (p. 14) equality, harmony, balance, and the cycles of life. After the preview, have students find each word boldfaced above, read aloud the sentence, and briefly discuss the meaning.
Reading and Reciprocal Teaching (10–15 minutes) *Note: After students check their predictions, they model Summarize, with you modeling if needed. Then they model all other strategies in any order, using their Strategy Notes. Model for them as needed. Samples are provided.*	▶ Refer to Posters 2 and 3. Remind students to use these strategies as they read. ▶ **Purpose-setting** Students read to check their predictions. ▶ **Silent Reading** pp. 4–9. Remind students to use SG p. 38 to help them model strategies. ▶ **After reading, students check** to see if their predictions were verified. ***Teacher Models*** • **CLARIFY** *I'm not sure what this word (point to **tiošpaye** on p. 7) means. I look it up in the glossary. I find out that it's pronounced /**tee/osh/pa/yay**/, and it means an extended family of parents and children, grandparents, aunts, uncles, and cousins. Now I understand.*	▶ **Purpose-setting** Students read to check their predictions. ▶ **Silent Reading** pp. 10–15. Remind students to use SG p. 38 to help them model strategies. ▶ **After reading, students check** to see if their predictions were verified. ***Teacher Models*** • **SUMMARIZE** *Kevin is committed to preserving Lakota culture. He plays music, dances with hoops, and tells the stories of his people. Circles (hoops) have great significance in all areas of Lakota life.* • **CLARIFY/PHONICS** *To figure out this word (point to **enchantment** on page 10), I break it into three chunks: **en**, **chant**, and **ment**. When I blend them together, I get **en/chant/ment**. It makes sense.*
Responding/ Reflecting (5 minutes) *Note: Assign the lesson homework (SG p. 39) at the end of each lesson.*	▶ **Main Ideas and Details** Using Poster 9 and SG p. 37, help students fill in one main idea and its supporting details from this section of *Lakota Hoop Dancer*. ▶ **Respond** Students discuss, complete, and share Reflection #1 on SG p. 39. ▶ **Strategies Discussion** (Posters 2, 3) **Prompt:** *When did you use CLARIFY? How did CLARIFY help you?*	▶ **Main Ideas and Details** Help students add to their Main Idea and Details Charts (SG p. 37). ▶ **Respond** Students discuss, complete, and share Reflection #2 on SG p. 39: *Why is dancing so important to Kevin?* ▶ **Strategies Discussion** (Posters 2, 3) **Prompt:** *When did you use QUESTION? How did it help you?*

Lakota Hoop Dancer	Lesson 3	Lesson 4
Revisiting (5 minutes) *Note: Do an Oral Reading Check only when you are concerned about a student's decoding or fluency.*	▶ **Students reread previously read *SOAR TO SUCCESS* books.** • Have students reread silently for fluency. • Have one student read silently and retell a section of a book. Note comprehension. (Use passages and protocols for Retellings, TM pp. R44–R45.)	▶ **Group Conference** Students discuss independent reading. **Prompt:** *Summarize the most interesting part of the book you are reading right now.* Remind students to keep up their book logs and to bring them to Group Conference for reference.
Reviewing (5 minutes)	▶ **Students discuss** strategies they have used with other classroom reading. ▶ **Students Summarize** Students use the book and their Main Ideas and Details Charts to summarize.	▶ **Students discuss** strategies they have used with other classroom reading. ▶ **Students Summarize** Students use the book and their Main Ideas and Details Charts to summarize.
Rehearsing (5–10 minutes)	▶ **Students Predict** Based on pages 10–15, students predict what they might learn in the next section. Record their predictions. ▶ **Cooperative Preview/Vocabulary** Have partners preview pages 16–23, noting chapter titles, photos, and captions. If needed, coach as follows: *pp. 16–19* Kevin made 16 hoops from a long vine called **rattan** (p. 16). It is a **pliable** (p. 18) material. *pp. 20–21* Kevin also prepared his **regalia** (p. 20), or outfit. It has **geometric** (p. 21) designs. *pp. 22–23* Kevin is also a grass dancer. This dance imitates the tall prairie grass which is almost **extinct** (p. 22). After the preview, have students find each word boldfaced above, read aloud the sentence, and briefly discuss the meaning.	▶ **Students Predict** Based on pages 16–23, students predict what they might learn in the final section. Record their predictions. ▶ **Independent Preview/Vocabulary** Have students independently preview pages 24–31, noting chapter titles, photos, and captions. If they come to words they don't know, remind them to use CLARIFY/PHONICS and the dictionary. (These words may be difficult for some students: **continuity**, **rhythmic**, **deftly**, p. 26; **ignorance**, **interlinked**, p. 28; **sphere**, p. 29.) After the preview, have students find each word boldfaced above, read aloud the sentence, and briefly discuss the meaning.
Reading and Reciprocal Teaching (10–15 minutes) *Note: After students check their predictions, they model Summarize, with you modeling if needed. Then they model all other strategies in any order, using their Strategy Notes. Model for them as needed. Samples are provided.*	▶ Refer to Posters 2 and 3. Remind students to use these strategies as they read. ▶ **Purpose-setting** Students read to check their predictions. ▶ **Silent Reading** pp. 16–23. Remind students to use SG p. 38 to help them model strategies. ▶ **After reading, students check** to see if their predictions were verified. *Teacher Models* • **SUMMARIZE** *Each Lakota creates a unique version of the hoop dance. Kevin constructs his hoops exactly the way he wants them, using rattan and plastic tubing. He also designed an outfit that made a personal statement about him.*	▶ **Purpose-setting** Students read to check their predictions. ▶ **Silent Reading** pp. 24–31. Remind students to use SG p. 38 to help them model strategies. ▶ **After reading, students check** to see if their predictions were verified. *Teacher Models* • **SUMMARIZE** *Steady rhythms of a Lakota hoop dance come from drumbeats and singers. During his dance, Kevin uses his hoops to tell a story about life, using symbols of an eagle, butterfly, and more. He also teaches children to carry on the hoop dancing tradition.* • **QUESTION** *What kinds of messages do Kevin's hoop dances pass along to the audience?*
Responding/ Reflecting (5 minutes) *Note: Assign the lesson homework (SG p. 40) at the end of each lesson.*	▶ **Main Ideas and Details** Using Poster 9 and SG p. 37, help students fill in one main idea and its supporting details from this section of *Lakota Hoop Dancer*. ▶ **Respond** Students discuss, complete, and share Reflection #3 on SG p. 40: *Describe Kevin's regalia.* ▶ **Strategies Discussion** (Posters 2, 3) **Prompt:** *When did you use SUMMARIZE? How did it help you?*	▶ **Main Ideas and Details** Students complete their Charts (SG p. 37) and use them to update Poster 9 and to summarize the book orally. ▶ **Respond** Students discuss, complete, and share Reflection #4 on SG p. 40. ▶ **Home Connection** Students take home *Lakota Hoop Dancer* and the Home Connection letter.

Lakota Hoop Dancer

Name _____

Students use this page to jot down notes or questions as they read. Sample notes are shown.

Strategy Notes

Clarify

Lakota expression: Mitakuye oyasin p. 9

Black Elk p. 14

audiotapes p. 25

Predict

I predict that Kevin will wear his regalia when he performs his dance. p. 21

Question

What does Kevin's Indian name mean? p. 7

Who was Arlo Goodbear? p. 13

Summarize

Pages 10–12: Kevin is committed to preserving Lakota culture. When he was a boy, his uncles showed him all about their traditions, and he does the same for his children. He plays Northern Plains flute music, dances at powwows, and performs the hoop dance at exhibitions.

Lakota Hoop Dancer

Name _____

Sample responses are shown.

Main Ideas and Details

Title *Lakota Hoop Dancer*

1. Main idea Tradition and homeland are at the heart of Kevin's Lakota hoop dancing.

a. **Detail** Hoop dancing has been performed for generations.

b. Extended families live there together and share Lakota traditions.

c. The wide open plains inspire Kevin to create his dances.

d. The homeland prairie is like a giant hoop itself.

2. Kevin wants to keep Lakota traditions alive.

a. He takes his children along when he performs hoop dances.

b. He has learned three dialects of Lakota language.

c. He has collected and recorded Northern Plains flute music and stories.

d. He and his family attend powwows.

3. Kevin makes special hoops and regalia.

a. He uses 28 different hoops: 16 rattan hoops and 12 plastic tubing hoops

b. He makes all of his hoops to fit around his body.

c. He wraps each hoop in one of four colors significant in Lakota tradition.

d. His outfit or regalia is a personal statement.

4. Hoop dancing depends on songs, symbols, and fun.

a. A hoop dance needs a song with a steady drumbeat.

b. Kevin makes the hoops look like the sun and moon, flowers, eagles, and other shapes.

c. Indian children learn to dance as soon as they can walk.

d. Kevin interlinks hoops and makes a road.

Lakota Hoop Dancer

Name _____

Students use this page to think about their reading and prepare for discussion. It should not be used for assessment. Sample responses are shown.

REFLECTION 3 Describe the regalia Kevin wears.

He wears an apron and leggings fringed with leather that sways when he moves like the prairie grasses of his homeland. He wears a headband made of beads with the same design as the moccasins he wears. He wears a shirt with ribbons on it. He wears a beaded belt.

HOMEWORK 3 Write a description of a regalia that makes a personal statement about you.

REFLECTION 4 Circle one of the strategies you used.

Strategy Box		
Predict	Summarize	Clarify	Question

How did this strategy help you?
Using Question helped me to learn more details about why Kevin is a Lakota hoop dancer and how he prepares for his dance.

HOMEWORK 4 Do research to find out more about the Lakota people. What name did Europeans use to refer to them? Write down this name and two other interesting facts about the Lakota.

40 Level 8, Book 9, *Lakota Hoop Dancer*

Lakota Hoop Dancer

Name _____

Students use this page to think about their reading and to prepare for discussion. It should not be used for assessment. Sample responses are shown.

REFLECTION 1 What does Kevin mean when he says the prairie is a hoop of life?

When he stands on the prairie, he can see the horizon stretch all the way around him, like a hoop. He notices all the living things that are inside that hoop, and so he calls it a "hoop of life."

HOMEWORK 1 Write a letter to a child your age living in the Lakota homeland. Explain how your homeland is similar to or different from the Lakota homeland.

REFLECTION 2 Why is dancing so important to Kevin?

To Kevin, the traditions of his ancestors are very important. Dancing is one of these traditions. Dancing is something he can do with other Lakotas at powwows to share their heritage.

HOMEWORK 2 List some of the things that the hoop represents to American Indian people.

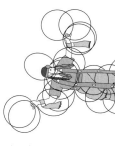

Level 8, Book 9, *Lakota Hoop Dancer* 39

Tunnels, Tracks, and Trains: Building a Subway

by Joan Hewett   Photographs by Richard Hewett

*S*ummary: This book provides an inside look at the construction of the Los Angeles subway system.

Materials

Lesson 1	Lesson 2	Lesson 3
• Previously read books • *Tunnels, Tracks, and Trains* pp. 4–10 • Posters 2, 3, 5 • Student Guide (SG) pp. 41–43 • Strategy Prompts, SG pp. 89–91 • Markers	• Independent reading books • *Tunnels, Tracks, and Trains* pp. 11–17 • Posters 2, 3, 5 • Student Guide (SG) pp. 41–43 • Strategy Prompts, SG pp. 89–91 • Markers	• Previously read books • *Tunnels, Tracks, and Trains* pp. 18–25 • Posters 2, 3, 5 • Student Guide (SG) pp. 41–42, 44 • Strategy Prompts, SG pp. 89–91 • Markers
Lesson 4	**Lesson 5**	**Lesson 6**
• Independent reading books • *Tunnels, Tracks, and Trains* pp. 26–31 • Posters 2, 3, 5 • Student Guide (SG) pp. 41–42, 44 • Strategy Prompts, SG pp. 89–91 • Markers	• Previously read books • *Tunnels, Tracks, and Trains* pp. 32–39 • Posters 2, 3, 5 • Student Guide (SG) pp. 41–42, 45 • Strategy Prompts, SG pp. 89–91 • Markers	• Independent reading books • *Tunnels, Tracks, and Trains* pp. 40–47 • Posters 2, 3, 5 • Student Guide (SG) pp. 41–42, 45 • Strategy Prompts, SG pp. 89–91 • Markers • Home Connection letter

Note: It is not necessary for students to know or be held responsible for all the facts presented in the book. The purpose of these lessons is to help students learn strategies for comprehending informational text.

Scaffolding

Strong Teacher Support	Moderate Teacher Support	Student Independence
	For Book 10 (Category IV), continue to coach and model as you encourage students to practice using strategies independently.	

Help with Phonics and Decoding Longer Words: For students who need explicit instruction, see the Optional Lesson on page R191 of the Teacher's Resource File in this manual.

Lesson Overview

	Lesson 1	**Lesson 2**	**Lesson 3**
Revisiting (5 minutes)	• Previously read books: Retelling	• Group Conference: Independent Reading	• Previously read books: Retelling
Reviewing (5 minutes)	• Review Reciprocal Teaching Strategies (Posters 2, 3)	• Students Discuss Strategies • Students Summarize	• Students Discuss Strategies • Students Summarize
Rehearsing (5–10 minutes)	• Introduce the Book • K-W-L (Poster 5, SG p. 41) • Guided Preview, pp. 4–10 Key Vocabulary: *construction, excavation, archaeologist, artifacts* • K-W-L/Question (Poster 5, SG p. 41)	• Cooperative Preview, pp. 11–17 Key Vocabulary: *boring, surveyors, reinforced, makeshift* • K-W-L/Question (Poster 5, SG p. 41)	• Cooperative Preview, pp. 18–25 Key Vocabulary: *stagnant, grueling, precast* • K-W-L/Question (Poster 5, SG p. 41)
Reading and Reciprocal Teaching (10–15 minutes)	• Silent Reading • Check Questions • Students Model Strategies • Teacher Models SUMMARIZE, QUESTION	• Silent Reading • Check Questions • Students Model Strategies • Teacher Models CLARIFY/PHONICS	• Silent Reading • Check Questions • Students Model Strategies • Teacher Models SUMMARIZE, CLARIFY
Responding/ Reflecting (5 minutes)	• K-W-L (Poster 5, SG p. 41) • Reflection #1 (SG p. 43) • Strategies Discussion (Posters 2, 3) • Homework 1	• K-W-L (Poster 5, SG p. 41) • Reflection #2 (SG p. 43) • Strategies Discussion (Posters 2, 3) • Homework 2	• K-W-L (Poster 5, SG p. 41) • Reflection #3 (SG p. 44) • Strategies Discussion (Posters 2, 3) • Homework 3

(Continued on next page)

Lesson Overview

	Lesson 4	Lesson 5	Lesson 6
Revisiting (5 minutes)	• Group Conference: Independent Reading	• Previously read books: Retelling	• Group Conference: Independent Reading
Reviewing (5 minutes)	• Students Discuss Strategies • Students Summarize	• Students Model Strategies • Students Summarize	• Students Discuss Strategies • Students Summarize
Rehearsing (5–10 minutes)	• Cooperative Preview, pp. 26–31 Key Vocabulary: *sure-footed, temporary, architectural* • K-W-L/Question (Poster 5, SG p. 41)	• Independent Preview, pp. 32–39 Key Vocabulary: *anchored, ventilating, flatbed, installations, experimentation, sleight of eye, fiber-optic* • K-W-L/Question (Poster 5, SG p. 41)	• Independent Preview, pp. 40–47 Key Vocabulary: *technology, instantaneously, apprehended, girders, endurance, throttle, accelerating, residential, subterranean* • K-W-L/Question (Poster 5, SG p. 41)
Reading and Reciprocal Teaching (10–15 minutes)	• Silent Reading • Check Questions • Students Model Strategies • Teacher Models SUMMARIZE, QUESTION	• Silent Reading • Check Questions • Students Model Strategies • Teacher Models SUMMARIZE, QUESTION, PREDICT	• Silent Reading • Check Questions • Students Model Strategies • Teacher Models SUMMARIZE, CLARIFY
Responding/ Reflecting (5 minutes)	• K-W-L (Poster 5, SG p. 41) • Reflection #4 (SG p. 44) • Strategies Discussion (Posters 2, 3) • Homework 4	• K-W-L (Poster 5, SG p. 41) • Reflection #5 (SG p. 45) • Strategies Discussion (Posters 2, 3) • Homework 5	• K-W-L (Poster 5, SG p. 41) • Reflection #6 (SG p. 45) • Homework 6 • Home Connection letter

Tunnels, Tracks, and Trains

	Lesson 1	Lesson 2
Revisiting (5 minutes) *Note: Do an Oral Reading Check only when you are concerned about a student's decoding or fluency.*	► **Students reread previously read *SOAR TO SUCCESS* books.** • Have students reread silently for fluency; assign each a different strategy to model in Reviewing. • Have one student read silently and retell a section of a book. Note comprehension. (Use passages and protocols for Retellings, TM pp. R46–R47.)	► **Group Conference** Students discuss independent reading. **Prompt:** *Describe a funny event or unusual fact from your book.* Remind students to keep up their book logs and to bring them to Group Conference for reference.
Reviewing (5 minutes)	► **Students review Reciprocal Teaching strategies.** (Posters 2, 3) Students discuss strategies used with *Lakota Hoop Dancer* and other classroom reading, and model strategies they used in Revisiting.	► **Students discuss** strategies they have used with other classroom reading. ► **Students Summarize** Students use the book and their K-W-L Charts (SG p. 41) to summarize pp. 4–10.
Rehearsing (5–10 minutes) *Note: After the Guided Preview in Lesson 1, hand out books.*	► **Introduce the Book** Show the cover and title page. Ask students what they think the book will be about. ► **K-W-L** Ask students what they know about trains and subways. Help them fill in the **K** column on their K-W-L Charts (SG p. 41). ► **Guided Preview/Vocabulary** pp. 4–10. *pp. 4–7* (Show photo on page 5.) What stage of **construction** (p. 4) is this? *p. 8* **Excavation** continues, and this trench—called a cut—is dug. What is the purpose of the wall? *pp. 9–10* Roberta Greenwood is an **archaeologist** (p. 9), a person who studies past times and cultures. She was assigned to check out **artifacts** (p. 9) that have been unearthed at the dig sites. ► **K-W-L/Question** Students write questions about trains and tunnels under **W** on their K-W-L Charts.	► **Cooperative Preview/Vocabulary** Have partners preview pages 11–17, noting section headings and photos. If needed, coach as follows: *pp. 11–13* Workers are going to dig up the park. They want to install equipment under it, and begin **boring** (p. 11) from there. They have to drain the lake. *pp. 14–15* **Surveyors** identify points where the earth will have to be **reinforced**. *pp. 16–17* Digging equipment is brought in on a **makeshift** (p. 17) road. What do you think happens to the newly dug dirt? After the preview, have students find each word boldfaced above, read aloud the sentence, and briefly discuss the meaning. ► **K-W-L/Question** Help students add questions to the **W** column on their K-W-L Charts (SG p. 41).
Reading and Reciprocal Teaching (10–15 minutes) *Note: After students check their questions, they model Summarize, with you modeling if needed. Then they model all other strategies in any order, using their Strategy Notes. Model for them as needed. Samples are provided.*	► Refer to Posters 2 and 3. Remind students to use these strategies as they read. ► **Purpose-setting** Students read to answer their **W** questions. ► **Silent Reading** pp. 4–10. Remind students to use SG p. 42 to help them model strategies. ► **After reading, students check** to see which of their **W** questions were answered. *Teacher Models* • **SUMMARIZE** Los Angeles is building its first subway system. Union Station is now being built by "cut and cover" construction. An archaeologist oversees the preservation of artifacts found at the site. • **QUESTION** Why use "cut and cover" construction?	► **Purpose-setting** Students read to answer their **W** questions. ► **Silent Reading** pp. 11–17. Remind students to use SG p. 42 to help them model strategies. ► **After reading, students check** to see which of their **W** questions were answered. *Teacher Models* • **CLARIFY/PHONICS** *I am not sure how to pronounce this word* (point to **contamination** on page 13). *I break it into chunks I know. I know the ending,* **nation**. *When I blend the chunks* **c-o-n** *and* **t-a-m**, *and* **i** *with the ending, I get* **con/tam/i/nation**. *I look up the meaning in the dictionary. It makes sense.*
Responding/ Reflecting (5 minutes) *Note: Assign the lesson homework (SG p. 43) at the end of each lesson.*	► **K-W-L** Students add to their K-W-L Charts (SG p. 41). ► **Respond** Students discuss, complete, and share Reflection #1 on SG p. 43: *What do objects found at this dig site tell about the people who lived here?* ► **Strategies Discussion** (Posters 2, 3) **Prompt:** *When did you use QUESTION? How did it help you?*	► **K-W-L** Students add to their K-W-L Charts (SG p. 41). ► **Respond** Students discuss, complete, and share Reflection #2 on SG p. 43: *Write a few sentences telling how the construction affects MacArthur Park.* ► **Strategies Discussion** (Posters 2, 3) **Prompt:** *When did you use PREDICT? How did PREDICT help you?*

	Lesson 3	**Lesson 4**
Revisiting (5 minutes) *Note: Do an Oral Reading Check only when you are concerned about a student's decoding or fluency.*	▶ **Students reread previously read *SOAR TO SUCCESS* books.** • Have students reread silently for fluency. • Have one student read silently and retell a section of a book. Note comprehension. (Use passages and protocols for Retellings, TM pp. R46–R47.)	▶ **Group Conference** Students discuss independent reading. **Prompt:** *Describe one of the characters in your book. What do you like or dislike about that character?* Remind students to keep up their book logs and to bring them to Group Conference for reference.
Reviewing (5 minutes)	▶ **Students discuss** strategies they have used with other classroom reading. ▶ **Students Summarize** Students use the book and their K-W-L Charts (SG p.41) to summarize pp. 11–17.	▶ **Students discuss** strategies they have used with other classroom reading. ▶ **Students Summarize** Students use the book and their K-W-L Charts (SG p.41) to summarize pp. 18–25.
Rehearsing (5–10 minutes)	▶ **Cooperative Preview/Vocabulary** Have partners preview pages 18–25, noting section headings and photos. If needed, coach as follows: *pp. 18–19* The boring machine is 180 feet long with huge fans that pull **stagnant** (p. 19) air out of the tunnel. *pp. 20–21* Jack Bowling is one of the miners. He has a tiring and **grueling** (p. 20) job. *pp. 22–25* The boring machine digs a 24-foot-diameter tunnel. Behind it, miners line the hole with **precast** (p. 22) concrete rings, formed ahead of time. After the preview, have students find each word boldfaced above, read aloud the sentence, and briefly discuss the meaning. ▶ **K-W-L/Question** Help students add questions to the **W** column on their K-W-L Charts (SG p. 41).	▶ **Cooperative Preview/Vocabulary** Have partners preview pages 26–31, noting section headings and photos. If needed, coach as follows: *p. 26* Why do these workers need to be **sure-footed**? *pp. 27–29* Above ground, crews get the buildings and streets ready for construction. They build a **temporary** (p. 28) road over torn-up streets. *pp. 30–31* A designer plans the inside of the station using models and **architectural** (p. 31) drawings. How big do you think a typical subway station is? After the preview, have students find each word boldfaced above, read aloud the sentence, and briefly discuss the meaning. ▶ **K-W-L/Question** Help students add questions to the **W** column on their K-W-L Charts (SG p. 41).
Reading and Reciprocal Teaching (10–15 minutes) *Note: After students check their questions, they model Summarize, with you modeling if needed. Then they model all other strategies in any order, using their Strategy Notes. Model for them as needed. Samples are provided.*	▶ **Purpose-setting** Students read to answer their **W** questions. ▶ **Silent Reading** pp. 18–25. Remind students to use SG p. 42 to help them model strategies. ▶ **After reading, students check** to see which of their **W** questions were answered. *Teacher Models* • **SUMMARIZE** *Now a giant boring machine is brought into the dig site. Teams of miners are digging the subway tunnel and laying track. They work both during the day and night.* • **CLARIFY** *I'm not sure what* **derring-do** *means on page 20.* **Derring** *sounds a little bit like* **daring***. When I reread, I see that Jack is describing how his father was daring.* **Derring-do** *has to do with being daring.*	▶ **Purpose-setting** Students read to answer their **W** questions. ▶ **Silent Reading** pp. 26–31. Remind students to use SG p. 42 to help them model strategies. ▶ **After reading, students check** to see which of their **W** questions were answered. *Teacher Models* • **SUMMARIZE** *Workers lay down a plastic lining and steel beams, and pour the tunnel's concrete floor. At night, they secure the streets around the construction. A designer plans the inside of the station.* • **QUESTION** *What is* decking?
Responding/Reflecting (5 minutes) *Note: Assign the lesson homework (SG p. 44) at the end of each lesson.*	▶ **K-W-L** Students add to their K-W-L Charts (SG p. 41). ▶ **Respond** Students discuss, complete, and share Reflection #3 on SG p. 44: *Using information from this section, make a timeline of events showing how the boring machine is constructed and used.* ▶ **Strategies Discussion** (Posters 2, 3) Ask students how strategies have helped them so far.	▶ **K-W-L** Students add to their K-W-L Charts (SG p. 41). ▶ **Respond** Students discuss, complete, and share Reflection #4 on SG p. 44: *Write a few sentences explaining why construction continues at night.* ▶ **Strategies Discussion** (Posters 2, 3) **Prompt:** *When did you use CLARIFY? How did CLARIFY help you?*

	Lesson 5	Lesson 6
Revisiting (5 minutes) *Note: Do an Oral Reading Check only when you are concerned about a student's decoding or fluency.*	▶ **Students reread previously read *SOAR TO SUCCESS* books.** • Have students reread silently for fluency; assign each a different strategy to model in Reviewing. • Have one student read silently and retell a section of a book. Note comprehension. (Use passages and protocols for Retellings, TM pp. R46–R47.)	▶ **Group Conference** Students discuss independent reading. **Prompt:** *What is the main topic or problem in your book?* Remind students to keep up their book logs and to bring them to Group Conference for reference.
Reviewing (5 minutes)	▶ **Students model** strategies they used in Revisiting. ▶ **Students Summarize** Students use the book and their K-W-L Charts (SG p. 41) to summarize pp. 26–31.	▶ **Students discuss** strategies they have used with other classroom reading. ▶ **Students Summarize** Students use the book and their K-W-L Charts (SG p. 41) to summarize pp. 32–39.
Rehearsing (5–10 minutes)	▶ **Independent Preview/Vocabulary** Have students independently preview pages 32–39, noting section headings and photos. If they come to words they don't know, remind them to use CLARIFY/PHONICS and the dictionary. (These words may be difficult for some students: **anchored**, p. 32; **ventilating**, p. 34; **flatbed**, p. 36; **installations**, **experimentation**, p. 37; **sleight of eye**, **fiber-optic**, p. 38.) After the preview, have students find each word boldfaced above, read aloud the sentence, and briefly discuss the meaning. ▶ **K-W-L/Question** Help students add questions to the **W** column on their K-W-L Charts (SG p. 41).	▶ **Independent Preview/Vocabulary** Have students independently preview pages 40–47, noting section headings and photos. If they come to words they don't know, remind them to use CLARIFY/PHONICS and the dictionary. (These words may be difficult for some students: **technology**, **instantaneously**, p. 40; **apprehended**, p. 41; **girders**, p. 42; **endurance**, p. 44; **throttle**, **accelerating**, p. 45, **residential**, **subterranean**, p. 47.) After the preview, have students find each word boldfaced above, read aloud the sentence, and briefly discuss the meaning. ▶ **K-W-L/Question** Help students add questions to the **W** column on their K-W-L Charts (SG p. 41).
Reading and Reciprocal Teaching (10–15 minutes) *Note: After students check their questions, they model Summarize, with you modeling if needed. Then they model all other strategies in any order, using their Strategy Notes. Model for them as needed. Samples are provided.*	▶ **Purpose-setting** Students read to answer their **W** questions. ▶ **Silent Reading** pp. 32–39. Remind students to use SG p. 42 to help them model strategies. ▶ **After reading, students check** to see which of their **W** questions were answered. *Teacher Models* • **SUMMARIZE** *A walkway is built and a special platform for tracks is anchored. Systems are installed and the station is fully constructed. A subway artist oversees installation of the art.* • **QUESTION** *What is a hot rail?* • **PREDICT** *I predict that a special artist will be commissioned to decorate this station.*	▶ **Purpose-setting** Students read to answer their **W** questions. ▶ **Silent Reading** pp. 40–47. Remind students to use SG p. 42 to help them model strategies. ▶ **After reading, students check** to see which of their **W** questions were answered. *Teacher Models* • **SUMMARIZE** *Technicians watch over the subway system with a computer fiber-optic system connected to a complex wall of monitors. The boring machine breaks into the station. The trains prepare to run along the tracks.* • **CLARIFY** *I don't understand what it means to* **put the new trains through their paces** *on p. 47. Then I read that the first train whizzes through the tunnel. "Paces" must be like practice runs.*
Responding/ Reflecting (5 minutes) *Note: Assign the lesson homework (SG p. 45) at the end of each lesson.*	▶ **K-W-L** Students add to their K-W-L Charts (SG p. 41). ▶ **Respond** Students discuss, complete, and share Reflection #5 on SG p. 45: *Summarize some of the final work that's needed to complete the subway station.* ▶ **Strategies Discussion** (Posters 2, 3) **Prompt:** *When did you use SUMMARIZE? How did it help you?*	▶ **K-W-L** Students add to their K-W-L Charts (SG p. 41). ▶ **Respond** Students discuss, complete, and share Reflection #6 on SG p. 45: *Circle the section you liked best. Which strategy most helped you to read that section and why?* ▶ **Home Connection** Students take home *Tunnels, Tracks, and Trains* and the Home Connection letter.

Tunnels, Tracks, and Trains

Name _____

Strategy Notes

Students use this page to jot down notes or questions as they read. It should not be used for assessment. Sample notes are shown.

Clarify

park reconstruction p. 12

front-end loader p. 17

reinforce p. 27

Predict

Letelier will complete an unusual mural for this station and maybe other

stations. p. 37

Question

What is "cut and cover" construction? p. 8

What's the difference between a safety engineer and a field engineer? p. 16

How do these train operators get this job? p. 45

Summarize

Pages 18–19: The boring machine is being assembled. It is aligned with the

proposed tunnel. It has a front and back section. The shield bores the hole.

A mechanical arm puts the dirt onto a conveyor belt. Fans suck stagnant air

out of the tunnel, and a gas detector checks for harmful gases.

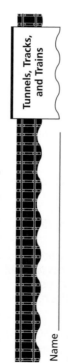

Tunnels, Tracks, and Trains

Name _____

Sample responses are shown.

K-W-L Chart

Title *Tunnels, Tracks, and Trains*

What I **K**now	What I **W**ant to Find Out	What I **L**earned
A subway is a speedy form of transportation. Subway trains usually run under the ground. Subways are found in big cities.	**Pages 4–10** How long will it take to finish the subway?	**Page 4** It will take 20 years.
	Pages 11–17 How big is the outer wall of the subway?	**Page 14** The wall is almost six-stories tall.
	Pages 18–25 How far can the boring machine move forward in one day?	**Page 21** The machine can go 30 or more feet a day.
	Pages 26–31 How do designers make models of stations?	**Page 31** They use computers and hand-made 3-D models.
	Pages 32–39 What brings fresh air into the subway?	**Page 34** Huge fans carry fresh air below.
	Pages 40–47 How does the train collect electricity from the third rail?	**Page 45** There is a special "shoe" at the bottom of the train car.

Tunnels, Tracks, and Trains

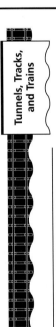

Name _____

Students use this page to think about their reading and to prepare for discussion. Sample responses are shown.

REFLECTION 1

What do objects found at this dig site tell about the people who lived here?

Most of the people who lived here were Chinese. Special objects like porcelain dolls, marbles, dominoes, and rusted Chinese coins were found. These objects tell what people did. Household objects, like steamers, spoons, teapots, toothbrushes, and a spittoon, tell how people lived and ate.

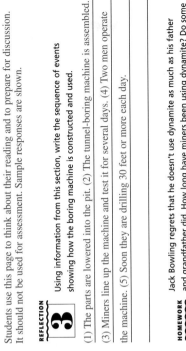

HOMEWORK 1

A subway is a useful form of transportation. List four reasons that make this statement true.

REFLECTION 2

Write a few sentences telling how the construction affects MacArthur Park.

A fence is put up around the park to keep people out. Geese and ducks are moved from the lake. Trees are uprooted. The water in the lake is drained and bad soil is removed. When the station is finished, the park will be planted again and a new lake will be created.

HOMEWORK 2

Pretend you are the project manager on this job for a day. Work is behind schedule and over budget. What do you tell your staff? Write a letter to your employees explaining the situation.

Level 8, Book 10, *Tunnels, Tracks, and Trains* 43

Tunnels, Tracks, and Trains

Name _____

Students use this page to think about their reading and to prepare for discussion. It should not be used for assessment. Sample responses are shown.

REFLECTION 3

Using information from this section, write the sequence of events showing how the boring machine is constructed and used.

(1) The parts are lowered into the pit. (2) The tunnel-boring machine is assembled. (3) Miners line up the machine and test it for several days. (4) Two men operate the machine. (5) Soon they are drilling 30 feet or more each day.

HOMEWORK 3

Jack Bowling regrets that he doesn't use dynamite as much as his father and grandfather did. How long have miners been using dynamite? Do some research, then write a few sentences explaining when and by whom dynamite was invented.

REFLECTION 4

Write a few sentences about why construction continues at night.

Construction continues at night because there are fewer people on the streets. Roads can be closed off and torn up at night.

HOMEWORK 4

Pretend you have been given the assignment to design a subway station. Write a list of things you would want to include in your design. Why are they important?

44 Level 8, Book 10, *Tunnels, Tracks, and Trains*

Tunnels, Tracks, and Trains

Name _____

Students use this page to think about their reading and to prepare for discussion. It should not be used for assessment. Sample responses are shown.

REFLECTION 5

Summarize some of the final work that's needed to complete the subway station.

Cables for power and pipes for water are installed. A narrow walkway is built for

use in case of an emergency. A special platform for train rails is put into place.

The "hot rail" is installed when the tunnel is almost operational. Gas and fire

alarm systems are installed. Artists install their artwork.

HOMEWORK 5

You have been selected to create art for this subway station. Write a description of what you would create.

REFLECTION 6

 Circle the section you liked best in *Tunnels, Tracks, and Trains*.

Pages 4–10
An archaeological dig is underway.

Pages 11–17
construction site in the park

Pages 18–24
The boring machine is assembled.

Pages 25–31
reinforcing an area and designing a station

Pages 32–39
finishing work and decorating

Pages 40–48
Central control brings on the trains.

Which strategy helped you most to read that section and why?

Question helped me understand how all the different workers worked together

successfully on this project.

HOMEWORK 6

Imagine you are sitting inside the central control room observing the monitors. Write a description of what you might see during a rush hour.

Level 8, Book 10, *Tunnels, Tracks, and Trains* **45**

Gloria Estefan: Cuban-American Singing Star

by Fernando Gonzalez

*S*ummary: The life of Gloria Estefan, the popular Hispanic-American singer, is traced from her childhood in Cuba and the United States through her adulthood, when she performed with the Miami Sound Machine and made a triumphant recovery from a life-threatening accident.

Materials

Lesson 1	Lesson 2	Lesson 3	Lesson 4
• Previously read books	• Independent reading books	• Previously read books	• Independent reading books
• *Gloria Estefan* pp. 5–8	• *Gloria Estefan* pp. 8–14	• *Gloria Estefan* pp. 15–25	• *Gloria Estefan* pp. 25–29
• Posters 2, 3, 8	• Posters 2, 3, 8	• Posters 2, 3, 8	• Posters 2, 3, 8
• Student Guide (SG) p. 46–48	• Student Guide (SG) p. 46–48	• Student Guide (SG) p. 46–47, 49	• Student Guide (SG) p. 46–47, 49
• Strategy Prompts, SG pp. 89–91	• Strategy Prompts, SG pp. 89–91	• Strategy Prompts, SG pp. 89–91	• Strategy Prompts, SG pp. 89–91
• Markers	• Markers	• Markers	• Markers
			• Home Connection letter

Scaffolding

Strong Teacher Support	Moderate Teacher Support	Student Independence
	For Book 11 (Category IV), continue to coach and model as you encourage students to practice using strategies independently.	

Help with Phonics and Decoding Longer Words: For students who need explicit instruction, see the Optional Lesson on page R192 of the Teacher's Resource File in this manual.

Lesson Overview

	Lesson 1	Lesson 2	Lesson 3	Lesson 4
Revisiting (5 minutes)	• Previously read books: Retelling	• Group Conference: Independent Reading	• Previously read books: Retelling	• Group Conference: Independent Reading
Reviewing (5 minutes)	• Review Reciprocal Teaching Strategies (Posters 2, 3)	• Students Discuss Strategies • Students Summarize	• Students Discuss Strategies • Students Summarize	• Students Discuss Strategies • Students Summarize
Rehearsing (5–10 minutes)	• Introduce the Book • Students Predict • Guided Preview, pp. 5–8 Key Vocabulary: *disconnected, procedure*	• Students Predict • Cooperative Preview, pp. 8–14 Key Vocabulary: *exiles, Cuban Revolution, prejudice, percussion*	• Students Predict • Cooperative Preview, pp. 15–25 Key Vocabulary: *cultures, overtone, achievement, crossover*	• Students Predict • Independent Preview, pp. 25–29 Key Vocabulary: *organization, bouquets, telethon, ethnic*
Reading and Reciprocal Teaching (10–15 minutes)	• Silent Reading • Check Predictions • Students Model Strategies • Teacher Models CLARIFY/PHONICS	• Silent Reading • Check Predictions • Students Model Strategies • Teacher Models SUMMARIZE, QUESTION	• Silent Reading • Check Predictions • Students Model Strategies • Teacher Models SUMMARIZE, QUESTION	• Silent Reading • Check Predictions • Students Model Strategies • Teacher Models SUMMARIZE, CLARIFY
Responding/ Reflecting (5 minutes)	• Event Map (Poster 8, SG p. 46) • Reflection #1 (SG p. 48) • Strategies Discussion (Posters 2, 3) • Homework 1	• Event Map (Poster 8, SG p. 46) • Reflection #2 (SG p. 48) • Strategies Discussion (Posters 2, 3) • Homework 2	• Event Map (Poster 8, SG p. 46) • Reflection #3 (SG p. 49) • Strategies Discussion (Posters 2, 3) • Homework 3	• Event Map (Poster 8, SG p. 46) • Reflection #4 (SG p. 49) • Homework 4 • Home Connection letter

Gloria Estefan	Lesson 1	Lesson 2
Revisiting (5 minutes) *Note: Do an Oral Reading Check only when you are concerned about a student's decoding or fluency.*	▶ **Students reread previously read *SOAR TO SUCCESS* books.** • Have students reread silently for fluency; assign each to choose a strategy to model in Reviewing. • Have one student read silently and retell a section of a book. Note comprehension. (Use passages and protocols for Retellings, TM pp. R48–R49.)	▶ **Group Conference** Students discuss independent reading. **Prompt:** *What questions would you like to ask the author about the book you are reading?* Remind students to keep up their book logs and to bring them to Group Conference for reference.
Reviewing (5 minutes)	▶ **Students review Reciprocal Teaching strategies.** (Posters 2, 3) Students discuss strategies used with *Tunnels, Tracks, and Trains* and other classroom reading, and model strategies they used in Revisiting.	▶ **Students discuss** strategies they have used with other classroom reading. ▶ **Students Summarize** Students use the book and their Event Maps (SG p.46) to summarize pp. 5–8.
Rehearsing (5–10 minutes) *Note: After the Guided Preview in Lesson 1, hand out books.*	▶ **Introduce the Book** Show the cover, title page, and author's name. Point out the time line of events at the back of the book. ▶ **Students Predict** Ask students what they think the book will be about. Record their predictions. ▶ **Guided Preview/Vocabulary** pp. 5–8 (top). *pp. 5–6* Gloria Estefan had been traveling with her band when their bus got into an accident. Gloria broke her back and couldn't move. She said she felt **disconnected** (p. 6) from her own body. *p. 7* Gloria chose to go through a long, difficult **procedure** in which doctors operated on her back, rather than spend six months in a body cast. *p. 8* Doctors said it would be several years before Estefan got better.	▶ **Students Predict** Based on pages 5–8, students predict what might happen next. Record predictions. ▶ **Cooperative Preview/Vocabulary** Have partners preview pp. 8 (bottom)–14, noting section headings, photos, and captions. If needed, coach as follows: *p. 8–9* Gloria and her family were Cuban **exiles** (p. 8). They came to the U.S. because of the **Cuban Revolution** (p. 9), a struggle for power in Cuba. *pp. 10–11* Gloria's family was often treated badly and knew **prejudice** (p. 11). How might she have felt? *pp. 12–14* Gloria joined a band and sang and played **percussion** (p. 14) instruments. She graduated college and married band member Emilio. After the preview, have students find each word boldfaced above, read aloud the sentence, and briefly discuss the meaning.
Reading and Reciprocal Teaching (10–15 minutes) *Note: After students check their predictions, they model Summarize. Then they model all other strategies in any order, using their Strategy Notes. Have students do most of the modeling, but help as needed. Samples are provided.*	▶ Refer to Posters 2 and 3. Remind students to use these strategies as they read. ▶ **Purpose-setting** Students read to check their predictions. ▶ **Silent Reading** pp. 5–8 (top). Remind students to use SG p. 47 to help them model strategies. ▶ **After reading, students check** to see if their predictions were verified. **Teacher Models** • **CLARIFY/PHONICS** *I don't recognize this word* (point to **determination** on page 8), *so I try breaking it into chunks. I know* **d-e** *is pronounced* /dee/. *I can sound out* **t-e-r**, **m-i-n**, *and* **a**, *and I recognize* **-t-i-o-n**. *When I blend them, I get* **de/ter/min/a/tion**. *I look it up in the dictionary and see that it means "a strong intention or goal."*	▶ **Purpose-setting** Students read to check their predictions. ▶ **Silent Reading** pp. 8 (bottom)–14. Remind students to use SG p. 47 to help them model strategies. ▶ **After reading, students check** to see if their predictions were verified. **Teacher Models** • **SUMMARIZE** *Gloria was born in Cuba. Her family came to the U.S. with other Cuban exiles who disagreed with Castro. Her music helped her overcome her sadness at feeling out of place. She started singing with the band Miami Sound Machine.* • **QUESTION** *Why does the song "Ferry Cross the Mersey" have special meaning for Gloria?*
Responding/ Reflecting (5 minutes) *Note: Assign the lesson homework (SG p. 48) at the end of each lesson.*	▶ **Event Map** Display Poster 8. Help students fill in events 1 and 2 on their own Event Maps (SG p. 46). ▶ **Respond** Students discuss, complete, and share Reflection #1 on SG p. 48: *Describe the scene at Gloria's bus accident.* ▶ **Strategies Discussion** (Posters 2, 3) **Prompt:** *When did you use CLARIFY? How did CLARIFY help you?*	▶ **Event Map** Using Event Map Poster 8, help students update their own Event Maps (SG p. 46). ▶ **Respond** Students discuss, complete, and share Reflection #2 on SG p. 48: *Why did Gloria feel out of place in Miami?* ▶ **Stratigies Discussion** (Posters 2, 3) **Prompt:** *When did you use SUMMARIZE? How did it help you?*

Gloria Estefan	Lesson 3	Lesson 4
Revisiting (5 minutes) *Note: Do an Oral Reading Check only when you are concerned about a student's decoding or fluency.*	▶ **Students reread previously read *SOAR TO SUCCESS* books.** • Have students reread silently for fluency. • Have one student read silently and retell a section of a book. Note comprehension. (Use passages and protocols for Retellings, TM pp. R48–R49.)	▶ **Group Conference** Students discuss independent reading. **Prompt:** *How do you predict your book will end? Why?* Remind students to keep up their book logs and to bring them to Group Conference for reference.
Reviewing (5 minutes)	▶ **Students discuss** strategies they have used with other classroom reading. ▶ **Students Summarize** Students use the book and their Event Maps (SG p. 46) to summarize pp. 8–14.	▶ **Students discuss** strategies they have used with other classroom reading. ▶ **Students Summarize** Students use the book and their Event Maps (SG p. 46) to summarize pp. 15–25.
Rehearsing (5–10 minutes)	▶ **Students Predict** Based on pages 8–14, students predict what might happen next. Record predictions. ▶ **Cooperative Preview/Vocabulary** Have partners preview pages 15–25 (top), noting section headings, photos, and captions. If needed, coach as follows: *pp. 15–17* Gloria and Emilio began to mix their own music with Cuban music, reflecting the Spanish, African, and French **cultures** (p. 17) of Cuba. *pp. 18–20* The Miami Sound Machine played *salsa* songs that had an American **overtone** (p. 19). *pp. 21–24* The band was proud of its **achievement** (p. 21) and soon made a **crossover** (p. 21)—appealing to both Spanish- and English-speaking listeners. After the preview, have students find each word boldfaced above, read aloud the sentence, and briefly discuss the meaning.	▶ **Students Predict** Based on pages 15–25, students predict what might happen in the final section. Record their predictions. ▶ **Independent Preview/Vocabulary** Have students independently preview pages 25 (bottom)–29, noting section headings, photos, and captions. If they come to words they don't know, remind them to use CLARIFY/ PHONICS and the dictionary. (These words may be difficult for some students: **organization**, **bouquets** p. 25; **telethon**, **ethnic**, p. 29). After the preview, have students find each word boldfaced above, read aloud the sentence, and briefly discuss the meaning.
Reading and Reciprocal Teaching (10–15 minutes) *Note: After students check their predictions, they model Summarize. Then they model all other strategies in any order, using their Strategy Notes. Have students do most of the modeling, but help as needed. Samples are provided.*	▶ **Purpose-setting** Students read to check their predictions. ▶ **Silent Reading** pp. 15–25 (top). Remind students to use SG p. 47 to help them model strategies. ▶ **After reading, students check** to see if their predictions were verified. ***Teacher Models*** • **SUMMARIZE** *Gloria and her husband, Emilio, created a new mix of Cuban and American music. They were signed by CBS Records. They worked to get as wide an audience as possible. Fans loved Gloria's style.* • **QUESTION** *Why did Emilio quit the band in 1985?*	▶ **Purpose-setting** Students read to check their predictions. ▶ **Silent Reading** pp. 25 (bottom)–29. Remind students to use SG p. 47 to help them model strategies. ▶ **After reading, students check** to see if their predictions were verified. ***Teacher Models*** • **SUMMARIZE** *Estefan was at the peak of her success when the bus accident happened. Her recovery was difficult but she worked hard to get well. During her recovery she wrote 25 new songs and, after several months, she performed again.* • **CLARIFY** *On page 25, how could Gloria have felt a positive "physical energy" around her? I see in the next paragraph that she was getting flowers and wishes from thousands of fans. She felt the energy of the fans.*
Responding/ Reflecting (5 minutes) *Note: Assign the lesson homework (SG p. 49) at the end of each lesson.*	▶ **Event Map** Using Event Map Poster 8, help students update their own Event Maps (SG p. 46). ▶ **Respond** Students discuss, complete, and share Reflection #3 on SG p. 49: *Explain what finally made Gloria Estefan such a success.* ▶ **Strategies Discussion** (Posters 2, 3) **Prompt:** *When did you use QUESTION? How did it help you?*	▶ **Event Map** Have students complete their Event Maps (SG p. 46). ▶ **Respond** Students discuss, complete, and share Reflection #4 on SG p. 49: *Circle the section you liked best. Which strategy helped you the most? Why?* ▶ **Home Connection** Students take home *Gloria Estefan* and the Home Connection letter.

Gloria Estefan

Name _____

Students use this page to jot down notes or questions as they read. It should not be used for assessment. Sample notes are shown.

Strategy Notes

Clarify

inspiration p. 18

portable keyboard p. 27

Predict

Gloria Estefan will make an important contribution to music. p. 21

Question

Who is Nayib? p. 5

How did Estefan's husband and son survive the accident? pp. 5–6

Summarize

Pages 12–14: Gloria learns to play the guitar and sings and plays for hours in her room. The Cuban and American cultures begin to come together in her music. She joins Miami Sound Machine. She earns a degree in psychology from the University of Miami and marries band member Emilio.

Gloria Estefan

Name _____

Sample responses are shown.

Event Map

Title
Gloria Estefan: Cuban-American Singing Star

Event 1
Gloria is born in Havana, Cuba, and the family soon moves to the United States.

Event 2
Gloria joins the Miami Sound Machine band.

Event 3
Gloria graduates from college and marries band member Emilio.

Event 4
CBS Records signs a contract with the band.

Event 5
The band becomes popular with Spanish-speaking people.

Event 6
Gloria and the band reach a crossover audience of English- and Spanish-speaking fans.

Event 7
Gloria is seriously injured in a bus accident.

Event 8
Through hard work and determination, Gloria recovers in only months and regains her career.

Gloria Estefan

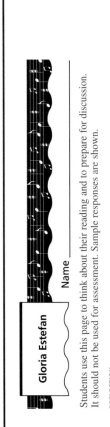

Name _____

Students use this page to think about their reading and to prepare for discussion. It should not be used for assessment. Sample responses are shown.

REFLECTION 1
Describe the scene at Gloria's bus accident.

The streets were icy and slick and it was snowing hard. While she was stopped in traffic, a truck smashed into Gloria's bus, pushing it into another truck. She was thrown to the floor of the bus.

HOMEWORK 1
Write a short letter in which Gloria tells a close friend how her recovery is going.

REFLECTION 2
Why did Gloria feel out of place in Miami?

She was often the only Latina in her class, and there was also a lot of prejudice against Cubans.

HOMEWORK 2
Write an advertisement promoting the Miami Sound Machine.

Gloria Estefan

Name _____

Students use this page to think about their reading and to prepare for discussion. It should not be used for assessment. Sample responses are shown.

REFLECTION 3
Explain what finally made Gloria Estefan and the Miami Sound Machine such a success.

The songs on their new album included pop and rock songs in English with Cuban rhythms. They attracted English- and Spanish-speaking listeners. Audiences liked Estefan's style of singing and dancing.

HOMEWORK 3
Do research to find out more about Latin music. Write the names of two other Latin singers or groups who have found crossover success.

REFLECTION 4
Circle the section you liked best in *Gloria Estefan*.

Pages 5–8	Pages 8–14	Pages 15–23	Pages 24–29
Gloria's accident	All about Cuba, Gloria's birthplace	Emilio and Gloria's musical style	Gloria's speedy recovery

Which strategy helped you the most to read that section? Why?

Summarize helped me keep track of the different influences in the music.

HOMEWORK 4
Write a few sentences about how her accident made Gloria stronger than before.

What Are You Figuring Now?: A Story About Benjamin Banneker

by Jeri Ferris Illustrations by Amy Johnson

*S*ummary: Benjamin Banneker was an African American farmer, self-taught mathematician, astronomer, and the assistant surveyor for the new capital city of the United States in 1791. This is his biography.

Materials

Lesson 1	Lesson 2	Lesson 3
• Previously read books • *What Are You Figuring Now?* pp. 6–15 • Posters 2, 3, 8 • Student Guide (SG) pp. 50–52 • Strategy Prompts, SG pp. 89–91 • Markers	• Independent reading books • *What Are You Figuring Now?* pp. 16–20 • Posters 2, 3, 8 • Student Guide (SG) pp. 50–52 • Strategy Prompts, SG pp. 89–91 • Markers	• Previously read books • *What Are You Figuring Now?* pp. 21–29 • Posters 2, 3, 8 • Student Guide (SG) pp. 50–51, 53 • Strategy Prompts, SG pp. 89–91 • Markers
Lesson 4	**Lesson 5**	**Lesson 6**
• Independent reading books • *What Are You Figuring Now?* pp. 30–39 • Posters 2, 3, 8 • Student Guide (SG) pp. 50–51, 53 • Strategy Prompts, SG pp. 89–91 • Markers	• Previously read books • *What Are You Figuring Now?* pp. 40–46 • Posters 2, 3, 8 • Student Guide (SG) pp. 50–51, 54 • Strategy Prompts, SG pp. 89–91 • Markers	• Independent reading books • *What Are You Figuring Now?* pp. 47–58 • Posters 2, 3, 8 • Student Guide (SG) pp. 50–51, 54 • Strategy Prompts, SG pp. 89–91 • Markers • Home Connection letter

Note: It is not necessary for students to know or be held responsible for all the facts presented in the book. The purpose of these lessons is to help students learn strategies for comprehending informational text.

Scaffolding

Strong Teacher Support	Moderate Teacher Support	Student Independence
	For Book 12 (Category IV), continue to coach and model as you encourage students to practice using strategies independently.	

Help with Phonics and Decoding Longer Words: For students who need explicit instruction, see the Optional Lesson on page R193 of the Teacher's Resource File in this manual.

Lesson Overview

	Lesson 1	Lesson 2	Lesson 3
Revisiting (5 minutes)	• Previously read books: Retelling	• Group Conference: Independent Reading	• Previously read books: Retelling
Reviewing (5 minutes)	• Review Reciprocal Teaching Strategies (Posters 2, 3)	• Students Discuss Strategies • Students Summarize	• Students Discuss Strategies • Students Summarize
Rehearsing (5–10 minutes)	• Introduce the Book • Students Predict • Guided Preview, pp. 6–15 Key Vocabulary: *tobacco, goose-quill*	• Students Predict • Cooperative Preview, pp. 16–20 Key Vocabulary: *hominy, penknife, hornbook*	• Students Predict • Cooperative Preview, pp. 21–29 Key Vocabulary: *complicated, memorized*
Reading and Reciprocal Teaching (10–15 minutes)	• Silent Reading • Check Predictions • Students Model Strategies • Teacher Models SUMMARIZE, PREDICT	• Silent Reading • Check Predictions • Students Model Strategies • Teacher Models SUMMARIZE, CLARIFY	• Silent Reading • Check Predictions • Students Model Strategies • Teacher Models SUMMARIZE, PREDICT, QUESTION
Responding/ Reflecting (5 minutes)	• Event Map (Poster 8, SG p. 50) • Reflection #1 (SG p. 52) • Strategies Discussion (Posters 2, 3) • Homework 1	• Event Map (Poster 8, SG p. 50) • Reflection #2 (SG p. 52) • Strategies Discussion (Posters 2, 3) • Homework 2	• Event Map (Poster 8, SG p. 50) • Reflection #3 (SG p. 53) • Strategies Discussion (Posters 2, 3) • Homework 3

(Continued on next page)

Lesson Overview

	Lesson 4	Lesson 5	Lesson 6
Revisiting (5 minutes)	• Group Conference: Independent Reading	• Previously read books: Retelling	• Group Conference: Independent Reading
Reviewing (5 minutes)	• Students Discuss Strategies • Students Summarize	• Students Model Strategies • Students Summarize	• Students Discuss Strategies • Students Summarize
Rehearsing (5–10 minutes)	• Students Predict • Cooperative Preview, pp. 30–39 Key Vocabulary: *revolutionary, independence, surveying, astronomy, eclipse*	• Students Predict • Independent Preview, pp. 40–46 Key Vocabulary: *capital, calculations, observation, latitude, longitude, spokes*	• Students Predict • Independent Preview, pp. 47–58 Key Vocabulary: *saddlebags, elegant, waistcoat, accomplishments, abolition, remedies, ingenious*
Reading and Reciprocal Teaching (10–15 minutes)	• Silent Reading • Check Predictions • Students Model Strategies • Teacher Models SUMMARIZE, QUESTION	• Silent Reading • Check Predictions • Students Model Strategies • Teacher Models SUMMARIZE, QUESTION, PREDICT	• Silent Reading • Check Predictions • Students Model Strategies • Teacher Models CLARIFY/PHONICS
Responding/ Reflecting (5 minutes)	• Event Map (Poster 8, SG p. 50) • Reflection #4 (SG p. 53) • Strategies Discussion (Posters 2, 3) • Homework 4	• Event Map (Poster 8, SG p. 50) • Reflection #5 (SG p. 54) • Strategies Discussion (Posters 2, 3) • Homework 5	• Event Map (Poster 8, SG p. 50) • Reflection #6 (SG p. 54) • Homework 6 • Home Connection letter

What Are You Figuring Now?	Lesson 1	Lesson 2
Revisiting (5 minutes) *Note: Do an Oral Reading Check only when you are concerned about a student's decoding or fluency.*	▸ **Students reread previously read** *SOAR TO SUCCESS* **books.** • Have students reread silently for fluency. This time, have students choose a strategy to model in Reviewing. • Have one student read silently and retell a section of a book. Note comprehension. (Use passages and protocols for Retellings, TM pp. R50–R51.)	▸ **Group Conference** Students discuss independent reading. **Prompt:** *Describe one of the characters or people in your book. What do you like or dislike about that character or person?* Remind students to keep up their book logs and to bring them to Group Conference for reference.
Reviewing (5 minutes)	▸ **Students review Reciprocal Teaching strategies.** (Posters 2, 3) Students discuss strategies used with *Gloria Estefan* and other classroom reading, and model strategies they used in Revisiting.	▸ **Students discuss** strategies they have used with other classroom reading. ▸ **Students Summarize** Students use the book and their Event Maps (SG p. 50) to summarize pp. 6–15.
Rehearsing (5–10 minutes) *Note: **After** the Guided Preview in Lesson 1, hand out books.*	▸ **Introduce the Book** Show the cover, title page, author's and illustrator's names. *This is Benjamin Banneker. What is he doing?* ▸ **Students Predict** Ask students what they think the book will be about. Record their predictions. ▸ **Guided Preview/Vocabulary** pp. 6–15. *pp. 6–8* In 1736, Benjamin worked on his grandmother's farm. In this picture he is picking caterpillars off **tobacco** (p. 6) leaves. Why would he need to do that? *pp. 9–10* Benjamin's Grandma Molly told him his family's history. His father and grandfather were both freed slaves. Benjamin started learning to write with a **goose-quill** (p. 11) pen. *pp. 11–15* Benjamin's father bought his own farm. Why might he want to do that?	▸ **Students Predict** Based on pages 6–15, students predict what might happen next. Record predictions. ▸ **Cooperative Preview/Vocabulary** Have partners preview pages 16–20, noting the illustrations. If needed, coach as follows: *p. 16* Benjamin's mother makes a special meal, including rabbit and **hominy**, to celebrate Benjamin's going to school. *pp. 17–18* Grandma Molly gives Benjamin a quill pen and a **penknife** (p. 17) to take to school. What else will he need? *pp. 19–20* At school, Benjamin reads from a **hornbook** (p. 19). What else will he do at school? After the preview, have students find each word boldfaced above, read aloud the sentence, and briefly discuss the meaning.
Reading and Reciprocal Teaching (10–15 minutes) *Note: After students check their predictions, they model Summarize. Then they model all other strategies in any order, using their Strategy Notes. Have students do most of the modeling, but help as needed. Samples are provided.*	Refer to Posters 2 and 3. Remind students to use these strategies as they read. ▸ **Purpose-setting** Students read to check their predictions. ▸ **Silent Reading** pp. 6–15. Remind students to use SG p. 51 to help them model strategies. ▸ **After reading, students check** to see if their predictions were verified. *Teacher Models* • **SUMMARIZE** *In 1736, six-year-old Benjamin Banneker worked on his family's tobacco farm. He loved to count. His father, a freed slave, bought his own land.* • **PREDICT** *I predict that Benjamin will go to school to learn more about numbers.*	▸ **Purpose-setting** Students read to check their predictions. ▸ **Silent Reading** pp. 16–20. Remind students to use SG p. 51 to help them model strategies. ▸ **After reading, students check** to see if their predictions were verified. *Teacher Models* • **SUMMARIZE** *A Quaker farmer opened a school nearby and Benjamin was one of eleven students who attended. Benjamin learned all he could there.* • **CLARIFY** *On page 20, what does the phrase* **he soaked up** *learning mean? I know how* **dry ground soaks up rain**—*it's like a sponge. The phrase must mean that Benjamin takes in everything he studies.*
Responding/ Reflecting (5 minutes) *Note: Assign the lesson homework (SG p. 52) at the end of each lesson.*	▸ **Event Map** Display Poster 8. Help students fill in events 1 and 2 on their own Event Maps (SG p. 50). ▸ **Respond** Students discuss, complete, and share Reflection #1 on SG p. 52: *List some ways that Grandma Molly influenced Benjamin.* ▸ **Strategies Discussion** (Posters 2, 3) **Prompt:** *When did you use PREDICT? How did PREDICT help you?*	▸ **Event Map** Using Event Map Poster 8, help students update their own Event Maps (SG p. 50). ▸ **Respond** Students discuss, complete, and share Reflection #2 on SG p. 52: *Write a few sentences that explain why Benjamin was proud.* ▸ **Strategies Discussion** (Posters 2, 3) Ask students how strategies have helped them so far.

What Are You Figuring Now?

	Lesson 3	Lesson 4
Revisiting (5 minutes) *Note: Do an Oral Reading Check only when you are concerned about a student's decoding or fluency.*	▶ **Students reread previously read *SOAR TO SUCCESS* books.** • Have students reread silently for fluency. • Have one student read silently and retell a section of a book. Note comprehension. (Use passages and protocols for Retellings, TM pp. R50–R51.)	▶ **Group Conference** Students discuss independent reading. **Prompt:** *Describe a funny event or unusual fact from your book.* Remind students to keep up their book logs and to bring them to Group Conference for reference.
Reviewing (5 minutes)	▶ **Students discuss** strategies they have used with other classroom reading. ▶ **Students Summarize** Students use the book and their Event Maps (SG p. 50) to summarize pp. 16–20.	▶ **Students discuss** strategies they have used with other classroom reading. ▶ **Students Summarize** Students use the book and their Event Maps (SG p. 50) to summarize pp. 21–29.
Rehearsing (5–10 minutes)	▶ **Students Predict** Based on pages 16–20, students predict what might happen in the next section. Record their predictions. ▶ **Cooperative Preview/Vocabulary** Have partners preview pages 21–29, noting the illustrations. If needed, coach as follows: *p. 21* Benjamin made up **complicated** math problems for himself. He helped his neighbors with reading and numbers. Why would a farmer need numbers? *pp. 24–29* Benjamin borrowed a watch. He **memorized** (p. 25) how all the pieces fit together, then built his own out of wood. After the preview, have students find each word boldfaced above, read aloud the sentence, and briefly discuss the meaning.	▶ **Students Predict** Based on pages 21–29, students predict what might happen next. Record predictions. ▶ **Cooperative Preview/Vocabulary** Have partners preview pages 30–39, noting the illustrations. If needed, coach as follows: *pp. 30–32* Benjamin met the Ellicott brothers, who recognized him as the man who built a clock. *pp. 33–34* In 1775, Benjamin learned about the **revolutionary** (p. 34) war and the colonists' fight to gain **independence** (p. 34). *pp. 35–39* Benjamin helped a friend study. He learned **surveying** (p. 35) and **astronomy** (p. 36). He learned enough to predict an **eclipse** (p. 38). After the preview, have students find each word boldfaced above, read aloud the sentence, and briefly discuss the meaning.
Reading and Reciprocal Teaching (10–15 minutes) *Note: After students check their predictions, they model Summarize. Then they model all other strategies in any order, using their Strategy Notes. Have students do most of the modeling, but help as needed. Samples are provided.*	▶ **Purpose-setting** Students read to check their predictions. ▶ **Silent Reading** pp. 21–29. Remind students to use SG p. 51 to help them model strategies. ▶ **After reading, students check** to see if their predictions were verified. ***Teacher Models*** • **SUMMARIZE** *Benjamin went into town to talk with friends. He borrowed a watch and studied it so he could make his own clock out of wood.* • **PREDICT** *I predict that Benjamin will master other subjects and will do other things in addition to farming.* • **QUESTION** *Why did Benjamin use wood to make his clock?*	▶ **Purpose-setting** Students read to check their predictions. ▶ **Silent Reading** pp. 30–39. Remind students to use SG p. 51 to help them model strategies. ▶ **After reading, students check** to see if their predictions were verified. ***Teacher Models*** • **SUMMARIZE** *At age 40, Benjamin met the Ellicotts, Quaker brothers building a mill nearby. He talked with them about the colonists' fight for independence. He learned how to survey and learned astronomy. He predicted an eclipse.* • **QUESTION** *How did Benjamin feel about the issue of independence for the colonies?*
Responding/ Reflecting (5 minutes) *Note: Assign the lesson homework (SG p. 53) at the end of each lesson.*	▶ **Event Map** Using Event Map Poster 8, help students update their own Event Maps (SG p. 50). ▶ **Respond** Students discuss, complete, and share Reflection #3 on SG p. 53: *Why might Benjamin have wanted to build his own clock?* ▶ **Strategies Discussion** (Posters 2, 3) **Prompt:** *When did you use CLARIFY? How did CLARIFY help you?*	▶ **Event Map** Using Event Map Poster 8, help students update their own Event Maps (SG p. 50). ▶ **Respond** Students discuss, complete, and share Reflection #4 on SG p. 53: *What did Benjamin think about the Declaration of Independence?* ▶ **Strategies Discussion** (Posters 2, 3) **Prompt:** *When did you use QUESTION? How did it help you?*

What Are You Figuring Now?	Lesson 5	Lesson 6
Revisiting (5 minutes) *Note: Do an Oral Reading Check only when you are concerned about a student's decoding or fluency.*	► **Students reread previously read *SOAR TO SUCCESS* books.** • Have students reread silently for fluency; remind them to choose a strategy to model in Reviewing. • Have one student read silently and retell a section of a book. Note comprehension. (Use passages and protocols for Retellings, TM pp. R50–R51.)	► **Group Conference** Students discuss independent reading. **Prompt:** *What is the main topic or problem in your book?* Remind students to keep up their book logs and to bring them to Group Conference for reference.
Reviewing (5 minutes)	► **Students model** strategies they used in Revisiting. ► **Students Summarize** Students use the book and their Event Maps (SG p. 50) to summarize pp. 30–39.	► **Students discuss** strategies they have used with other classroom reading. ► **Students Summarize** Students use the book and their Event Maps (SG p. 50) to summarize pp. 40–46.
Rehearsing (5–10 minutes)	► **Students Predict** Based on pages 30–39, students predict what might happen in the next section. Record their predictions. ► **Independent Preview/Vocabulary** Have students independently preview pages 40–46, noting the illustrations. If they come to words they don't know, remind them to use CLARIFY/PHONICS and the dictionary. (These words may be difficult for some students: **capital**, **calculations**, p. 40; **observation**, **latitude**, **longitude**, p. 43; **spokes**, p. 46.) After the preview, have students find each word boldfaced above, read aloud the sentence, and briefly discuss the meaning.	► **Students Predict** Based on pages 40–46, students predict what might happen in the final section. Record their predictions. ► **Independent Preview/Vocabulary** Have students independently preview pages 47–58, noting the illustrations. If they come to words they don't know, remind them to use CLARIFY/PHONICS and the dictionary. (These words may be difficult for some students: **saddlebags**, p. 47; **elegant**, p. 50; **waistcoat**, **accomplishments**, **abolition**, p. 51; **remedies**, p. 54; **ingenious**, p. 56.) After the preview, have students find each word boldfaced above, read aloud the sentence, and briefly discuss the meaning.
Reading and Reciprocal Teaching (10–15 minutes) *Note: After students check their predictions, they model Summarize. Then they model all other strategies in any order, using their Strategy Notes. Have students do most of the modeling, but help as needed. Samples are provided.*	► **Purpose-setting** Students read to check their predictions. ► **Silent Reading** pp. 40–46. Remind students to use SG p. 51 to help them model strategies. ► **After reading, students check** to see if their predictions were verified. ***Teacher Models*** • **SUMMARIZE** *In 1790, a capital city for America was about to be built. Benjamin was the chief assistant surveyor.* • **QUESTION** *Why was Banjamin's heart beating so fast when he met George Washington?* • **PREDICT** *I predict that Benjamin Banneker will become famous after helping to build the capital city.*	► **Purpose-setting** Students read to check their predictions. ► **Silent Reading** pp. 47–58. Remind students to use SG p. 51 to help them model strategies. ► **After reading, students check** to see if their predictions were verified. ***Teacher Models*** • **CLARIFY/PHONICS** *I'm not sure how to pronounce this word* (point to **academy** on page 54). *I know the chunks* **a**, **cad**, *and* **em**, *and* **y** *has a long* **e** *sound. Together, they make* **a/cad/em/y**. *I look it up in the dictionary and find that an academy is a "group of scholars."*
Responding/ Reflecting (5 minutes) *Note: Assign the lesson homework (SG p. 54) at the end of each lesson.*	► **Event Map** Using Event Map Poster 8, help students update their own Event Maps (SG p. 50). ► **Respond** Students discuss, complete, and share Reflection #5 on SG p. 54: *Why was Benjamin so nervous about meeting George Washington?* ► **Strategies Discussion** (Posters 2, 3) **Prompt:** *When did you use SUMMARIZE? How did it help you?*	► **Event Map** Have students complete their Event Maps (SG p. 50). ► **Respond** Students discuss, complete, and share Reflection #6 on SG p. 54: *Circle the section you liked best. Which strategy most helped you?* ► **Home Connection** Students take home *What Are You Figuring Now?* and the Home Connection letter.

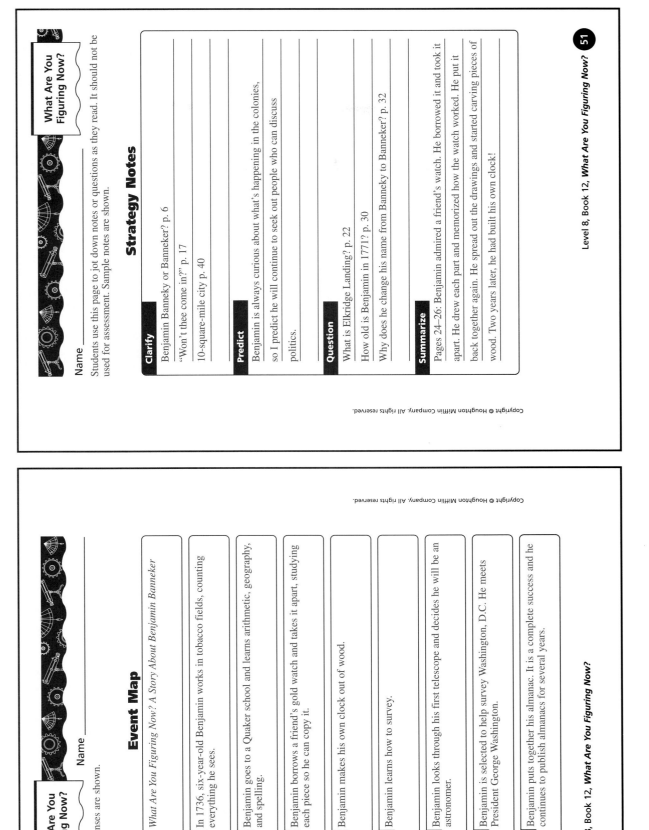

Name _____

Students use this page to jot down notes or questions as they read. It should not be used for assessment. Sample notes are shown.

Strategy Notes

Clarify

Benjamin Banneky or Banneker? p. 6

"Won't thee come in?" p. 17

10-square-mile city p. 40

Predict

Benjamin is always curious about what's happening in the colonies, so I predict he will continue to seek out people who can discuss politics.

Question

What is Elkridge Landing? p. 22

How old is Benjamin in 1771? p. 30

Why does he change his name from Banneky to Banneker? p. 32

Summarize

Pages 24–26: Benjamin admired a friend's watch. He borrowed it and took it apart. He drew each part and memorized how the watch worked. He put it back together again. He spread out the drawings and started carving pieces of wood. Two years later, he had built his own clock!

Level 8, Book 12, *What Are You Figuring Now?* **51**

Name _____

Sample responses are shown.

Event Map

Title *What Are You Figuring Now? A Story About Benjamin Banneker*

Event 1 In 1736, six-year-old Benjamin works in tobacco fields, counting everything he sees.

Event 2 Benjamin goes to a Quaker school and learns arithmetic, geography, and spelling.

Event 3 Benjamin borrows a friend's gold watch and takes it apart, studying each piece so he can copy it.

Event 4 Benjamin makes his own clock out of wood.

Event 5 Benjamin learns how to survey.

Event 6 Benjamin looks through his first telescope and decides he will be an astronomer.

Event 7 Benjamin is selected to help survey Washington, D.C. He meets President George Washington.

Event 8 Benjamin puts together his almanac. It is a complete success and he continues to publish almanacs for several years.

50 Level 8, Book 12, *What Are You Figuring Now?*

What Are You Figuring Now?

Name _____

Students use this page to think about their reading and to prepare for discussion. It should not be used for assessment. Sample responses are shown.

REFLECTION 1

List some ways that Grandma Molly influenced Benjamin.

(1) She told him stories about her home in England and coming to America. (2) Molly taught him hundreds of numbers. (3) Molly told Benjamin the story of his father, who was a freed slave. (4) Molly helped him learn to write and read.

HOMEWORK 1

Life in 1736 was very different than it is today. Write a paragraph comparing and contrasting Benjamin's life with details from your life today.

REFLECTION 2

Write a few sentences that explain why Benjamin was proud.

Benjamin was proud to have his farm. He was also proud to be a free black man. He was learning in school and making himself a better person.

HOMEWORK 2

Do research to find out more about schools in America in the early 1700s. Write three interesting things that you find out.

What Are You Figuring Now?

Name _____

Students use this page to think about their reading and to prepare for discussion. It should not be used for assessment. Sample responses are shown.

REFLECTION 3

Why might Benjamin have wanted to build his own clock?

He couldn't afford a clock of his own. Also, building a clock would help him understand how clocks work.

HOMEWORK 3

Write about the qualities that made Benjamin a good clockmaker.

REFLECTION 4

What did Benjamin think about the Declaration of Independence?

The Declaration of Independence says "All men are created equal." Benjamin's family was made up of freed slaves so he knew how important freedom was.

He didn't understand why some Americans were still slaves.

HOMEWORK 4

Benjamin liked talking about current events with the Ellicotts. Write a short dialogue between Benjamin and two other characters.

What Are You Figuring Now?

Name _____

Students use this page to think about their reading and to prepare for discussion. It should not be used for assessment. Sample responses are shown.

REFLECTION

5

Why was Benjamin so nervous about meeting George Washington?

Benjamin was nervous because Washington was a great man and a hero. He was

also a very important man because he was President of the United States.

_____

_____

HOMEWORK

5

Pretend you are a newspaper editor writing a feature story about Benjamin Banneker's career. What would you write? What is your headline?

REFLECTION

6

Circle the section you liked best in *What Are You Figuring Now?*

Pages 6–15 Learns to count	**Pages 16–20** Goes to school	**Pages 21–29** Makes a clock
Pages 30–39 Becomes astronomer	**Pages 40–45** Surveys nation's Capital	**Pages 46–58** Finishes almanacs

Which strategy most helped you read that section?

Question helped me to understand Benjamin's determination to become

an astronomer. I asked questions to understand why he would farm all day in

the sun and study all night by candlelight.

HOMEWORK

6

Read the afterword on pages 59–62. Write a summary of Benjamin's life after he stopped making almanacs.

54 Level 8, Book 12, *What Are You Figuring Now?*

Lightning

by Stephen Kramer

Photographs by Warren Faidley

*S*ummary: This book provides the reader with the scientific explanation of how lightning is formed, what types of lightning there are, and what safety measures should be taken in a thunderstorm. The book includes a glossary and a collection of fascinating facts about lightning.

Note: It is not necessary for students to know or be held responsible for all the facts presented in the book. The purpose of these lessons is to help students learn strategies for comprehending informational text.

Materials

Lesson 1	Lesson 2	Lesson 3

• Previously read books
• *Lightning* pp. 6–11
• Posters 2, 3, 5
• Student Guide (SG) pp. 55–57
• Strategy Prompts,
  SG pp. 87–89
• Markers
	• Independent reading books
	• *Lightning* pp. 12–17
	• Posters 2, 3, 5
	• Student Guide (SG) pp. 55–57
	• Strategy Prompts,
	  SG pp. 87–89
	• Markers
		• Previously read books
		• *Lightning* pp. 18–27
		• Posters 2, 3, 5
		• Student Guide (SG) pp. 55–56, 58
		• Strategy Prompts,
		  SG pp. 87–89
		• Markers

Lesson 4	**Lesson 5**	**Lesson 6**

• Independent reading books
• *Lightning* pp. 28–35
• Posters 2, 3, 5
• Student Guide (SG) pp. 55–56, 58
• Strategy Prompts,
  SG pp. 87–89
• Markers
	• Previously read books
	• *Lightning* pp. 36–41
	• Posters 2, 3, 5
	• Student Guide (SG) pp. 55–56, 59
	• Strategy Prompts,
	  SG pp. 87–89
	• Markers
		• Independent reading books
		• *Lightning* pp. 42–47
		• Posters 2, 3, 5
		• Student Guide (SG) pp. 55–56, 59
		• Strategy Prompts,
		  SG pp. 87–89
		• Markers
		• Home Connection letter

Scaffolding

Strong Teacher Support	Moderate Teacher Support	Student Independence
	For Book 13 (Category IV), continue to coach and model as you encourage students to practice using strategies independently.	

Help with Phonics and Decoding Longer Words: For students who need explicit instruction, see the Optional Lesson on page R194 of the Teacher's Resource File in this Manual.

Lesson Overview

	Lesson 1	Lesson 2	Lesson 3
Revisiting (5 minutes)	• Previously read books: Retelling	• Group Conference: Independent Reading	• Previously read books: Retelling
Reviewing (5 minutes)	• Review Reciprocal Teaching Strategies (Posters 2, 3)	• Students Discuss Strategies • Students Summarize	• Students Discuss Strategies • Students Summarize
Rehearsing (5–10 minutes)	• Introduce the Book • K-W-L (Poster 5, SG p. 55) • Guided Preview pp. 6–11 Key Vocabulary: *bolts, mystery, particles, electrons* • K-W-L/Question (Poster 5, SG p. 55)	• Guided Preview, pp. 12–17 Key Vocabulary: *slivers, collisions, sideways* • K-W-L/Question (Poster 5, SG p. 55)	• Cooperative Preview, pp. 18–27 Key Vocabulary: *instruments, flickers, analysis* • K-W-L/Question (Poster 5, SG p. 55)
Reading and Reciprocal Teaching (10–15 minutes)	• Silent Reading • Check Questions • Students Model Strategies • Teacher Models SUMMARIZE, QUESTION	• Silent Reading • Check Questions • Students Model Strategies • Teacher Models SUMMARIZE, CLARIFY	• Silent Reading • Check Questions • Students Model Strategies • Teacher Models SUMMARIZE
Responding/ Reflecting (5 minutes)	• K-W-L (Poster 5, SG p. 55) • Reflection #1 (SG p. 57) • Strategies Discussion (Posters 2, 3) • Homework 1	• K-W-L (Poster 5, SG p. 55) • Reflection #2 (SG p. 57) • Strategies Discussion (Posters 2, 3) • Homework 2	• K-W-L (Poster 5, SG p. 55) • Reflection #3 (SG p. 58) • Strategies Discussion (Posters 2, 3) • Homework 3

(Continued on next page)

Lesson Overview

	Lesson 4	Lesson 5	Lesson 6
Revisiting (5 minutes)	• Group Conference: Independent Reading	• Previously read books: Retelling	• Group Conference: Independent Reading
Reviewing (5 minutes)	• Students Discuss Strategies • Students Summarize	• Students Model Strategies • Students Summarize	• Students Discuss Strategies • Students Summarize
Rehearsing (5–10 minutes)	• Cooperative Preview, pp. 28–35 Key Vocabulary: *echoes, thunderheads, eventually* • K-W-L/Question (Poster 5, SG p. 55)	• Independent Preview, pp. 36–41 Key Vocabulary: *equator, illusions, blurred, motionless* • K-W-L/Question (Poster 5, SG p. 55)	• Independent Preview, pp. 42–47 Key Vocabulary: *emergencies, crouch, sacred, atmosphere* • K-W-L/Question (Poster 5, SG p. 55)
Reading and Reciprocal Teaching (10–15 minutes)	• Silent Reading • Check Questions • Students Model Strategies • Teacher Models SUMMARIZE, CLARIFY	• Silent Reading • Check Questions • Students Model Strategies • Teacher Models CLARIFY/PHONICS, CLARIFY, PREDICT	• Silent Reading • Check Questions • Students Model Strategies • Teacher Models SUMMARIZE, QUESTION
Responding/ Reflecting (5 minutes)	• K-W-L (Poster 5, SG p. 55) • Reflection #4 (SG p. 58) • Strategies Discussion (Posters 2, 3) • Homework 4	• K-W-L (Poster 5, SG p. 55) • Reflection #5 (SG p. 59) • Strategies Discussion (Posters 2, 3) • Homework 5	• K-W-L (Poster 5, SG p. 55) • Reflection #6 (SG p. 59) • Homework 6 • Home Connection letter

Lightning	**Lesson 1**	**Lesson 2**
Revisiting (5 minutes) *Note: Do an Oral Reading Check only when you are concerned about a student's decoding or fluency.*	▶ **Students reread previously read *SOAR TO SUCCESS* books.** • Have students reread silently for fluency. Remind them to choose a strategy to model in Reviewing. • Have one student read silently and retell a section of a book. Note comprehension. (Use passages and protocols for Retellings, TM pp. R52–R53.)	▶ **Group Conference** Students discuss independent reading. **Prompt:** *Summarize the most interesting part of the book you are reading now.* Remind students to keep up their book logs and to bring them to Group Conference for reference.
Reviewing (5 minutes)	▶ **Students review Reciprocal Teaching strategies.** (Posters 2, 3) Students discuss strategies used with *What Are You Figuring Now?* and other classroom reading, and model strategies they used in Revisiting.	▶ **Students discuss** strategies they have used with other classroom reading. ▶ **Students Summarize** Students use the book and their K-W-L Charts (SG p. 55) to summarize pp. 6–11.
Rehearsing (5–10 minutes) *Note: **After** the Guided Preview in Lessons 1 and 2, hand out books.* *Note: To keep the emphasis on comprehension, students should not be held responsible for pronunciation of scientific terms.*	▶ **Introduce the Book** Show the cover, title, and author's name. Point out the glossary on p. 48. Ask students what they might learn from this book. ▶ **K-W-L** Ask students what they know about lightning. Help them fill in the **K** column on their K-W-L Charts (SG p. 55). ▶ **Guided Preview/Vocabulary** pp. 6–11. *pp. 6–8* What sound usually accompanies lightning **bolts** (p. 8) like these? *p. 9* Scientists now know a lot about lightning, but it used to be a **mystery**. *pp. 10–11* Lightning is caused by tiny **particles** (p. 10) in an atom called **electrons** (p. 10). What do you think the blue lines in the diagram show? ▶ **K-W-L/Question** Students write questions about lightning under **W** on their K-W-L Charts (SG p. 55).	▶ **Guided Preview/Vocabulary** pp. 12–17 *pp. 12–13* Strong winds can hurl the water in a cloud up to the top, freezing it into **slivers** (p. 12) of ice or lumps of hail. What is hail like? When there are **collisions** (p. 12) between these different bits of ice, electrons get pulled down by falling pieces of hail. In the diagram, what charge is there at the bottom of the cloud? *pp. 14–15* Lightning usually shoots downwards, but it can also shoot **sideways**. Read the caption. In what direction is this lightning (point to photo on page 15) traveling? *pp. 16–17* Lightning that strikes the ground causes the most damage. Why might that be? ▶ **K-W-L/Question** Help students add questions to the **W** column on their K-W-L Charts (SG p. 55).
Reading and Reciprocal Teaching (10–15 minutes) *Note: After students check their questions, they model Summarize. Then they model all other strategies in any order, using their Strategy Notes. Have students do most of the modeling, but help as needed. Samples are provided.*	▶ Refer to Posters 2 and 3. Remind students to use these strategies as they read. ▶ **Purpose-setting** Students read to answer their **W** questions. ▶ **Silent Reading** pp. 6–11. Remind students to use SG p. 56 to help them model strategies. ▶ **After reading, students check** to see which of their **W** questions were answered. ***Teacher Models*** • **SUMMARIZE** *Lightning is very powerful and used to be a mystery. It is an electric spark that occurs in thunderstorms. It is caused by the motion of electrons, the negative particles in atoms, as they move from one place to another.* • **QUESTION** *What instruments do scientists use to study lightning?*	▶ **Purpose-setting** Students read to answer their **W** questions. ▶ **Silent Reading** pp. 12–17. Remind students to use SG p. 56 to help them model strategies. ▶ **After reading, students check** to see which of their **W** questions were answered. ***Teacher Models*** • **SUMMARIZE** *During a thunderstorm, the base of a cloud gets a negative charge. The electrons are attracted to positive charges on the ground or in other parts of the cloud. The attraction can cause a flow of electrons to the positive charges. This flow of electrons is lightning.* • **CLARIFY** *I wasn't sure if lightning could travel upward, but the photo on page 15 shows how that happens.*
Responding/ Reflecting (5 minutes) *Note: Assign the lesson homework (SG p. 57) at the end of each lesson.*	▶ **K-W-L** Students add to their K-W-L Charts (SG p. 55). ▶ **Respond** Students discuss, complete, and share Reflection #1 on SG p. 57: *What is lightning, and how does it make light?* ▶ **Strategies Discussion** (Posters 2, 3) **Prompt:** *When did you use CLARIFY? How did CLARIFY help you?*	▶ **K-W-L** Students add to their K-W-L Charts (SG p. 55). ▶ **Respond** Students discuss, complete, and share Reflection #2 on SG p. 57: *Why does lightning strike when the base of a thundercloud has a negative charge and the ground has a positive charge?* ▶ **Strategies Discussion** (Posters 2, 3) Ask students how strategies have helped them.

Lightning	Lesson 3	Lesson 4
Revisiting (5 minutes) *Note: Do an Oral Reading Check only when you are concerned about a student's decoding or fluency.*	▶ **Students reread previously read *SOAR TO SUCCESS* books.** • Have students reread silently for fluency. • Have one student read silently and retell a section of a book. Note comprehension. (Use passages and protocols for Retellings, TM pp. R52–R53.)	▶ **Group Conference** Students discuss independent reading. **Prompt:** *Show and discuss any photographs shown in the book you are reading.* Remind students to keep up their book logs and to bring them to Group Conference for reference.
Reviewing (5 minutes)	▶ **Students discuss** strategies they have used with other classroom reading. ▶ **Students Summarize** Students use the book and their K-W-L Charts (SG p. 55) to summarize pp. 12–17.	▶ **Students discuss** strategies they have used with other classroom reading. ▶ **Students Summarize** Students use the book and their K-W-L Charts (SG p. 55) to summarize pp. 18–27.
Rehearsing (5–10 minutes) *Note: To keep the emphasis on comprehension, students should not be held responsible for pronunciation of scientific terms.*	▶ **Cooperative Preview/Vocabulary** Have partners preview pages 18–27, noting section headings, photos, captions, and diagrams. If needed, coach as follows: *pp. 18–21* Scientists use many different **instruments** (p. 19) to measure and track lightning. pp. 22–25 Lightning usually has four parts that take place in order. Most of the light comes from the return stroke. Lightning that **flickers** (p. 25) has several return strokes. *pp. 26–27* Scientists use **analysis** of photos to learn more about how it works. After the Preview, have students find each word boldfaced above, read aloud the sentence, and briefly discuss the meaning. ▶ **K-W-L/Question** Help students add questions to the **W** column on their K-W-L Charts (SG p. 55).	▶ **Cooperative Preview/Vocabulary** Have partners preview pages 28–35, noting section headings, photos, and captions. If needed, coach as follows: *pp. 28–29* The heat of lightning expands air so fast that it causes the sound of thunder that often **echoes** (p. 29) off mountains. *pp. 30–31* Most lightning comes from **thunderheads** (p. 30), towering clouds seen in thunderstorms. *pp. 32–35* Thunderheads grow from smaller clouds. **Eventually** (p. 33) they are so tall that they reach air cold enough to freeze water. After the Preview, have students find each word boldfaced above, read aloud the sentence, and briefly discuss the meaning. ▶ **K-W-L/Question** Help students add questions to the **W** column on their K-W-L Charts (SG p. 55).
Reading and Reciprocal Teaching (10–15 minutes) *Note: After students check their questions, they model Summarize. Then they model all other strategies in any order, using their Strategy Notes. Have students do most of the modeling, but help as needed. Samples are provided.*	▶ **Purpose-setting** Students read to answer their **W** questions. ▶ **Silent Reading** pp. 18–27. Remind students to use SG p. 56 to help them model strategies. ▶ **After reading, students check** to see which of their **W** questions were answered. ***Teacher Models*** • **SUMMARIZE** *Scientists use various instruments to find out what happens in a bolt of lightning. As electrons move down toward the ground, positive charges move to meet them. A lightning channel connects the cloud and the ground along the path that is formed. Then electrons rush through the path so fast that the air around them glows. This creates most of the light we see in lightning.*	▶ **Purpose-setting** Students read to answer their **W** questions. ▶ **Silent Reading** pp. 28–35. Remind students to use SG p. 56 to help them model strategies. ▶ **After reading, students check** to see which of their **W** questions were answered. ***Teacher Models*** • **SUMMARIZE** *The path of lightning gets so hot that the air expand very quickly. This explosion of air makes the sound of thunder. Most lightning forms from huge, tall clouds called thunderheads, which form on warm days from smaller clouds.* • **CLARIFY** *On page 29, I read that thunder is the sound made by lightning. I wondered how light could make sound, but then I read on and discovered that the heat really causes the sound.*
Responding/ Reflecting (5 minutes) *Note: Assign the lesson homework (SG p. 58) at the end of each lesson.*	▶ **K-W-L** Students add to their K-W-L Charts (SG p. 55). ▶ **Respond** Students discuss, complete, and share Reflection #3 on SG p. 58: *What are some of the instruments that scientists use to study lightning?* ▶ **Strategies Discussion** (Posters 2, 3) **Prompt:** *When did you use SUMMARIZE? How did it help you?*	▶ **K-W-L** Students add to their K-W-L Charts (SG p. 55). ▶ **Respond** Students discuss, complete, and share Reflection #4 on SG p. 58: *How do thunderhead clouds form?* ▶ **Strategies Discussion** (Posters 2, 3) **Prompt:** *When did you use PREDICT? How did PREDICT help you?*

Lightning	Lesson 5	Lesson 6
Revisiting (5 minutes) *Note: Do an Oral Reading Check only when you are concerned about a student's decoding or fluency.*	▶ **Students reread previously read *SOAR TO SUCCESS* books.** • Have students reread silently for fluency. Remind them to choose a strategy to model in Reviewing. • Have one student read silently and retell a section of a book. Note comprehension. (Use passages and protocols for Retellings, TM pp. R52–R53.)	▶ **Group Conference** Students discuss independent reading. **Prompt:** *Would you recommend your book to others? Why or why not?* Remind students to keep up their book logs and to bring them to Group Conference for reference.
Reviewing (5 minutes)	▶ **Students model** strategies they used in Revisiting. ▶ **Students Summarize** Students use the book and their K-W-L Charts (SG p. 55) to summarize pp. 28–35.	▶ **Students discuss** strategies they have used with other classroom reading. ▶ **Students Summarize** Students use the book and their K-W-L Charts (SG p. 55) to summarize pp. 36–41.
Rehearsing (5–10 minutes) *Note: To keep the emphasis on comprehension, students should not be held responsible for pronunciation of scientific terms.*	▶ **Independent Preview/Vocabulary** Have students independently preview pages 36–41, noting section headings, charts, photos, and captions. If they come to words they don't know, remind them to use CLARIFY/PHONICS and the dictionary. (These words may be difficult for some students: **equator**, p. 36; **illusions**, **blurred**, p. 40; **motionless**, p.41) After the Preview, have students find each word boldfaced above, read aloud the sentence, and briefly discuss the meaning. ▶ **K-W-L/Question** Help students add questions to the **W** column on their K-W-L Charts (SG p. 55).	▶ **Independent Preview/Vocabulary** Have students independently preview pages 42–47, noting section headings, photos, and captions. If they come to words they don't know, remind them to use CLARIFY/PHONICS and the dictionary. (These words may be difficult for some students: **emergencies**, p. 42; **crouch**, p. 43; **sacred**, p. 46, **atmosphere**, p. 47.) After the Preview, have students find each word boldfaced above, read aloud the sentence, and briefly discuss the meaning. ▶ **K-W-L/Question** Help students add questions to the **W** column on their K-W-L Charts (SG p. 55).
Reading and Reciprocal Teaching (10–15 minutes) *Note: After students check their questions, they model Summarize. Then they model all other strategies in any order, using their Strategy Notes. Have students do most of the modeling, but help as needed. Samples are provided.*	▶ **Purpose-setting** Students read to answer their **W** questions. ▶ **Silent Reading** pp. 36–41. Remind students to use SG p. 56 to help them model strategies. ▶ **After reading, students check** to see which of their **W** questions were answered. ***Teacher Models*** • **CLARIFY** *I used the map key on page 37 to help me see which countries have the most lightning.* • **CLARIFY/PHONICS** *To figure out this word* (point to the word **comparison** on p. 36), *I break it into chunks* **c-o-m, p-a-r, i,** *and* **s-o-n.** *When I blend the chunks, I get the word* **com/par/i/son.** *It makes sense in the sentence.* • **PREDICT** *I predict that in the next section we will read about people who have been struck by lightning.*	▶ **Purpose-setting** Students read to answer their **W** questions. ▶ **Silent Reading** pp. 42–47. Remind students to use SG p. 56 to help them model strategies. ▶ **After reading, students check** to see which of their **W** questions were answered. ***Teacher Models*** • **SUMMARIZE** *Although we don't know everything about lightning, we do know how to stay safe in a thunderstorm. Taking shelter in a building or a car is the best defense. Outdoors, people shouldn't stay in water, and should avoid being near very tall objects.* • **QUESTION** *Where should you shelter if you get caught in a lightning storm?*
Responding/ Reflecting (5 minutes) *Note: Assign the lesson homework (SG p. 59) at the end of each lesson.*	▶ **K-W-L** Students add to their K-W-L Charts (SG p. 55). ▶ **Respond** Students discuss, complete, and share Reflection #5 on SG p. 59: *The nearer the equator, the more thunderstorms there are. Why?* ▶ **Strategies Discussion** (Posters 2, 3) **Prompt:** *When did you use QUESTION? How did it help you?*	▶ **K-W-L** Students add to their K-W-L Charts (SG p. 55). ▶ **Respond** Students discuss, complete, and share Reflection #6 on SG pp. 59: *Circle a strategy that helped you read* Lightning. *How did it help you?* ▶ **Home Connection** Students take home *Lightning* and the Home Connection letter.

Lightning

Name _____

Students use this page to jot down notes or questions as they read. It should not be used for assessment. Sample notes are shown.

Strategy Notes

Clarify

How can lightning travel upward? p. 15

sensors p. 21

Cars are metal, but they're safe places in a storm. p. 42

Predict

I'll learn about different kinds of lightning; I already know that there's heat lightning. pp. 38–39

Question

What makes the noise of thunder? p. 29

Why does lightning hit tall objects? p. 43

Summarize

Pages 12–17: The water at the top of a cloud becomes ice. It falls downward, hitting tiny slivers of ice floating upward. Some of the electrons from the small pieces are caught by the falling ice, and reach the bottom of the cloud. If they get attracted to positive charges on the ground, they may shoot through the air and make lightning.

Lightning

Name _____

Sample responses are shown.

K-W-L Chart

Title *Lightning*

What I **K**now	What I **W**ant to Find Out	What I **L**earned
Lightning is a kind of electricity.	**Pages 6–11** What makes the light in lightning?	**Pages 6–11** Electrons move so fast that the air glows.
It can be dangerous.	**Pages 12–17** Why does lightning travel from clouds to the ground?	**Pages 12–17** Electrons in clouds are attracted to positive charges on the ground.
When lightning strikes, you can hear thunder.	**Pages 18–27** How fast does lightning travel from the sky to the ground?	**Pages 18–27** In a return stroke, it moves up to 60,000 miles per second.
Lightning strikes from the sky.	**Pages 28–35** What makes the sound we hear when we hear thunder?	**Pages 28–35** Lightning heats the air so much it expands explosively.
	Pages 36–41 Where is lightning the most common?	**Pages 36–41** Most lightning occurs near the equator.
	Pages 42–47 Do airplanes get hit by lightning?	**Pages 42–47** Yes, every 5–10,000 hours of flying.

Lightning

Name _____

Students use this page to think about their reading and to prepare for discussion. It should not be used for assessment. Sample responses are shown.

REFLECTION 3
What are some of the instruments that scientists use to study lightning? How are they helpful?

Scientists send rockets into thunderstorms. They use cameras and computers. They also use lightning sensors. They have shown that lightning usually has four main parts.

HOMEWORK 3
Draw a picture of lightning striking the ground. Label the lightning channel and the branches.

REFLECTION 4
How do thunderhead clouds form?

On warm, sunny days, clouds can form. Sometimes they join together, and the air all around rushes into them. They get taller and taller until they reach very cold air, which turns the moisture in the top of the cloud into ice.

HOMEWORK 4
Write a short paragraph explaining to a younger person why the sound of thunder reaches a person after he or she sees lightning.

58 Level 8, Book 13, *Lightning*

Lightning

Name _____

Students use this page to think about their reading and to prepare for discussion. It should not be used for assessment. Sample responses are shown.

REFLECTION 1
What is lightning, and how does it make light?

Lightning is a big electric spark. Electrons moving very fast through the air make the air glow.

HOMEWORK 1
Write a description of a lightning storm you have seen. What did it look like? What did it sound like?

REFLECTION 2
Why does lightning strike when the base of a thundercloud has a negative charge and the ground has a positive charge?

The two opposite charges are attracted. Electrons, which have a negative charge, rush from the cloud to the ground, which has a positive charge.

HOMEWORK 2
Lightning strikes are dangerous. Make a chart naming three other kinds of weather that can threaten safety, explaining how they are dangerous. Do research to gather information for your chart.

Level 8, Book 13, *Lightning* **57**

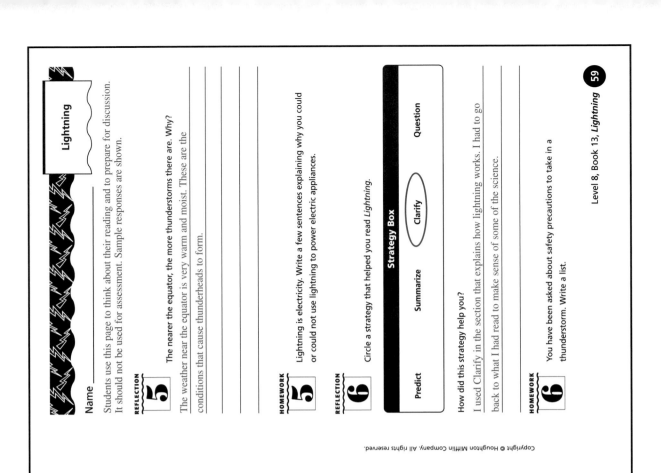

Lightning

Name _____

Students use this page to think about their reading and to prepare for discussion. It should not be used for assessment. Sample responses are shown.

REFLECTION 5

The nearer the equator, the more thunderstorms there are. Why?

The weather near the equator is very warm and moist. These are the

conditions that cause thunderheads to form.

HOMEWORK 5

Lightning is electricity. Write a few sentences explaining why you could or could not use lightning to power electric appliances.

REFLECTION 6

Circle a strategy that helped you read *Lightning*.

Strategy Box

Predict	Summarize	Clarify	Question

How did this strategy help you?

I used Clarify in the section that explains how lightning works. I had to go

back to what I had read to make sense of some of the science.

HOMEWORK 6

You have been asked about safety precautions to take in a thunderstorm. Write a list.

Level 8, Book 13, *Lightning* **59**

Sports Lab: How Science Has Changed Sports

by Robert Sheely with Louis Bourgeois

Materials

Lesson 1	Lesson 2	Lesson 3
• Previously read books • *Sports Lab* pp. 1–6 • Posters 2, 3, 9 • Student Guide (SG) pp. 60–62 • Strategy Prompts, SG pp. 89–91 • Markers	• Independent reading books • *Sports Lab* pp. 7–14 • Posters 2, 3, 9 • Student Guide (SG) pp. 60–62 • Strategy Prompts, SG pp. 89–91 • Markers	• Previously read books • *Sports Lab* pp. 15–23 • Posters 2, 3, 9 • Student Guide (SG) pp. 60–61, 63 • Strategy Prompts, SG pp. 89–91 • Markers
Lesson 4	**Lesson 5**	**Lesson 6**
• Independent reading books • *Sports Lab* pp. 24–31 • Posters 2, 3, 9 • Student Guide (SG) pp. 60–61, 63 • Strategy Prompts, SG pp. 89–91 • Markers	• Previously read books • *Sports Lab* pp. 32–41 • Posters 2, 3, 9 • Student Guide (SG) pp. 60–61, 64 • Strategy Prompts, SG pp. 89–91 • Markers	• Independent reading books • *Sports Lab* pp. 42–47 • Posters 2, 3, 9 • Student Guide (SG) pp. 60–61, 64 • Strategy Prompts, SG pp. 89–91 • Markers • Home Connection letter

*S*ummary: A step-by-step look at how medical and technological advances in science have changed sports, how athletes use these advances to improve their performance, and how they sometimes misuse these advances.

Note: It is not necessary for students to know or be held responsible for all the facts presented in the book. The purpose of these lessons is to help students learn strategies for comprehending informational text.

Scaffolding

Strong Teacher Support	Moderate Teacher Support	Student Independence
		For Book 14 (Category V), encourage students to model and practice using strategies at every opportunity. Coach and model as needed.

Help with Phonics and Decoding Longer Words: For students who need explicit instruction, see the Optional Lesson on page R195 of the Teacher's Resource File in this manual.

Lesson Overview

	Lesson 1	**Lesson 2**	**Lesson 3**
Revisiting (5 minutes)	• Previously read books: Retelling	• Group Conference: Independent Reading	• Previously read books: Retelling
Reviewing (5 minutes)	• Review Reciprocal Teaching Strategies (Posters 2, 3)	• Students Discuss Strategies • Students Summarize	• Students Discuss Strategies • Students Summarize
Rehearsing (5–10 minutes)	• Introduce the Book • Students Predict • Guided Preview, pp. 1–6 Key Vocabulary: *Olympics, springiness, arthroscopy, ultrasound*	• Students Predict • Cooperative Preview, pp. 7–14 Key Vocabulary: *determination, aerodynamics, principles, opponent*	• Students Predict • Cooperative Preview, pp. 15–23 Key Vocabulary: *vault, techniques, visualization, meditation, psychologists, biofeedback*
Reading and Reciprocal Teaching (10–15 minutes)	• Silent Reading • Check Questions • Students Model Strategies • Teacher Models CLARIFY/PHONICS	• Silent Reading • Check Questions • Students Model Strategies • Teacher Models CLARIFY, QUESTION	• Silent Reading • Check Questions • Students Model Strategies • Teacher Models SUMMARIZE, CLARIFY/PHONICS
Responding/ Reflecting (5 minutes)	• Main Ideas and Details (Poster 9, SG p. 60) • Reflection #1 (SG p. 62) • Strategies Discussion (Posters 2, 3) • Homework 1	• Main Ideas and Details (Poster 9, SG p. 60) • Reflection #2 (SG p. 62) • Strategies Discussion (Posters 2, 3) • Homework 2	• Main Ideas and Details (Poster 9, SG p. 60) • Reflection #3 (SG p. 63) • Strategies Discussion (Posters 2, 3) • Homework 3

(Continued on next page)

Lesson Overview

	Lesson 4	**Lesson 5**	**Lesson 6**
Revisiting (5 minutes)	• Group Conference: Independent Reading	• Previously read books: Retelling	• Group Conference: Independent Reading
Reviewing (5 minutes)	• Students Discuss Strategies • Students Summarize	• Students Model Strategies • Students Summarize	• Students Discuss Strategies • Students Summarize
Rehearsing (5–10 minutes)	• Students Predict • Independent Preview, pp. 24–32 Key Vocabulary: *rhythm, potential, flexibility, resistance, stamina, nutritionists, physiology, efficient*	• Students Predict • Independent Preview, pp. 33–42 Key Vocabulary: *cartilage, ligaments, preventative, acronym, compression, elevation, resonance, structures, incision, cruciate, plica*	• Students Predict • Independent Preview, pp. 43–48 Key Vocabulary: *reputation, anabolic steroids, amphetamines, testosterone, amateur*
Reading and Reciprocal Teaching (10–15 minutes)	• Silent Reading • Check Questions • Students Model Strategies • Teacher Models CLARIFY/PHONICS, PREDICT	• Silent Reading • Check Questions • Students Model Strategies • Teacher Models SUMMARIZE, QUESTION	• Silent Reading • Check Questions • Students Model Strategies • Teacher Models SUMMARIZE, CLARIFY
Responding/ Reflecting (5 minutes)	• Main Ideas and Details (Poster 9, SG p. 60) • Reflection #4 (SG p. 63) • Strategies Discussion (Posters 2, 3) • Homework 4	• Main Ideas and Details (Poster 9, SG p. 60) • Reflection #5 (SG p. 64) • Strategies Discussion (Posters 2, 3) • Homework 5	• Main Ideas and Details (Poster 9, SG p. 60) • Reflection #6 (SG p. 64) • Homework 6 • Home Connection letter

Sports Lab	Lesson 1	Lesson 2
Revisiting (5 minutes) *Note: Do an Oral Reading Check only when you are concerned about a student's decoding or fluency.*	▶ **Students reread previously read *SOAR TO SUCCESS* books.** • Have students reread silently for fluency. Remind them to choose a strategy to model in Reviewing. • Have one student read silently and retell a section of a book. Note comprehension. (Use passages and protocols for Retellings, TM pp. R54–R55.)	▶ **Group Conference** Students discuss independent reading. **Prompt:** *If your book has illustrations, how do they help you as you read? If it doesn't, what would help you as you read?* Remind students to keep up their book logs and to bring them to Group Conference for reference.
Reviewing (5 minutes)	▶ **Students review Reciprocal Teaching strategies.** (Posters 2, 3) Students discuss strategies used with *Lightning* and other classroom reading, and model strategies they used in Revisiting.	▶ **Students discuss** strategies they have used with other classroom reading. ▶ **Students Summarize** Students use the book and their Main Ideas and Details Charts to summarize.
Rehearsing (5–10 minutes) *Note: **After** the Guided Preview in Lesson 1, hand out books.*	▶ **Introduce the Book** Show the cover, title page, authors' names, timeline (pp. 57–58), and glossary. ▶ **Students Predict** Ask students what they think the book will be about. Record their predictions. ▶ **Guided Preview/Vocabulary** pp. 1–6. *pp. 1–2* In 1991, Mike Powell (see photo) broke the world long jump record that had been set at the 1968 Mexico City **Olympics** (p. 1). *p. 3* Today's pole-vaulting poles are made out of fiberglass and have more **springiness**. *pp. 4–5* Techniques such as **arthroscopy** and **ultrasound** help athletes recover from injuries. Look at this chart. What has happened over the years?	▶ **Students Predict** Based on pages 1–6, students predict what they might learn in the next section. Record their predictions. ▶ **Cooperative Preview/Vocabulary** Have partners preview pages 7–14, noting the chapter title, photos, captions, and diagrams. If needed, coach as follows: *pp. 7–8* Jack Morris beat the Braves in the World Series with **determination**. *pp. 9–11* **Aerodynamics** (p. 9) is the science that studies how objects move through the air. Scientific **principles** (p. 9) determine how a ball moves. *pp. 12–14* How can a tennis player use the different spins on page 11 against an **opponent** (p. 12)? After the preview, have students find each word boldfaced above, read aloud the sentence, and briefly discuss the meaning.
Reading and Reciprocal Teaching (10–15 minutes) *Note: After students check their predictions, they model Summarize. Then they model all other strategies in any order, using their Strategy Notes. Have students do most of the modeling, but help as needed. Samples are provided.*	▶ Refer to Posters 2 and 3. Remind students to use these strategies as they read. ▶ **Purpose-setting** Students read to check predictions. ▶ **Silent Reading** pp. 1–6. Remind students to use SG p. 61 to help them model strategies. ▶ **After reading, students check** to see if their predictions were verified. ***Teacher Models*** • **CLARIFY/PHONICS** *I don't know this word* (point to **manufacturers** on page 3). *I know the first chunk, **man**. I'll pronounce the **u** as **you** and **f-a-c** like **back**. Now I blend them with **t-u-r** and **e-r-s** to get **man/u/fac/tur/ers**. I reread the sentence and it sounds right. I look it up in the dictionary and see that it means "a person or company that makes things."*	▶ **Purpose-setting** Students read to check their predictions. ▶ **Silent Reading** pp. 7–14. Remind students to use SG p. 61 to help them model strategies. ▶ **After reading, students check** to see if their predictions were verified. ***Teacher Models*** • **CLARIFY** *On page 8, I'm not sure what **the threat on first base had lost its bite** means. I know **threat** is danger. The **bite** is the danger the runner on first might score. But with two outs he's much less likely to score. He's less dangerous, so the threat has **lost its bite.*** • **QUESTION** *What would happen if golf balls were smooth?*
Responding/Reflecting (5 minutes) *Note: Assign the lesson homework (SG p. 62) at the end of each lesson.*	▶ **Main Ideas and Details** Using Poster 9 and SG p. 60, help students fill in one main idea and its supporting details from this section of *Sports Lab*. ▶ **Respond** Students discuss, complete, and share Reflection #1 on SG p. 62. ▶ **Strategies Discussion** (Posters 2, 3) **Prompt:** *When did you use SUMMARIZE? How did it help you?*	▶ **Main Ideas and Details** Help students add to their Main Ideas and Details Charts (SG p. 60). ▶ **Respond** Students discuss, complete, and share Reflection #2 on SG p. 62: *Pick a pitcher and research his best pitch. Describe how he spins the bell.* ▶ **Strategies Discussion** (Posters 2, 3) **Prompt:** *When did you use CLARIFY? How did CLARIFY help?*

Sports Lab	Lesson 3	Lesson 4
Revisiting (5 minutes) *Note: Do an Oral Reading Check only when you are concerned about a student's decoding or fluency.*	▸ **Students reread previously read *SOAR TO SUCCESS* books.** • Have students reread silently for fluency. • Have one student read silently and retell a section of a book. Note comprehension. (Use passages and protocols for Retellings, TM pp. R54–R55.)	▸ **Group Conference** Students discuss independent reading. **Prompt:** *Do you want to read more books by this author or on the same subject? Why or why not?* Remind students to keep up their book logs and to bring them to Group Conference for reference.
Reviewing (5 minutes)	▸ **Students discuss** strategies they have used with other classroom reading. ▸ **Students Summarize** Students use the book and their Main Ideas and Details Charts to summarize.	▸ **Students discuss** strategies they have used with other classroom reading. ▸ **Students Summarize** Students use the book and their Main Ideas and Details Charts to summarize.
Rehearsing (5–10 minutes)	▸ **Students Predict** Based on pages 7–14, students predict what they might learn in the next section. Record their predictions. ▸ **Cooperative Preview/Vocabulary** Have partners preview pages 15–23, noting the chapter title and section headings. If needed, coach as follows: *pp. 15–18* Mary Lou Retton made a perfect **vault** (p. 15) at the Olympics. How do you think she prepared for it? *pp. 19–23* Athletes learn **techniques** (p. 19) like **visualization** (p. 19) and **meditation** (p. 20). **Psychologists** (p. 20) teach them **biofeedback** (p. 21). Have you heard of these techniques before? After the preview, have students find each word boldfaced above, read aloud the sentence, and briefly discuss the meaning.	▸ **Students Predict** Based on pages 15–23, students predict what they might learn in the next section. Record their predictions. ▸ **Independent Preview/Vocabulary** Have students independently preview pages 24–31, noting the chapter title and photo. If they come to words they don't know, remind them to use CLARIFY/PHONICS and the dictionary. (These words may be difficult for some students: **rhythm**, p. 25; **potential**, **flexibility**, **resistance**, **stamina**, p. 27; **nutritionists**, **physiology**, p. 28; **efficient**, p. 30.) After the preview, have students find each word boldfaced above, read aloud the sentence, and briefly discuss the meaning.
Reading and Reciprocal Teaching (10–15 minutes) *Note: After students check their predictions, they model Summarize. Then they model all other strategies in any order, using their Strategy Notes. Have students do most of the modeling, but help as needed. Samples are provided.*	▸ **Purpose-setting** Students read to check their predictions. ▸ **Silent Reading** pp. 15–23. Remind students to use SG p. 61 to help them model strategies. ▸ **After reading, students check** to see if their predictions were verified. ***Teacher Models*** • **SUMMARIZE** *Today, athletes use techniques like visualization, meditation and biofeedback to help them perform.* • **CLARIFY/PHONICS** *To figure out this word (**somersaults** on page 15), I look for chunks. I think **s-o-m-e-r** is probably two chunks—**som** and **er**. I think **s-a-u-l-t-s** is one chunk and that it rhymes with **faults**. I try saying /**sum/er/saltz**/. It sounds right.*	▸ **Purpose-setting** Students read to check their predictions. ▸ **Silent Reading** pp. 24–31. Remind students to use SG p. 61 to help them model strategies. ▸ **After reading, students check** to see if their predictions were verified. ***Teacher Models*** • **CLARIFY/PHONICS** *I am not sure how to pronounce this word* (point to **capacities** on page 28). *First I break it into chunks: **c-a**, **p-a**, and a word I know—**cities**. I try putting all the chunks together and saying /**kay/pay/citeez**/. It doesn't sound right. I try again and say /**kuh/pa/citeez**/. It sounds right. The word is **capacities**.* • **PREDICT** *I predict we will read about other challenges athletes face in the next section.*
Responding/ Reflecting (5 minutes) *Note: Assign the lesson homework (SG p. 63) at the end of each lesson.*	▸ **Main Ideas and Details** Help students add to their Main Ideas and Details Charts (SG p. 60). ▸ **Respond** Students discuss, complete, and share Reflection #3 on SG p. 63: *Write a paragraph describing how you could use visualization.* ▸ **Strategies Discussion** (Posters 2, 3) **Prompt:** *When did you use QUESTION? How did it help you?*	▸ **Main Ideas and Details** Help students add to their Main Ideas and Details Charts (SG p. 60). ▸ **Respond** Students discuss, complete, and share Reflection #4 on SG p. 63: *Write a dialogue in which Nicole and John discuss their skating performances.* ▸ **Strategies Discussion** (Posters 2, 3) Ask students how strategies have helped them so far.

Sports Lab	Lesson 5	Lesson 6
Revisiting (5 minutes) *Note: Do an Oral Reading Check only when you are concerned about a student's decoding or fluency.*	▸ **Students reread previously read *SOAR TO SUCCESS* books.** • Have students reread silently for fluency. Remind them to choose a strategy to model in Reviewing. • Have one student read silently and retell a section of a book. Note comprehension. (Use passages and protocols for Retellings, TM pp. R54–R55.)	▸ **Group Conference** Students discuss independent reading. **Prompt:** *Summarize what has happened in your book so far.* Remind students to keep up their book logs and to bring them to Group Conference for reference.
Reviewing (5 minutes)	▸ **Students model** strategies they used in Revisiting. ▸ **Students Summarize** Students use the book and their Main Ideas and Details Charts (SG p. 60) to summarize pp. 24–31.	▸ **Students discuss** strategies they have used with other classroom reading. ▸ **Students Summarize** Students use the book and their Main Ideas and Details Charts to summarize.
Rehearsing (5–10 minutes)	▸ **Students Predict** Based on pages 24–31, students predict what they might learn in the next section. Record their predictions. ▸ **Independent Preview/Vocabulary** Have students independently preview pages 32–41, noting the chapter title, photo, and bulleted list. If they come to words they don't know, remind them to use CLARIFY/PHONICS and the dictionary. (These words may be difficult for some students: **cartilage**, **ligaments**, p. 34; **preventative**, p. 35; **acronym**, **compression**, **elevation**, p. 36; **resonance**, **structures**, **incision**, p.37; **cruciate**, p. 38; **plica**, p. 39.) After the preview, have students find each word boldfaced above, read aloud the sentence, and briefly discuss the meaning.	▸ **Students Predict** Based on pages 32–41, students predict what they might learn in the next section. Record their predictions. ▸ **Independent Preview/Vocabulary** Have students independently preview pages 42–47, noting the chapter title, photos, and caption. If they come to words they don't know, remind them to use CLARIFY/PHONICS and the dictionary. (These words may be difficult for some students: **reputation**, **anabolic steroids**, p. 43; **amphetamines**, p. 44; **testosterone**, p. 45; **amateur**, p. 47.) After the preview, have students find each word boldfaced above, read aloud the sentence, and briefly discuss the meaning.
Reading and Reciprocal Teaching (10–15 minutes) *Note: After students check their predictions, they model Summarize. Then they model all other strategies in any order, using their Strategy Notes. Have students do most of the modeling, but help as needed. Samples are provided.*	▸ **Purpose-setting** Students read to check their predictions. ▸ **Silent Reading** pp. 32–41. Remind students to use SG p. 61 to help them model strategies. ▸ **After reading, students check** to see if their predictions were verified. *Teacher Models* • **SUMMARIZE** *Runner Joan Benoit injured her knee while training for the Olympic trials. A new technique called arthroscopic surgery repaired her knee and allowed her to compete in the trials just two weeks later.* • **QUESTION** *What does the National Athletic Trainers' Association suggest young athletes do to avoid injuries?*	▸ **Purpose-setting** Students read to check predictions. ▸ **Silent Reading** pp. 42–47. Remind students to use SG p. 61 to help them model strategies. ▸ **After reading, students check** to see if their predictions were verified. *Teacher Models* • **SUMMARIZE** *Sometimes the same things that make athletes better and stronger can work against them. Some athletes take dangerous drugs that improve their performance in the short run but do severe damage in the long run.* • **CLARIFY** *I didn't understand what this word* (point to **out-anythinged** on page 43) *meant. But then I reread the sentence and saw the other words **out-ran** and **out-hit**. Now I understand. The speaker could do anything better than anyone else.*
Responding/ Reflecting (5 minutes) *Note: Assign the lesson homework (SG p. 64) at the end of each lesson.*	▸ **Main Ideas and Details** Help students add to their Main Ideas and Details Charts (SG p. 60). ▸ **Respond** Students discuss, complete, and share Reflection #5 on SG p. 64: *Write a paragraph telling how doctors use RICE.* ▸ **Strategies Discussion** (Posters 2, 3) **Prompt:** *When did you use PREDICT? How did PREDICT help you?*	▸ **Main Ideas and Details** Students complete their Main Ideas and Details Charts and use them to update Poster 9 and to summarize the book orally. ▸ **Respond** Students discuss, complete, and share Reflection #6 on SG p. 64. ▸ **Home Connection** Students take home *Sports Lab* and the Home Connection letter.

Name _____

Main Ideas and Details Chart (continued)

4. The USOC Training Center helps athletes improve their performance.
   a. Athletes get medical tests and physical exams.
   b. Nutritionists evalute the athletes' diets.
   c. Psychologists aid the athletes' mental preparation.
   d. _____

5. Improved medical techniques lessen the effects of injuries.
   a. Weight- and cross-training strengthen muscles and prevent injuries.
   b. Minor injuries are immediately treated with Rest, Ice, Compression, and Elevation.
   c. MRIs are safer than X-rays and provide better information about injuries.
   d. Arthroscopic surgery is less invasive than conventional surgery.

6. Some athletes may misuse science and medicine.
   a. Lyle Alzado used steroids and died of brain cancer.
   b. Steroids have a medical use, but can severely damage healthy bodies.
   c. Steroids are banned from the Olympics and other sports.
   d. Ben Johnson was stripped of his medal and lost millions in endorsements.

Name _____

Sample responses are shown.

Main Ideas and Details

Title *Sports Lab: How Science Has Changed Sports*

1. **Main idea** Modern advances in science improve athletes' performances.
   a. **Detail** Manufactured track surfaces help people run faster and jump farther.
   b. New materials like fiberglass improve sports equipment like pole-vault poles.
   c. Trainers use sensors and computers to analyze an athlete's performance.
   d. Medical advances help athletes recover more quickly from injuries.

2. The way a ball spins as it moves through the air affects its path.
   a. A baseball with backspin will be held up by the air beneath it.
   b. A baseball with topspin will drop sharply.
   c. A baseball with sidespin will follow a curved path.
   d. Tennis players put spin on the ball to affect the way it bounces.

3. Mental attitude can affect athletic performance.
   a. Mary Lou Retton used visualization to prepare for her perfect Olympic vault.
   b. Visualizing a procedure or routine helps your muscles learn it.
   c. Meditation helps an athlete relax and prepare for a performance.
   d. Biofeedback uses a computer to help an athlete learn how to relax.

(Continued on next page)

Sports Lab

Name _____

Students use this page to jot down notes or questions as they read. It should not be used for assessment. Sample notes are shown.

Strategy Notes

Clarify

first Olympic games 1896 p. 2

Biofeedback computer makes a musical tone when body relaxes. p. 21

first fitness laboratory at Harvard University in 1919 p. 35

Predict

I predict that sports medicine and technology will continue to make advances that help athletes move faster and get stronger. p. 4

Question

Why did Joan Benoit ignore the pain in her knee? p. 34

Why should healthy people not take anabolic steroids? p. 46

Summarize

Pages 43–44: Lyle Alzado was a great football player who thought he could become better by taking anabolic steroids. The drugs made him strong, but out-of-control and violent. He got brain cancer, presumably from that drug use. He spoke out against the use of anabolic steroids until his death in 1992.

Sports Lab

Name _____

Students use this page to think about their reading and to prepare for discussion. It should not be used for assessment. Sample responses are shown.

REFLECTION 1

A runner doesn't use much equipment. How can technology improve a runner's performance?

A runner runs on a track surface that can be manufactured to improve performance.

HOMEWORK 1

A runner's shoes can also be designed to help him or her run faster.

Imagine you are a reporter witnessing Mike Powell's record-breaking long jump. Write an article describing the event.

REFLECTION 2

Explain how the study of aerodynamics has changed sports.

The study of aerodynamics has allowed us to know how and why a ball curves in its path through the air. Pitchers can develop pitches that are harder to hit.

HOMEWORK 2

Pick a baseball pitcher and do research to find out what his best pitch or pitches are. Then describe how he spins the ball to achieve that pitch.

REFLECTION 3

Why might mental attitude be important to someone who isn't an athlete?

A person with a positive mental attitude has a better chance of accomplishing goals and realizing success.

HOMEWORK 3

Write a paragraph describing how you could use visualization to make yourself a better student.

Sports Lab

Name

Students use this page to think about their reading and to prepare for discussion. It should not be used for assessment. Sample responses are shown.

REFLECTION 4

Why do you think Nicole and John's coach met with the psychologists too?

The coach might have been able to give the psychologists information about Nicole and John's mental state.

HOMEWORK 4

Pretend you are in the room when Nicole and John meet with the psychologist. Write a dialogue during which they discuss past and future skating performances.

REFLECTION 5

Why can patients recover so much more quickly from arthroscopic surgery than from conventional surgery?

Conventional surgery requires opening up a large section of the body so the surgeon can work. Arthroscopic surgery only requires a tiny incision.

HOMEWORK 5

Imagine you are an athlete who has been injured on the playing field. Write a paragraph telling how the sports doctors help you. How do they use RICE?

REFLECTION 6

Which strategy most helped you to read *Sports Lab?*

Clarify and Clarify/Phonics both helped me to understand the sports terms and explanations about drugs and dangerous practices.

HOMEWORK 6

What is the moral of Ben Johnson's story? Why is it important for young athletes to pay attention to his story? How could this help someone who is not an athlete?

64 Level 8, Book 14, *Sports Lab*

On the Court with...Lisa Leslie

by Matt Christopher

*S*ummary: *On the Court* is a biography of Lisa Leslie, one of the star players for the Los Angeles Sparks of the Women's National Basketball Association.

Note: It is not necessary for students to know or be held responsible for all the facts presented in the book.

Note: This book has been divided into meaningful chunks for reading. Some lessons may need to be extended over more than one day to allow students time to complete the reading. Adjust as needed.

Materials

Lesson 1	Lesson 2	Lesson 3	Lesson 4
• Previously read books • *On the Court with...Lisa Leslie* pp. 1–13 • Posters 2, 3, 8 • Student Guide (SG) pp. 65–67 • Strategy Prompts, SG pp. 89–91 • Markers	• Independent reading books • *On the Court with...Lisa Leslie* pp. 14–24 • Posters 2, 3, 8 • Student Guide (SG) pp. 65–67 • Strategy Prompts, SG pp. 89–91 • Markers	• Previously read books • *On the Court with...Lisa Leslie* pp. 25–36 • Posters 2, 3, 8 • Student Guide (SG) pp. 65–66, 68 • Strategy Prompts, SG pp. 89–91 • Markers	• Independent reading books • *On the Court with...Lisa Leslie* pp. 37–55 • Posters 2, 3, 8 • Student Guide (SG) pp. 65–66, 68 • Strategy Prompts, SG pp. 89–91 • Markers
Lesson 5	**Lesson 6**	**Lesson 7**	**Lesson 8**
• Previously read books • *On the Court with...Lisa Leslie* pp. 56–66 • Posters 2, 3, 8 • Student Guide (SG) pp. 65–66, 69 • Strategy Prompts, SG pp. 89–91 • Markers	• Independent reading books • *On the Court with...Lisa Leslie* pp. 67–84 • Posters 2, 3, 8 • Student Guide (SG) pp. 65–66, 69 • Strategy Prompts, SG pp. 89–91 • Markers	• Previously read books • *On the Court with...Lisa Leslie* pp. 85–97 • Posters 2, 3, 8 • Student Guide (SG) pp. 65–66, 70 • Strategy Prompts, SG pp. 89–91 • Markers	• Independent reading books • *On the Court with...Lisa Leslie* pp. 98–109 • Posters 2, 3, 8 • Student Guide (SG) pp. 65–66, 70 • Strategy Prompts, SG pp. 89–91 • Markers • Home Connection letter

Scaffolding

Strong Teacher Support	Moderate Teacher Support	Student Independence
		For Book 15 (Category V), continue to coach and model as you encourage students to practice using strategies independently.

Help with Phonics and Decoding Longer Words: For students who need explicit instruction, see the Optional Lesson on page R196 of the Teacher's Resource File in this manual.

Lesson Overview

	Lesson 1	Lesson 2	Lesson 3	Lesson 4
Revisiting (5 minutes)	• Previously read books: Retelling	• Group Conference: Independent Reading	• Previously read books: Retelling	• Group Conference: Independent Reading
Reviewing (5 minutes)	• Review Reciprocal Teaching Strategies (Posters 2, 3)	• Students Discuss Strategies • Students Summarize	• Students Discuss Strategies • Students Summarize	• Students Discuss Strategies • Students Summarize
Rehearsing (5–10 minutes)	• Introduce the Book • Students Predict • Guided Preview, pp. 1–13 Key Vocabulary: *exasperated, jeers, long-hauler, bunk, lay-up*	• Students Predict • Cooperative Preview, pp. 14–24 Key Vocabulary: *fundamentals, perennial, aggressors, mesmerized*	• Students Predict • Cooperative Preview, pp. 25–36 Key Vocabulary: *scholarships, slam-dunk, squander, respectable*	• Students Predict • Cooperative Preview, pp. 37–55 Key Vocabulary: *prestigious, designated, controversial*
Reading and Reciprocal Teaching (10–15 minutes)	• Silent Reading • Check Predictions • Students Model Strategies • Teacher Models CLARIFY/PHONICS	• Silent Reading • Check Predictions • Students Model Strategies • Teacher Models SUMMARIZE, PREDICT	• Silent Reading • Check Predictions • Students Model Strategies • Teacher Models CLARIFY/PHONICS	• Silent Reading • Check Predictions • Students Model Strategies • Teacher Models SUMMARIZE, CLARIFY
Responding/ Reflecting (5 minutes)	• Event Map (Poster 8, SG p. 65) • Reflection #1 (SG p. 67) • Strategies Discussion (Posters 2, 3) • Homework 1	• Event Map (Poster 8, SG p. 65) • Reflection #2 (SG p. 67) • Strategies Discussion (Posters 2, 3) • Homework 2	• Event Map (Poster 8, SG p. 65) • Reflection #3 (SG p. 68) • Strategies Discussion (Posters 2, 3) • Homework 3	• Event Map (Poster 8, SG p. 65) • Reflection #4 (SG p. 68) • Strategies Discussion (Posters 2, 3) • Homework 4

(Continued on next page)

Lesson Overview

	Lesson 5	**Lesson 6**	**Lesson 7**	**Lesson 8**
Revisiting (5 minutes)	• Previously read books: Retelling	• Group Conference: Independent Reading	• Previously read books: Retelling	• Group Conference: Independent Reading
Reviewing (5 minutes)	• Students Model Strategies • Students Summarize	• Students Discuss Strategies • Students Summarize	• Students Discuss Strategies • Students Summarize	• Students Discuss Strategies • Students Summarize
Rehearsing (5–10 minutes)	• Students Predict • Independent Preview, pp. 56–66 Key Vocabulary: *collegiate, embroiled, negotiate, bittersweet*	• Students Predict • Independent Preview, pp. 67–84 Key Vocabulary: *stipend, berth, blitzing, consecutive, stint, splays, cosmopolitan*	• Students Predict • Independent Preview, pp. 85–97 Key Vocabulary: *aftermath, aberration, agility, rout, dogged, impromptu*	• Students Predict • Independent Preview, pp. 98–109 Key Vocabulary: *ecstatic, circumference, fledgling, inaugural, outmaneuvered*
Reading and Reciprocal Teaching (10–15 minutes)	• Silent Reading • Check Predictions • Students Model Strategies • Teacher Models SUMMARIZE, QUESTION	• Silent Reading • Check Predictions • Students Model Strategies • Teacher Models CLARIFY/PHONICS	• Silent Reading • Check Predictions • Students Model Strategies • Teacher Models SUMMARIZE, CLARIFY	• Silent Reading • Check Predictions • Students Model Strategies • Teacher Models CLARIFY/PHONICS, QUESTION
Responding/ Reflecting (5 minutes)	• Event Map (Poster 8, SG p. 65) • Reflection #5 (SG p. 69) • Strategies Discussion (Posters 2, 3) • Homework 5	• Event Map (Poster 8, SG p. 65) • Reflection #6 (SG p. 69) • Strategies Discussion (Posters 2, 3) • Homework 6	• Event Map (Poster 8, SG p. 65) • Reflection #7 (SG p. 70) • Strategies Discussion (Posters 2, 3) • Homework 7	• Event Map (Poster 8, SG p. 65) • Reflection #8 (SG p. 70) • Homework 8 • Home Connection letter

Lisa Leslie	Lesson 1	Lesson 2
Revisiting (5 minutes) *Note: Do an Oral Reading Check only when you are concerned about a student's decoding or fluency.*	▸ **Students reread previously read *SOAR TO SUCCESS* books.** • Have students reread silently for fluency. Remind them to choose a strategy to model in Reviewing. • Have one student read silently and retell a section of a book. Note comprehension. (Use passages and protocols for Retellings, TM pp. R56–R57.)	▸ **Group Conference** Students discuss independent reading. **Prompt:** *Why do you think the author decided to write the book you are reading?* Remind students to keep up their book logs and to bring them to Group Conference for reference.
Reviewing (5 minutes)	▸ **Students review Reciprocal Teaching strategies.** (Posters 2, 3) Students discuss strategies used with *Sports Lab* and other classroom reading, and model strategies they used in Revisiting.	▸ **Students discuss** strategies they have used with other classroom reading. ▸ **Students Summarize** Students use the book and their Event Maps (SG p. 54) to summarize pp. 1–13.
Rehearsing (5–10 minutes) *Note: **After** the Guided Preview in Lesson 1, hand out books.* *Note: To keep the emphasis on comprehension, students should not be held responsible for pronunciation of proper names or places.*	▸ **Introduce the Book** Show the cover, title page, and author's name. Explain that this is a book about WNBA player Lisa Leslie. Point out the 12 pages of photos, statistics, and career highlights at the end of the book. ▸ **Students Predict** Ask students what they think they will learn about Lisa Leslie. Record their predictions. ▸ **Guided Preview/Vocabulary** pp. 1–13. *pp. 1–5* Young Lisa became **exasperated** (p. 1), or fed up, with people asking, "Do you play basketball?" *pp. 6–11* Lisa ignored the **jeers** (p. 9), or teasing, from others. Lisa's mother worked as a **long-hauler** (p. 9), driving a truck long distances. Summers, Lisa and her sisters slept in the truck's **bunk** (p. 9). *pp. 12–13* In junior high, Lisa didn't even know how to shoot a **lay-up** (p. 13).	▸ **Students Predict** Based on pages 1–13, students predict what might happen next. Record predictions. ▸ **Cooperative Preview/Vocabulary** Have partners preview pages 14–24, noting the chapter title. If needed, coach as follows: *pp. 14–17* Lisa's cousin Craig taught Lisa the **fundamentals** (p. 16), or basics, of playing basketball. *pp. 18–22* Lisa joined her high school team, **perennial** (p. 18) champs in the L.A. area. In Lisa's sophomore year, however, they lost the state tournament when the opposing team became the **aggressors** (p. 22). *pp. 23–24* Lisa was **mesmerized** (p. 23) when she saw the U.S. women's team play a game. After the preview, have students find each word boldfaced above, read aloud the sentence, and briefly discuss the meaning.
Reading and Reciprocal Teaching (10–15 minutes) *Note: After students check their predictions, they model Summarize. Then they model all other strategies in any order, using their Strategy Notes. Have students do most of the modeling, but help as needed. Samples are provided.*	▸ Refer to Posters 2 and 3. Remind students to use these strategies as they read. ▸ **Purpose-setting** Students read to check their predictions. ▸ **Silent Reading** pp. 1–13. Remind students to use SG p. 66 to help them model strategies. ▸ **After reading, students check** to see if their predictions were verified. ***Teacher Models*** • **CLARIFY/PHONICS** *To figure out this word* (point to **opportunity** on page 4), *I looked at letter patterns to divide it into chunks:* **op**, **por**, **tu**, **ni**, *and an ending I recognize:* **-t-y.** *I blend the chunks and get* **op/por/tu/ni/ty.** *It sounds right.*	▸ **Purpose-setting** Students read to check their predictions. ▸ **Silent Reading** pp. 14–24. Remind students to use SG p. 66 to help them model strategies. ▸ **After reading, students check** to see if their predictions were verified. ***Teacher Models*** • **SUMMARIZE** *Lisa's cousin Craig put her through a workout routine and helped her to learn more about basketball. She got stronger and joined the Morningside Monarchs team. She decided that one day she would win a gold medal in the Olympics.* • **PREDICT** *I predict that Lisa will go on to play successful basketball throughout high school.*
Responding/Reflecting (5 minutes) *Note: Assign the lesson homework (SG p. 67) at the end of each lesson.*	▸ **Event Map** Display Poster 8. Help students fill in events 1 and 2 on their own Event Maps (SG p. 65). ▸ **Respond** Students discuss, complete, and share Reflection #1 on SG p. 67: *How did being tall affect the way Lisa was treated?* ▸ **Strategies Discussion** (Posters 2, 3) **Prompt:** *When did you use CLARIFY? How did CLARIFY help you?*	▸ **Event Map** Using Event Map Poster 8, help students update their own Event Maps (SG p. 65). ▸ **Respond** Students discuss, complete, and share Reflection #2 on SG p. 67: *What things did Craig Simpson do to help Lisa get in better shape?* ▸ **Strategies Discussion** (Posters 2, 3) **Prompt:** *When did you use QUESTION? How did it help you?*

Lisa Leslie	Lesson 3	Lesson 4
Revisiting (5 minutes) *Note: Do an Oral Reading Check only when you are concerned about a student's decoding or fluency.*	▶ **Students reread previously read SOAR TO SUCCESS books.** • Have students reread silently for fluency. • Have one student read silently and retell a section of a book. Note comprehension. (Use passages and protocols for Retellings, TM pp. R56–R57.)	▶ **Group Conference** Students discuss independent reading. **Prompt:** *What is your book about? Tell us about your favorite part so far.* Remind students to keep up their book logs and to bring them to Group Conference for reference.
Reviewing (5 minutes)	▶ **Students discuss** strategies they have used with other classroom reading. ▶ **Students Summarize** Students use the book and their Event Maps (SG p. 54) to summarize pp. 14–24.	▶ **Students discuss** strategies they have used with other classroom reading. ▶ **Students Summarize** Students use the book and their Event Maps (SG p. 54) to summarize pp. 25–36.
Rehearsing (5–10 minutes) *Note: To keep the emphasis on comprehension, students should not be held responsible for pronunciation of proper names or places.*	▶ **Students Predict** Based on pages 14–24, students predict what might happen in the next section. Record their predictions. ▶ **Cooperative Preview/Vocabulary** Have partners preview pages 25–36, noting the chapter title. If needed, coach as follows: *pp. 25–32* Lisa was so good that many colleges offered her basketball **scholarships** (p. 25). She was the first girl to **slam-dunk** (p. 28) the ball. *pp. 32–34* This time, the Monarchs didn't **squander** (p. 33) their lead. They won the championship. *pp. 35–36* Lisa played on the U.S. junior team, which finished with a **respectable** (p. 36) win-loss record. After the preview, have students find each word boldfaced above, read aloud the sentence, and briefly discuss the meaning.	▶ **Students Predict** Based on pages 25–36, students predict what might happen in the next section. Record their predictions. ▶ **Cooperative Preview/Vocabulary** Have partners preview pages 37–55, noting chapter titles. If needed, coach as follows: *p. 37* Lisa was chosen best girls' basketball player and won the **prestigious** (p. 37) Dial award. *pp. 38–51* Once, the coach **designated** (p. 39) Lisa as the girl for all teammates to throw the ball to. She nearly broke the record for points in a game in only half a game. *pp. 52–55* Lisa's first score on the **controversial** (p. 53) SATs was not high enough. After the preview, have students find each word boldfaced above, read aloud the sentence, and briefly discuss the meaning.
Reading and Reciprocal Teaching (10–15 minutes) *Note: After students check their predictions, they model Summarize. Then they model all other strategies in any order, using their Strategy Notes. Have students do most of the modeling, but help as needed. Samples are provided.*	▶ **Purpose-setting** Students read to check their predictions. ▶ **Silent Reading** pp. 25–36. Remind students to use SG p. 66 to help them model strategies. ▶ **After reading, students check** to see if their predictions were verified. ***Teacher Models*** • **CLARIFY/PHONICS** *To figure out the word on page 30* (point to **philosophical**), *I look at letter patterns to break the word into chunks:* **p-h-i, l-o, s-o, p-h-i-c,** *and* **a-l**. *When I blend the chunks, I try* /fie/loe/soe/fik/uhl/. *It doesn't sound right. Then I try* /fi/luh/sah/fik/ull/. *It makes sense.*	▶ **Purpose-setting** Students read to check their predictions. ▶ **Silent Reading** pp. 37–55. Remind students to use SG p. 66 to help them model strategies. ▶ **After reading, students check** to see if their predictions were verified. ***Teacher Models*** • **SUMMARIZE** *Because of Lisa, the Monarchs were the #1 ranked girls' basketball team in California. Lisa decided to go to USC. She had to take the SAT three times to qualify for entry into USC.* • **CLARIFY** *On page 47, the phrase* **saddled with foul trouble** *makes me think of a horse saddle, which is heavy. When Lisa played too aggressively, she had a lot of fouls called against her. The trouble this caused weighed heavily on her.*
Responding/ Reflecting (5 minutes) *Note: Assign the lesson homework (SG p. 68) at the end of each lesson.*	▶ **Event Map** Using Event Map Poster 8, help students update their own Event Maps (SG p. 65). ▶ **Respond** Students discuss, complete, and share Reflection #3 on SG p. 68: *How was Lisa intimidating on the basketball court? Explain.* ▶ **Strategies Discussion** (Posters 2, 3) **Prompt:** *When did you use PREDICT? How did PREDICT help you?*	▶ **Event Map** Using Event Map Poster 8, help students update their own Event Maps (SG p. 65). ▶ **Respond** Students discuss, complete, and share Reflection #4 on SG p. 68: *What were some of the things Lisa felt affected her SAT score?* ▶ **Strategies Discussion** (Posters 2, 3) Ask students how strategies have helped them so far.

Lisa Leslie	Lesson 5	Lesson 6
Revisiting (5 minutes) *Note: Do an Oral Reading Check only when you are concerned about a student's decoding or fluency.*	▶ **Students reread previously read *SOAR TO SUCCESS* books.** • Have students reread silently for fluency. Remind them to choose a strategy to model in Reviewing. • Have one student read silently and retell a section of a book. Note comprehension. (Use passages and protocols for Retellings, TM pp. R56–R57.)	▶ **Group Conference** Students discuss independent reading. **Prompt:** *What is the main topic or problem in your book?* Remind students to keep up their book logs and to bring them to Group Conference for reference.
Reviewing (5 minutes)	▶ **Students model** strategies they used in Revisiting. ▶ **Students Summarize** Students use the book and their Event Maps (SG p. 54) to summarize pp. 37–55.	▶ **Students discuss** strategies they have used with other classroom reading. ▶ **Students Summarize** Students use the book and their Event Maps (SG p. 54) to summarize pp. 56–66.
Rehearsing (5–10 minutes) *Note: To keep the emphasis on comprehension, students should not be held responsible for pronunciation of proper names or places.*	▶ **Students Predict** Based on pages 37–55, students predict what might happen in the next section. Record their predictions. ▶ **Independent Preview/Vocabulary** Have students independently preview pages 56–66, noting the chapter title. If they come to words they don't know, remind them to use CLARIFY/PHONICS and the dictionary. (These words may be difficult for some students: **collegiate**, p. 56; **embroiled**, p. 61; **negotiate**, **bittersweet**, p. 62.) After the preview, have students find each word boldfaced above, read aloud the sentence, and briefly discuss the meaning.	▶ **Students Predict** Based on pages 56–66, students predict what might happen in the next section. Record their predictions. ▶ **Independent Preview/Vocabulary** Have students independently preview pages 67–84, noting chapter titles. If they come to words they don't know, remind them to use CLARIFY/PHONICS and the dictionary. (These words may be difficult for some students: **stipend**, p. 68; **berth**, p. 69; **blitzing**, p. 70; **consecutive**, p. 71; **stint**, p. 72; **splays**, p. 74; **cosmopolitan**, p. 75.) After the preview, have students find each word boldfaced above, read aloud the sentence, and briefly discuss the meaning.
Reading and Reciprocal Teaching (10–15 minutes) *Note: After students check their predictions, they model Summarize. Then they model all other strategies in any order, using their Strategy Notes. Have students do most of the modeling, but help as needed. Samples are provided.*	▶ **Purpose-setting** Students read to check their predictions. ▶ **Silent Reading** pp. 56–66. Remind students to use SG p. 66 to help them model strategies. ▶ **After reading, students check** to see if their predictions were verified. ***Teacher Models*** • **SUMMARIZE** *Lisa was starting center as a freshman. For four years Lisa won awards, broke records, and was even named team captain. Lisa was chosen All-American and women's basketball player of year.* • **QUESTION** *Why isn't women's college basketball taken as seriously as men's?*	▶ **Purpose-setting** Students read to check their predictions. ▶ **Silent Reading** pp. 67–84. Remind students to use SG p. 66 to help them model strategies. ▶ **After reading, students check** to see if their predictions were verified. ***Teacher Models*** • **CLARIFY/PHONICS** *How do I pronounce* (point to **athleticism** on page 41) *this word? I try looking for parts I know. I see **athlet**. I know it has to do with **athlete**. I know **-cism** is an ending. I try **ath/let/i/cism**. It sounds right, and it makes sense.*
Responding/ Reflecting (5 minutes) *Note: Assign the lesson homework (SG p. 69) at the end of each lesson.*	▶ **Event Map** Have students update their own Event Maps (SG p. 65). ▶ **Respond** Students discuss, complete, and share Reflection #5 on SG p. 69: *Briefly summarize what happened at USC with Coach Stanley.* ▶ **Strategies Discussion** (Posters 2, 3) **Prompt:** *When did you use CLARIFY/PHONICS? How did it help you?*	▶ **Event Map** Have students update their own Event Maps (SG p. 65). ▶ **Respond** Students discuss, complete, and share Reflection #6 on SG p. 69: *What important lessons did Lisa learn during the match against Brazil?* ▶ **Strategies Discussion** (Posters 2, 3) **Prompt:** *When did you use CLARIFY? How did CLARIFY help you?*

Lisa Leslie	Lesson 7	Lesson 8
Revisiting (5 minutes) *Note: Do an Oral Reading Check only when you are concerned about a student's decoding or fluency.*	▶ **Students reread previously read SOAR TO SUCCESS books.** • Have students reread silently for fluency. • Have one student read silently and retell a section of a book. Note comprehension. (Use passages and protocols for Retellings, TM pp. R56–R57.)	▶ **Group Conference** Students discuss independent reading. **Prompt:** *Would you recommend your book to someone else? Why or why not?* Remind students to keep up their book logs and to bring them to Group Conference for reference.
Reviewing (5 minutes)	▶ **Students discuss** strategies they have used with other classroom reading. ▶ **Students Summarize** Students use the book and their Event Maps (SG p. 54) to summarize pp. 67–84.	▶ **Students discuss** strategies they have used with other classroom reading. ▶ **Students Summarize** Students use the book and their Event Maps (SG p. 54) to summarize pp. 85–97.
Rehearsing (5–10 minutes) *Note: To keep the emphasis on comprehension, students should not be held responsible for pronunciation of proper names or places.*	▶ **Students Predict** Based on pages 67–84, students predict what might happen in the next section. Record their predictions. ▶ **Independent Preview/Vocabulary** Have students independently preview pages 85–97, noting the chapter title. If they come to words they don't know, remind them to use CLARIFY/PHONICS and the dictionary. (These words may be difficult for some students: **aftermath**, p. 90; **aberration**, p. 91; **agility**, p. 93; **rout**, **dogged**, p. 96; **impromptu**, p. 97.) After the preview, have students find each word boldfaced above, read aloud the sentence, and briefly discuss the meaning.	▶ **Students Predict** Based on pages 85–97, students predict what might happen in the final section. Record their predictions. ▶ **Independent Preview/Vocabulary** Have students independently preview pages 98–109, noting the chapter title. If they come to words they don't know, remind them to use CLARIFY/PHONICS and the dictionary. (These words may be difficult for some students: **ecstatic**, p. 98; **circumference**, p. 101; **fledgling**, p. 102; **inaugural**, p. 103; **outmaneuvered**, p. 105.) After the preview, have students find each word boldfaced above, read aloud the sentence, and briefly discuss the meaning.
Reading and Reciprocal Teaching (10–15 minutes) *Note: After students check their predictions, they model Summarize. Then they model all other strategies in any order, using their Strategy Notes. Have students do most of the modeling, but help as needed. Samples are provided.*	▶ **Purpose-setting** Students read to check their predictions. ▶ **Silent Reading** pp. 85–97. Remind students to use SG p. 66 to help them model strategies. ▶ **After reading, students check** to see if their predictions were verified. ***Teacher Models*** • **SUMMARIZE** *At the 1996 Olympic Games in Atlanta, fans gave a lot of support to women's basketball. The U.S. team won its rematch with Brazil!* • **CLARIFY** *On page 87, I don't understand what a **bullet pass** is. I know that a bullet travels very quickly. It must mean that the ball was thrown hard and travelled quickly.*	▶ **Purpose-setting** Students read to check their predictions. ▶ **Silent Reading** pp. 98–109. Remind students to use SG p. 66 to help them model strategies. ▶ **After reading, students check** to see if their predictions were verified. ***Teacher Models*** • **CLARIFY/PHONICS** *I am not sure how to pronounce this word* (point to **effervescent** on page 99). *I start with chunks I know. I recognize the chunk **cent** at the end. I try looking at other letter patterns. ef/fer/ves/cent. It makes sense. I look it up in the dictionary and see that it means "bubbly."* • **QUESTION** *When does Lisa try modeling?*
Responding/ Reflecting (5 minutes) *Note: Assign the lesson homework (SG p. 70) at the end of each lesson.*	▶ **Event Map** Have students update their own Event Maps (SG p. 65). ▶ **Respond** Students discuss, complete, and share Reflection #7 on SG p. 70: *Why was it so important to Lisa to be a positive role model?* ▶ **Strategies Discussion** (Posters 2, 3) **Prompt:** *When did you use SUMMARIZE? How did it help you?*	▶ **Event Map** Have students complete their Event Maps (SG p. 65). ▶ **Respond** Students discuss, complete, and share Reflection #8 on SG p. 70: *Explain how each strategy helped you read this book.* ▶ **Home Connection** Students take home *Lisa Leslie* and the Home Connection letter.

On the Court with . . . Lisa Leslie

Name _____

Students use this page to jot down notes or questions as they read. It should not be used for assessment. Sample notes are shown.

Strategy Notes

Clarify

21.3 points, 12.2 rebounds, and 6.1 blocked shots at
Morningside games p. 20
the consensus pick p. 37

Predict

Lisa will win a gold medal at the Olympics. p. 84

Question

Why does Coach Stanley want to leave USC? p. 60

Summarize

Pages 49–51: Lisa's little sister had chicken pox. In the game against
Berkeley, Lisa was feverish and nauseous. She realized she had the early
stages of chicken pox. Still she managed to play, score points, and remain
under control.

(66) Level 8, Book 15, *On the Court with . . . Lisa Leslie*

On the Court with . . . Lisa Leslie

Name _____

Sample responses are shown.

Event Map

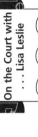

Title
On the Court with . . . Lisa Leslie

Event 1
Lisa played her first basketball game.

Event 2
Lisa joined her high school girls' basketball team.

Event 3
Lisa made the Olympic Festival junior team and was part of its starting lineup.

Event 4
After taking the SAT three times, Lisa was accepted to USC.

Event 5
In her junior year, Lisa played for the U.S. national team and was named Best Female Athlete of the Year.

Event 6
Lisa joined a professional Italian team in order to keep playing basketball.

Event 7
Lisa won a gold medal as part of the USA Women's Basketball team at the 1996 Olympics.

Event 8
Lisa joined the WNBA, playing on the Los Angeles Sparks team.

Level 8, Book 15, *On the Court with . . . Lisa Leslie* (65)

On the Court with . . . Lisa Leslie

Name _____

Students use this page to think about their reading and to prepare for discussion. It should not be used for assessment. Sample responses are shown.

REFLECTION 3

How was Lisa intimidating on the basketball court? Explain.

Lisa was intimidating because she was an aggressive player and could cover different areas of the court well. In school she was known as "Dunkin'" for her slam-dunk shots. When she played internationally, she got most of the rebounds, free throws, and steals per game. People were afraid to throw a ball upcourt because she always seemed to be in the ball's way.

HOMEWORK 3

You have been sent to the Olympic festival and the Junior World Championships on behalf of your school newspaper. Write a short editorial about the women basketball players you're watching—especially Lisa Leslie.

REFLECTION 4

What were some of the things Lisa felt affected her SAT score?

She blamed the fact that she went to a poor, urban school and hadn't gotten as good an education, and that students at her school used old textbooks. She felt the test was biased.

HOMEWORK 4

You are watching the game between Morningside and Berkeley. Describe how Lisa almost broke the record of most points in a single game. What stopped her from achieving her goal?

On the Court with . . . Lisa Leslie

Name _____

Students use this page to think about their reading and to prepare for discussion. Sample responses are shown.

REFLECTION 1

How did being tall affect the way Lisa was treated?

Because Lisa was tall, everyone always asked her if she played basketball. She was teased a lot as she grew up and felt embarrassed, but her mother told her to be proud of being tall. Sometimes Lisa and her sister modeled for charm school fashion shows and stores. When she went to junior high, basketball coaches noticed Lisa because she was so tall.

HOMEWORK 1

Describe how Lisa's mother encouraged her daughters to feel about themselves. Do you think this attitude contributed to Lisa's future successes? Why?

REFLECTION 2

What things did Craig Simpson do to help Lisa get in better shape?

He asked Lisa to do sit-ups and push-ups, and to jump rope. She needed gym exercises to increase her strength. Then Craig helped Lisa learn skills such as dribbling and passing. He also worked with her on improving her jump shots and hook shots. Eventually he had Lisa play games with guys at his gym.

HOMEWORK 2

Lisa was willing to do what her cousin Craig asked her to do. What does that tell you about Lisa?

On the Court with . . . Lisa Leslie

Name _____

Students use this page to think about their reading and to prepare for discussion. It should not be used for assessment. Sample responses are shown.

REFLECTION 7

Why was it so important to Lisa to be a positive role model?

Lisa wanted to show that a woman could be strong and beautiful. She knew that young girls would look up to her and she took that seriously. In addition to playing basketball, she also modeled for magazines. She showed many different sides of herself to her fans.

HOMEWORK 7

Do research to find out how the U.S. Women's Basketball team did at the last Olympics. Write a short paragraph telling what medals, if any, they won, and whether Lisa Leslie was on the team.

REFLECTION 8

Explain how each strategy helped you read *On the Court with...Lisa Leslie.*

Strategy Box			
Predict	Summarize	Clarify	Question

Clarify helped me to understand basketball terms.
Question helped me to figure out what *outmaneuvered* meant on page 105.
Predict helped me guess what Lisa would do next in her career.
Summarize helped me keep track of all the events in Lisa's career.

HOMEWORK 8

What lessons and rewards from Lisa's life would you want to share with your friends?

70 Level 8, Book 15, *On the Court with . . . Lisa Leslie*

On the Court with . . . Lisa Leslie

Name _____

Students use this page to think about their reading and to prepare for discussion. It should not be used for assessment. Sample responses are shown.

REFLECTION 5

Briefly summarize what happened at USC with Coach Stanley.

Coach Stanley wanted to be paid the same as the men's basketball coach. The athletic director said he would raise her salary, but then backed down. Stanley complained publicly and was fired. Her fight put Lisa and her teammates in a difficult position. The team threatened to leave, too, but in the end they stayed and got a new coach, Cheryl Miller.

HOMEWORK 5

How is Lisa Leslie a pioneer in women's basketball? Write a short list of reasons.

REFLECTION 6

What important lessons did Lisa learn during the match against Brazil?

Lisa learned that sometimes you can play hard and still lose the match. She learned that experience matters. Most importantly, she learned that she needed to become a better *international* player.

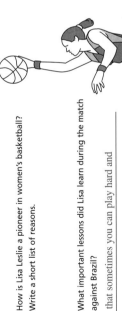

HOMEWORK 6

Pretend you are Lisa giving a press conference during which you announce your goals for the upcoming national team's world tour. Write a statement to the press which says what you hope to accomplish.

Level 8, Book 15, *On the Court with . . . Lisa Leslie* 69

An Even Break

by Sid Hite

*S*ummary: To earn money, 12-year-old Frisk gets the coveted summer job of managing the local pool room and, in the end-of-the-season tournament, proves his skill with a cue stick.

Note: This book has been divided into meaningful chunks for reading. Some lessons may need to be extended over more than one day to allow students enough time to complete the reading. Adjust as needed.

Materials

Lesson 1	Lesson 2	Lesson 3
• Previously read books • *An Even Break* pp. 3–14 • Posters 2, 3, 4 • Student Guide (SG) pp. 71–73 • Strategy Prompts, SG pp. 89–91 • Markers	• Independent reading books • *An Even Break* pp. 15–25 • Posters 2, 3, 4 • Student Guide (SG) pp. 71–73 • Strategy Prompts, SG pp. 89–91 • Markers	• Previously read books • *An Even Break* pp. 26–36 • Posters 2, 3, 4 • Student Guide (SG) pp. 71–72, 74 • Strategy Prompts, SG pp. 89–91 • Markers

Lesson 4	Lesson 5	Lesson 6	Lesson 7
• Independent reading books • *An Even Break* pp. 37–48 • Posters 2, 3, 4 • Student Guide (SG) pp. 71–72, 74 • Strategy Prompts, SG pp. 89–91 • Markers	• Previously read books • *An Even Break* pp. 49–62 • Posters 2, 3, 4 • Student Guide (SG) pp. 71–72, 75 • Strategy Prompts, SG pp. 89–91 • Markers	• Independent reading books • *An Even Break* pp. 63–74 • Posters 2, 3, 4 • Student Guide (SG) pp. 71–72, 75 • Strategy Prompts, SG pp. 89–91 • Markers	• Previously read books • *An Even Break* pp. 75–90 • Posters 2, 3, 4 • Student Guide (SG) pp. 71–72, 76 • Strategy Prompts, SG pp. 89–91 • Markers • Home Connection letter

Scaffolding

Strong Teacher Support	Moderate Teacher Support	Student Independence
		For Book 16 (Category V), encourage students to model and practice using strategies at every opportunity. Coach and model as needed.

Help with Phonics and Decoding Longer Words: For students who need explicit instruction, see the Optional Lesson on page R197 of the Teacher's Resource File in this manual.

Lesson Overview

	Lesson 1	Lesson 2	Lesson 3	Lesson 4
Revisiting (5 minutes)	• Previously read books: Retelling	• Group Conference: Independent Reading	• Previously read books: Retelling	• Group Conference: Independent Reading
Reviewing (5 minutes)	• Review Reciprocal Teaching Strategies (Posters 2, 3)	• Students Discuss Strategies • Students Summarize	• Students Discuss Strategies • Students Summarize	• Students Discuss Strategies • Students Summarize
Rehearsing (5–10 minutes)	• Introduce the Book • Students Predict • Guided Preview, pp. 3–14 Key Vocabulary: *rambunctious, perplexed, coveted*	• Students Predict • Cooperative Preview, pp. 15–25 Key Vocabulary: *scrupulous, volatile, rudiments*	• Students Predict • Cooperative Preview, pp. 26–36 Key Vocabulary: *prerogative, bachelor, matinee*	• Students Predict • Cooperative Preview, pp. 37–48 Key Vocabulary: *trill, dispute, perpetual*
Reading and Reciprocal Teaching (10–15 minutes)	• Silent Reading • Check Predictions • Students Model Strategies • Teacher Models SUMMARIZE	• Silent Reading • Check Predictions • Students Model Strategies • Teacher Models CLARIFY, PREDICT	• Silent Reading • Check Predictions • Students Model Strategies • Teacher Models SUMMARIZE, PREDICT	• Silent Reading • Check Predictions • Students Model Strategies • Teacher Models CLARIFY
Responding/ Reflecting (5 minutes)	• Story Map (Poster 4, SG p. 71) • Reflection #1 (SG p. 73) • Strategies Discussion (Posters 2, 3) • Homework 1	• Story Map (Poster 4, SG p. 71) • Reflection #2 (SG p. 73) • Strategies Discussion (Posters 2, 3) • Homework 2	• Story Map (Poster 4, SG p. 71) • Reflection #3 (SG p. 74) • Strategies Discussion (Posters 2, 3) • Homework 3	• Story Map (Poster 4, SG p. 71) • Reflection #4 (SG p. 74) • Strategies Discussion (Posters 2, 3) • Homework 4

(Continued on next page)

Lesson Overview

	Lesson 5	Lesson 6	Lesson 7
Revisiting (5 minutes)	• Previously read books: Retelling	• Group Conference: Independent Reading	• Previously read books: Retelling
Reviewing (5 minutes)	• Students Model Strategies • Students Summarize	• Students Discuss Strategies • Students Summarize	• Students Discuss Strategies • Students Summarize
Rehearsing (5–10 minutes)	• Students Predict • Independent Preview, pp. 49–62 Key Vocabulary: *gregarious, speculation, ruminations, pundits, piety, gratuities, expectant*	• Students Predict • Independent Preview, pp. 63–74 Key Vocabulary: *facade, reassurance, frugal, eliminated, besieged, relinquishing, careening, chagrin, blatant*	• Students Predict • Independent Preview, pp. 75–90 Key Vocabulary: *sentimental, succession, flabbergasted, exude, empathetic, ambiguously, abate, fathom, tempered, accolades*
Reading and Reciprocal Teaching (10–15 minutes)	• Silent Reading • Check Predictions • Students Model Strategies • Teacher Models SUMMARIZE, CLARIFY	• Silent Reading • Check Predictions • Students Model Strategies • Teacher Models CLARIFY/PHONICS	• Silent Reading • Check Predictions • Students Model Strategies • Teacher Models SUMMARIZE, QUESTION
Responding/ Reflecting (5 minutes)	• Story Map (Poster 4, SG p. 71) • Reflection #5 (SG p. 75) • Strategies Discussion (Posters 2, 3) • Homework 5	• Story Map (Poster 4, SG p. 71) • Reflection #6 (SG p. 75) • Strategies Discussion (Posters 2, 3) • Homework 6	• Story Map (Poster 4, SG p. 71) • Reflection #7 (SG p. 76) • Homework 7 • Home Connection letter

An Even Break	Lesson 1	Lesson 2
Revisiting (5 minutes) *Note: Do an Oral Reading Check only when you are concerned about a student's decoding or fluency.*	▶ **Students reread previously read *SOAR TO SUCCESS* books.** • Have students reread silently for fluency. Remind them to choose a strategy to model in Reviewing. • Have one student read silently and retell a section of a book. Note comprehension. (Use passages and protocols for Retellings, TM pp. R58–R59.)	▶ **Group Conference** Students discuss independent reading. **Prompt:** *How is your book different from the last book you read? Which do you like better? Why?* Remind students to keep up their book logs and to bring them to Group Conference for reference.
Reviewing (5 minutes)	▶ **Students review Reciprocal Teaching strategies** (Posters 2, 3). Students discuss strategies used with *On the Court with…Lisa Leslie* and other classroom reading, and model strategies they used in Revisiting.	▶ **Students discuss** strategies they have used with other classroom reading. ▶ **Students Summarize** Students use the book and their Story Maps (SG p. 71) to summarize pp. 3–14.
Rehearsing (5–10 minutes) *Note: After the Guided Reading in Lesson 1, hand out books.*	▶ **Introduce the Book** Show the cover, title, and author's name. ▶ **Students Predict** Ask students what they think the book will be about. Record their predictions. ▶ **Guided Preview/Vocabulary** pp. 3–14. *pp. 3–6* Twelve-year-old Francis got the nickname Frisk because he was a **rambunctious** (p. 4) child. *pp. 7–9* Frisk was **perplexed** (p. 7) because he knew Shelly wanted to buy a house. *pp. 10–14* Billy Compton owned a hardware store with a poolroom. How do you think Frisk got the **coveted** (p. 13) job of poolroom manager?	▶ **Students Predict** Based on pages 3–14, students predict what might happen in the next section. Record their predictions. ▶ **Cooperative Preview/Vocabulary** Have partners preview pp. 15–25 by reading the first and last paragraphs of each chapter and by skimming the text. If needed, coach as follows: *pp. 15–16* Frisk was **scrupulous** (p. 15) about his work. But he had to deal with Teddy Wald, a **volatile** (p. 15), or explosive, customer. *pp. 17–21* Dan Breedon, the best pool player in town, taught Frisk the **rudiments** (p. 18) of the game. *pp. 22–25* Frisk saved tips and spent little money. After the preview, have students find each word boldfaced above, read aloud the sentence, and briefly discuss the meaning.
Reading and Reciprocal Teaching (10–15 minutes) *Note: After students check their predictions, they model Summarize. Then they model all other strategies in any order, using their Strategy Notes. Have students do most of the modeling, but help as needed. Samples are provided.*	▶ Refer to Posters 2 and 3. Remind students to use these strategies as they read. ▶ **Purpose-setting** Students read to check their predictions. ▶ **Silent Reading** pp. 3–14. Remind students to use SG p. 72 to help them model strategies. ▶ **After reading, students check** to see if their predictions were verified. ***Teacher Models*** • **SUMMARIZE** *Frisk lived in Wilma with his mother, Shelly. They were poor, but Shelly dreamed of getting her own house one day. Frisk decided to get a job. He was hired as manager of the Back Room, a poolroom in Billy Compton's hardware store.*	▶ **Purpose-setting** Students read to check their predictions. ▶ **Silent Reading** pp. 15–25. Remind students to use SG p. 72 to help them model strategies. ▶ **After reading, students check** to see if their predictions were verified. ***Teacher Models*** • **CLARIFY** *I'm not too sure what **red hair brushed into submission** means on page 22. The word **submission** makes me think of giving in, so I think it must mean that Frisk had unruly hair that he brushed into being neat.* • **PREDICT** *I predict that Frisk will get caught up in the Wilma Eight-Ball Tournament.*
Responding/ Reflecting (5 minutes) *Note: Assign the lesson homework (SG p. 73) at the end of each lesson.*	▶ **Story Map** (Poster 7) Review the parts of a story. Have students fill in **Setting** on their Story Maps (SG p. 71). ▶ **Respond** Students discuss, complete, and share Reflection #1 on SG p. 73. ▶ **Strategies Discussion** (Posters 2, 3) **Prompt:** *When did you use PREDICT? How did PREDICT help you?*	▶ **Story Map** Have students update their Story Maps (SG p. 71). ▶ **Respond** Students discuss, complete, and share Reflection #2 on SG p. 73: *How does Frisk win the respect of the customers in the Back Room?* ▶ **Strategies Discussion** (Posters 2, 3) **Prompt:** *When did you use CLARIFY? How did CLARIFY help you?*

An Even Break	Lesson 3	Lesson 4
Revisiting (5 minutes) *Note: Do an Oral Reading Check only when you are concerned about a student's decoding or fluency.*	▶ **Students reread previously read *SOAR TO SUCCESS* books.** • Have students reread silently for fluency. • Have one student read silently and retell a section of a book. Note comprehension. (Use passages and protocols for Retellings, TM pp. R58–R59.)	▶ **Group Conference** Students discuss independent reading. **Prompt:** *Why do you think the author decided to write the book you are reading?* Remind students to keep up their book logs and to bring them to Group Conference for reference.
Reviewing (5 minutes)	▶ **Students discuss** strategies they have used with other classroom reading. ▶ **Students Summarize** Students use the book and their Story Maps (SG p. 71) to summarize pp. 15–25.	▶ **Students discuss** strategies they have used with other classroom reading. ▶ **Students Summarize** Students use the book and their Story Maps (SG p. 71) to summarize pp. 26–36.
Rehearsing (5–10 minutes)	▶ **Students Predict** Based on pages 15–25, students predict what might happen in the next section. Record their predictions. ▶ **Cooperative Preview/Vocabulary** Have partners preview pp. 26–36 by reading the first and last paragraphs of each chapter and by skimming the text. If needed, coach as follows: *pp. 26–29* Frisk says it's Teddy's **prerogative** (p. 27) to be a jerk if he wants to. *pp. 30–36* Frisk suspected that his **bachelor** (p. 32) friend Dan was interested in his mother. He got them together to see a **matinee** (p. 34) of the movie *Dr. Zhivago.* After the preview, have students find each word boldfaced above, read aloud the sentence, and briefly discuss the meaning.	▶ **Students Predict** Based on pages 26–36, students predict what might happen next. Record predictions. ▶ **Cooperative Preview/Vocabulary** Have partners preview pp. 37–48 by reading the first and last paragraphs of each chapter and by skimming the text. If needed, coach as follows: *pp. 37–42* Frisk heard a **trill** (p. 38) in his mother's voice when Dan arrived at the movies. *pp. 43–46* As the pool tournament got closer, Frisk had a **dispute** (p. 43) with a player and he had his **perpetual** (p. 43) problems with Teddy Wald. *pp. 47–48* Frisk practiced pool, even when Dan couldn't. After the preview, have students find each word boldfaced above, read aloud the sentence, and briefly discuss the meaning.
Reading and Reciprocal Teaching (10–15 minutes) *Note: After students check their predictions, they model Summarize. Then they model all other strategies in any order, using their Strategy Notes. Have students do most of the modeling, but help as needed. Samples are provided.*	▶ **Purpose-setting** Students read to check their predictions. ▶ **Silent Reading** pp. 26–36. Remind students to use SG p. 72 to help them model strategies. ▶ **After reading, students check** to see if their predictions were verified. ***Teacher Models*** • **SUMMARIZE** *Teddy Wald taunts Frisk in the Back Room. Frisk decides that Dan and Shelly like each other, and he hatches a plot to bring them together. But first, he goes fishing with Pepper.* • **PREDICT** *I predict that Frisk's set-up for Dan and Shelly will be a success.*	▶ **Purpose-setting** Students read to check their predictions. ▶ **Silent Reading** pp. 37–48. Remind students to use SG p. 72 to help them model strategies. ▶ **After reading, students check** to see if their predictions were verified. ***Teacher Models*** • **CLARIFY** *I didn't understand what **one could see dreams etched in the faces of the Back Room regulars** meant on page 47. Then I reread the sentence and I looked up **etch** in the dictionary. It means "to cut deep lines into," so I guess the dreams of winning are deep in the men's faces.*
Responding/ Reflecting (5 minutes) *Note: Assign the lesson homework (SG p. 74) at the end of each lesson.*	▶ **Story Map** Have students add to the **Major Events** box on their Story Maps (SG p. 71). ▶ **Respond** Students discuss, complete, and share Reflection #3 on SG p. 74: *What kind of a person is Dan Breedon? Describe his relationship with Frisk.* ▶ **Strategies Discussion** (Posters 2, 3) **Prompt:** *When did you use SUMMARIZE? How did it help you?*	▶ **Story Map** Have students add to the **Major Events** box on their Story Maps (SG p. 71). ▶ **Respond** Students discuss, complete, and share Reflection #4 on SG p. 74: *Summarize the interactions at the theater among Dan, Shelly, and Frisk.* ▶ **Strategies Discussion** (Posters 2, 3) **Prompt:** *When did you use QUESTION? How did it help you?*

An Even Break	**Lesson 5**	**Lesson 6**
Revisiting (5 minutes) *Note: Do an Oral Reading Check only when you are concerned about a student's decoding or fluency.*	▶ **Students reread previously read** *SOAR TO SUCCESS* **books.** • Have students reread silently for fluency. Remind them to choose a strategy to model in Reviewing. • Have one student read silently and retell a section of a book. Note comprehension. (Use passages and protocols for Retellings, TM pp. R58–R59.)	▶ **Group Conference** Students discuss independent reading. **Prompt:** *Describe one of the people or characters in your book. What is he or she like? What do you like or dislike about the person or character?* Remind students to keep up their book logs and to bring them to Group Conference for reference.
Reviewing (5 minutes)	▶ **Students model** strategies they used in Revisiting. ▶ **Students Summarize** Students use the book and their Story Maps (SG p. 71) to summarize pp. 37–48.	▶ **Students discuss** strategies they have used with other classroom reading. ▶ **Students Summarize** Students use the book and their Story Maps (SG p. 71) to summarize pp. 49–62.
Rehearsing (5–10 minutes)	▶ **Students Predict** Based on pages 37–48, students predict what might happen in the next section. Record their predictions. ▶ **Independent Preview/Vocabulary** Have students independently preview pages 49–62 by reading the first and last paragraphs of each chapter and by skimming the text. If they come to words they don't know, remind them to use CLARIFY/PHONICS and the dictionary. (These words may be difficult for some students: **gregarious**, **speculation**, **ruminations**, **pundits**, p. 50; **piety**, p. 52; **gratuities**, p. 58; **expectant**, p. 60.) After the preview, have students find each word boldfaced above, read aloud the sentence, and briefly discuss the meaning.	▶ **Students Predict** Based on pages 49–62, students predict what might happen in the next section. Record their predictions. ▶ **Independent Preview/Vocabulary** Have students independently preview pp. 63–74 by reading the first and last paragraphs of each chapter and by skimming the text. If they come to words they don't know, remind them to use CLARIFY/PHONICS and the dictionary. (These words may be difficult for some students: **facade**, p. 64; **reassurance**, p. 66; **frugal**, p. 68; **eliminated**, **besieged**, p. 69; **relinquishing**, p. 71; **careening**, p. 72; **chagrin**, **blatant**, p. 74.) After the preview, have students find each word boldfaced above, read aloud the sentence, and briefly discuss the meaning.
Reading and Reciprocal Teaching (10–15 minutes) *Note: After students check their predictions, they model Summarize. Then they model all other strategies in any order, using their Strategy Notes. Have students do most of the modeling, but help as needed. Samples are provided.*	▶ **Purpose-setting** Students read to check their predictions. ▶ **Silent Reading** pp. 49–62. Remind students to use SG p. 72 to help them model strategies. ▶ **After reading, students check** to see if their predictions were verified. *Teacher Models* • **SUMMARIZE** *Frisk goes fishing and has a run-in with Teddy Wald, but Teddy's dad breaks it up. The pool tournament starts and a mysterious contestant, B. Ferris, shows up. She's a girl!* • **CLARIFY** *I'm not too sure what **wrestle himself to sleep** means on page 57. I reread the paragraph and see that Frisk has trouble sleeping. He is probably tossing and turning, which is like wrestling.*	▶ **Purpose-setting** Students read to check their predictions. ▶ **Silent Reading** pp. 63–74. Remind students to use SG p. 72 to help them model strategies. ▶ **After reading, students check** to see if their predictions were verified. *Teacher Models* • **CLARIFY/PHONICS** *To figure out this word* (point to **consolation** on page 71)*, I look for chunks I know. I know the chunk **con**. I look at the letters and break the middle into **so** and **la**, giving the vowels the long sounds. I know the ending **-t-i-o-n**, which sounds like /**shun**/. I blend all the chunks together and get **con/so/la/tion**. The word makes sense.*
Responding/ Reflecting (5 minutes) *Note: Assign the lesson homework (SG p. 75) at the end of each lesson.*	▶ **Story Map** Have students add to the **Major Events** box on their Story Maps (SG p. 71). ▶ **Respond** Students discuss, complete, and share Reflection #5 on SG p. 75: *Which section did you like best so far in* An Even Break? ▶ **Strategies Discussion** (Posters 2, 3) **Prompt:** *When did you use CLARIFY/PHONICS? How did it help you?*	▶ **Story Map** Have students add to the **Major Events** box on their Story Maps (SG p. 71). ▶ **Respond** Students discuss, complete, and share Reflection #6 on SG p. 75: *Describe how the mood in the Back Room changes.* ▶ **Strategies Discussion** (Posters 2, 3) Ask students how strategies have helped them so far.

Revisiting
(5 minutes)

Note: Do an Oral Reading Check only when you are concerned about a student's decoding or fluency.

▶ **Students reread previously read *SOAR TO SUCCESS* books.**
- Have students reread silently for fluency.
- Have one student read silently and retell a section of a book. Note comprehension. (Use passages and protocols for Retellings, TM pp. R58–R59.)

Reviewing
(5 minutes)

▶ **Students discuss** strategies they have used with other classroom reading.
▶ **Students Summarize** Students use the book and their Story Maps (SG p. 71) to summarize pp. 63–74.

Rehearsing
(5–10 minutes)

▶ **Students Predict** Based on pages 63–74, students predict what might happen in the final section. Record their predictions.
▶ **Independent Preview/Vocabulary** Have students independently preview pp. 75–90 by reading the first and last paragraphs of each chapter and by skimming the text. If they come to words they don't know, remind them to use CLARIFY/PHONICS and the dictionary. (These words may be difficult for some students: **sentimental**, p. 75; **succession**, p. 76; **flabbergasted**, **exude**, p. 77; **empathetic**, p. 78; **ambiguously**, p. 79; **abate**, **fathom**, p. 80; **tempered**, p. 82; **accolades**, p. 86.)
After the preview, have students find each word boldfaced above, read aloud the sentence, and briefly discuss the meaning.

Reading and Reciprocal Teaching
(10–15 minutes)

Note: After students check their predictions, they model Summarize. Then they model all other strategies in any order, using their Strategy Notes. Have students do most of the modeling, but help as needed. Samples are provided.

▶ **Purpose-setting** Students read to check their predictions.
▶ **Silent Reading** pp. 75–90. Remind students to use SG p. 72 to help them model strategies.
▶ **After reading, students check** to see if their predictions were verified.

Teacher Models
- **SUMMARIZE** *Dan is called away for an emergency, so he asks Frisk to fill in for him. The tournament final is Frisk versus Beverly. Everyone in the poolroom is rooting for Frisk. When he wins, he offers the money to his mother.*
- **QUESTION** *Why does Beverly feel that Frisk "puts a dent in her optimism"?*

Responding/ Reflecting
(5 minutes)

Note: Assign the lesson homework (SG p. 76) at the end of the lesson.

▶ **Story Map** Have students fill in the **Outcome** box on their Story Maps (SG p. 71).
▶ **Respond** Students discuss, complete, and share Reflection #7 on SG p. 76: *Why did Frisk believe that no one would feel sorry for him anymore?*
▶ **Home Connection** Students take home *An Even Break* and the Home Connection letter.

An Even Break

Name _____

Students use this page to jot down notes or questions as they read. It should not be used for assessment. Sample notes are shown.

Strategy Notes

Clarify

Aunt Rachel gave Francis the nickname Frisk. p. 4

Turkey Scratch p. 35

Predict

Frisk will set up Shelly and Dan when they go to see *Dr. Zhivago*. p. 31

Question

What did the Eight-Ball Tournament raise money for? p. 22

What did Frisk use to help him make shots when he couldn't reach? p. 45

Summarize

Pages 52–55 Frisk went fishing late one evening at the Turkey Scratch River. Teddy showed up and snatched Frisk's rod from him. Frisk didn't react and felt helpless. Suddenly Teddy's father, Frank, showed up. He barked at his son and demanded that Frisk get his rod back.

An Even Break

Name _____

Sample responses are shown.

Story Map

Title

An Even Break

Setting

Downtown Wilma; inside the Back Room

Characters

Francis (Frisk) Tilden, Shelly Tilden, Dan Breedon, Billy Compton, Pepper Parker, Teddy Wade, Beverly Ferris, the regulars at the poolroom

Problem

Frisk and his mother are poor and do not have the money for things they want. He takes a job at the poolroom, but the regulars pick on him.

Major Events   (May vary)

1. Much to his surprise, Frisk gets hired as the manager of the Back Room, a poolroom at the back of Compton's hardware store.
2. Everyone in the Back Room, especially Teddy Wald, picks on Frisk because he's underage and skinny.
3. Dan Breedon, the best pool player in town, teaches Frisk how to play the game like a champ.
4. Frisk notices Dan's attraction to his mother, and tries to encourage it.
5. After fishing with Pepper, Frisk has an encounter with Teddy Wade.
6. The day of the billiard tournament arrives and everyone comes—including one contestant who is a girl, Beverly Ferris.
7. The final round is Dan Breedon versus Beverly Ferris, but Dan gets called away on an emergency.
8. Dan asks Frisk to fill in for him and play the final games.
9. Frisk agrees to play—and wins.

Outcome

By winning the Wilma Eight-Ball Tournament, Frisk earns the respect of the regulars, including Teddy Wade; he also makes extra money to buy a bike.

An Even Break

Name _____

Students use this page to think about their reading and to prepare for discussion. It should not be used for assessment. Sample responses are shown.

REFLECTION 3

3. What kind of a person was Dan Breedon? Describe his relationship with Frisk.

Dan was a kind teacher and friend to Frisk. He always seems to be around when Frisk needed help. Dan's relationship with Frisk became complicated when Dan became interested in Frisk's mother. But Frisk knew Dan was a good man, so he wanted his mother and Dan to be more than friends.

HOMEWORK 3

3. Imagine you were there when Teddy Wald started pushing Frisk around in the Back Room. What did the two say to each other? Summarize their encounter in a few sentences.

REFLECTION 4

4. Summarize the interaction at the movie theater between Dan, Shelly, and Frisk.

From the moment Dan showed up there was tension. The three of them sat together at the movie with Frisk in the middle. Shelly was crying at the sad parts, but Frisk fell asleep. After the movie ended, Dan walked them home like a "bona fide" gentleman.

HOMEWORK 4

4. Frisk said there are two kinds of people in the world (page 44). Which kind of person are you? Explain.

(74) Level 8, Book 16, *An Even Break*

An Even Break

Name _____

Students use this page to think about their reading and to prepare for discussion. It should not be used for assessment. Sample responses are shown.

REFLECTION 1

1. The Back Room had strict rules for the players. Why do you think these rules were so important?

The rules were important because there were lots of teenage boys hanging out in the poolroom, and teenage boys can sometimes cause trouble. Having strict rules helps stop trouble before it starts.

HOMEWORK 1

1. Frisk was described as "persistent as an aching tooth" when he went looking for a job at the Back Room. Write a short dialogue that shows Frisk asking Billy Compton for the Back Room manager job.

REFLECTION 2

2. How did Frisk win the respect of the customers in the Back Room? Frisk won everyone's respect by being patient and not ever losing his temper. They got used to him.

HOMEWORK 2

2. There are many reasons why Frisk loves the game of pool. What games do you enjoy that much? Pick one game and write a short paragraph telling why you like it.

Level 8, Book 16, *An Even Break* (73)

An Even Break

Name _____

Students use this page to think about their reading and to prepare for discussion. It should not be used for assessment. Sample responses are shown.

REFLECTION 7

Why did Frisk believe that no one in Wilma would feel sorry for him and his mother anymore?

Frisk and his mom were going to move into a house like everyone else; Frisk was going to have a bike to ride, like other kids; Frisk had earned everyone's respect by winning the pool tournament.

HOMEWORK 7

Make a list of all the qualities that you think make Frisk a special character. What do you like or dislike the most about Frisk? Explain in a short paragraph.

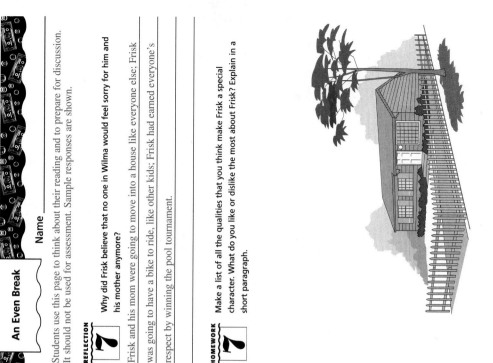

76 Level 8, Book 16, *An Even Break*

An Even Break

Name _____

Students use this page to think about their reading and to prepare for discussion. It should not be used for assessment. Sample responses are shown.

REFLECTION 5

Which section did you like best so far in *An Even Break*?

Pages 3–14	Pages 15–25	Pages 26–36
Arrived in Wilma	Got job at Back Room	Got to know Dan

Pages 37–48	Pages 49–62
The movies	The tournament starts

Which strategy most helped you to read that section?
Predict helped me anticipate the big game, just like the characters in the story did, so it helped me imagine the mood.

HOMEWORK 5

Why did the run-in with Teddy and his father change Frisk's opinion of Teddy? How did the book show you this? Explain in a short paragraph.

REFLECTION 6

Describe how the mood in the Back Room changed from the first to the third round of the tournament.

At the start of the tournament, everyone chuckled at Beverly because she was a girl. But then Mike White lost to her and everyone saw that she was a good player. When she made it to the finals, everyone was jittery but happy to be there, including Teddy Wald.

HOMEWORK 6

How do you play eight-ball? Do research to find the rules, then write a paragraph explaining them.

Level 8, Book 16, *An Even Break*

75

El Duque: The Story of Orlando Hernandez

by Kenneth LaFreniere

*S*ummary: A biography of the New York Yankees pitcher "El Duque" who defected from Cuba after achieving great success on the Cuban national team.

Materials

Lesson 1	Lesson 2	Lesson 3
• Previously read books • *El Duque* pp. 9–15 • Posters 2, 3, 8 • Student Guide (SG) pp. 77–79 • Strategy Prompts, SG pp. 89–91 • Markers	• Independent reading books • *El Duque* pp. 16–29 • Posters 2, 3, 8 • Student Guide (SG) pp. 77–79 • Strategy Prompts, SG pp. 89–91 • Markers	• Previously read books • *El Duque* pp. 30–43 • Posters 2, 3, 8 • Student Guide (SG) pp. 77–78, 80 • Strategy Prompts, SG pp. 89–91 • Markers

Lesson 4	Lesson 5	Lesson 6	Lesson 7
• Independent reading books • *El Duque* pp. 44–57 • Posters 2, 3, 8 • Student Guide (SG) pp. 77–78, 80 • Strategy Prompts, SG pp. 89–91 • Markers	• Previously read books • *El Duque* pp. 58–71 • Posters 2, 3, 8 • Student Guide (SG) pp. 77–78, 81 • Strategy Prompts, SG pp. 89–91 • Markers	• Independent reading books • *El Duque* pp. 72–84 • Posters 2, 3, 8 • Student Guide (SG) pp. 77–78, 81 • Strategy Prompts, SG pp. 89–91 • Markers	• Previously read books • *El Duque* pp. 85–95 • Posters 2, 3, 8 • Student Guide (SG) pp. 77–78, 82 • Strategy Prompts, SG pp. 89–91 • Markers • Home Connection letter

Note: It is not necessary for students to know or be held responsible for all the facts presented in the book. The purpose of these lessons is to help students learn strategies for comprehending informational text.

Note: This book has been divided into meaningful chunks for reading. Some lessons may need to be extended over more than one day to allow students enough time to complete the reading. Adjust as needed.

Scaffolding

Strong Teacher Support	Moderate Teacher Support	Student Independence
		For Book 17 (Category VI), encourage students to model and practice using strategies at every opportunity. Coach and model as needed.

Help with Phonics and Decoding Longer Words: For students who need explicit instruction, see the Optional Lesson on page R198 of the Teacher's Resource File in this manual.

Lesson Overview

	Lesson 1	Lesson 2	Lesson 3	Lesson 4
Revisiting (5 minutes)	• Previously read books: Retelling	• Group Conference: Independent Reading	• Previously read books: Retelling	• Group Conference: Independent Reading
Reviewing (5 minutes)	• Review Reciprocal Teaching Strategies (Posters 2, 3)	• Students Discuss Strategies • Students Summarize	• Students Discuss Strategies • Students Summarize	• Students Discuss Strategies • Students Summarize
Rehearsing (5–10 minutes)	• Introduce the Book • Students Predict • Guided Preview, pp. 9–15 Key Vocabulary: *trademark, obstacles*	• Students Predict • Cooperative Preview, pp. 16–29 Key Vocabulary: *pastime, mechanics, moonlighting, privileges, defector*	• Students Predict • Independent Preview, pp. 30–43 Key Vocabulary: *unforgivable, suspicious, interrogation, dominant, harassing, clamored, surveillance*	• Students Predict • Independent Preview, pp. 44–57 Key Vocabulary: *vessel, capsized miraculously, buoys, immigration, coverage, deport*
Reading and Reciprocal Teaching (10–15 minutes)	• Silent Reading • Check Predictions • Students Model Strategies • Teacher Models CLARIFY/PHONICS	• Silent Reading • Check Predictions • Students Model Strategies • Teacher Models SUMMARIZE, QUESTION	• Silent Reading • Check Predictions • Students Model Strategies • Teacher Models SUMMARIZE, QUESTION, PREDICT	• Silent Reading • Check Predictions • Students Model Strategies • Teacher Models CLARIFY/PHONICS
Responding/ Reflecting (5 minutes)	• Event Map (Poster 8, SG p. 77) • Reflection #1 (SG p. 79) • Strategies Discussion (Posters 2, 3) • Homework 1	• Event Map (Poster 8, SG p. 77) • Reflection #2 (SG p. 79) • Strategies Discussion (Posters 2, 3) • Homework 2	• Event Map (Poster 8, SG p. 77) • Reflection #3 (SG p. 80) • Strategies Discussion (Posters 2, 3) • Homework 3	• Event Map (Poster 8, SG p. 77) • Reflection #4 (SG p. 80) • Strategies Discussion (Posters 2, 3) • Homework 4

(Continued on next page)

Lesson Overview

	Lesson 5	**Lesson 6**	**Lesson 7**
Revisiting (5 minutes)	• Previously read books: Retelling	• Group Conference: Independent Reading	• Previously read books: Retelling
Reviewing (5 minutes)	• Students Model Strategies • Students Summarize	• Students Discuss Strategies • Students Summarize	• Students Discuss Strategies • Students Summarize
Rehearsing (5–10 minutes)	• Students Predict • Independent Preview, pp. 58–71 Key Vocabulary: *interpreter, commotion, deceptive, rivals, invigorated*	• Students Predict • Independent Preview, pp. 72–84 Key Vocabulary: *status, accomplishment, advantage, hostile, momentum, champagne*	• Students Predict • Independent Preview, pp. 85–95 Key Vocabulary: *receptions, intimidated, eminence, reunited, confetti, serenaded*
Reading and Reciprocal Teaching (10–15 minutes)	• Silent Reading • Check Predictions • Students Model Strategies • Teacher Models SUMMARIZE, CLARIFY	• Silent Reading • Check Predictions • Students Model Strategies • Teacher Models SUMMARIZE, PREDICT	• Silent Reading • Check Predictions • Students Model Strategies • Teacher Models SUMMARIZE, CLARIFY
Responding/ Reflecting (5 minutes)	• Event Map (Poster 8, SG p. 77) • Reflection #5 (SG p. 81) • Strategies Discussion (Posters 2, 3) • Homework 5	• Event Map (Poster 8, SG p. 77) • Reflection #6 (SG p. 81) • Strategies Discussion (Posters 2, 3) • Homework 6	• Event Map (Poster 8, SG p. 77) • Reflection #7 (SG p. 82) • Homework 7 • Home Connection letter

El Duque	Lesson 1	Lesson 2
Revisiting (5 minutes) *Note: Do an Oral Reading Check only when you are concerned about a student's decoding or fluency.*	▶ **Students reread previously read *SOAR TO SUCCESS* books.** • Have students reread silently for fluency. Remind them to choose a strategy to model in Reviewing. • Have one student read silently and retell a section of a book. Note comprehension. (Use passages and protocols for Retellings, TM pp. R60–R61.)	▶ **Group Conference** Students discuss independent reading. **Prompt:** *Why did you decide to read this book? Are you glad that you chose it? Why or why not?* Remind students to keep up their book logs and to bring them to Group Conference for reference.
Reviewing (5 minutes)	▶ **Students review Reciprocal Teaching strategies.** (Posters 2, 3) Students discuss strategies used with *An Even Break* and other reading in and out of school, and model strategies they used in Revisiting.	▶ **Students discuss** strategies they have used with other reading in and out of school. ▶ **Students Summarize** Students use the book and their Event Maps (SG p. 77) to summarize pp. 9–15.
Rehearsing (5–10 minutes) *Note: **After** the Guided Preview in Lesson 1, hand out books.*	▶ **Introduce the Book** Show the cover, title page, author's name, and chapter titles. Show the photo section, and mention it covers El Duque's entire career. ▶ **Students Predict** Ask students what they think the book will be about. Record their predictions. ▶ **Guided Preview/Vocabulary** pp. 9–15. *pp. 9–10* In 1998, the crowd at Yankee Stadium cheered as El Duque went into his **trademark** (p. 10) windup for the first time. (Show cover photo.) Describe the windup. What's unusual about it? *pp. 11–12* El Duque's real name is Orlando Hernandez. He was born in Cuba. His father, Arnaldo, was a great pitcher whose nickname was "El Duque"–The Duke. *pp. 13–15* El Duque overcame many **obstacles** (p. 13), such as terrible poverty. He played and practiced all the time. What does this say about his character?	▶ **Students Predict** Based on pages 9–15, students predict what might happen next. Record predictions. ▶ **Cooperative Preview/Vocabulary** Have partners preview pp. 16–29, noting the chapter titles. If needed, coach as follows: *pp. 16–19* In Cuba, baseball isn't just a **pastime** (p. 16), it is a source of national pride. Orlando becomes a star and teaches Livan the **mechanics** (p. 19) of pitching. *pp. 20–23* El Duque starts **moonlighting** (p. 20)– earning extra money. On the national team, he has certain **privileges** (p. 21), like owning a car. *pp. 24–29* Livan thinks about leaving. As a **defector** (p. 26), he would never be able to return home. After the preview, have students find each word boldfaced above, read aloud the sentence, and briefly discuss the meaning.
Reading and Reciprocal Teaching (10–15 minutes) *Note: After students check their predictions, they model Summarize. Then they model all other strategies in any order, using their Strategy Notes. Have students do most of the modeling, but help as needed. Samples are provided.*	▶ Refer to Posters 2 and 3. Remind students to use these strategies as they read. ▶ **Purpose-setting** Students read to check their predictions. ▶ **Silent Reading** pp. 9–15. Remind students to use SG p. 78 to help them model strategies. ▶ **After reading, students check** to see if their predictions were verified. ***Teacher Models*** • **CLARIFY/PHONICS** *To figure out this word* (point to **fundamentals** on page 14), *I start with a word I know at the beginning,* **fun**. *A chunk in the middle,* **ment**, *is pronounced like* **meant**. *I can sound out the chunks* **da** *and* **als**. *When I blend them together, I get* **fun/da/ment/als**. *It makes sense.*	▶ **Purpose-setting** Students read to check their predictions. ▶ **Silent Reading** pp. 16–29. Remind students to use SG p. 78 to help them model strategies. ▶ **After reading, students check** to see if their predictions were verified. ***Teacher Models*** • **SUMMARIZE** *Orlando's steady training pays off, and he becomes a baseball star in Cuba. He gets the nickname El Duque, after his father. Orlando gets married and has two children. His brother decides to defect, but El Duque stays in Cuba.* • **QUESTION** *Did Livan mind being called* El Duquecito *and always being compared to his older brother?*
Responding/ Reflecting (5 minutes) *Note: Assign the lesson homework (SG p. 79) at the end of each lesson.*	▶ **Event Map** Display Poster 8. Help students fill in events 1 and 2 on their own Event Maps (SG p. 77). ▶ **Respond** Students discuss, complete, and share Reflection #1 on SG p. 79: *How did Orlando and his friends afford baseball equipment?* ▶ **Strategies Discussion** (Posters 2, 3) **Prompt:** *When did you use CLARIFY? How did CLARIFY help you?*	▶ **Event Map** Using Event Map Poster 8, help students update their own Event Maps (SG p. 77). ▶ **Respond** Students discuss, complete, and share Reflection #2 on SG p. 79: *Summarize the reasons that Orlando's pitching style is unique.* ▶ **Strategies Discussion** (Posters 2, 3) Ask students how strategies have helped them so far.

El Duque	Lesson 3	Lesson 4
Revisiting (5 minutes) *Note: Do an Oral Reading Check only when you are concerned about a student's decoding or fluency.*	▸ **Students reread previously read *SOAR TO SUCCESS* books.** • Have students reread silently for fluency. • Have one student read silently and retell a section of a book. Note comprehension. (Use passages and protocols for Retellings, TM pp. R60–R61.)	▸ **Group Conference** Students discuss independent reading. **Prompt:** *Describe a funny event or unusual fact from your book.* Remind students to keep up their book logs and to bring them to Group Conference for reference.
Reviewing (5 minutes)	▸ **Students discuss** strategies they have used with other reading in and out of school. ▸ **Students Summarize** Students use the book and their Event Maps (SG p. 77) to summarize pp. 16–29.	▸ **Students discuss** strategies they have used with other reading in and out of school. ▸ **Students Summarize** Students use the book and their Event Maps (SG p. 77) to summarize pp. 30–43.
Rehearsing (5–10 minutes)	▸ **Students Predict** Based on pages 16–29, students predict what might happen in the next section. Record their predictions. ▸ **Independent Preview/Vocabulary** Have students independently preview pages 30–43, noting the chapter titles. If they come to words they don't know, remind them to use CLARIFY/PHONICS and the dictionary. (These words may be difficult for some students: **unforgivable**, p. 31; **suspicious**, **interrogation**, p. 32; **dominant**, p. 34; **harassing**, p. 39; **clamored**, p. 41; **surveillance**, p. 42.) After the preview, have students find each word boldfaced above, read aloud the sentence, and briefly discuss the meaning.	▸ **Students Predict** Based on pages 30–43, students predict what might happen in the next section. Record their predictions. ▸ **Independent Preview/Vocabulary** Have students independently preview pages 44–57, noting the chapter titles. If they come to words they don't know, remind them to use CLARIFY/PHONICS and the dictionary. (These words may be difficult for some students: **vessel**, p. 46; **capsized**, p. 47; **miraculously**, p. 49; **buoys**, p. 50; **immigration**, **coverage**, p. 51; **deport**, p. 52.) After the preview, have students find each word boldfaced above, read aloud the sentence, and briefly discuss the meaning.
Reading and Reciprocal Teaching (10–15 minutes) *Note: After students check their predictions, they model Summarize. Then they model all other strategies in any order, using their Strategy Notes. Have students do most of the modeling, but help as needed. Samples are provided.*	▸ **Purpose-setting** Students read to check predictions. ▸ **Silent Reading** pp. 30–43. Remind students to use SG p. 78 to help them model strategies. ▸ **After reading, students check** to see if their predictions were verified. *Teacher Models* • **SUMMARIZE** *After Livan's defection, life in Cuba becomes unbearable for El Duque. He is not allowed to play baseball, he loses his wife, and he takes a cut in pay at his job. While Livan enjoys success and makes millions playing ball for a U.S. team, El Duque loses almost everything.* • **QUESTION** *Why did El Duque continue to work out every day after he was banned from playing?* • **PREDICT** *I predict that El Duque will defect to the United States.*	▸ **Purpose-setting** Students read to check their predictions. ▸ **Silent Reading** pp. 44–57. Remind students to use SG p. 78 to help them model strategies. ▸ **After reading, students check** to see if their predictions were verified. *Teacher Models* • **CLARIFY/PHONICS** *To figure out this word* (point to **negotiate** on page 54), *I break the word into chunks. I know the chunks **go** and **ate**. The chunck **n-e** is probably pronounced /**nuh**/, and **t-i** might be /**tie**/. I try putting them all together: /**nuh/go/tie/ate**/. That doesn't sound right, so I try /**nuh/go/shee/ate**/. I recognize it. It makes sense.*
Responding/ Reflecting (5 minutes) *Note: Assign the lesson homework (SG p. 80) at the end of each lesson.*	▸ **Event Map** Using Event Map Poster 8, help students update their own Event Maps (SG p. 77). ▸ **Respond** Students discuss, complete, and share Reflection #3 on SG p. 80: *How does El Duque know he will "never play baseball in Cuba again"?* ▸ **Strategies Discussion** (Posters 2, 3) **Prompt:** *When did you use CLARIFY/PHONICS? How did it help you?*	▸ **Event Map** Using Event Map Poster 8, help students update their own Event Maps (SG p. 77). ▸ **Respond** Students discuss, complete, and share Reflection #4 on SG p. 80: *What do the color photos tell you about El Duque's personality?* ▸ **Strategies Discussion** (Posters 2, 3) **Prompt:** *When did you use PREDICT? How did PREDICT help you?*

El Duque	Lesson 5	Lesson 6
Revisiting (5 minutes) *Note: Do an Oral Reading Check only when you are concerned about a student's decoding or fluency.*	▸ **Students reread previously read SOAR TO SUCCESS books.** • Have students reread silently for fluency. Remind them to choose a strategy to model in Reviewing. • Have one student read silently and retell a section of a book. Note comprehension. (Use passages and protocols for Retellings, TM pp. R60–R61.)	▸ **Group Conference** Students discuss independent reading. **Prompt:** *What questions would you like to ask the author about the book you are reading?* Remind students to keep up their book logs and to bring them to Group Conference for reference.
Reviewing (5 minutes)	▸ **Students model** strategies they used in Revisiting. ▸ **Students Summarize** Students use the book and their Event Maps (SG p. 77) to summarize pp. 44–57.	▸ **Students discuss** strategies they have used with other reading in and out of school. ▸ **Students Summarize** Students use the book and their Event Maps (SG p. 77) to summarize pp. 58–71.
Rehearsing (5–10 minutes)	▸ **Students Predict** Based on pages 44–57, students predict what might happen in the next section. Record their predictions. ▸ **Independent Preview/Vocabulary** Have students independently preview pages 58–71, noting the chapter titles. If they come to words they don't know, remind them to use CLARIFY/PHONICS and the dictionary. (These words may be difficult for some students: **interpreter**, p. 58; **commotion**, p. 59; **deceptive**, p. 64; **rivals**, p. 70; **invigorated**, p. 71.) After the preview, have students find each word boldfaced above, read aloud the sentence, and briefly discuss the meaning.	▸ **Students Predict** Based on pages 58–71, students predict what might happen in the next section. Record their predictions. ▸ **Independent Preview/Vocabulary** Have students independently preview pages 72–84, noting the chapter titles. If they come to words they don't know, remind them to use CLARIFY/PHONICS and the dictionary. (These words may be difficult for some students: **status**, p. 73; **accomplishment**, p. 76; **advantage**, p. 80; **hostile**, p. 82; **momentum**, **champagne**, p. 83.) After the preview, have students find each word boldfaced above, read aloud the sentence, and briefly discuss the meaning.
Reading and Reciprocal Teaching (10–15 minutes) *Note: After students check their predictions, they model Summarize. Then they model all other strategies in any order, using their Strategy Notes. Have students do most of the modeling, but help as needed. Samples are provided.*	▸ **Purpose-setting** Students read to check predictions. ▸ **Silent Reading** pp. 58–71. Remind students to use SG p. 78 to help them model strategies. ▸ **After reading, students check** to see if their predictions were verified. **Teacher Models** • **SUMMARIZE** *During a TV interview, El Duque is reunited with Livan. He enjoys the benefits that American baseball players have; but he misses his children. He starts in the Triple A league, but quickly works his way up to the majors.* • **CLARIFY** *I can't remember what this word* (point to **panchalo** on page 63) *means, so I flip back the pages. On page 19, I reread that it is a Spanish word that means "strike out." Now I understand. The fans want him to strike out batters.*	▸ **Purpose-setting** Students read to check their predictions. ▸ **Silent Reading** pp. 72–84. Remind students to use SG p. 78 to help them model strategies. ▸ **After reading, students check** to see if their predictions were verified. **Teacher Models** • **SUMMARIZE** *In one year, El Duque goes from being harassed in Cuba to being a hero in America. He pitches very well, and the Yankees make it to the World Series.* • **PREDICT** *I predict that El Duque will start and win a game in the World Series championships.*
Responding/ Reflecting (5 minutes) *Note: Assign the lesson homework (SG p. 81) at the end of each lesson.*	▸ **Event Map** Using Event Map Poster 8, help students update their own Event Maps (SG p. 77). ▸ **Respond** Students discuss, complete, and share Reflection #5 on SG p. 81: *Describe the relationship between El Duque and his Yankees teammates.* ▸ **Strategies Discussion** (Posters 2, 3) **Prompt:** *When did you use QUESTION? How did QUESTION help you?*	▸ **Event Map** Using Event Map Poster 8, help students update their own Event Maps (SG p. 77). ▸ **Respond** Students discuss, complete, and share Reflection #6 on SG p. 81: *Write a newspaper article profiling El Duque.* ▸ **Strategies Discussion** (Posters 2, 3) **Prompt:** *When did you use SUMMARIZE? How did it help you?*

El Duque	**Lesson 7**

Revisiting
(5 minutes)

Note: Do an Oral Reading Check only when you are concerned about a student's decoding or fluency.

▶ **Students reread previously read** *SOAR TO SUCCESS* **books.**
- Have students reread silently for fluency.
- Have one student read silently and retell a section of a book. Note comprehension. (Use passages and protocols for Retellings, TM pp. R60–R61.)

Reviewing
(5 minutes)

▶ **Students discuss** strategies they have used with other reading in and out of school.
▶ **Students Summarize** Students use the book and their Event Maps (SG p. 77) to summarize pp. 72–84.

Rehearsing
(5–10 minutes)

▶ **Students Predict** Based on pages 72–84, students predict what might happen in the final section. Record their predictions.
▶ **Independent Preview/Vocabulary** Have students independently preview pages 85–97, noting the chapter titles. If they come to words they don't know, remind them to use CLARIFY/PHONICS and the dictionary. (These words may be difficult for some students: **receptions**, p. 87; **intimidated**, **eminence**, p. 90; **reunited**, p. 93; **confetti**, **serenaded**, p. 95.)
After the preview, have students find each word boldfaced above, read aloud the sentence, and briefly discuss the meaning.

Reading and Reciprocal Teaching
(10–15 minutes)

Note: After students check their predictions, they model Summarize. Then they model all other strategies in any order, using their Strategy Notes. Have students do most of the modeling, but help as needed. Samples are provided.

▶ **Purpose-setting** Students read to check predictions.
▶ **Silent Reading** pp. 85–97. Remind students to use SG p. 78 to help them model strategies.
▶ **After reading, students check** to see if their predictions were verified.

Teacher Models
- **SUMMARIZE** *El Duque gets to pitch at the World Series. The Yankees win. His family is given permission to celebrate the win in the U.S.*
- **CLARIFY** *I don't know what this word* (point to **countrymen** on page 85) *means. I know that* **country** *is the opposite of* **city***, but that doesn't help. So I look it up in the dictionary. I find out that* **countryman** *means "a person from the same country as another." So El Duque's countrymen are people from Cuba.*

Responding/ Reflecting
(5 minutes)

Note: Assign the lesson homework (SG p. 82) at the end of the lesson.

▶ **Event Map** Have students complete their Event Maps (SG p. 77).
▶ **Respond** Students discuss, complete, and share Reflection #7 on SG p. 82: *Circle a strategy that helped you to read* El Duque. *How did it help you?*
▶ **Home Connection** Students take home *El Duque* and the Home Connection letter.

El Duque

Name _____

Strategy Notes

Students use this page to jot down notes or questions as they read. It should not be used for assessment. Sample notes are shown.

Clarify

"El Duque"? p. 9

first-ever gold medal in baseball p. 23

Paul O'Neill catches ball twice? p. 88

Predict

I predict that El Duque will play in the World Series. p. 79

Question

Why does Livan decide to defect? pp. 25–26

Why does El Duque go to Costa Rica instead of the United States? p. 52

Summarize

Pages 58–59: El Duque arrives in the United States and is mobbed by fans. He is reunited with Noris. He gives a press conference in which he explains why he left Cuba. In the middle of the press conference, he is reunited with Livan. He is so happy that he cannot stop crying.

El Duque

Name _____

Event Map

Sample responses are shown.

Title
El Duque

Event 1
Orlando Hernandez is raised by his single mother in Cuba.

Event 2
He becomes a baseball star and gets the nickname "El Duque."

Event 3
His brother Livan decides to defect from Cuba.

Event 4
Cuban officials make life hard for El Duque.

Event 5
El Duque finally decides he must also defect. He escapes to Costa Rica.

Event 6
He is reunited with his brother Livan.

Event 7
El Duque moves from the Triple-A league to the Major League as a starting pitcher for the Yankees.

Event 8
With El Duque pitching well, the Yankees win the World Series. El Duque's family is permitted to come to New York to celebrate.

El Duque

Name _____

Students use this page to think about their reading and to prepare for discussion. It should not be used for assessment. Sample responses are shown.

HOMEWORK 1

Although Orlando and his friends could not afford equipment, they found ways to play baseball. How?

They used broomsticks for bats and a large cork for a ball. There were no baseball diamonds, so they played in any open field they could find.

HOMEWORK 1

Orlando was very close to his mother and his brother. How do you imagine these relationships made him a stronger person and better baseball player?

HOMEWORK 2

Describe El Duque's unique pitching position.

(1) He starts by lifting his knee nearly to his ear.

(2) He curls his upper body into a ball.

(3) While most pitchers have one or two release points, he has six.

HOMEWORK 2

Compare and contrast the ways the Cuban and American baseball leagues are organized. Which do you think is better? Why?

El Duque

Name _____

Students use this page to think about their reading and to prepare for discussion. It should not be used for assessment. Sample responses are shown.

HOMEWORK 3

How does El Duque know he will "never play baseball in Cuba again?"

It's been clear for some time that the Cuban government has been punishing him for Livan's defection—taking away things like his car and his nice house. But when they warn him about talking to the media during the Pope's visit, he realizes they are afraid of what he might do. And that means they'll never let him receive public attention or play baseball again.

HOMEWORK 3

When El Duque sees Livan play in the World Series, he says "his victory is my victory." What do you think he means?

HOMEWORK 4

Look through color photos and read the captions. What do they tell you about El Duque's personality?

El Duque is almost always smiling. He likes to be around his fans and other people and he is very generous with them, especially children. When he isn't playing ball, he also finds time to see and talk to his family as much as possible. He seems like a kind, thoughtful, hard-working player.

HOMEWORK 4

Find Cuba and Costa Rica on a map. Draw your own map showing a route El Duque and the others might have taken.

El Duque

Name _____

Students use this page to think about their reading and to prepare for discussion. It should not be used for assessment. Sample responses are shown.

REFLECTION 7

Circle a strategy that helped you to read *El Duque*.

Strategy Box

Predict   Summarize   (Clarify)   Question

Explain how you used this strategy.

Clarify helped me learn the differences between the way American baseball is organized and the way Cuban baseball is organized—as well as the similarities, too.

HOMEWORK 7

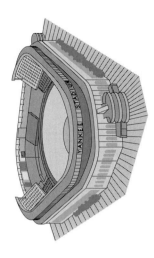

Of all his successes, which do you think was El Duque's *greatest victory*? Why?

82   Level 8, Book 17, *El Duque*

El Duque

Name _____

Students use this page to think about their reading and to prepare for discussion. It should not be used for assessment. Sample responses are shown.

HOMEWORK 5

Describe the relationship between El Duque and his teammates on the Yankees.

His teammates respect him for his amazing pitching talent, as well as for all the hardships he's had to go through.

HOMEWORK 5

What do you think makes someone into a hero? Make a list of all the reasons you think El Duque should or should not be called a hero.

REFLECTION 6

What does El Duque mean when he says, "When you can't pitch with your arm, you have to pitch with your heart"?

El Duque knows all of the physical skills that are needed to be a strong pitcher, but he also knows how much a pitcher has to love the game and really want to win.

HOMEWORK 6

El Duque is heading to the World Series! Write a newspaper article profiling this amazing pitcher. Explain why he is one of the Yankees' most valuable assets for winning the championship.

Level 8, Book 17, *El Duque*   81

Marisol and Magdalena: The Sound of our Sisterhood

by Veronica Chambers

*S*ummary: When Marisol is sent to Panama to learn more about her homeland, she is separated from her best friend, Magdalena.

Note: This book has been divided into meaningful chunks for reading. Some lessons may need to be extended over more than one day to allow students enough time to complete the reading. Adjust as needed.

Materials

Lesson 1	Lesson 2	Lesson 3	Lesson 4
• Previously read books • *Marisol and Magdalena* pp. 1–17 • Posters 2, 3, 4 • Student Guide (SG) pp. 74–76 • Strategy Prompts, SG pp. 87–89 • Markers	• Independent reading books • *Marisol and Magdalena* pp. 18–36 • Posters 2, 3, 4 • Student Guide (SG) pp. 74–76 • Strategy Prompts, SG pp. 87–89 • Markers	• Previously read books • *Marisol and Magdalena* pp. 37–54 • Posters 2, 3, 4 • Student Guide (SG) pp. 74–75, 77 • Strategy Prompts, SG pp. 87–89 • Markers	• Independent reading books • *Marisol and Magdalena* pp. 55–71 • Posters 2, 3, 4 • Student Guide (SG) pp. 74–75, 77 • Strategy Prompts, SG pp. 87–89 • Markers
Lesson 5	**Lesson 6**	**Lesson 7**	**Lesson 8**
• Previously read books • *Marisol and Magdalena* pp. 72–89 • Posters 2, 3, 4 • Student Guide (SG) pp. 74–75, 78 • Strategy Prompts, SG pp. 87–89 • Markers	• Independent reading books • *Marisol and Magdalena* pp. 90–103 • Posters 2, 3, 4 • Student Guide (SG) pp. 74–75, 78 • Strategy Prompts, SG pp. 87–89 • Markers	• Previously read books • *Marisol and Magdalena* pp. 104–123 • Posters 2, 3, 4 • Student Guide (SG) pp. 74–75, 79 • Strategy Prompts, SG pp. 87–89 • Markers	• Independent reading books • *Marisol and Magdalena* pp. 124–141 • Posters 2, 3, 4 • Student Guide (SG) pp. 74–75, 79 • Strategy Prompts, SG pp. 87–89 • Markers • Home Connection letter

Scaffolding

Strong Teacher Support	Moderate Teacher Support	Student Independence
		For Book 18 (Category VI), encourage students to model and practice using strategies at every opportunity. Coach and model as needed.

Help with Phonics and Decoding Longer Words: For students who need explicit instruction, see the Optional Lesson on page R199 of the Teacher's Resource File in this manual.

Lesson Overview

	Lesson 1	Lesson 2	Lesson 3	Lesson 4
Revisiting (5 minutes)	• Previously read books: Retelling	• Group Conference: Independent Reading	• Previously read books: Retelling	• Group Conference: Independent Reading
Reviewing (5 minutes)	• Review Reciprocal Teaching Strategies (Posters 2, 3)	• Students Discuss Strategies • Students Summarize	• Students Discuss Strategies • Students Summarize	• Students Discuss Strategies • Students Summarize
Rehearsing (5–10 minutes)	• Introduce the Book • Students Predict • Guided Preview, pp. 1–17 Key Vocabulary: *Panamanian, quinceañera*	• Students Predict • Cooperative Preview, pp. 18–36 Key Vocabulary: *piñata, swiveling*	• Students Predict • Independent Preview, pp. 37–54 Key Vocabulary: *grudge, semester, tantrums, convertible*	• Students Predict • Independent Preview, pp. 55–71 Key Vocabulary: *whirlwind, heritage, sarcastically, novena, valentine, astronaut*
Reading and Reciprocal Teaching (10–15 minutes)	• Silent Reading • Check Predictions • Students Model Strategies • Teacher Models QUESTION, CLARIFY	• Silent Reading • Check Predictions • Students Model Strategies • Teacher Models SUMMARIZE, CLARIFY/PHONICS	• Silent Reading • Check Predictions • Students Model Strategies • Teacher Models SUMMARIZE, PREDICT	• Silent Reading • Check Predictions • Students Model Strategies • Teacher Models SUMMARIZE, CLARIFY/PHONICS
Responding/ Reflecting (5 minutes)	• Story Map (Poster 8, SG p. 83) • Reflection #1 (SG p. 85) • Strategies Discussion (Posters 2, 3) • Homework 1	• Story Map (Poster 8, SG p. 83) • Reflection #2 (SG p. 85) • Strategies Discussion (Posters 2, 3) • Homework 2	• Story Map (Poster 8, SG p. 83) • Reflection #3 (SG p. 86) • Strategies Discussion (Posters 2, 3) • Homework 3	• Story Map (Poster 8, SG p. 83) • Reflection #4 (SG p. 86) • Strategies Discussion (Posters 2, 3) • Homework 4

(Continued on next page)

Lesson Overview

	Lesson 5	Lesson 6	Lesson 7	Lesson 8
Revisiting (5 minutes)	• Previously read books: Retelling	• Group Conference: Independent Reading	• Previously read books: Retelling	• Group Conference: Independent Reading
Reviewing (5 minutes)	• Students Model Strategies • Students Summarize	• Students Discuss Strategies • Students Summarize	• Students Discuss Strategies • Students Summarize	• Students Discuss Strategies • Students Summarize
Rehearsing (5–10 minutes)	• Students Predict • Independent Preview, pp. 72–89 Key Vocabulary: *doilies, cashmere, poise, antennae, wares, plunged, chlorine, sync*	• Students Predict • Independent Preview, pp. 90–103 Key Vocabulary: *dreadlocks, mimicking, hybrid, cretin, senile, abundance*	• Students Predict • Independent Preview, pp. 104–123 Key Vocabulary: *psyched, comfy, pulsated, monogram, choreographing, obsession*	• Students Predict • Independent Preview, pp. 124–141 Key Vocabulary: *consequences, congas, trampoline, bargain, hysterically*
Reading and Reciprocal Teaching (10–15 minutes)	• Silent Reading • Check Predictions • Students Model Strategies • Teacher Models SUMMARIZE, CLARIFY/PHONICS	• Silent Reading • Check Predictions • Students Model Strategies • Teacher Models SUMMARIZE, QUESTION	• Silent Reading • Check Predictions • Students Model Strategies • Teacher Models SUMMARIZE, PREDICT	• Silent Reading • Check Predictions • Students Model Strategies • Teacher Models SUMMARIZE, CLARIFY
Responding/ Reflecting (5 minutes)	• Story Map (Poster 8, SG p. 83) • Reflection #5 (SG p. 87) • Strategies Discussion (Posters 2, 3) • Homework 5	• Story Map (Poster 8, SG p. 83) • Reflection #6 (SG p. 87) • Strategies Discussion (Posters 2, 3) • Homework 6	• Story Map (Poster 8, SG p. 83) • Reflection #7 (SG p. 88) • Strategies Discussion (Posters 2, 3) • Homework 7	• Story Map (Poster 8, SG p. 83) • Reflection #8 (SG p. 88) • Homework 8 • Home Connection letter

Marisol and Magdalena

	Lesson 1	Lesson 2
Revisiting (5 minutes) *Note: Do an Oral Reading Check only when you are concerned about a student's decoding or fluency.*	► **Students reread previously read *SOAR TO SUCCESS* books.** • Have students reread silently for fluency. Remind them to choose a strategy to model in Reviewing. • Have one student read silently and retell a section of a book. Note comprehension. (Use passages and protocols for Retellings, TM pp. R62–R63.)	► **Group Conference** Students discuss independent reading. **Prompt:** *Why do you think the author decided to write the book you are reading?* Remind students to keep up their book logs and to bring them to Group Conference for reference.
Reviewing (5 minutes)	► **Students review Reciprocal Teaching strategies.** (Posters 2, 3) Students discuss strategies used with *El Duque* and other reading in and out of school, and model strategies they used in Revisiting.	► **Students discuss** strategies they have used with other reading in and out of school. ► **Students Summarize** Students use the book and their Story Maps (SG p. 74) to summarize pp. 1–17.
Rehearsing (5–10 minutes) *Note: **After** the Guided Preview in Lesson 1, hand out books.*	► **Introduce the book.** Show the cover, title page, and author's name. ► **Students Predict** Ask students what they think the book will be about. Record their predictions. ► **Guided Preview/Vocabulary** pp. 1–17. *pp. 1–7* Marisol and Magda come from **Panamanian** (p. 2) families–they were born in New York, but Magda's older brothers and sisters were born in Panama. Their mothers speak Spanish to each other. *pp. 7–9* Magda's sister Evelyn is getting ready for her **quinceañera** (p. 7), which is like a "sweet fifteen" party. *pp. 10–17* Marisol and Magda talk about boys they like. What else might they do at a sleepover?	► **Students Predict** Based on pages 1–17, students predict what might happen in the next section. Record their predictions. ► **Cooperative Preview/Vocabulary** Have partners preview pages 18–36 by reading the first and last paragraphs of each chapter and by skimming the text. If needed, coach as follows: *pp. 18–27* At the party, the children hit at a **piñata** (p. 20). The adults dance, **swiveling** (p. 23) their hips to the music. Tia China gives Marisol dancing lessons. Why does Roxana make fun of Marisol? *pp. 28–36* Marisol and Magda sit at the same lunch table as Stephen Cardoza, the boy Magda likes. After the preview, have students find each word boldfaced above, read aloud the sentence, and briefly discuss the meaning.
Reading and Reciprocal Teaching (10–15 minutes) *Note: After students check their predictions, they model Summarize. Then they model all other strategies in any order, using their Strategy Notes. Have students do most of the modeling, but help as needed. Samples are provided.*	► Refer to Posters 2 and 3. Remind students to use these strategies as they read. ► **Purpose-setting** Students read to check their predictions. ► **Silent Reading** pp. 1–17. Remind students to use SG p. 84 to help them model strategies. ► **After reading, students check** to see if their predictions were verified. ***Teacher Models*** • **QUESTION** *Why does Marisol want to have her own quince?* • **CLARIFY** *On page 17, I don't know what **tias** means, so I look back. On page 1, Marisol calls Magda's mother "Tia Luisa." The word on page 17 seems to refer to relatives. Magda's mother isn't a relative, but Marisol might call her "Aunt Luisa." Maybe **tias** means "aunts."*	► **Purpose-setting** Students read to check their predictions. ► **Silent Reading** pp. 18–36. Remind students to use SG p. 84 to help them model strategies. ► **After reading, students check** to see if their predictions were verified. ***Teacher Models*** • **SUMMARIZE** *Marisol gets back at Roxana. Magda talks to the boy she likes. Marisol studies and makes dinner for herself and her mother.* • **CLARIFY/PHONICS** *I don't know this word (point to **impersonation** on page 31). I know **i-m-** is a prefix; **person** is a word I know; **a** is probably long; and I know that **-t-i-o-n** is /**shun**/. I blend them together and I get **im/person/a/tion**, and it makes sense.*
Responding/ Reflecting (5 minutes) *Note: Assign the lesson homework (SG p. 85) at the end of each lesson.*	► **Story Map** (Poster 7) Review the parts of a story. Have students fill in **Setting** on their Story Maps. ► **Respond** Students discuss, complete, and share Reflection #1 on SG p. 85: *What role does food play in the family's gathering?* ► **Strategies Discussion** (Posters 2, 3) **Prompt:** *How did you use SUMMARIZE? How did it help you?*	► **Story Map** Have students update their Story Maps (SG p. 83). ► **Respond** Students discuss, complete, and share Reflection #2 on SG p. 85: *Describe the relationship between Roxana and Marisol.* ► **Strategies Discussion** (Posters 2, 3) **Prompt:** *How did you use CLARIFY? How did CLARIFY help you?*

Marisol and Magdalena	Lesson 3	Lesson 4
Revisiting (5 minutes) *Note: Do an Oral Reading Check only when you are concerned about a student's decoding or fluency.*	▶ **Students reread previously read SOAR TO SUCCESS books.** • Have students reread silently for fluency. • Have one student read silently and retell a section of a book. Note comprehension. (Use passages and protocols for Retellings, TM pp. R62–R63.)	▶ **Group Conference** Students discuss independent reading. **Prompt:** *How do you predict your book will end? Why do you think that?* Remind students to keep up their book logs and to bring them to Group Conference for reference.
Reviewing (5 minutes)	▶ **Students discuss** strategies they have used with other reading in and out of school. ▶ **Students Summarize** Students use the book and their Story Maps (SG p. 74) to summarize pp. 18–36.	▶ **Students discuss** strategies they have used with other reading in and out of school. ▶ **Students Summarize** Students use the book and their Story Maps (SG p. 74) to summarize pp. 37–54.
Rehearsing (5–10 minutes)	▶ **Students Predict** Based on pages 18–36, students predict what might happen in the next section. Record their predictions. ▶ **Independent Preview/Vocabulary** Have students independently preview pages 37–54 by reading the first and last paragraphs of each chapter and by skimming the text. If they come to words they don't know, remind them to use CLARIFY/PHONICS and the dictionary. (These words may be difficult for some students: **grudge**, p. 37; **semester**, p. 42; **tantrums**, p. 45; **convertible**, p. 51.) After the preview, have students find each word boldfaced above, read aloud the sentence, and briefly discuss the meaning.	▶ **Students Predict** Based on pages 37–54, students predict what might happen in the next section. Record their predictions. ▶ **Independent Preview/Vocabulary** Have students independently preview pages 55–71 by reading the first and last paragraphs of each chapter and by skimming the text. If they come to words they don't know, remind them to use CLARIFY/PHONICS and the dictionary. (These words may be difficult for some students: **whirlwind**, p. 57; **heritage**, p. 58; **sarcastically**, p. 60; **novena**, p. 61; **valentine**, p. 66; **astronaut**, p. 70.) After the preview, have students find each word boldfaced above, read aloud the sentence, and briefly discuss the meaning.
Reading and Reciprocal Teaching (10–15 minutes) *Note: After students check their predictions, they model Summarize. Then they model all other strategies in any order, using their Strategy Notes. Have students do most of the modeling, but help as needed. Samples are provided.*	▶ **Purpose-setting** Students read to check their predictions. ▶ **Silent Reading** pp. 37–54. Remind students to use SG p. 84 to help them model strategies. ▶ **After reading, students check** to see if their predictions were verified. ***Teacher Models*** • **SUMMARIZE** *On the last day of school, Magda tells Marisol what she overheard: Marisol will be moving to Panama. Later, Marisol's mother tells her she'll be staying in Panama for a year. Marisol is upset, but secretly hopes to find her father there.* • **PREDICT** *I predict that Marisol will go to Panama and end up liking it there.*	▶ **Purpose-setting** Students read to check predictions. ▶ **Silent Reading** pp. 55–71. Remind students to use SG p. 84 to help them model strategies. ▶ **After reading, students check** to see if their predictions were verified. ***Teacher Models*** • **SUMMARIZE** *Marisol prepares for Panama. Magda is upset that she's leaving. Tia Julia drives Marisol, her mother, and Magda to the airport.* • **CLARIFY/PHONICS** *I don't know how to pronounce this word (point to **gibberish** on page 58). I'll try breaking it into chunks. I know **b-e-r** from words like **rubber**, and **i-s-h** rhymes with **wish**. The first chunk could be pronounced with a soft **g** or a hard **g**. Both sound right, so I check the dictionary. It says to use the soft sound: /**jib**/**buhr**/**ish**/.*
Responding/ Reflecting (5 minutes) *Note: Assign the lesson homework (SG p. 86) at the end of each lesson.*	▶ **Story Map** Have students add to the **Major Events** box on their Story Maps (SG p. 83). ▶ **Respond** Students discuss, complete, and share Reflection #3 on SG p. 86: *What good things might happen to Marisol in Panama?* ▶ **Strategies Discussion** (Posters 2, 3) **Prompt:** *How did you use PREDICT? How did PREDICT help you?*	▶ **Story Map** Have students add to the **Major Events** box on their Story Maps (SG p. 83). ▶ **Respond** Students discuss, complete, and share Reflection #4 on SG p. 86: *What is Marisol feeling as she rides to the airport?* ▶ **Strategies Discussion** (Posters 2, 3) Ask students how strategies have helped them so far.

Marisol and Magdalena	Lesson 5	Lesson 6
Revisiting (5 minutes) *Note: Do an Oral Reading Check only when you are concerned about a student's decoding or fluency.*	▶ **Students reread previously read *SOAR TO SUCCESS* books.** • Have students reread silently for fluency. Remind them to choose a strategy to model in Reviewing. • Have one student read silently and retell a section of a book. Note comprehension. (Use passages and protocols for Retellings, TM pp. R62–R63.)	▶ **Group Conference** Students discuss independent reading. **Prompt:** *Summarize what has happened in your book so far.* Remind students to keep up their book logs and to bring them to Group Conference for reference.
Reviewing (5 minutes)	▶ **Students model** strategies they used in Revisiting. ▶ **Students Summarize** Students use the book and their Story Maps (SG p. 74) to summarize pp. 55–71.	▶ **Students discuss** strategies they have used with other reading in and out of school. ▶ **Students Summarize** Students use the book and their Story Maps (SG p. 74) to summarize pp. 72–89.
Rehearsing (5–10 minutes)	▶ **Students Predict** Based on pages 55–71, students predict what might happen in the next section. Record their predictions. ▶ **Independent Preview/Vocabulary** Have students independently preview pages 72–89 by reading the first and last paragraphs of each chapter and by skimming the text. If they come to words they don't know, remind them to use CLARIFY/PHONICS and the dictionary. (These words may be difficult for some students: **doilies**, p. 74; **cashmere**, p. 75; **poise**, p. 77; **antennae**, p. 80; **wares**, p. 83; **plunged**, **chlorine**, **sync**, p. 89.) After the preview, have students find each word boldfaced above, read aloud the sentence, and briefly discuss the meaning.	▶ **Students Predict** Based on pages 72–89, students predict what might happen in the next section. Record their predictions. ▶ **Independent Preview/Vocabulary** Have students independently preview pages 90–103 by reading the first and last paragraphs of each chapter and by skimming the text. If they come to words they don't know, remind them to use CLARIFY/PHONICS and the dictionary. (These words may be difficult for some students: **dreadlocks**, p. 91; **mimicking**, p. 92; **hybrid**, p. 95; **cretin**, p. 96; **senile**, p. 100; **abundance**, p. 102.) After the preview, have students find each word boldfaced above, read aloud the sentence, and briefly discuss the meaning.
Reading and Reciprocal Teaching (10–15 minutes) *Note: After students check their predictions, they model Summarize. Then they model all other strategies in any order, using their Strategy Notes. Have students do most of the modeling, but help as needed. Samples are provided.*	▶ **Purpose-setting** Students read to check predictions. ▶ **Silent Reading** pp. 72–89. Remind students to use SG p. 84 to help them model strategies. ▶ **After reading, students check** to see if their predictions were verified. ***Teacher Models*** • **SUMMARIZE** *Abuela picks Marisol up at the Panama City airport. She introduces her to the neighbors and takes her to the market. Marisol is worried about speaking Spanish. Her new friend Ana tries to help her out. She starts school.* • **CLARIFY/PHONICS** *To figure out this word (**immersion** on page 85), I break it into chunks. I recognize the chunk **i-m-** and the ending **-s-i-o-n**. The chunk **m-e-r** looks like it rhymes with **her**. I put the chunks together and get **im/mer/sion**, which makes sense.*	▶ **Purpose-setting** Students read to check their predictions. ▶ **Silent Reading** pp. 90–103. Remind students to use SG p. 84 to help them model strategies. ▶ **After reading, students check** to see if their predictions were verified. ***Teacher Models*** • **SUMMARIZE** *Marisol meets a cute boy named Rubén at school. Ana tells her that he will ask her out because she is the "cool American exchange student." Abuela and Marisol spend time together talking about family. Marisol wants to find her father.* • **QUESTION** *How does Marisol feel to be the cool student instead of the one everyone teases?*
Responding/ Reflecting (5 minutes) *Note: Assign the lesson homework (SG p. 87) at the end of each lesson.*	▶ **Story Map** Have students add to the **Major Events** box on their Story Maps (SG p. 83). ▶ **Respond** Students discuss, complete, and share Reflection #5 on SG p. 87: *What do Marisol and Ana have in common? How are they different?* ▶ **Strategies Discussion** (Posters 2, 3) **Prompt:** *How did you use SUMMARIZE? How did it help you?*	▶ **Story Map** Have students add to the **Major Events** box on their Story Maps (SG p. 83). ▶ **Respond** Students discuss, complete, and share Reflection #6 on SG p. 87: *Describe Marisol's father, Lucho. What do you think he was like?* ▶ **Strategies Discussion** (Posters 2, 3) **Prompt:** *How did you use CLARIFY? How did CLARIFY help you?*

	Lesson 7	**Lesson 8**
Revisiting (5 minutes) *Note: Do an Oral Reading Check only when you are concerned about a student's decoding or fluency.*	▶ **Students reread previously read *SOAR TO SUCCESS* books.** • Have students reread silently for fluency. • Have one student read silently and retell a section of a book. Note comprehension. (Use passages and protocols for Retellings, TM pp. R62–R63.)	▶ **Group Conference** Students discuss independent reading. **Prompt:** *Do you want to read more books by this author or on this same subject? Why or why not?* Remind students to keep up their book logs and to bring them to Group Conference for reference.
Reviewing (5 minutes)	▶ **Students discuss** strategies they have used with other reading in and out of school. ▶ **Students Summarize** Students use the book and their Story Maps (SG p. 74) to summarize pp. 90–103.	▶ **Students discuss** strategies they have used with other reading in and out of school. ▶ **Students Summarize** Students use the book and their Story Maps (SG p. 74) to summarize pp. 104–123.
Rehearsing (5–10 minutes)	▶ **Students Predict** Based on pages 90–103, students predict what might happen in the next section. Record their predictions. ▶ **Independent Preview/Vocabulary** Have students independently preview pages 104–123 by reading the first and last paragraphs of each chapter and by skimming the text. If they come to words they don't know, remind them to use CLARIFY/PHONICS and the dictionary. (These words may be difficult for some students: **psyched**, p. 107; **comfy**, p. 108; **pulsated**, p. 112; **monogram**, p. 115; **choreographing**, p. 117; **obsession**, p. 120.) After the preview, have students find each word boldfaced above, read aloud the sentence, and briefly discuss the meaning.	▶ **Students Predict** Based on pages 104–123, students predict what might happen in the final section. Record their predictions. ▶ **Independent Preview/Vocabulary** Have students independently preview pages 124–141 by reading the first and last paragraphs of each chapter and by skimming the text. If they come to words they don't know, remind them to use CLARIFY/PHONICS and the dictionary. (These words may be difficult for some students: **consequences**, p. 124; **congas**, p. 125; **trampoline**, p. 128; **bargain**, p. 136; **hysterically**, p. 141.) After the preview, have students find each word boldfaced above, read aloud the sentence, and briefly discuss the meaning.
Reading and Reciprocal Teaching (10–15 minutes) *Note: After students check their predictions, they model Summarize. Then they model all other strategies in any order, using their Strategy Notes. Have students do most of the modeling, but help as needed. Samples are provided.*	▶ **Purpose-setting** Students read to check their predictions. ▶ **Silent Reading** pp. 104–123. Remind students to use SG p. 84 to help them model strategies. ▶ **After reading, students check** to see if their predictions were verified. ***Teacher Models*** • **SUMMARIZE** *Ana and Marisol go to look for Lucho. They only find Lucho's brother, but he gives Marisol a handkerchief with her Papi's monogram on it. Marisol realizes that she is very happy in Panama. Through everything, Marisol keeps sending letters to Magda.* • **PREDICT** *I predict that Marisol will impress Roxana with her experiences in Panama.*	▶ **Purpose-setting** Students read to check their predictions. ▶ **Silent Reading** pp. 124–141. Remind students to use SG p. 84 to help them model strategies. ▶ **After reading, students check** to see if their predictions were verified. ***Teacher Models*** • **SUMMARIZE** *Marisol dances well enough to qualify for the show. Rubén asks her to be his girlfriend. Abuela meets Rubén and likes him. And Mami and Magda will be coming to visit at Christmas.* • **CLARIFY** *On page 125, what does **the rhythms popped like hot oil in a frying pan** mean? I know that oil bounces around in a hot frying pan. I guess it means that the dance rhythms jump and bounce a lot.*
Responding/Reflecting (5 minutes) *Note: Assign the lesson homework (SG p. 88) at the end of each lesson.*	▶ **Story Map** Have students add to the **Major Events** box on their Story Maps (SG p. 83). ▶ **Respond** Students discuss, complete, and share Reflection #7 on SG p. 88: *Do you think the man at the Wilcox building told Marisol the truth? Why?* ▶ **Strategies Discussion** (Posters 2, 3) **Prompt:** *How did you use PREDICT? How did PREDICT help you?*	▶ **Story Map** Have students fill in the **Outcome** box on their Story Maps (SG p. 83). ▶ **Respond** Students discuss, complete, and share Reflection #8 on SG p. 88: *Circle a strategy that helped you. Explain how you used this strategy.* ▶ **Home Connection** Students take home *Marisol and Magdalena* and the Home Connection letter.

Marisol and Magdalena

Name _____

Strategy Notes

Students use this page to jot down notes or questions as they read. It should not be used for assessment. Sample notes are shown.

Clarify

quinceañera = Sweet Fifteen p. 7

Little crosses around their necks = Marisol and Magdalena will stay friends forever. p. 71

Predict

I predict that Marisol will become friends with Ana. p. 80

Question

Why doesn't Marisol want to have a joint quince with Magda? p. 8

Why does Mami ask Marisol not to look for Lucho in Panama? pp. 60–61

Summarize

Pages 131–133: Marisol's dance teacher chooses Marisol to perform. Rubén is picked, too. He writes Marisol a note that says she is the prettiest girl in school. He asks if he can be her boyfriend. Later, Marisol realizes she doesn't miss her father so much any more.

84 Level 8, Book 18, *Marisol and Magdalena*

Marisol and Magdalena

Name _____

Sample responses are shown.

Story Map

Title

Marisol and Magdalena

Setting

Brooklyn, New York and Panama

Characters

Marisol, Magdalena, Mami (Inez), Tia Luisa, Tio Ricardo, Junior Vasquez, Roxana, Tia Alicia, Tia China, Tia Julia, Abuela, Ana, Rubén

Problem

Marisol has to leave her best friend, Magda, and her home in New York and move to Panama.

Major Events   (May vary)

1. Marisol and Magdalena help Tia Luisa serve frituras.
2. Roxana picks on Marisol because she can't dance salsa that well.
3. On the last day of school, Marisol finds out that she has to move to Panama.
4. Marisol decides that if she has to go to Panama, she will look for her father, Lucho, there.
5. Marisol prepares for her trip. She says her good-byes to family and friends, including Magda.
6. Marisol arrives in Panama and is picked up by her Abuela.
7. Marisol meets a new friend, Ana.
8. Marisol starts school in Panama.
9. She develops a crush on a boy named Rubén at school.
10. Marisol and Ana go to the Wilcox Building to look for her father.
11. Marisol finds out that Mami and Magda are coming to visit her.

Outcome

Marisol learns about her Panamanian heritage and makes new friends while keeping a strong bond with her best friend in Brooklyn, New York.

Level 8, Book 18, *Marisol and Magdalena* **83**

Name _____

Students use this page to think about their reading and to prepare for discussion. It should not be used for assessment. Sample responses are shown.

REFLECTION 1

What role does food play in the family's gathering?

Food brings the family together. Whenever anyone comes over to the Rosarios' house, they end up in the kitchen where Tía Luisa is cooking. Making food is a way for everyone to get together. Panamanians from all over the neighborhood call Luisa to place their orders for traditional food.

HOMEWORK 1

Write a diary entry in which Marisol describes her feelings about her father, Lucho.

REFLECTION 2

Describe the relationship between Roxana and Marisol.

Roxana is always making fun of Marisol because she was born in the United States and not in Panama. Marisol feels like she isn't as good as Roxana.

HOMEWORK 2

Pretend that you are Marisol. You have made dinner, and you are waiting for Mami to come home from her class. Write a poem that expresses your feelings.

Level 8, Book 18, *Marisol and Magdalena* **85**

Name _____

Students use this page to think about their reading and to prepare for discussion. It should not be used for assessment. Sample responses are shown.

REFLECTION 3

What good things might happen to Marisol in Panama?

She might learn to be more confident. She might learn more about her Panamanian heritage. She might learn to speak better Spanish. She might find her father.

HOMEWORK 3

Write a few sentences to explain why Marisol's photographs are so important to her.

REFLECTION 4

What is Marisol feeling as she rides to the airport?

She is nervous and frightened because she doesn't know what life will be like in Panama. She is afraid her friends and family in New York will forget her.

HOMEWORK 4

What is the meaning of "the sound of our sisterhood"?

86 Level 8, Book 18, *Marisol and Magdalena*

Marisol and Magdalena

Name _____

Students use this page to think about their reading and to prepare for discussion. It should not be used for assessment. Sample responses are shown.

REFLECTION 7

Do you think the man at the Wilcox Building told Marisol the truth? Why or why not?

No, I don't. I don't have any real reason to think he is lying, but I can't help wondering why he has Lucho's handkerchief. Maybe he really is Lucho after all.

HOMEWORK 7

What has Marisol learned about herself in Panama? Write down the reasons why you think her experiences have been an important milestone in her life.

REFLECTION 8

Circle a strategy that helped you to read *Marisol and Magdalena*.

Strategy Box

Predict	Summarize	Clarify	Question

Explain how you used this strategy.

I used Predict because I was trying to figure out how Marisol would balance her old life in New York with her new life in Panama. I wanted to predict which friends would be the most important to her.

HOMEWORK 8

Write a summary of what happened at the dance rehearsal. How did Marisol's experiences there reflect how much her life had changed?

88 Level 8, Book 18, *Marisol and Magdalena*

Marisol and Magdalena

Name _____

Students use this page to think about their reading and to prepare for discussion. It should not be used for assessment. Sample responses are shown.

REFLECTION 5

What do Marisol and Ana have in common? How are they different?

Ana dresses differently. She wears bright pink dresses and orange sunglasses. Ana speaks Spanish very quickly, unlike Marisol. But they both have had best friends they were separated from. Marisol left Magda in New York, and Ana's best friend moved away to Nicaragua.

HOMEWORK 5

Do research to find out more about Panama. Write a short description of Panama City and of the countryside.

REFLECTION 6

Describe Marisol's father, Lucho. What do you think he was like?

I think he was very romantic, and he liked living a fun life. But he didn't like responsibility, and couldn't act like a grown-up.

HOMEWORK 6

Write another letter home from Marisol to Magda. Tell her more details about Ana, Rubén, and her new Panamanian school.

Level 8, Book 18, *Marisol and Magdalena* **87**

SOAR TO SUCCESS

Teacher's Resource File
Contents

Summary of Research Report

A Study of the Effectiveness of an Intervention Program Designed to Accelerate Reading for Struggling Readers in the Upper Grades

Project SUCCESS Researchers

J. David Cooper
Ball State University
Muncie, Indiana

Janet McWilliams
Literacy Consultant
Fair Oaks, California

Lynne Pistochini
San Juan Unified School District
Carmichael, California

Irene Boschken
San Juan Unified School District
Carmichael, California

Research Consultant

Larry Henriksen
Ball State University
Muncie, Indiana

December, 1997

Introduction

A continuing goal of educators is to ensure that all students learn to read successfully. In order to achieve this goal, many schools have developed an approach known as intervention to help students struggling in the process of learning to read. A reading intervention program is one that prevents failure or stops it as quickly as possible. There have been many successful early intervention programs for students in the primary grades (Hiebert & Taylor, 1994).

Teachers in grade three and above also find themselves faced with many students who have low reading achievement. Results of the *National Assessment of Educational Progress* document that there are many students in the upper grades who are reading below level (Mullis, Campbell, & Farstrup, 1993). There is clearly a need for research-based instructional programs designed specifically to accelerate reading for below-level readers in the upper grades.

The purpose of this study was to test the effectiveness of a reading intervention model designed specifically for upper-grade students who are struggling readers. This plan, known as Project SUCCESS, was designed to accelerate reading progress for students by using authentic literature sequenced in complexity, reciprocal teaching, and graphic organizers. The 40-minute daily lessons of Project SUCCESS were delivered in addition to the regular quality classroom reading instruction.

Background

The development of Project SUCCESS began with the researchers summarizing what they knew about four major areas:

1. Characteristics and needs of struggling readers in grade three and above

2. Lessons learned from early intervention programs

3. Instructional strategies proven to be successful with upper-grade students

4. Materials used for instruction with struggling readers in the upper grades

This summarizing process was followed by a review of existing literature and research in relation to each area. It was concluded that:

- For upper-grade students who need intervention, the focus should be on the application of decoding skills and strategies and on developing comprehension.

- The structured, fast-paced type of lessons used in early intervention seem appropriate for upper-grade students.

- Reciprocal teaching and graphic organizers have proven to be effective in accelerating the reading of upper-grade students. Scaffolding is an important part of this successful instruction.

- The most appropriate materials for upper-grade intervention are authentic literature that is sequenced from simple to complex to help students accelerate their reading.

The Instructional Plan for Project SUCCESS

The instructional plan for Project SUCCESS is presented in Table 1 with a description and rationale for each component. During the 1995–1996 school year, this model was field-tested and revised by two teachers and eleven fourth-grade students reading considerably below level. After approximately 90 days of instruction, the students gained an average of 3.0 levels in retelling and 2.4 levels in oral reading as measured by the *Basic Reading Inventory* (Johns, 1994). It was concluded that with this amount of growth, the model should be tested more carefully to see if similar gains would be obtained in a more controlled situation.

Procedures

Persons attending a national presentation of Project SUCCESS at the International Reading Association conference in May 1996 were invited to submit proposals to become research sites for the 1996–97 national research study of Project SUCCESS. Proposals had to include a description of need, background of teachers, commitment of school or district, and a coaching plan to support teachers during the project. Thirteen sites submitted plans that were accepted.

Table 1

The Project SUCCESS Instructional Plan

Component	Description	Rationale
Revisiting (5 minutes)	• Students reread, alone or with a partner, previously read Project SUCCESS books. • Teacher works with individual students to take a retelling, take a running record, or coach their reading. OR • Teacher and students hold a group conference over independently read books.	• Builds fluency • Develops comprehension (Samuels, 1979; 1997) • Builds the connection between learning to read and independent reading (Anderson, Wilson, Fielding, 1988; Center for the Study of Reading, n.d.)
Reviewing (5 minutes)	• Students summarize previous day's reading, using graphic organizers. • Students and teacher discuss strategies used and share examples of their use beyond Project SUCCESS.	• Develops comprehension • Keeps students focused on the same four strategies
Rehearsing (5–10 minutes)	• Teacher does a quick text walk, guided preview, cooperative preview, or independent preview for text to be read. • Students may predict, question, or start a K-W-L chart.	• Builds background specifically for the text to be read (Clay, 1979; 1985; 1991) • Sets purpose for reading
Reading and Reciprocal Teaching (15 minutes)	• Students silently read a meaningful chunk of text to verify predictions or answer questions. • Following reading, reciprocal teaching is employed, with the students and teacher taking turns assuming the role of teacher to model these four strategies: SUMMARIZE QUESTION CLARIFY PREDICT	• Applies strategies and develops comprehension (Pearson, 1984) • Develops students' abilities to construct meaning (Palincsar & Brown, 1984a; 1984b; 1986; Palincsar, 1984)

Responding/Reflecting (5 minutes)	• Students do one or more of the following:
	   Make a written response
	   Complete graphic organizers
	   Reflect on strategies
	   Discuss and share
		• Develops comprehension
		• Develops use of strategies (Sweet, 1993)

Population The population for the study was a group of fourth-grade students identified as considerably below-level readers in 24 different schools within the 13 sites. Sites ranged from major metropolitan areas to rural areas. A total of 38 teachers taught Project SUCCESS.

Selecting the Sample The samples for the research groups (Project SUCCESS) and the control groups were randomly selected. Teachers were given guidelines to identify fourth-grade students who were reading considerably below level. Table 2 shows the number of students in the initial sample and the number of students in the final sample. The final sample was reduced due to mobility of students and inaccurate scoring of tests.

Table 2

Sample for National Study

		Project SUCCESS		Control	
Sample	Total	Males	Females	Males	Females
Initial	409	112	107	97	93
Final	345	94	91	83	77

Testing Two instruments were selected to use as pre- and posttests in this study: the *Qualitative Reading Inventory-II* (QRI-II) (Leslie & Caldwell, 1995) and the *Gates-MacGinitie Reading Tests* (MacGinitie & MacGinitie, 1989). The pretesting occurred within the first three weeks of school and the posttesting took place during the first two weeks of March 1997.

Research Questions This study sought answers to two research questions:

1. Is there a difference in the retelling, questions, oral reading, vocabulary, and comprehension raw-score means between the Project SUCCESS group and the control group?

2. Is there a difference in the retelling, questions, oral reading, vocabulary, and comprehension raw-score means between Project SUCCESS students taught as an in-class group, as a pullout group, or as an extended-day group?

Training, Treatment, and Monitoring The teachers who were to be the Project SUCCESS teachers were given two days of intensive training. During this training teachers were taught how to use

- the Project SUCCESS instructional model

- reciprocal teaching

- the lessons provided for each book designated for fourth grade

The treatment started at varying times due to different starting dates for each school. Each teacher was asked to teach the Project SUCCESS groups for 40 minutes per day for four or five days each week. A record of the number of days taught and the number of books completed was kept by all Project SUCCESS teachers. The control groups were given the instruction from their regular reading program. Some of the control-group students were given additional support through Title 1 or other support programs; no attempt was made to control this factor.

Data Analysis Procedures Data from this study were analyzed using raw scores because such scores are more easily interpreted by consumers of research when the objective is to compare group means. The use of raw scores avoids many of the problems associated with interpreting transformed scores.

The control and SUCCESS groups and locations (two groups) were compared relative to the pretest scores using the Hotelling T2 statistic (reported as an F statistic). This same procedure was used to test differences between subgroup posttest means. Univariate F statistics were interpreted if multivariate F statistics were significant. A strength of relationship index was computed where appropriate. Finally, a t statistic was used to compare time means for the two location subgroups. A detailed report of the results can be found in the final report of the research project (Cooper et al., 1997).

The results of this research project are generalizable to the fourth-grade population studied. Because the research sites represented a variety of geographic regions and locations, the results should be representative of the country as a whole. Furthermore, because the randomization procedures followed resulted in equivalent research and control groups at the beginning of the study, it is safe to assume that these results can be replicated in other situations.

Discussion

Research Question 1 The results relative to Research Question 1 do show that it is possible to accelerate the reading of struggling fourth graders in a relatively short amount of time (40 minutes per day for an average of 75.8 days, in addition to regular classroom instruction). Four of the five measures yielded significant differences. Only the Gates-MacGinitie Vocabulary Subtest did not show significance. This may be due to the way in which vocabulary is measured with this instrument.

Reciprocal teaching is a critical part of the Project SUCCESS instructional model. Other researchers have found that the use of this instructional strategy results in relatively large gains in reading comprehension for students in a short amount of time (Rosenshine & Meister, 1994). Another important benefit of reciprocal teaching is the effect it seems to have on students' fluency as measured by oral reading.

The students in this study did show a significant gain in oral reading, which is a measure of their application of phonics and other decoding skills. This same pattern has been noted by other researchers (Rosenshine & Meister, 1994). This gain in application of phonics and decoding is explainable in two ways. First, the CLARIFY strategy of reciprocal teaching provides a natural place to teach students to apply phonics and other decoding skills as they read. This was emphasized heavily throughout the Project SUCCESS lessons by using a strategy called CLARIFY—Think About Words with scaffolded amounts of teacher modeling.

The second explanation for the gains in oral reading relates to the overall structure of the Project SUCCESS lessons. The REVISITING step of the lessons provides time for many repeated readings. As other researchers have shown (Samuels, 1979; 1997), repeated reading does result in improved fluency or oral reading.

Research Question 2 The results relative to Research Question 2 do show that there were no overall statistically significant differences in the results obtained with a pullout or in-class location for the instruction. The pullout groups did perform significantly better on answering questions, oral reading, and comprehension. This suggests that pullout programs may have some positive results even though they are not the answer to all educational needs.

Another factor relative to location of treatment was time. Again, no significant differences in amounts of time devoted to instruction were found in relation to location. The most time for instruction was given by the extended-day teacher (only one teacher) and the least time by the in-class teacher. This is explained, in part, by the fact that classroom teachers have so many factors that can interfere with their day that they are more likely to skip special group instruction with the in-class model. Also, the reports from in-class teachers showed that they sometimes experienced difficulty in managing the in-class groups. The extended-day model needs to be explored more fully with a much larger sample.

Students' Acceleration to Level The goal of intervention instruction is to get students "up to level" and to get them out of the program. A greater proportion of Project SUCCESS students were reading at level as operationally defined in this study than were control group students. The researchers found that it was difficult for teachers to drop students from the program even though the students appeared to meet the criteria for being released. There seems to be a "remedial syndrome" or "fear-of-letting-go syndrome" that is shared by many intervention teachers. This may be a result of the teachers having operated as remedial teachers in the past.

While a greater percentage of Project SUCCESS students were up to level, it should also be noted that there was considerable variability from site to site. This appears to be explained in part by the teacher variable. As the researchers observed teachers at different sites, differences in teaching style were clearly apparent.

General Observations Numerous observations were made by the researchers throughout this study. Three types merit discussion: student motivation, teacher training and coaching, and the qualities of teachers who should be intervention teachers.

Student motivation was high throughout the study. Some teachers were concerned at the beginning of the study that students might become bored with the repetition or might be insulted by some of the easy books. The situation was very much to the contrary. Students loved the books, and other students in the classroom wanted to know when they could read them. The repetition and fast pace of the lessons appeared to keep the students on task and excited. The researchers felt that the students were reading successfully (many for the first time in their educational careers) and seeing themselves grow in reading. This success also resulted in many positive notes and responses from parents and other family members.

Another observation made by the researchers was that training was essential in helping teachers learn to use Project SUCCESS. All teachers attended the two-day training institute. This was essential to helping teachers get started, learn to use reciprocal teaching, and teach the lessons. The structured Project SUCCESS lessons themselves were also a part of the training process. It was observed that as teachers taught the lessons, they got better at teaching them and needed to refer to the lessons less and less. Many teachers reviewed the training video throughout the project in order to hone their teaching skills. Finally, ongoing coaching was important in helping teachers make the strategies of Project SUCCESS their own. Coaching varied from site to site. However, it was clear that coaching contributed to helping teachers learn to teach this upper-grade intervention model.

Finally, as teachers in the research project were observed, it was clearly evident that some teachers do not respond positively to the structure and fast pace of intervention lessons. Therefore, school districts should keep this idea in mind as they select the teachers who are to become the intervention teachers.

Conclusions

Based on the results of this study, the following conclusions are warranted:

1. It is possible to accelerate the reading of struggling fourth graders in a relatively short amount of time. The lessons required for this intervention must meet the following criteria:

   - Utilize authentic literature sequenced from simple to complex

   - Be fast-paced

   - Incorporate reciprocal teaching and graphic organizers

   - Be taught 40 minutes per day in addition to classroom instruction

   - Follow the model developed in this study

2. The intervention instruction is likely to be equally effective if delivered as an in-class program or as a pullout program. There was not enough evidence to draw conclusions about the extended-day model. The in-class model poses problems relative to classroom management for some teachers.

3. Teachers who become upper-grade intervention teachers must be selected with care because not all teachers respond equally well to the structured process of intervention instruction.

4. Training and coaching are essential components in helping teachers learn the type of model utilized in Project SUCCESS.

Evidence of Success in Middle Schools Between the time of the national study on which this research report was based and the time of the publication of Levels 7 and 8 of *SOAR TO SUCCESS*, middle schools reported substantial gains using Level 6 of this program. They used Level 6 or they used the *SOAR TO SUCCESS* lesson plans with books from Level 6 as well as leveled books chosen for relevance to seventh or eighth graders. One district had the following results:

Gains in Years After One Semester of *SOAR TO SUCCESS*, Measured by Pretests and Posttests Using the Gates-MacGinitie Reading Tests			
Grade	Comprehension	Vocabulary	Total
6	1.77	.61	1.10
7	2.44	.78	1.50
8	2.48	.99	1.65

Research Bibliography

Allington, R. L., & Walmsley, S. A. (Eds.). (1995). *No quick fix: Rethinking literacy programs in America's elementary schools.* New York: Teachers College Press.

Anderson, R. C., Wilson, P. T., & Fielding, L. G. (1988). Growth in reading and how children spend their time outside of school. *Reading Research Quarterly, 23,* 285–303.

Burns, P. C., & Roe, B. D. (1989). *Informal reading inventory* (3rd ed.). Boston: Houghton Mifflin.

Carter, C. (1997). Why reciprocal teaching? *Educational Leadership, 54*(6), 64–68.

Clay, M. M. (1979). *Reading: The patterning of complex behavior* (2nd ed.). Portsmouth, NH: Heinemann.

Clay, M. M. (1985). *The early detection of reading difficulties* (3rd ed.). Portsmouth, NH: Heinemann.

Clay, M. M. (1991). *Becoming literate: The construction of inner control.* Portsmouth, NH: Heinemann.

Collins, A., Brown, J. S., & Newman, S. E. (1987). *Cognitive apprenticeship: Teaching the craft of reading, writing and mathematics* (Tech. Rep. No. 403). Champaign: University of Illinois at Urbana-Champaign, Center for the Study of Reading.

Cooper, J. D., Boschken, I., McWilliams, J., & Pistochini, L. (1997). Project SUCCESS: A study of the effectiveness of an intervention program designed to accelerate reading for struggling readers in the upper grades. Unpublished.

Cunningham, P. M., & Cunningham, J. W. (1992). Making words: Enhancing the invented spelling-decoding connection. *The Reading Teacher, 46*(2), 106–115.

Ekwall, E. E., & Shanker, J. L. (1993). *Ekwall/Shanker reading inventory* (3rd ed.). Boston: Allyn & Bacon.

Heimlich, J. E., & Pittelman, S. D. (1986). *Semantic mapping:* Classroom applications. Newark, DE: International Reading Association.

Hiebert, E. H. (1994). Reading recovery in the United States: What difference does it make to an age cohort? *Educational Researcher, 23*(9), 15–25.

Hiebert, E. H., & Taylor, B. M. (Eds.). (1994). *Getting reading right from the start: Effective early literacy interventions.* Boston: Allyn and Bacon.

Johns, J. J. (1994). *Basic reading inventory* (4th ed.). Dubuque, IA: Kendall/Hunt.

Joyce, B. R., & Showers, B. (1981). Transfer of training: The contribution of "coaching." *Journal of Education, 16*(2), 163–172.

Leslie, L., & Caldwell, J. (1995). *Qualitative reading inventory, II.* New York: HarperCollins.

MacGinitie, W. H., & MacGinitie, R. K. (1989). *Gates-MacGinitie reading tests* (3rd ed.). Chicago: Riverside.

Mullis, I. V. S., Campbell, J. R., & Farstrup, A. E. (1993). *NAEP 1992 reading report card for the nation and the states: Data from the national and trial state assessments.* Washington, DC: U.S. Department of Education, National Center for Educational Statistics.

Palincsar, A. S. (1984). The quest for meaning from expository text: A teacher-guided journey. In G. Duffy, L. R. Roehler, & J. Mason (Eds.), *Comprehension instruction: Perspectives and suggestions* (pp. 251–264). New York: Longman.

Palincsar, A. S. & Brown, A. L. (1986). Interactive teaching to promote independent learning from text. *The Reading Teacher, 39*(8), 771–777.

Palincsar, A., & Brown, A. (1985). Reciprocal teaching: A means to a meaningful end. In J. Osborn, P. T. Wilson, & R. C. Anderson (Eds.), *Reading education: Foundations for a literate America* (pp. 299–310). Lexington, MA: D. C. Heath.

Palincsar, A. S., & Brown, A. L. (1984a). *A means to a meaningful end: Recommendations for the instruction of poor comprehenders.* Champaign: University of Illinois at Urbana-Champaign, Center for the Study of Reading, reprint.

Palincsar, A. S., & Brown, A. L. (1984b). Reciprocal teaching of comprehension-fostering and comprehension-monitoring activities. *Cognition and Instruction, 1*(2), 117–175.

Pearson, P. D. (1984). *Reading comprehension instruction: Six necessary changes* (Reading Education Rep. No. 54).

Champaign: University of Illinois at Urbana-Champaign, Center for the Study of Reading.

Pearson, P. D. (1985). Changing the face of reading comprehension instruction. *The Reading Teacher,* 38(8), 724–738.

Pehrsson, R. S., & Robinson, H. A. (1985). *The semantic organizer approach to writing and reading instruction.* Rockville, MD: Aspen Systems Corp.

Peterson, B. (1991). Selecting books for beginning readers. In D. E. DeFord, C. A. Lyons, & G. S. Pinnell (Eds.), *Bridges to literacy: Learning from reading recovery* (pp. 119–147). Portsmouth, NH: Heinemann.

Pikulski, J. J. (1991). The transition years: The middle school. In J. Flood, J. M. Jensen, D. Lapp, & J. R. Squire (Eds.), *Handbook of research on teaching the English language arts* (pp. 303–319). New York: Macmillan.

Pikulski, J. J. (1994). Preventing reading failure: A review of five effective programs. *The Reading Teacher,* 48(1), 30–39.

Pinnell, G. S., Fried, M. D., & Estice, R. M. (1990). Reading recovery: Learning how to make a difference. *The Reading Teacher,* 43, 282–295.

Rosenshine, B., & Meister, C. (1994). Reciprocal teaching: A review of the research. *Review of Educational Research,* 64(4), 479–530.

Samuels, S. J. (1979/1997). The method of repeated readings. *The Reading Teacher,* 50(5), 376–381.

Showers, B., Joyce, B., & Bennett, B. (1987). Synthesis of research on staff development: A framework for future study and a state-of-the-art analysis. *Educational Leadership,* 45(3), 77–87.

Sparks, D., & Hirsh, S. (1997). *A new vision for staff development.* Alexandria, VA: Association for Supervision and Curriculum Development.

Swartz, S. L., & Klein, A. F. (Eds.) (1997). *Research in reading recovery.* Portsmouth, NH: Heinemann.

Swearingen, R., & Allen, D. (1997). *Classroom assessment of reading processes.* Boston: Houghton Mifflin.

Sweet, A. P. (1993). *State of the art: Transforming ideas for teaching and learning to read.* Washington, DC: U.S. Department of Education, Office of Research.

Teachers and independent reading: Suggestions for the classroom. (1990). Champaign: University of Illinois at Urbana-Champaign, Center for the Study of Reading.

Vygotsky, L. S. (1978). *Mind in society: The development of higher psychological processes.* Cambridge, MA: Harvard University Press.

Bibliography of Books for Level 8 Students

✪ Multicultural

The following books are grouped into categories according to the criteria for selecting and sequencing books that are described in Section 1 of this Teacher's Manual.

Category I

Wild Horse Winter
by Tetsuya Honda
Chronicle 1992 (32p) also paper
A herd of wild horses survives a raging blizzard during a harsh winter.

✪ The First Strawberries: A Cherokee Story
by Joseph Bruchac
Dial 1993 (32p) also paper
A story about a quarrel teaches that friendship and respect are as sweet as strawberries.

Toad Overload
by Patricia Siebert
Millbrook 1996 (32p)
When Australian farmers import huge toads to control crop pests, they inadvertently start a toad explosion.

✪ The Song of Mu Lan
by Jeanne M. Lee
Front Street 1995 (32p)
Taking her father's place in the Emperor's army, Mu Lan disguises herself as a man and rides off to war.

Category II

Praying Mantis
by Rebecca Stefoff
Benchmark 1997 (32p)
Color photographs and text bring to life the fascinating world of a predatory insect.

Giants in the Land
by Diana Appelbaum
Houghton 1993 (32p) also paper
Cut down to build ships, pine trees as tall as apartment buildings disappeared from New England during colonial days.

✪ Richard Wright and the Library Card
by William Miller
Lee & Low 1997 (32p) also paper
In the segregated South, a teenager who became a famous writer finds a way to borrow the books he loves from the library.

The Pumpkin Runner
by Dianne Arnold
Dial 1998 (32p)
In a story inspired by a real event, an old farmer enters and wins a road race hundreds of miles long.

Rare Treasure: Mary Anning and Her Remarkable Discoveries
by Don Brown
Houghton 1999 (32p)
Self taught paleontologist Mary Anning first discovered important fossils when she was a young girl.

Category III

America's Champion Swimmer: Gertrude Ederle
by David A. Adler
Harcourt 2000 (32p)
In 1926 Gertrude Ederle became the first woman to swim the English Channel.

✪ Slugger Season: McGwire and Sosa
by Laura Driscoll
Grosset 1998 (32p) also paper
In the exciting 1998 baseball season, both Sammy Sosa and Mark McGwire break a 37-year-old home run record.

Who's That Stepping on Plymouth Rock?
by Jean Fritz
Paperstar 1998 (32p)
The story of how the historic monument Plymouth Rock was moved, dropped, broken, and cemented back together.

✪ Tea with Milk
by Allen Say
Houghton 1999 (32p)
May has a difficult time adjusting to her new life when her parents move from San Francisco to Japan.

Big Cats
by Seymour Simon
Harper 1994 (40p) also paper
An introduction to lions, jaguars, and other big cats in their natural habitats.

✪ **Luis Munoz Marin: Father of Modern Puerto Rico**
by Linda and Charles George
Children's 1999 (48p)
Marin, the first elected governor of Puerto Rico, worked to unite people and to improve their living conditions.

Category IV

Dive!
by Sylvia Earle
Nat'l Geo 1999 (64p)
The author relates some of her adventures studying and exploring the world's oceans.

The Snake Scientist
by Sy Montgomery
Houghton 1999 (48p)
A close-up look at a scientist's work with the 18,000 garter snakes that emerge en masse from caves in Canada every spring.

West by Covered Wagon: Retracing the Pioneer Trails
by Dorothy Hinshaw Patent
Walker 1995 (32p)
A group of people called the Westmont Wagoneers celebrate the pioneer spirit by recreating a wagon train journey.

Once a Wolf
by Stephen R. Swinburne
Houghton 1999 (48p)
A brief history of the relationship between man and wolf is followed by an account of the wolves' return to Yellowstone Park.

Category V

Christopher Reeve
by Libby Hughes
Dillon Press 1998 (70p)
A biography of the well-known actor who played Superman and was later paralyzed in a horseback-riding accident.

✪ **Neate to the Rescue**
by Debbi Chocolate
Just Us 1992 (96p) paper
Naimah and her junior high school friends work together to help Naimah's mother win reelection to the city council.

Earthquakes
by Sally M. Walker
Carolrhoda 1996 (48p)
Photos and factual information explain the geographical phenomena and its impact on people.

The Final Cut
by Fred Bowen
Peachtree 1999 (112p)
Four eighth-graders find their friendship tested when two of them make the basketball team and two do not.

To the Top of the World: Adventures with Arctic Wolves
by Jim Brandenberg
Walker 1995 (44p)
The author-photographer tells of his experiences during the summer he lived among white wolves in the Arctic.

Category VI

✪ **Fire in Their Eyes**
by Karen Magnuson Beil
Harcourt 1999 (64p)
Highly trained individuals called fire jumpers risk their lives fighting wildfires all over the United States.

✪ **Black Star, Bright Dawn**
by Scott O'Dell
Houghton 1988 (144p)
An Inuit girl faces many challenges when she takes her father's place in the 1,172-mile Iditarod.

Knots in My Yo-Yo String: The Autobiography of a Kid
by Jerry Spinelli
Knopf 1988 (148p) also paper
The Newbery Medal–winning author presents a humorous account of his childhood in Pennsylvania.

✪ **Discovering the Inca Ice Maiden**
by Johan Reinhard
Nat'l Geo 1998 (48p)
A first-person account of the discovery of an over 500-year-old ice mummy on a mountain in Peru.

The Music of Dolphins
by Karen Hesse
Scholastic 1996 (181p) also paper
Using words she has just learned, Mila tells the story of how she was raised by dolphins.

SOAR TO **SUCCESS**

Jack and Jill Hurt Fetching Water

Jack and Jill, a brother and sister from 3 Story Lane, had an accident today while fetching a pail of water. The children were climbing the hill to the town well when Jack tripped on a shoelace and fell down. Jill, who was also holding on to the pail, came tumbling after. Jack was treated for a broken crown. Jill suffered a skinned knee. Get-well cards may be sent to Mother Goose Hospital.

SOAR TO SUCCESS

Reading Time

Revisiting
5 minutes

Discuss our self-selected books with teacher.

Reviewing
5 minutes

Summarize what we read yesterday.

Rehearsing
5–10 minutes

Think about what we will read today.

Reading
10–15 minutes

—Read and discuss.
—Take turns being the teacher.

Responding/Reflecting
5 minutes

—Write in Student Guide.
—Talk about strategies we used.

SOAR TO SUCCESS

Strategies for Success

Clarify
Reread or discuss words or points that were not clear.

Predict
What will happen or what will we learn?

Question
After reading, ask a question for others to answer.

Summarize
Tell what we read.

SOAR TO SUCCESS

Clarify/Phonics: Think About Words

When you come to a word you don't know:

1. Look for the largest chunks you know
(syllables, prefixes, suffixes).
Try to say the word.

2. Look at the letters and think about the sounds.
Try to sound out the word.

3. Reread the sentence.
Does it make sense?

SOAR TO **SUCCESS**

Story Map

Title

Setting

Characters

Problem

Major Events

Outcome

K-W-L Chart

Title

What I **K**now	What I **W**ant to Find Out	What I **L**earned

Semantic Map

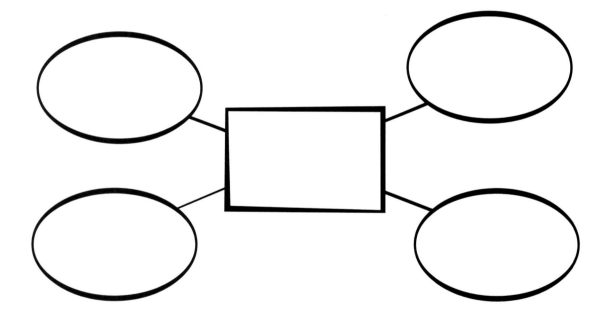

Story Frame

Pages _____
Setting _____
Characters _____
Event _____

Pages _____
Setting _____
Characters _____
Event _____

Pages _____
Setting _____
Characters _____
Event _____

Pages _____
Setting _____
Characters _____
Event _____

Pages _____
Setting _____
Characters _____
Event _____

SOAR TO **SUCCESS**

Event Map

Title

Event 1

Event 2

Event 3

Event 4

Event 5

Event 6

Event 7

Event 8

Main Ideas and Details

Title _____

1. Main idea _____
   a. Detail _____
   b. _____
   c. _____
   d. _____

2. _____
   a. _____
   b. _____
   c. _____
   d. _____

3. _____
   a. _____
   b. _____
   c. _____
   d. _____

4. _____
   a. _____
   b. _____
   c. _____
   d. _____

Clarify/Phonics — How to Say a Word

When I come to a word I can't say, I look for chunks I know. If I still don't know the word, I look for letter sounds. I blend together what I know. Then I read the sentence to see if it fits. . . .

Clarify — A Word Meaning

When I come to a word I don't know, I look at the pictures or read to the end of the sentence to get the meaning. Then I reread the sentence to see if it makes sense. . . .

Clarify — An Idea

When I don't understand an idea, I reread, read ahead, or look at pictures to figure it out. I reread the sentence to see if it makes sense. . . .

Predict

When I predict, I use what I have read or the pictures to tell what will happen next or what I will learn. . . .

Question

When I question, I ask something that can be answered as I read or after I finish reading. . . .

Summarize

When I summarize, I tell in my own words the important things I have read. . . .

Name _____

Book Log

Title	Author	Date Completed	Comments

Student Log Sheet for REVISITING

SOAR TO SUCCESS

Student Name	Date Assessment Text Used	Date Assessment Text Used	Date Assessment Text Used	Date Assessment Text Used	Date Assessment Text Used	Date Assessment Text Used	Date Assessment Text Used
1.							
2.							
3.							
4.							
5.							
6.							
7.							

Retelling Protocol for *A Beauty of a Plan*

Name _____ **Date** _____

Directions to the Teacher: Do not tell the student the title of the book. Ask the student to reread pages 2 through 10 silently and be ready to retell the key points in his or her own words. Ask the student to close the book before retelling. As the student retells the information, number the key items in the space provided. The order of the retelling does not affect the score. **Do not prompt** until the student has told all that he or she can recall from the rereading.

If the student leaves out key points, prompt by using the statements/questions provided. You may reword or adjust prompts to suit your situation. Complete the scoring and observation guide.

Directions to the Student: "You have read this book before. Reread pages 2–10 silently now. When you are finished, I want you to retell the key points in your words."

Retelling Response Summary		Scoring Guide		
	Number Correct		**Unprompted**	**Prompted + Unprompted**
Unprompted	_____			
Prompted	_____			
Unprompted + Prompted	_____	Acceptable	4–6	4–6
		Unacceptable	0–3	0–3

Observation Guide

(Check items that apply)

_____ Retelling smooth and connected; reflected a good summary
_____ Retelling disorganized
_____ Required no prompting
_____ Gave only the important ideas
_____ Gave important ideas plus details
_____ Told unnecessary details
_____ Could not tell without prompting
_____ Showed signs of misreading words (Example: Kept saying "solen" instead of "salon")

_____

_____

_____ Other

_____

_____

_____

Unprompted Retelling (Number in order given.)	Key Points	Prompts (Use after unprompted retelling, if needed.)	Prompted Retelling (Check items correctly given.)
_____	1. Sheila and Michael finish their shop project.	1. What are Sheila and Michael doing at the beginning of the section?	_____
_____	2. Michael asks Sheila what their next project will be.	2. What does Michael say about their next project?	_____
_____	3. Sheila says she doesn't know yet, but she'll plan something.	3. What has Sheila planned for the next project?	_____
_____	4. Sheila goes to Grandma's beauty shop.	4. Where does Sheila go after school?	_____
_____	5. Sheila goes upstairs to fold towels.	5. Why does Sheila go upstairs?	_____
_____	6. Grandma asks Sheila to drop shop class.	6. What does Grandma ask Sheila to do at school?	_____

## Book 2

Retelling Protocol for *The Lost Expedition*

• •

Name _____   **Date** _____

Directions to the Teacher: Do not tell the student the title of the book. Ask the student to reread pages 14 through 17 silently and be ready to retell the key points in his or her own words. Ask the student to close the book before retelling. As the student retells the information, number the key items in the space provided. The order of the retelling does not affect the score. **Do not prompt** until the student has told all that he or she can recall from the rereading.

If the student leaves out key points, prompt by using the statements/questions provided. You may reword or adjust prompts to suit your situation. Complete the scoring and observation guide.

Directions to the Student: "You have read this book before. Reread pages 14–17 silently now. When you are finished, I want you to retell the key points in your words."

Retelling Response Summary		Scoring Guide	
Number Correct		**Unprompted**	**Prompted + Unprompted**
Unprompted _____			
Prompted _____	Acceptable	6–8	6–8
Unprompted + Prompted _____	Unacceptable	0–6	0–5

Observation Guide

(Check items that apply)

_____ Retelling smooth and connected; reflected a good summary
_____ Retelling disorganized
_____ Required no prompting
_____ Gave only the important ideas
_____ Gave important ideas plus details
_____ Told unnecessary details
_____ Could not tell without prompting
_____ Showed signs of misreading words (Example: Kept saying "floods" instead of "floes")

_____
_____

_____ Other

_____
_____
_____

Unprompted Retelling (Number in order given.)	Key Points	Prompts (Use after unprompted retelling, if needed.)	Prompted Retelling (Check items correctly given.)
_____	1. Shackleton ordered his men to abandon ship.	1. What did Shackleton order the men to do?	_____
_____	2. They took the lifeboats and some supplies from the ship.	2. What did the crew take from the ship?	_____
_____	3. The crew set up a camp on the ice.	3. Where did they live after they abandoned the ship?	_____
_____	4. The *Endurance* sank.	4. What happened to the ship?	_____
_____	5. Shackleton wanted to get his men off the ice floes and onto dry land.	5. What did Shackleton want to do after the ship sank?	_____
_____	6. The ice would melt as weather got warmer.	6. What would happen to the ice as the weather changed?	_____
_____	7. The men would walk across the ice field.	7. How would the crew get across the ice field?	_____
_____	8. They took supplies and the lifeboats.	8. What did the men take with them?	_____

## Book 3

Retelling Protocol for *Owl*

● ●

Name _____ **Date** _____

Directions to the Teacher: Do not tell the student the title of the book. Ask the student to reread pages 12 through 21 silently and be ready to retell the key points in his or her own words. Ask the student to close the book before retelling. As the student retells the information, number the key items in the space provided. The order of the retelling does not affect the score. **Do not prompt** until the student has told all that he or she can recall from the rereading.

If the student leaves out key points, prompt by using the statements/questions provided. You may reword or adjust prompts to suit your situation. Complete the scoring and observation guide.

Directions to the Student: "You have read this book before. Reread pages 12–21 silently now. When you are finished, I want you to retell the key points in your words."

Retelling Response Summary		Scoring Guide		
	Number Correct		**Unprompted**	**Prompted + Unprompted**
Unprompted	_____			
Prompted	_____	Acceptable	5–7	5–7
Unprompted + Prompted	_____	Unacceptable	0–4	0–4
Observation Guide				

(Check items that apply)

_____ Retelling smooth and connected; reflected a good summary
_____ Retelling disorganized
_____ Required no prompting
_____ Gave only the important ideas
_____ Gave important ideas plus details
_____ Told unnecessary details
_____ Could not tell without prompting
_____ Showed signs of misreading words (Example: Kept saying "owltees" instead of "owlets")
       _____
       _____
_____ Other
       _____
       _____
       _____

Unprompted Retelling (Number in order given.)	Key Points	Prompts (Use after unprompted retelling, if needed.)	Prompted Retelling (Check items correctly given.)
_____	1. Mother and father owls spend most of their time catching food for their large families.	1. What do mother and father owls do most of the time?	_____
_____	2. Baby owlets are born with soft, fluffy white feathers that gradually turn darker.	2. How do baby owlets change?	_____
_____	3. Owls live all over the world— from rain forests to snowfields to deserts. (**Note**: Details of specific habitats are not required.)	3. Where do owls live?	_____
_____	4. Barn owls live in barns and many other places.	4. Where do barn owls live?	_____
_____	5. The great horned owl and the long-eared owl are big owls that have tufts of feathers that look like horns or ears.	5. What can you tell me about some big owls?	_____
_____	6. Elf owls are the smallest owls; they live in Mexico and the Southwest. (**Note**: Students need mention only one of these locations.)	6. What are the smallest owls, and where do they live?	_____
_____	7. Saw-whet and pygmy owls are also very small. (**Note**: Students need mention only one of these owls by name.)	7. What are some other small owls?	_____

## Book 4

Retelling Protocol for *The Babe & I*

• •

Name _____ **Date** _____

Directions to the Teacher: **Do not tell the student the title of the book.** Ask the student to reread pages 11 through 19 silently and be ready to retell the key points in his or her own words. Ask the student to close the book before retelling. As the student retells the information, number the key items in the space provided. The order of the retelling does not affect the score. **Do not prompt** until the student has told all that he or she can recall from the rereading.

If the student leaves out key points, prompt by using the statements/questions provided. You may reword or adjust prompts to suit your situation. Complete the scoring and observation guide.

Directions to the Student: "You have read this book before. Reread pages 11–19 silently now. When you are finished, I want you to retell the key points in your words."

Retelling Response Summary		Scoring Guide		
	Number Correct		**Unprompted**	**Prompted + Unprompted**
Unprompted	_____			
Prompted	_____	Acceptable	5–7	5–7
Unprompted + Prompted	_____	Unacceptable	0–4	0–4

Observation Guide

(Check items that apply)

_____ Retelling smooth and connected; reflected a good summary
_____ Retelling disorganized
_____ Required no prompting
_____ Gave only the important ideas
_____ Gave important ideas plus details
_____ Told unnecessary details
_____ Could not tell without prompting
_____ Showed signs of misreading words (Example: Kept saying "news" instead of "newsie")
_____
_____
_____ Other
_____
_____
_____

Unprompted Retelling (Number in order given.)	Key Points	Prompts (Use after unprompted retelling, if needed.)	Prompted Retelling (Check items correctly given.)
_____	1. The boy and his friend Jacob saw the boy's father selling apples on the street.	1. Who did the boy and Jacob see on the street?	_____
_____	2. The boy had thought that his father had a job.	2. Why was the boy surprised to see his father selling apples?	_____
_____	3. The boy joined Jacob selling newspapers to make money.	3. What did the boy decide to do?	_____
_____	4. They went to Yankee Stadium to sell the papers.	4. Where did the boy and Jacob go with the papers?	_____
_____	5. Jacob knew a good way to sell papers—he called out the news about Babe Ruth.	5. How did Jacob sell newspapers?	_____
_____	6. The boy gave the money he made to his mother.	6. What did the boy do with the money he made?	_____
_____	7. The boy's father returned in the evening and pretended he had been at the office.	7. What happened when the boy's father returned home?	_____

Retelling Protocol for *Journey Home*

Name _____ **Date** _____

Directions to the Teacher: Do not tell the student the title of the book. Ask the student to reread pages 26 through 29 silently and be ready to retell the key points in his or her own words. Ask the student to close the book before retelling. As the student retells the information, number the key items in the space provided. The order of the retelling does not affect the score. **Do not prompt** until the student has told all that he or she can recall from the rereading.

If the student leaves out key points, prompt by using the statements/questions provided. You may reword or adjust prompts to suit your situation. Complete the scoring and observation guide.

Directions to the Student: "You have read this book before. Reread pages 26–29 silently now. When you are finished, I want you to retell the key points in your words."

Retelling Response Summary		Scoring Guide		
	Number Correct		**Unprompted**	**Prompted + Unprompted**
Unprompted	_____			
Prompted	_____	Acceptable	6–8	6–8
Unprompted + Prompted	_____	Unacceptable	0–5	0–5

Observation Guide

(Check items that apply)

_____ Retelling smooth and connected; reflected a good summary
_____ Retelling disorganized
_____ Required no prompting
_____ Gave only the important ideas
_____ Gave important ideas plus details
_____ Told unnecessary details
_____ Could not tell without prompting
_____ Showed signs of misreading words (Example: Kept saying "tare" instead of "tear")

_____

_____

_____ Other

_____

_____

Unprompted Retelling (Number in order given.)	Key Points	Prompts (Use after unprompted retelling, if needed.)	Prompted Retelling (Check items correctly given.)
_____	1. Mom shows the old man her picture, and a tear falls down his cheek.	1. What does Mom do when she meets the old man?	_____
_____	2. The old man cannot speak English.	2. Why does the girl have to translate for the old man?	_____
_____	3. Mom's own father made the kite.	3. Who made Mom's kite?	_____
_____	4. Mom's mother and father had been killed when the village was bombed.	4. What had happened to Mom's parents?	_____
_____	5. The old man had found Mom in the rubble under the kite.	5. Where did the man find Mom?	_____
_____	6. The old man carried Mom and the kite to the orphanage.	6. Where did he take Mom?	_____
_____	7. After the war, the old man tried to find Mom, but the orphanage was gone.	7. Did the old man try to find Mom after the war?	_____
_____	8. The old man told Mom the name she had been given when she was born.	8. What did the old man tell Mom about herself?	_____

## Book 6

Retelling Protocol for *Cal Ripken, Jr.: Play Ball!*

Name _____   **Date** _____

Directions to the Teacher: Do not tell the student the title of the book. Ask the student to reread pages 15 through 22 silently and be ready to retell the key points in his or her own words. Ask the student to close the book before retelling. As the student retells the information, number the key items in the space provided. The order of the retelling does not affect the score. **Do not prompt** until the student has told all that he or she can recall from the rereading.

If the student leaves out key points, prompt by using the statements/questions provided. You may reword or adjust prompts to suit your situation. Complete the scoring and observation guide.

Directions to the Student: "You have read this book before. Reread pages 15–22 silently now. When you are finished, I want you to retell the key points in your words."

Retelling Response Summary		Scoring Guide		
	Number Correct		**Unprompted**	**Prompted + Unprompted**
Unprompted	_____			
Prompted	_____	Acceptable	6–8	6–8
Unprompted + Prompted	_____	Unacceptable	0–5	0–5

Observation Guide

(Check items that apply)

_____ Retelling smooth and connected; reflected a good summary
_____ Retelling disorganized
_____ Required no prompting
_____ Gave only the important ideas
_____ Gave important ideas plus details
_____ Told unnecessary details
_____ Could not tell without prompting
_____ Showed signs of misreading words (Example: Kept saying "leejiz" instead of "leagues")
  _____
  _____
_____ Other
  _____
  _____

Unprompted Retelling (Number in order given.)	Key Points	Prompts (Use after unprompted retelling, if needed.)	Prompted Retelling (Check items correctly given.)
_____	1. Cal's dad took a job with the Orioles, so he was home more.	1. What was good about Cal's dad's new job?	_____
_____	2. Cal played baseball in high school.	2. What did Cal do in high school?	_____
_____	3. Cal's dad helped him improve his hitting.	3. Did Cal and his dad do anything together?	_____
_____	4. Cal worked hard to solve a challenging math problem.	4. What did Cal do in class?	_____
_____	5. Cal was drafted by the Orioles.	5. What happened to Cal after high school?	_____
_____	6. Cal played in the minor leagues.	6. Where did Cal first play professional baseball?	_____
_____	7. During the winter, Cal played in Florida and Puerto Rico.	7. Where did Cal play during the winter?	_____
_____	8. Cal's last game in the minor leagues was the longest game in baseball history.	8. What was special about Cal's last game in the minor leagues?	_____

## Book 7

Retelling Protocol for *Mountains*

....

Name _____ **Date** _____

Directions to the Teacher: Do not tell the student the title of the book. Ask the student to reread pages 28 through 32 silently and be ready to retell the key points in his or her own words. Ask the student to close the book before retelling. As the student retells the information, number the key items in the space provided. The order of the retelling does not affect the score. **Do not prompt** until the student has told all that he or she can recall from the rereading.

If the student leaves out key points, prompt by using the statements/questions provided. You may reword or adjust prompts to suit your situation. Complete the scoring and observation guide.

Directions to the Student: "You have read this book before. Reread pages 28–32 silently now. When you are finished, I want you to retell the key points in your words."

Retelling Response Summary		Scoring Guide		
	Number Correct		**Unprompted**	**Prompted + Unprompted**
Unprompted	_____			
Prompted	_____	Acceptable	4–6	4–6
Unprompted + Prompted	_____	Unacceptable	0–3	0–3

Observation Guide

(Check items that apply)

_____ Retelling smooth and connected; reflected a good summary
_____ Retelling disorganized
_____ Required no prompting
_____ Gave only the important ideas
_____ Gave important ideas plus details
_____ Told unnecessary details
_____ Could not tell without prompting
_____ Showed signs of misreading words (Example: Kept saying "habits" instead of "habitats")
_____
_____
_____ Other
_____
_____
_____

Unprompted Retelling (Number in order given.)	Key Points	Prompts (Use after unprompted retelling, if needed.)	Prompted Retelling (Check items correctly given.)
_____	1. The higher slopes have low-growing plants, not trees.	1. Are there many trees above the timberline on a mountain?	_____
_____	2. Small animals and sure-footed goats can live on the high slopes.	2. What kinds of animals can live on the high slopes?	_____
_____	3. The air contains less oxygen.	3. Why is it hard to breathe high up on a mountain?	_____
_____	4. Herd animals provide milk, meat, and wool.	4. What do herd animals provide for mountain people?	_____
_____	5. Terraces are small fields that are cut into the steep sides of mountains.	5. What are terraces?	_____
_____	6. Farms and cities depend on mountain lakes for drinking water.	6. Why do farms and cities depend on mountain lakes?	_____

## Book 8

Retelling Protocol for *Jesse Jackson: I Am Somebody!*

●●

Name _____ **Date** _____

Directions to the Teacher: Do not tell the student the title of the book. Ask the student to reread pages 23 through 28 silently and be ready to retell the key points in his or her own words. Ask the student to close the book before retelling. As the student retells the information, number the key items in the space provided. The order of the retelling does not affect the score. **Do not prompt** until the student has told all that he or she can recall from the rereading.

If the student leaves out key points, prompt by using the statements/questions provided. You may reword or adjust prompts to suit your situation. Complete the scoring and observation guide.

Directions to the Student: "You have read this book before. Reread pages 23–28 silently now. When you are finished, I want you to retell the key points in your words."

Retelling Response Summary		Scoring Guide		
Number Correct			**Unprompted**	**Prompted + Unprompted**
Unprompted _____				
Prompted _____		Acceptable	6–8	6–8
Unprompted + Prompted _____		Unacceptable	0–5	0–5

Observation Guide

(Check items that apply)

_____ Retelling smooth and connected; reflected a good summary
_____ Retelling disorganized
_____ Required no prompting
_____ Gave only the important ideas
_____ Gave important ideas plus details
_____ Told unnecessary details
_____ Could not tell without prompting
_____ Showed signs of misreading words (Example: Kept saying "breadbresket" instead of "breadbasket")

_____
_____

_____ Other
_____
_____
_____

Unprompted Retelling (Number in order given.)	Key Points	Prompts (Use after unprompted retelling, if needed.)	Prompted Retelling (Check items correctly given.)
_____	1. In Chicago, Jackson started Operation Breadbasket.	1. What organization did Jackson start in Chicago?	_____
_____	2. Operation Breadbasket's goal was to bring bread, money, and income to black and poor people in Chicago.	2. What was the goal of Operation Breadbasket?	_____
_____	3. Jackson told people to boycott stores that didn't hire black people.	3. What did Jackson tell people to do if a store didn't hire blacks?	_____
_____	4. Because of the boycotts, stores lost business and were forced to hire blacks.	4. What happened when people stopped shopping at a store?	_____
_____	5. Jackson continued to preach on Saturday mornings.	5. What did Jackson still find time to do even after working on Operation Breadbasket?	_____
_____	6. Dr. King was shot.	6. What happened to Dr. King?	_____
_____	7. Many young African Americans rioted.	7. What was the reaction across the country to the murder?	_____
_____	8. Jackson called for a nonviolent response.	8. What did Jackson do in response to the rioting?	_____

## Book 9

Retelling Protocol for *Lakota Hoop Dancer*

• •

Name _____ **Date** _____

Directions to the Teacher: Do not tell the student the title of the book. Ask the student to reread pages 7 through 15 silently and be ready to retell the key points in his or her own words. Ask the student to close the book before retelling. As the student retells the information, number the key items in the space provided. The order of the retelling does not affect the score. **Do not prompt** until the student has told all that he or she can recall from the rereading.

If the student leaves out key points, prompt by using the statements/questions provided. You may reword or adjust prompts to suit your situation. Complete the scoring and observation guide.

Directions to the Student: "You have read this book before. Reread pages 7–15 silently now. When you are finished, I want you to retell the key points in your words."

Retelling Response Summary		Scoring Guide		
Number Correct			**Unprompted**	**Prompted + Unprompted**
Unprompted	_____			
Prompted	_____	Acceptable	5–7	5–7
Unprompted + Prompted	_____	Unacceptable	0–4	0–4

Observation Guide

(Check items that apply)

_____ Retelling smooth and connected; reflected a good summary
_____ Retelling disorganized
_____ Required no prompting
_____ Gave only the important ideas
_____ Gave important ideas plus details
_____ Told unnecessary details
_____ Could not tell without prompting
_____ Showed signs of misreading words (Example: Kept saying "prayer" instead of "prairie")
       _____
       _____
_____ Other
       _____
       _____
       _____

Unprompted Retelling (Number in order given.)	Key Points	Prompts (Use after unprompted retelling, if needed.)	Prompted Retelling (Check items correctly given.)
_____	1. Kevin Locke is an American Indian from the Lakota Nation.	1. Who is Kevin Locke?	_____
_____	2. Kevin lives on a reservation in South Dakota.	2. Where does Kevin live?	_____
_____	3. Kevin loves the prairie land upon which he lives.	3. How does Kevin feel about the land upon which he lives?	_____
_____	4. Kevin learned about Lakota traditions from traveling with his uncles and their friends.	4. How did Kevin learn about his nation's culture?	_____
_____	5. Kevin passes along Lakota traditions by teaching them to his own children and by performing the hoop dance all over the world.	5. How does Kevin keep Lakota traditions alive?	_____
_____	6. The hoop Kevin dances with stands for unity and equality. (**Note**: Accept a retelling that mentions at least two of these five: unity, equality, harmony, balance, and the cycle of life.)	6. What does a hoop stand for?	_____
_____	7. The Lakota believe circles have special meanings. They believe that when people gather in a circle, no one is left out.	7. What does a circle mean to the Lakota people?	_____

## Book 10

Retelling Protocol for *Tunnels, Tracks, and Trains: Building a Subway*

· ·

Name _____ **Date** _____

Directions to the Teacher: Do not tell the student the title of the book. Ask the student to reread pages 11 through 21 silently and be ready to retell the key points in his or her own words. Ask the student to close the book before retelling. As the student retells the information, number the key items in the space provided. The order of the retelling does not affect the score. **Do not prompt** until the student has told all that he or she can recall from the rereading.

If the student leaves out key points, prompt by using the statements/questions provided. You may reword or adjust prompts to suit your situation. Complete the scoring and observation guide.

Directions to the Student: "You have read this book before. Reread pages 11–21 silently now. When you are finished, I want you to retell the key points in your words."

Retelling Response Summary		Scoring Guide		
Number Correct			**Unprompted**	**Prompted + Unprompted**
Unprompted	_____			
Prompted	_____	Acceptable	5–7	5–7
Unprompted + Prompted	_____	Unacceptable	0–4	0–4

Observation Guide

(Check items that apply)

_____ Retelling smooth and connected; reflected a good summary
_____ Retelling disorganized
_____ Required no prompting
_____ Gave only the important ideas
_____ Gave important ideas plus details
_____ Told unnecessary details
_____ Could not tell without prompting
_____ Showed signs of misreading words (Example: Kept saying "boxing" instead of "boring")
_____
_____
_____ Other
_____
_____
_____

Unprompted Retelling (Number in order given.)	Key Points	Prompts (Use after unprompted retelling, if needed.)	Prompted Retelling (Check items correctly given.)
_____	1. MacArthur Park will become a center of subway activity for two years.	1. What will happen to MacArthur Park for two years?	_____
_____	2. The ducks and geese are moved from the park's lake to lakes in other parks.	2. What happens to the living things in the park?	_____
_____	3. Then the lake is drained.	3. What happens after the ducks and geese are moved?	_____
_____	4. Workers dig a huge pit in the park.	4. What do the workers do to the park?	_____
_____	5. They reinforce the walls of the pit and line it with cement.	5. How do they make sure the pit doesn't collapse?	_____
_____	6. The boring machine is lowered into the pit and assembled.	6. What happens inside the pit?	_____
_____	7. The boring machine begins to dig the tunnel.	7. What does the boring machine do?	_____

## Book 11

Retelling Protocol for *Gloria Estefan: Cuban-American Singing Star*

Name _____ **Date** _____

Directions to the Teacher: Do not tell the student the title of the book. Ask the student to reread pages 19 through 25 silently and be ready to retell the key points in his or her own words. Ask the student to close the book before retelling. As the student retells the information, number the key items in the space provided. The order of the retelling does not affect the score. **Do not prompt** until the student has told all that he or she can recall from the rereading.

If the student leaves out key points, prompt by using the statements/questions provided. You may reword or adjust prompts to suit your situation. Complete the scoring and observation guide.

Directions to the Student: "You have read this book before. Reread pages 19–25 silently now. When you are finished, I want you to retell the key points in your words."

Retelling Response Summary		Scoring Guide		
	Number Correct		**Unprompted**	**Prompted + Unprompted**
Unprompted	_____			
Prompted	_____	Acceptable	5–7	5–7
Unprompted + Prompted	_____	Unacceptable	0–4	0–4

Observation Guide

(Check items that apply)

_____ Retelling smooth and connected; reflected a good summary
_____ Retelling disorganized
_____ Required no prompting
_____ Gave only the important ideas
_____ Gave important ideas plus details
_____ Told unnecessary details
_____ Could not tell without prompting
_____ Showed signs of misreading words (Example: Kept saying "poplar" instead of "popular")
    _____
    _____
_____ Other
    _____
    _____
    _____

Unprompted Retelling (Number in order given.)	Key Points	Prompts (Use after unprompted retelling, if needed.)	Prompted Retelling (Check items correctly given.)
_____	1. The Miami Sound Machine got a record contract.	1. What did the band's local success lead to?	_____
_____	2. The band recorded songs in Spanish.	2. What kind of music did the band first record?	_____
_____	3. Estefan found a growing audience of Spanish-speaking people.	3. What audience did Estefan first have?	_____
_____	4. The band recorded "Dr. Beat" and it was popular with both Spanish- and English-speaking people.	4. What happened when the band recorded "Dr. Beat"?	_____
_____	5. The band recorded a crossover album.	5. What did the band do that gave them a larger audience?	_____
_____	6. Estefan and the band became popular all over the world.	6. Was the Miami Sound Machine popular only in the United States?	_____
_____	7. Gloria won the award for Songwriter of the Year.	7. Did Gloria gain any special recognition for songwriting?	_____

## Book 12

Retelling Protocol for *What Are You Figuring Now? Benjamin Banneker*

• •

Name _____ **Date** _____

Directions to the Teacher: Do not tell the student the title of the book. Ask the student to reread pages 35 through 39 silently and be ready to retell the key points in his or her own words. Ask the student to close the book before retelling. As the student retells the information, number the key items in the space provided. The order of the retelling does not affect the score. **Do not prompt** until the student has told all that he or she can recall from the rereading.

If the student leaves out key points, prompt by using the statements/questions provided. You may reword or adjust prompts to suit your situation. Complete the scoring and observation guide.

Directions to the Student: "You have read this book before. Reread pages 35–39 silently now. When you are finished, I want you to retell the key points in your words."

Retelling Response Summary		Scoring Guide		
Number Correct			**Unprompted**	**Prompted + Unprompted**
Unprompted _____				
Prompted _____		Acceptable	7–9	7–9
Unprompted + Prompted _____		Unacceptable	0–6	0–6
Observation Guide				

(Check items that apply)

_____ Retelling smooth and connected; reflected a good summary
_____ Retelling disorganized
_____ Required no prompting
_____ Gave only the important ideas
_____ Gave important ideas plus details
_____ Told unnecessary details
_____ Could not tell without prompting
_____ Showed signs of misreading words (Example: Kept saying "serving" instead of "surveying")
  _____
  _____
_____ Other
  _____
  _____

Unprompted Retelling (Number in order given.)	Key Points	Prompts (Use after unprompted retelling, if needed.)	Prompted Retelling (Check items correctly given.)
_____	1. The United States and Britain signed a peace treaty.	1. What happened to the nation at the beginning of the section?	_____
_____	2. Benjamin couldn't understand why a "free" country still allowed slavery.	2. What bothered Benjamin about the new United States?	_____
_____	3. George Ellicott studied surveying, but needed Benjamin's help with the math.	3. Why did George Ellicott come to Benjamin for help?	_____
_____	4. Benjamin learned surveying as he helped George.	4. What did Benjamin learn as he helped George?	_____
_____	5. Benjamin learned astronomy by helping his friend George learn astronomy.	5. Did Benjamin learn any other subjects?	_____
_____	6. George lent Benjamin astronomy books and instruments.	6. Did George give anything to Benjamin?	_____
_____	7. Benjamin used the telescope at night and ran the farm during the day.	7. How did Benjamin spend his days and nights?	_____
_____	8. Benjamin decided to write an almanac.	8. What did Benjamin decide to do?	_____
_____	9. For practice, Benjamin predicted an eclipse of the sun.	9. What did Benjamin do to show he could be an almanac-maker?	_____

## Book 13

Retelling Protocol for *Lightning*

●●

Name _____ **Date** _____

Directions to the Teacher: Do not tell the student the title of the book. Ask the student to reread pages 42 through 43 silently and be ready to retell the key points in his or her own words. Ask the student to close the book before retelling. As the student retells the information, number the key items in the space provided. The order of the retelling does not affect the score. **Do not prompt** until the student has told all that he or she can recall from the rereading.

If the student leaves out key points, prompt by using the statements/questions provided. You may reword or adjust prompts to suit your situation. Complete the scoring and observation guide.

Directions to the Student: "You have read this book before. Reread pages 42–43 silently now. When you are finished, I want you to retell the key points in your words."

Retelling Response Summary		Scoring Guide		
	Number Correct		**Unprompted**	**Prompted + Unprompted**
Unprompted	_____			
Prompted	_____	Acceptable	5–7	5–7
Unprompted + Prompted	_____	Unacceptable	0–4	0–4

Observation Guide

(Check items that apply)

_____ Retelling smooth and connected; reflected a good summary
_____ Retelling disorganized
_____ Required no prompting
_____ Gave only the important ideas
_____ Gave important ideas plus details
_____ Told unnecessary details
_____ Could not tell without prompting
_____ Showed signs of misreading words (Example: Kept saying "sheeler" instead of "shelter")
_____
_____
_____ Other
_____
_____
_____

Unprompted Retelling (Number in order given.)	Key Points	Prompts (Use after unprompted retelling, if needed.)	Prompted Retelling (Check items correctly given.)
_____	1. Lightning is very dangerous and kills hundreds of people a year.	1. Is lightning dangerous to people?	_____
_____	2. If you're near a thunderstorm, get inside a building or car if you can.	2. Where should you go if a thunderstorm is approaching?	_____
_____	3. Don't use electric appliances, and keep away from metal objects.	3. What shouldn't you use in a thunderstorm?	_____
_____	4. If you're swimming or on a boat, leave the water at once.	4. What should you do if you are in the water or on a boat in the water in a thunderstorm?	_____
_____	5. If you're in the open, stay as low as you can, because lightning hits tall objects.	5. What should you do in a thunderstorm if you can't reach shelter? Why?	_____
_____	6. Don't shelter near or under very tall objects.	6. What kind of shelter should you avoid in a thunderstorm?	_____
_____	7. Sometimes tingling tells you that lightning is about to strike, and you should crouch down but not lie down.	7. How can you tell if lightning will strike? What should you do?	_____

## Book 14

Retelling Protocol for *Sports Lab: How Science Has Changed Sports*

Name _____ **Date** _____

Directions to the Teacher: **Do not tell the student the title of the book.** Ask the student to reread pages 25 through 31 silently and be ready to retell the key points in his or her own words. Ask the student to close the book before retelling. As the student retells the information, number the key items in the space provided. The order of the retelling does not affect the score. **Do not prompt** until the student has told all that he or she can recall from the rereading.

If the student leaves out key points, prompt by using the statements/questions provided. You may reword or adjust prompts to suit your situation. Complete the scoring and observation guide.

Directions to the Student: "You have read this book before. Reread pages 25–31 silently now. When you are finished, I want you to retell the key points in your words."

Retelling Response Summary		Scoring Guide		
	Number Correct		**Unprompted**	**Prompted + Unprompted**
Unprompted	_____			
Prompted	_____	Acceptable	7–9	7–9
Unprompted + Prompted	_____	Unacceptable	0–6	0–6

Observation Guide

(Check items that apply)

_____ Retelling smooth and connected; reflected a good summary
_____ Retelling disorganized
_____ Required no prompting
_____ Gave only the important ideas
_____ Gave important ideas plus details
_____ Told unnecessary details
_____ Could not tell without prompting
_____ Showed signs of misreading words (Example: Kept saying "medicine" instead of "medical")
_____
_____
_____ Other
_____
_____
_____

Unprompted Retelling (Number in order given.)	Key Points	Prompts (Use after unprompted retelling, if needed.)	Prompted Retelling (Check items correctly given.)
_____	1. Nicole and John are competing in the Junior Nationals.	1. Who is the chapter about? What are they doing at the beginning?	_____
_____	2. They hope to earn a chance to enter the USOC Training Center program.	2. Is there a special reason they want to do well at the Junior Nationals?	_____
_____	3. They finish a disappointing seventh, but qualify for the program anyway.	3. What is the outcome?	_____
_____	4. First, they go through a medical exam.	4. What is the first thing that happens at the USOC Training Center?	_____
_____	5. A nutritionist examines everything they eat.	5. What does a nutritionist do with Nicole and John?	_____
_____	6. A physiologist studies their muscles and their training program.	6. What does a physiologist do with Nicole and John?	_____
_____	7. Nicole, John, and their coach meet with psychologists.	7. Who meets with the psychologists?	_____
_____	8. Coaches and trainers use computers and other technology to study how Nicole and John move.	8. Is technology used at the USOC Training Center?	_____
_____	9. Nicole and John are invited to compete at the Olympics Sports Festival.	9. Where are Nicole and John invited to compete?	_____

## Book 15

Retelling Protocol for *On the Court with . . . Lisa Leslie*

• •

Name _____ **Date** _____

Directions to the Teacher: Do not tell the student the title of the book. Ask the student to reread pages 92 through 97 silently and be ready to retell the key points in his or her own words. Ask the student to close the book before retelling. As the student retells the information, number the key items in the space provided. The order of the retelling does not affect the score. **Do not prompt** until the student has told all that he or she can recall from the rereading.

If the student leaves out key points, prompt by using the statements/questions provided. You may reword or adjust prompts to suit your situation. Complete the scoring and observation guide.

Directions to the Student: "You have read this book before. Reread pages 92–97 silently now. When you are finished, I want you to retell the key points in your words."

Retelling Response Summary		Scoring Guide		
	Number Correct		**Unprompted**	**Prompted + Unprompted**
Unprompted	_____			
Prompted	_____			
Unprompted + Prompted	_____	Acceptable	5–7	5–7
		Unacceptable	0–4	0–4

Observation Guide

(Check items that apply)

_____ Retelling smooth and connected; reflected a good summary
_____ Retelling disorganized
_____ Required no prompting
_____ Gave only the important ideas
_____ Gave important ideas plus details
_____ Told unnecessary details
_____ Could not tell without prompting
_____ Showed signs of misreading words (Example: Kept saying "fools" instead of "fouls")
_____
_____
_____ Other
_____
_____

Unprompted Retelling (Number in order given.)	Key Points	Prompts (Use after unprompted retelling, if needed.)	Prompted Retelling (Check items correctly given.)
_____	1. Both Brazil and the U.S. were undefeated heading into the Olympic final.	1. How many games had the U.S. and Brazil lost before the Olympic final?	_____
_____	2. The game between Brazil and the U.S. took place on the last night of the Olympics.	2. When was the rematch between Brazil and the U.S.?	_____
_____	3. The Americans got off to a slow start.	3. How did the U.S. play at the start of the game?	_____
_____	4. Brazil's first-string center was pulled from the game for fouls.	4. Which important player was taken out of the game?	_____
_____	5. Brazil's second-string center couldn't keep up with Lisa, and Lisa kept scoring.	5. How did Brazil's second-string center play against Lisa?	_____
_____	6. Everyone on the U.S. team got into the game and scored.	6. Did everyone on the U.S. team play?	_____
_____	7. The U.S. won the game.	7. Who won the game?	_____

## Book 16

Retelling Protocol for *An Even Break*

• •

Name _____ **Date** _____

Directions to the Teacher: Do not tell the student the title of the book. Ask the student to reread pages 52 through 55 silently and be ready to retell the key points in his or her own words. Ask the student to close the book before retelling. As the student retells the information, number the key items in the space provided. The order of the retelling does not affect the score. **Do not prompt** until the student has told all that he or she can recall from the rereading.

If the student leaves out key points, prompt by using the statements/questions provided. You may reword or adjust prompts to suit your situation. Complete the scoring and observation guide.

Directions to the Student: "You have read this book before. Reread pages 52–55 silently now. When you are finished, I want you to retell the key points in your words."

Retelling Response Summary		Scoring Guide		
	Number Correct		**Unprompted**	**Prompted + Unprompted**
Unprompted	_____			
Prompted	_____	Acceptable	6–8	6–8
Unprompted + Prompted	_____	Unacceptable	0–5	0–5

Observation Guide

(Check items that apply)

_____ Retelling smooth and connected; reflected a good summary
_____ Retelling disorganized
_____ Required no prompting
_____ Gave only the important ideas
_____ Gave important ideas plus details
_____ Told unnecessary details
_____ Could not tell without prompting
_____ Showed signs of misreading words (Example: Kept saying "finishing" instead of "fishing")
_____
_____
_____ Other
_____
_____
_____

Unprompted Retelling (Number in order given.)	Key Points	Prompts (Use after unprompted retelling, if needed.)	Prompted Retelling (Check items correctly given.)
_____	1. Frisk closed the Back Room at six and hurried home for his fishing gear.	1. What did Frisk do at six o'clock?	_____
_____	2. His mom didn't want him to go out fishing so late; she worried about him.	2. Why didn't Shelly want Frisk to go fishing?	_____
_____	3. Frisk enjoyed the sunset.	3. What did Frisk enjoy when he went fishing?	_____
_____	4. Teddy Wald came along and grabbed Frisk's fishing gear from him.	4. Who came along while Frisk was fishing?	_____
_____	5. Frisk waited to see what would happen next.	5. What did Frisk do when Teddy took the rod?	_____
_____	6. Teddy Wald's father came along in a truck.	6. Who came along?	_____
_____	7. Mr. Wald accused his son of taking the fishing gear from Frisk.	7. What did Mr. Wald accuse his son of?	_____
_____	8. Frisk protected Teddy and said he had lent him the gear to try.	8. What did Frisk do for Teddy?	_____

## Book 17

Retelling Protocol for *El Duque: The Story of Orlando Hernandez*

• •

Name _____ **Date** _____

Directions to the Teacher: Do not tell the student the title of the book. Ask the student to reread pages 44 through 50 silently and be ready to retell the key points in his or her own words. Ask the student to close the book before retelling. As the student retells the information, number the key items in the space provided. The order of the retelling does not affect the score. **Do not prompt** until the student has told all that he or she can recall from the rereading.

If the student leaves out key points, prompt by using the statements/questions provided. You may reword or adjust prompts to suit your situation. Complete the scoring and observation guide.

Directions to the Student: "You have read this book before. Reread pages 44–50 silently now. When you are finished, I want you to retell the key points in your words."

Retelling Response Summary		Scoring Guide		
	Number Correct		**Unprompted**	**Prompted + Unprompted**
Unprompted _____				
Prompted _____		Acceptable	6–8	6–8
Unprompted + Prompted _____		Unacceptable	0–5	0–5

Observation Guide

(Check items that apply)

_____ Retelling smooth and connected; reflected a good summary
_____ Retelling disorganized
_____ Required no prompting
_____ Gave only the important ideas
_____ Gave important ideas plus details
_____ Told unnecessary details
_____ Could not tell without prompting
_____ Showed signs of misreading words (Example: Kept saying "say" instead of "sea")

_____
_____

_____ Other

_____
_____
_____

Unprompted Retelling (Number in order given.)	Key Points	Prompts (Use after unprompted retelling, if needed.)	Prompted Retelling (Check items correctly given.)
_____	1. El Duque decides to defect.	1. What does El Duque decide to do at the beginning of the chapter?	_____
_____	2. On Christmas night, he and Noris attend a Christmas party. They eat as much as they can.	2. What do El Duque and Noris do on Christmas night?	_____
_____	3. At dawn, El Duque, Noris, and six others get into a homemade boat and head out to sea.	3. What happens at dawn the next day?	_____
_____	4. After eight or nine hours, the seas turn rough.	4. What happens after eight or nine hours at sea?	_____
_____	5. Noris gets sick, and everyone is worried.	5. How does this affect the defectors?	_____
_____	6. They land on an uninhabited island.	6. Do they find safety?	_____
_____	7. They survive by catching seafood and huddling together for warmth.	7. How do they survive on the island?	_____
_____	8. Finally, a U.S. Coast Guard helicopter rescues them.	8. How do they get off the island?	_____

## Book 18

Retelling Protocol for *Marisol and Magdalena: The Sound of Our Sisterhood*

Name _____ **Date** _____

Directions to the Teacher: Do not tell the student the title of the book. Ask the student to reread pages 72 through 81 silently and be ready to retell the key points in his or her own words. Ask the student to close the book before retelling. As the student retells the information, number the key items in the space provided. The order of the retelling does not affect the score. **Do not prompt** until the student has told all that he or she can recall from the rereading.

If the student leaves out key points, prompt by using the statements/questions provided. You may reword or adjust prompts to suit your situation. Complete the scoring and observation guide.

Directions to the Student: "You have read this book before. Reread pages 72–81 silently now. When you are finished, I want you to retell the key points in your words."

Retelling Response Summary		Scoring Guide		
Number Correct			**Unprompted**	**Prompted + Unprompted**
Unprompted	_____			
Prompted	_____	Acceptable	5–7	5–7
Unprompted + Prompted	_____	Unacceptable	0–4	0–4

Observation Guide

(Check items that apply)

_____ Retelling smooth and connected; reflected a good summary
_____ Retelling disorganized
_____ Required no prompting
_____ Gave only the important ideas
_____ Gave important ideas plus details
_____ Told unnecessary details
_____ Could not tell without prompting
_____ Showed signs of misreading words (Example: Kept saying "abeulah" instead of "Abuela")

_____

_____

_____ Other _____

_____

_____

_____

Unprompted Retelling (Number in order given.)	Key Points	Prompts (Use after unprompted retelling, if needed.)	Prompted Retelling (Check items correctly given.)
_____	1. Abuela meets her at the airport.	1. Who meets Marisol at the airport?	_____
_____	2. They go to Abuela's apartment.	2. Where does Abuela take Marisol?	_____
_____	3. Abuela tells Marisol she can be a kid; Abuela will do the cooking and cleaning.	3. What does Abuela tell Marisol she can do?	_____
_____	4. Marisol falls asleep thinking of her father.	4. What does Marisol think about as she falls asleep?	_____
_____	5. When she wakes up, the kitchen is full of strangers.	5. What is the first thing Marisol notices when she wakes up the next morning?	_____
_____	6. They turn out to be neighbors and friends of the family.	6. Who are these people?	_____
_____	7. Marisol meets Ana, a girl her own age who lives next door.	7. Is there anyone Marisol's age there?	_____

Oral Reading Check

Name _____   **Date** _____

A Beauty of a Plan
Book #1, pages 2–4 (96 words)

It was four o'clock on a sunny Wednesday afternoon. But there were still students hard at work at Meadow Middle School.

Mr. Flores ran the shop classes. Some days he let students stay late to work on their projects.

Sheila Ross and Michael DeWitt put the finishing touches on their cabinet.

"Wow!" Michael said. "This is our best work yet!"

Sheila and Michael cleaned up and got ready to go.

"Mr. Flores," said Sheila, "we're finished!"

Mr. Flores checked their work. "Looking good!" he said. "I can't wait to see the plans for your next project!"

Scoring Guide   _____ – _____ = _____
   Number of Miscues   Self-corrections   Miscues Counted

   _____ Acceptable: 0–10 miscues
   _____ Unacceptable: 11+ miscues

Observations   _____ fluent oral reading (See TM, page T48 for criteria.)
   _____ good self-correction strategies
   _____ needs to use phonics (_____)
   _____ needs to use structural elements (_____)
   _____ overuses context

Comments   _____
   _____
   _____
   _____

Oral Reading Check

Name _____ **Date** _____

The Lost Expedition
Book #2, pages 2–3 (98 words)

Antarctica is the coldest place on Earth. It is so cold that the seas surrounding the continent freeze over in winter, forming a solid ice pack. Even in summer, temperatures rarely rise above freezing, and huge sheets of ice called floes fill the water.

Yet, in the early 1900's, explorers were eager to travel to this harsh, icy continent. Each wanted to be the first to reach the South Pole.

One of these daring explorers was Ernest Shackleton. In 1907–1909, he was part of an expedition that came closer to the South Pole than anyone had before.

Scoring Guide _____ – _____ = _____
 Number of Miscues   Self-corrections   Miscues Counted

_____ Acceptable: 0–10 miscues
_____ Unacceptable: 11+ miscues

Observations
_____ fluent oral reading (See TM, page T48 for criteria.)
_____ good self-correction strategies
_____ needs to use phonics (_____)
_____ needs to use structural elements (_____)
_____ overuses context

Comments _____
_____
_____
_____

Oral Reading Check

Name _____ **Date** _____

Owl

Book #3, pages 7–10 (92 words)

There is a bird that flies when the moon is high. Like a shadow, it glides silently through the night forest.

It is the owl.

Owls spend the day in nests and hiding places. In the late afternoon they come out and look around them. Then, in the soft gray dusk, owls spread their wings and take off.

All owls are hunters. Some eat insects, birds, or fish. Most owls eat little animals like mice. Even in the dark, an owl's big eyes can see a mouse scurrying through a field below.

Scoring Guide   _____ − _____ = _____
                    Number of Miscues   Self-corrections   Miscues Counted

                    _____ Acceptable: 0–9 miscues
                    _____ Unacceptable: 10+ miscues

Observations   _____ fluent oral reading (See TM, page T48 for criteria.)
                    _____ good self-correction strategies
                    _____ needs to use phonics (_____)
                    _____ needs to use structural elements (_____)
                    _____ overuses context

Comments   _____
                    _____
                    _____
                    _____

Oral Reading Check

Name _____   **Date** _____

The Babe & I

Book #4, pages 5–7 (119 words)

For my birthday I was hoping my parents would give me a bicycle. They only gave me a dime. I was disappointed, but not surprised. It was 1932, in the midst of the Great Depression, and millions of people were out of work. We were lucky. My father had a job. But we never seemed to have much money. Where we lived, in the Bronx, New York, everyone was poor.

"Happy birthday," Dad said when I walked him outside. I watched him go off, carrying his briefcase and smiling.

My neighbor Jacob was tossing a ball and catching it. He threw it to me and shouted, "Give me a high one. I'm Babe Ruth, the world's greatest baseball player."

Scoring Guide   _____ − _____ = _____
                    Number of Miscues   Self-corrections   Miscues Counted

_____ Acceptable: 0–12 miscues
_____ Unacceptable: 13+ miscues

Observations   _____ fluent oral reading (See TM, page T48 for criteria.)
_____ good self-correction strategies
_____ needs to use phonics (_____)
_____ needs to use structural elements (_____)
_____ overuses context

Comments   _____
_____
_____
_____

Oral Reading Check

Name _____ **Date** _____

Journey Home

Book #5, pages 3–4 (109 words)

Mom and I are packing for our big trip to Vietnam. A long time ago when Mom was a baby she was left at an orphanage in Saigon during the Vietnam War. The nuns named her Trinh Nu Linh, but these days Mom is called Lin. Now, Mom's going back and taking me with her to help search for her birth family. I'm excited, but I'm also afraid of what we'll find when we get there.

I want to take the kite on my wall, but Mom says it's too fragile to make the journey. The kite was her only possession when she was adopted and brought to America.

Scoring Guide _____ – _____ = _____
                    Number of Miscues   Self-corrections   Miscues Counted

_____ Acceptable: 0–11 miscues
_____ Unacceptable: 12+ miscues

Observations _____ fluent oral reading (See TM, page T48 for criteria.)
_____ good self-correction strategies
_____ needs to use phonics (_____)
_____ needs to use structural elements (_____)
_____ overuses context

Comments _____
_____
_____
_____

Oral Reading Check

Name _____ **Date** _____

Cal Ripken, Jr.: Play Ball!
Book #6, page 5 (93 words)

The year was 1981. I was sitting on the Orioles bench waiting to play pro baseball.

Me? I thought. Sitting on the bench? I was not used to this. This wasn't what I had in mind. Not for the big leagues.

But the Baltimore Orioles had always been my favorite team. While I was growing up in Maryland in the 1960s and 1970s, they had one winning season after another. By 1981, they had been in five World Series, and they had won two championships.

It was my first year with the Orioles.

Scoring Guide

_____ – _____ = _____
Number of Miscues   Self-corrections   Miscues Counted

_____ Acceptable: 0–9 miscues
_____ Unacceptable: 10+ miscues

Observations

_____ fluent oral reading (See TM, page T48 for criteria.)
_____ good self-correction strategies
_____ needs to use phonics (_____)
_____ needs to use structural elements (_____)
_____ overuses context

Comments _____

_____

_____

_____

Oral Reading Check

Name _____ **Date** _____

Mountains

Book #7, pages 5–6 (107 words)

Mountains are a dramatic reminder of ages past and ages to come. They seem to be solid and unchanging, but they are not everlasting. Mountains are born, grow tall over the years, change their shapes, and are finally worn down and disappear into the earth from which they came. These processes take millions of years, but a million years in the life of our planet is like a few days in the life of a person.

Mountains are tall, but just how tall does one have to be to be called a mountain? The Himalayan Mountains in central Asia have at least fourteen peaks over 26,000 feet.

Scoring Guide _____ – _____ = _____
                Number of Miscues   Self-corrections   Miscues Counted

_____ Acceptable: 0–11 miscues
_____ Unacceptable: 12+ miscues

Observations
_____ fluent oral reading (See TM, page T48 for criteria.)
_____ good self-correction strategies
_____ needs to use phonics (_____)
_____ needs to use structural elements (_____)
_____ overuses context

Comments _____
_____
_____
_____

Oral Reading Check

Name _____ **Date** _____

Jesse Jackson, I Am Somebody!
Book #8, page 6 (95 words)

What would you do if you thought you were being treated unfairly at home or in school? What if your brother got to sit in the front seat of the car and you always had to sit in the back? What if some children in your class got brand-new books, and you had to use an old, torn paperback? What if you always had to play on the side of the playground without any swings? Would this be fair? Would it be "liberty and justice for all," like it says in the Pledge of Allegiance?

Scoring Guide

_____ – _____ = _____
Number of Miscues   Self-corrections   Miscues Counted

_____ Acceptable: 0–9 miscues
_____ Unacceptable: 10+ miscues

Observations

_____ fluent oral reading (See TM, page T48 for criteria.)
_____ good self-correction strategies
_____ needs to use phonics (_____)
_____ needs to use structural elements (_____)
_____ overuses context

Comments _____

_____

_____

_____

Oral Reading Check

Name _____   **Date** _____

Lakota Hoop Dancer
Book #9, page 5 (118 words)

Repeated strikes on the drum—like a heartbeat—and an intense, chantlike song draw people near. In the still, stubborn heat of a summer's day, an American Indian man performs a breathtaking dance for an eager audience. Red, yellow, and blue colors blur. His braided hair and the fringe on his outfit sway and snap. Hoops whirl.

People from many Indian Nations perform the hoop dance. No one knows for certain when or how the dance began. However, paintings of Lakota people dancing with hoops were made in the 1700s, and the dance was the subject of traditional Lakota songs that were recorded in the early 1900s. At that time, the hoop dance was called the rainbow dance.

Scoring Guide   _____ – _____ = _____
                              Number of Miscues   Self-corrections   Miscues Counted

                      _____ Acceptable: 0–12 miscues
                      _____ Unacceptable: 13+ miscues

Observations   _____ fluent oral reading (See TM, page T48 for criteria.)
                      _____ good self-correction strategies
                      _____ needs to use phonics (_____)
                      _____ needs to use structural elements (_____)
                      _____ overuses context

Comments   _____
                  _____
                  _____
                  _____

Oral Reading Check

Name _____ **Date** _____

Tunnels, Tracks, and Trains

Book #10, page 4 (116 words)

DANGER. Signs warn pedestrians to stay clear of construction. Jackhammering jolts the air. Massive backhoes, towering cranes, workers shoveling and measuring—construction crews are everywhere—downtown, midtown, and below the town! Los Angeles is getting a subway.

Big foreign cities like Moscow, Paris, Berlin, Tokyo, Mexico City, and London have subways. Boston has this country's earliest subway system; New York has the longest. There are under-grounds in Philadelphia, Chicago, San Francisco, Miami, Atlanta, and Washington, D.C.

Although city dwellers around the world ride subways, many people in Los Angeles find the idea strange. They are used to going everywhere by car. But the city is quickly becoming more densely populated, the freeways and streets more traffic-clogged.

Scoring Guide   _____ – _____ = _____
                     Number of Miscues   Self-corrections   Miscues Counted

                           _____ Acceptable: 0–12 miscues
                           _____ Unacceptable: 13+ miscues

Observations   _____ fluent oral reading (See TM, page T48 for criteria.)
                           _____ good self-correction strategies
                           _____ needs to use phonics (_____)
                           _____ needs to use structural elements (_____)
                           _____ overuses context

Comments   _____
_____
_____
_____

Oral Reading Check

Name _____ **Date** _____

Gloria Estefan

Book #11, page 5 (123 words)

It is hard to imagine Gloria Estefan stopping—even for a moment. On stage she leads the powerful ten-piece band, the Miami Sound Machine. In her concerts she sings, dances, jumps, and kicks her way from one side of the stage to the other. She is both star of the show and party host. She encourages her fans to join in, get up, sing along, and dance.

On March 20, 1990, however, everything stopped for Gloria Estefan—almost for good.

She had been traveling with her band around the United States, playing their music in many cities. That day, she was on a bus just outside the city of Scranton, Pennyslvania. It was snowing very hard. Estefan's bus stopped on an icy highway.

Scoring Guide _____ – _____ = _____
                   Number of Miscues   Self-corrections   Miscues Counted

_____ Acceptable: 0–12 miscues
_____ Unacceptable: 13+ miscues

Observations _____ fluent oral reading (See TM, page T48 for criteria.)
_____ good self-correction strategies
_____ needs to use phonics (_____)
_____ needs to use structural elements (_____)
_____ overuses context

Comments _____
_____
_____
_____

Oral Reading Check

Name _____ **Date** _____

What Are You Figuring Now, Benjamin Banneker?
Book #12, pages 6–8 (116 words)

In 1736, when wolves and wildcats (and the king of England) owned the Maryland woods, most folks lived on farms. Most of them didn't have clocks or watches or appointment books. They knew what day it was by looking at the almanac. They knew what time it was by looking at the sun.

On the Banneky farm in northern Maryland, it was three o'clock by the sun, and Benjamin Banneky was out working in the tobacco field. He heard the birds singing sleepily in the hickory trees. He knew the wolves and the wildcats were taking naps over in the woods. That's just what I'd like to do, thought Benjamin, feeling tired and hot and sticky.

Scoring Guide _____ – _____ = _____
Number of Miscues   Self-corrections   Miscues Counted

_____ Acceptable: 0–12 miscues
_____ Unacceptable: 13+ miscues

Observations _____ fluent oral reading (See TM, page T48 for criteria.)
_____ good self-correction strategies
_____ needs to use phonics (_____)
_____ needs to use structural elements (_____)
_____ overuses context

Comments _____
_____
_____
_____

Oral Reading Check

Name _____   **Date** _____

Lightning
Book #13, pages 6–8 (100 words)

Late in the evening, a dark cloud hangs in the sky. The air is calm. The birds are quiet. Even the blades of dry grass are still. Everything is hushed, waiting.

Suddenly a giant spark leaps through the air, connecting earth and sky. The spark flickers for an instant and disappears. There is a moment of silence. Then a tremendous CRACK rips through the quiet. Booming echoes follow, rolling across the land.

A thunderstorm drifts across the summer sky.

At any moment, there are about 1,800 thunderstorms happening around the world. About 100 lightning bolts strike the earth every second.

Scoring Guide   _____ – _____ = _____
                      Number of Miscues   Self-corrections   Miscues Counted

_____ Acceptable: 0–10 miscues
_____ Unacceptable: 11+ miscues

Observations   _____ fluent oral reading (See TM, page T48 for criteria.)
_____ good self-correction strategies
_____ needs to use phonics (_____)
_____ needs to use structural elements (_____)
_____ overuses context

Comments   _____
_____
_____
_____

Oral Reading Check

Name _____

Date _____

Sports Lab

Book #14, page 1   (128 words)

A feeling of electricity flashed through the stadium. The crowd seemed to sense that a record was about to be broken—a world record that had stood for over 23 years.

The scene was the 1991 World Track and Field Championships. United States athlete Mike Powell was challenging the world long jump record of 29 feet 2 inches. This was one of the longest-standing records in modern athletic competition. It had been set at the 1968 Mexico City Olympics by Bob Beamon of the United States.

Some people said it was the high altitude and thin air of Mexico City that allowed Bob Beamon to jump so far. And others said Beamon's record would never be broken. But Mike Powell was in Tokyo to challenge Beamon's world record.

Scoring Guide   _____ − _____ = _____

                       Number of Miscues   Self-corrections   Miscues Counted

                     _____ Acceptable: 0–13 miscues
                     _____ Unacceptable: 14+ miscues

Observations
     _____ fluent oral reading (See TM, page T48 for criteria.)
     _____ good self-correction strategies
     _____ needs to use phonics (_____)
     _____ needs to use structural elements (_____)
     _____ overuses context

Comments _____

_____

_____

_____

Oral Reading Check

Name _____ **Date** _____

On the Court with . . . Lisa Leslie

Book #15, page 1 (123 words)

"Why don't you play basketball?"

That was the last question twelve-year-old Lisa Leslie wanted to hear. She was just beginning the seventh grade in Carson, California, a city near Los Angeles, and she was already six feet, two inches tall. She wasn't very comfortable being so much taller than the other children her age. Nearly every day either a teacher or an older student walked up to her and, before they even said hello or introduced themselves, asked Lisa the same old question.

"Why don't you play basketball?"

Exasperated at being asked the same question over and over, Lisa often answered, "Because I hate it!" She was so tired of the question that she decided she hated basketball and never wanted to play.

Scoring Guide _____ – _____ = _____
              Number of Miscues   Self-corrections   Miscues Counted

_____ Acceptable: 0–12 miscues
_____ Unacceptable: 13+ miscues

Observations _____ fluent oral reading (See TM, page T48 for criteria.)
_____ good self-correction strategies
_____ needs to use phonics (_____)
_____ needs to use structural elements (_____)
_____ overuses context

Comments _____
_____
_____
_____

Oral Reading Check

Name _____   **Date** _____

An Even Break

Book #16, page 5 (95 words)

Frisk was four feet five inches tall, and skinny. He had large ears and a dimpled chin. Springing from his head was an unruly mass of red hair. His eyes were bright blue, he was speckled all over with freckles, and he had a high-pitched voice. Sometimes, much to his embarrassment, he squeaked when he got excited.

Frisk and Shelly lived in a four-room apartment in downtown Wilma. The apartment was located above Billy Compton's hardware store. If you could find the town, it was a cinch finding the store. Wilma had only one street.

Scoring Guide   _____ − _____ = _____
                     Number of Miscues   Self-corrections   Miscues Counted

_____ Acceptable: 0–9 miscues
_____ Unacceptable: 10+ miscues

Observations   _____ fluent oral reading (See TM, page T48 for criteria.)
                     _____ good self-correction strategies
                     _____ needs to use phonics (_____)
                     _____ needs to use structural elements (_____)
                     _____ overuses context

Comments   _____
                 _____
                 _____
                 _____

Oral Reading Check

Name _____   **Date** _____

El Duque
Book #17, page 9 (109 words)

June 3, 1998

New York City

He stood on the pitcher's mound at Yankee Stadium as thousands of fans cheered his name.

"Du-que! Du-que! Du-que!"

Although he hadn't yet thrown his first pitch, Orlando "El Duque" Hernandez was already a star. Now, standing in the center of the most famous baseball stadium in the world, he took a moment to let it all soak in. He gazed around the crowd with an expression of disbelief. People he had never seen before were rooting for him because they knew he had risked his life in order to be there. And now it was clear that he had finally made it.

Scoring Guide   _____ − _____ = _____
                     Number of Miscues   Self-corrections   Miscues Counted

          _____ Acceptable: 0–11 miscues
          _____ Unacceptable: 12+ miscues

Observations   _____ fluent oral reading (See TM, page T48 for criteria.)
                   _____ good self-correction strategies
                   _____ needs to use phonics (_____)
                   _____ needs to use structural elements (_____)
                   _____ overuses context

Comments   _____
               _____
               _____
               _____

Oral Reading Check

Name _____ **Date** _____

Marisol and Magdalena
Book #18, page 1 (122 words)

Do you know what it's like to be in a room full of people, but to feel completely alone? Outside of the noise and the talking and the eating—just apart from it, watching it all? That's how I felt tonight in the Rosarios' kitchen.

I've known the Rosario family since I was a little baby. I've been over to their house a million times. But tonight it was like noticing it all for the first time. Noticing not just what everything looked like, but how it all felt. When I stopped to think about it, I realized how happy it all made me—these same things, these same people, that I have seen over and over again, my whole life long.

Scoring Guide _____ – _____ = _____
  Number of Miscues   Self-corrections   Miscues Counted

_____ Acceptable: 0–12 miscues
_____ Unacceptable: 13+ miscues

Observations
_____ fluent oral reading (See TM, page T48 for criteria.)
_____ good self-correction strategies
_____ needs to use phonics (_____)
_____ needs to use structural elements (_____)
_____ overuses context

Comments _____
_____
_____
_____

Video Viewing Guide

Using the Viewing Guide

This guide has been designed to interact with the *SOAR TO SUCCESS* video by providing discussion prompts and teaching simulations to use after watching each section of the video. Read over the section prompts before viewing each segment.

After you discuss each section, list any remaining questions. These may be answered later in the video. For further clarity, you may need to consult with other teachers using *SOAR TO SUCCESS*.

SECTION 1 Overview

View Section 1 of the *SOAR TO SUCCESS* video. Then refer to your Teacher's Manual, pages T4–T12.

After viewing and discussing Section I, participants should

- understand the meaning of "intervention";
- understand the difference between early and intermediate intervention;
- know some of the reading behaviors of below-level readers in Grades 3 and above;
- be introduced to instructional strategies and goals of intervention;
- become acquainted with reciprocal teaching.

Discussion Prompts

1. List two or three key points you learned from this section of the video.
2. What is an intervention program?
3. How do intermediate and middle-school reading intervention differ from early intervention?
4. What does the research tell us about the needs of below-level readers in Grades 3 and above?
5. Define reciprocal teaching. List the four strategies, and describe each one.
6. Do the following exercises:
   A. Turn to pages T56–T57 and read each of the models. Decide whether it is QUESTION, SUMMARIZE, CLARIFY, or PREDICT. Compare and discuss.
   B. In your group, choose a short chunk of text from one of the books in your level of *SOAR TO SUCCESS*. Read it silently. Then write out one model for each of the four strategies. Compare and discuss.

SECTION 2
The Teaching Plan

View Section 2 of the *SOAR TO SUCCESS* video. Then refer to your Teacher's Manual, pages T13–T23.

After viewing and discussing Section 2, participants should

- know the five parts of the *SOAR TO SUCCESS* lesson plan and the rationale for each;
- understand how to interact with your students as you take turns applying the strategies to a specific book;
- become acquainted with the basic assessment pieces.

Discussion Prompts

1. List two or three key points you learned from this section of the video.

2. Complete the following chart by describing each part of the five-step instructional plan. (You may want to look back at the video as you do this.)

Plan Part	Describe What Happens
Revisiting	
Reviewing	
Rehearsing	
Reading and Reciprocal Teaching	
Responding/ Reflecting	

3. a. Describe how the teacher on the video does a Guided Preview.
   b. How does she introduce key vocabulary?

4. After the book is completed, what happens?

5. **Assessment** Name the two forms of assessment to use during Revisiting. (For additional information on assessment, see Section 6, pages T41–T51.)

SECTION 3
Staff Development and Coaching

View Section 3 of the *SOAR TO SUCCESS* video. Then refer to your Teacher's Manual, pages T24–T28.

After viewing and discussing Section 3, participants should

- be familiar with the various forms of staff development for *SOAR TO SUCCESS;*
- understand the importance of coaching;
- be introduced to the three types of coaching you can use;
- be able to develop a coaching plan based on your own needs and resources.

Discussion Prompts

1. List two or three points you learned from this section of the video.

2. List the four types of staff development support available for *SOAR TO SUCCESS.*

3. What are the three types of coaching?

4. Think back over what you learned from this section of the video. Review Teacher's Manual pages T24–T28. Develop your plans for
   - Staff Development
   - Ongoing Coaching

SECTION 4
Organizing and Managing
SOAR TO SUCCESS

View Section 4 of the *SOAR TO SUCCESS* video. Then refer to your Teacher's Manual, pages T29–T36.

After viewing and discussing Section 4, participants should

- be familiar with the various ways to use *SOAR TO SUCCESS* as a reading intervention program;
- understand which model best fits your school situation;
- be able to develop a plan for using independent activities.

Discussion Prompts

1. List two or three key points you learned from this section of the video.

2. List and discuss the three ways to use *SOAR TO SUCCESS.* Which is the best for your situation?

3. Helping students develop routines is an important part of managing *SOAR TO SUCCESS* within the classroom. List and discuss the four steps for managing the program by developing routines.

4. Develop a plan for how you will use and manage *SOAR TO SUCCESS.*

SOAR TO SUCCESS Coaching Form

Teacher		Coach	
School		Date	Starting/Stopping Time /
Book Title		Lesson No.	Level

Agreed Coaching Focus:

Time	Lesson Part	Observations/Questions/Suggestions/Reflections
	Revisiting (5 min.)	
	Reviewing (5 min.)	
	Rehearsing (5–10 min.)	
	Reading/ Reciprocal Teaching (10–15 min.)	
	Responding/ Reflecting (5 min.)	

Next Steps:

Monthly Meeting Survey Form

To _____   **From** _____

Topic: Suggestions for Monthly Meetings   **Date** _____

Please check the three monthly meeting topics that would be most helpful to you in our next few sessions:

☐ _____

☐ _____

☐ _____

☐ _____

☐ _____

☐ _____

☐ _____

☐ _____

☐ _____

☐ _____

☐ _____

☐ _____

List other topics that would help you:

_____

_____

_____

Observing and Selecting Students

School

Teacher(s)

SOAR TO SUCCESS Teacher

		Grade	Date	
		Grade	Month	
		Grade	Year	

Student	Age	Grade	Silent Reading	Standard Test Data	Timed Fluency Test or Other Oral Reading	Phonics/Decoding Screening Test			Candidate for *SOAR TO SUCCESS*
						SOAR	*SOAR +* Decoding Support	Phonics Intervention	Potential

 **Student Data Sheet**

| Name | | Age | Sex | Grade |

| Teacher | | School |

SOAR TO SUCCESS Teacher (if different from above)

Book Number	Category	Title	Comments
1	I	*A Beauty of a Plan*	
2	I	*The Lost Expedition*	
3	II	*Owl*	
4	II	*The Babe & I*	
5	III	*Journey Home*	
6	III	*Cal Ripken, Jr.*	
7	III	*Mountains*	
8	III	*Jesse Jackson*	
9	IV	*Lakota Hoop Dancer*	
10	IV	*Tunnels, Tracks, and Trains*	
11	IV	*Gloria Estefan*	
12	IV	*Benjamin Banneker*	
13	IV	*Lightning*	
14	V	*Sports Lab*	
15	V	*On the Court with . . . Lisa Leslie*	
16	V	*An Even Break*	
17	VI	*El Duque*	
18	VI	*Marisol and Magdalena*	

Student Record of Progress

Name _____ **Level** _____

Date Program Started _____ **Date Released** _____

Explanation of Release:

Informal Reading Inventory

Date	Score	Comments

Retellings

Book Title	Book No.	Category	Performance/Comments

Student Record of Progress page 2

Oral Reading Checks

Book Title	Book No.	Category	Performance/Comments

Books Completed

Book Title	Category	Date Completed	Performance/Comments
A Beauty of a Plan	I		
The Lost Expedition	I		
Owl	II		
The Babe & I	II		
Journey Home	III		
Cal Ripken, Jr.	III		
Mountains	III		
Jesse Jackson	III		
Lakota Hoop Dancer	IV		
Tunnels, Tracks, and Trains	IV		
Gloria Estefan	IV		
Benjamin Banneker	IV		
Lightning	IV		
Sports Lab	V		
On the Court with . . . Lisa Leslie	V		
An Even Break	V		
El Duque	VI		
Marisol and Magdalena	VI		

Comments:

Dear Family:

Your child has been given the opportunity to participate in the *SOAR TO SUCCESS* reading program. This program offers special instruction to help your child develop the confidence to read widely and independently.

It is very important that your child stay with the *SOAR TO SUCCESS* program from beginning to end. Each *SOAR TO SUCCESS* book builds on the progress made in previous books. If you think it is likely that your child will not be able to attend school regularly, please let me know now.

After reading each book, your child will bring home a Home Connection letter to celebrate the completion of the book. Encourage your child to retell the book. Then sign the Home Connection letter and send it back to me.

Please sign this letter, acknowledging that you have been informed about the *SOAR TO SUCCESS* program.

Finally, as often as possible, read with your child. Sharing this experience will make your child want to read more and read better.

Sincerely,

Teacher

_____
(signature of parent or guardian)

SOAR TO SUCCESS · Home Connection

Dear Family,

_____ has successfully read
        (student's name)

_____ .
        (title of book)

He/she would like to retell this book to someone at home. Please

return this letter to school by _____ .
                                (date)

_____ has retold the book to me.
        (student's name)

_____
            (signature)

_____
           (relationship)

Home Connection

Dear Family,

_____ has successfully read
      (student's name)

_____ .
      (title of book)

The Student Guide pages attached to this letter include a graphic

organizer with your child's notes about the book and a page (or

pages) with your child's written responses to the book. Use these

pages to have your child retell the story or key points which were

in the book, and discuss your child's reactions to the book.

Sincerely,

Teacher

Administering, Scoring, and Interpreting the Informal Reading Inventory

Overview

Purpose The Informal Reading Inventory (IRI) is an individually administered survey designed to help you determine students' progress over time and their strengths and needs in using reading skills and strategies.

Description The IRI materials consist of the following:

- **Teacher's Directions for Administering, Scoring, and Interpreting the Informal Reading Inventory** (the section you are reading)

- **Protocol Sheets and Passages, Forms A, B, and C**

The table on page R96 shows that for levels Preprimer/Primer–8 there are two complete sets of passages.

- **Form A** is usually given as a pretest.

- **Form B** is usually given as a posttest.

At each of levels 3–8, there is an extra passage:

- **Form C** (optional) is provided to use if you feel further testing is needed.

For each passage, there are the following blackline masters:

- **Protocol:** This sheet provides the directions to give the student, a place to record the student's retelling and score it, and a place to record the oral reading score.

- **Passage:** This is the passage that the student will read; the teacher holds a copy on which to record the student's oral reading.

- **Pages for summarizing results:** IRI Summary; Miscue Summary (optional)

Informal Reading Inventory Passages (18 passages)

Level	Form A: Passages	Form B: Passages	Form C: Passages
Preprimer/Primer Level	A Good-Looking Bear (Narrative)	A House for Cat (Narrative)	–
Level 1	No One Should Have Six Cats (Narrative)	If You Give a Moose a Muffin (Narrative)	–
Level 2	Ronald Morgan Goes to Bat (Narrative)	Arthur's Pet Business (Narrative)	–
Level 3	The *Titanic* (Expository)	Pompeii . . . Buried Alive! (Expository)	Halmoni and the Picnic (Narrative)
Level 4	The Case of the Missing Roller Skates (Narrative)	The Case of the Disgusting Sneakers (Narrative)	Pride in the City (Expository)
Level 5	To Space & Back (Expository)	Wolves (Expository)	Me, Mop, and the Moondance Kid (Narrative)
Level 6	Long Claws (Narrative)	The Pinballs (Narrative)	Tales Mummies Tell (Expository)
Level 7	The Importance of Pigeons in World War II (Expository)	Wolf Pack (Expository)	Sarah Bishop (Narrative)
Level 8	Look Back at the Sea (Narrative)	The Fuller Brush Man (Narrative)	Hot Air Balloons (Expository)

Administration and Scoring Procedures

Overview of Materials and Preparation

The table on page R97 gives you an overview of the materials and preparation needed for the IRI.

Administration Procedures

- The IRI is given individually for each student.
- The following is the order of testing for each passage read:
  1. The student reads the passage silently.
  2. The student retells the passage.
  3. The student answers questions as needed to complete the retelling.
  4. The student reads the passage orally.
  5. Move on to the next passage, if not at frustration level.

IRI Materials and Preparation

IRI Materials	Materials Needed by Student	Materials Needed by Teacher
Pretest (Form A) (Levels PP–8)	• Form A Passage to read	• Form A Protocol to mark • Form A Passage on which to write miscues
Posttest (Form B) (Levels PP–8)	• Form B Passage to read	• Form B Protocol to mark • Form B Passage on which to write miscues
IRI Summary		• IRI Summary sheet (page R152)
Optional (Form C) (Levels 3–8)	• Form C Passage to read	• Form C Protocol to mark • Form C Passage on which to write miscues
Preparation of Materials	Photocopy: • **1 copy of the Passage** for students to read from. TIP: Many teachers place the student's copy of each passage in an individual file folder or mount each passage on file folder stock.	Photocopy: • **For each student** to be tested, **1 copy of each Protocol and 1 copy of the Passage for the teacher to mark.** • **1 copy of the IRI Summary Sheet** (page R152) **for each student** tested.

Determining the Starting Point

1. If you have some idea about the student's reading level, drop one year below what you expect the reading level to be for the starting passage.

   Example: Mark's expected reading level: 2
   Starting Passage: Level 1

2. If you know nothing about the student's reading level, start with the first passage on the pretest.

   Example: Betty is new to your school.
   Starting Passage: Preprimer/Primer

3. It is better to start too low than to start too high. Students need to be as comfortable as possible with what they are reading to ensure that they do their best.

Administering the Passages

Retelling/Questions

- Using the Teacher Protocol Sheets for the Student Passages, read aloud the instructions. On page R99 is an example of the Preprimer/Primer passage for Form A.

- After the student silently reads the passage, ask him/her to retell what was read; note the score by the numbered retelling point or prompt question.

- After the retelling, ask any questions to elicit points not included in the retelling or not told fully. (See example on page R99.)

- Score the retelling/questioning by multiplying the number correct by 10. If you have two scores for a question—

Example:

Retelling	Questioning
1	2

—drop the lower score. **Each question must have only one score.**

- The comprehension score must be 75% or higher to be considered the student's instructional level.

Oral Reading

Next, ask the student to read aloud the passage that has just been read silently. Record miscues using the same coding procedure given for the Oral Reading Check. Self-corrections are not counted as miscues. (See Code for Marking an Oral Reading Check, Section 6, Assessment, page T47.)

Mark the Oral Reading Accuracy Chart. For the student to be considered at the instructional level in oral reading, he/she must score 95% or higher. (See the example on page R99.)

Deciding What to Do Next

If the student scored less than 75% in comprehension or 95% in oral reading on the initial passage used, drop to the next lower passage.

If the student scored at least 75% in comprehension and at least 95% in oral reading, continue with the next passage. The student illustrated on page R99 should continue on to the next passage.

Stopping the Testing

When a student scores less than 75% in comprehension and 95% in oral reading on the same passage, the testing should be stopped.

A House for Cat

"I need a ~~house~~ *horse* ^SC^," Cat said to Dog.

"You can go up in a tree," said Dog.

So Cat went up in a tree. But she did not like it.

"Too many birds," she said.

"This is not a good house for me."

Cat went back to Dog.

"I need a house with no birds," said Cat.

"There are no birds in the water," said Dog.

"You will like it in the water."

So Cat went in the water.

There ~~were~~ *was* no birds.

But she did not like it.

"Too many fish!" she said.

"This is (not) a good house for me."

Student Name _____

A House for Cat: Protocol
Preprimer/Primer Level

Say: I'm going to ask you to read part of a story about a cat who is looking for a place to live.

Sample background questions: Where do cats usually live? . . . What would make a good house for a cat? . . . What do cats like to eat?

Say: Read this part of the story silently. I will ask you to tell me what you have read, and then I will ask you some questions about the story.

(Student reads silently.)

Say: Tell me everything you can about the selection. (As student retells, for each numbered point that the student includes, write **2** or **1** by the **R** for a full or part-credit response. After the student has told all he/she remembers, ask only the questions needed to bring out any points omitted, and write **2** or **1** by the **Q** next to any point the student tells after being prompted by the question.)

1. **Cat needed a house.**
   What did Cat need?   R __2__
                                                         Q __2__

2. **First, Dog told Cat to go up to a tree.**
   What was the first place Dog told Cat to go?   R __1__
                                                         Q __2__

3. **Cat didn't like it because there were too many birds.**
   Why didn't Cat like the tree?   R __0__
                                                         Q __2__

4. **Next, Dog told Cat to go in the water.**
   What was the next place Dog told Cat to go?   R __2__
                                                         Q __0__

5. **Cat didn't like it because there were too many fish.**
   Why didn't Cat like the water?   R __0__
                                                         Q __0__

Say: Now, as you read this passage aloud, I'm going to mark some things that you say. We will go over them later.

	Retelling	Questioning
	2	
	1	2
	0	2
	2	0
x 10 =	_8_	_80_

2 = full-credit response
1 = part-credit response
0 = incorrect/not included

Oral Reading Accuracy
Number of words = 102
Each error = .98

# of errors	% score
1	99
2	98
3	97 (circled)
4	96
5	95
6	94
7	93
8	92
9	91
10	90

Student Score __97__ **%**

Summarizing and Interpreting Results

Using the Summary Sheets

Use the IRI Summary Sheet (blackline master, page R152) to compile each student's results. Complete all pertinent data and record the student's percentages for the passages read. On page R101 a sample sheet for Nelson Vazquez is shown.

Interpreting the Scores

The table below presents criteria that can be used to help you determine a student's reading levels. These criteria must always be used in relation to your observations and judgments. Lisa Jones is definitely frustrated on the third level passage. She is a strong reader on levels 1 and 2 even though level 2 is beginning to be difficult for her. Her independent level is Preprimer/Primer.

Placement Criteria for Reading Levels*

	Word Recognition		Comprehension
Independent	99%+	**AND**	90%+
Instructional	95%+	**AND**	75%+
Frustration	90% or less	**OR**	50% or less
Listening Comprehension			75%+

* Betts, E. A. (1946). *Foundations of Reading Instruction*. New York: American Books. (These are the most widely accepted reading level criteria. Some reading experts suggest that the word recognition criterion for the Instructional level can go as low as 90%.)

Analyzing Miscues

If you want to do so, you may analyze the miscues, using the Miscue Summary form presented as a blackline master on page R153.

IRI Summary

Student Nelson Vazquez   **Date** 1-21-01

School King   **Teacher** Wallis

Grade 8   **Examiner** Donald

☒ **Form A**   ☐ **Form B**   ☐ **Form C**

Observations/Notes

Passage Level	Comprehension Score (%)	Oral Reading Accuracy (%)	Comments
PP/P	99	99	
1	96	97	
2	91	89	
3	88	85	
4	70	80	
5	50	60	

Summary of Reading Levels (List the passage level.)

Independent PP/P-3   Instructional 4

Frustration 5   Listening

Overall Comments/Observations

Interest/Motivation *Showed real excitement about detective story*

Understanding of passages

Reading strategies *Stops frequently to clarify words*

Reading fluency *Smooth through Grade 3*

General comments

A Good-Looking Bear: Protocol
Preprimer/Primer Level

Say: I'm going to ask you to read part of a story about a little bear who doesn't like the way he looks.

Sample background questions: What do bears look like? . . . Why do you think a bear might not like how it looks? . . . One of the words in this story is "ridiculous." What do you think it means to look ridiculous?

Say: Read this part of the story silently. I will ask you to tell me what you have read, and then I will ask you some questions about the story.

(Student reads silently.)

Say: Tell me everything you can about the selection. (As student retells, for each numbered point that the student includes, write **2** or **1** by the **R** for a full or part-credit response. After the student has told all he/she remembers, ask only the questions needed to bring out any points omitted, and write **2** or **1** by the **Q** next to any point the student tells after being prompted by the question.)

1. **Little Bear asked his father if he looked good.**   R _____
   What did Little Bear ask his father?   Q _____

2. **He didn't think he looked good,** or **He didn't want to look like a bear.**   R _____
   What did Little Bear think of his own looks?   Q _____

3. **Little Bear went to Lion.**   R _____
   Who did Little Bear go to next?   Q _____

4. **He said he wanted to look like Lion.**   R _____
   What did Little Bear say to Lion?   Q _____

5. **Little Bear fixed himself up to look like a lion.**   R _____
   What did Little Bear do after he spoke to Lion?   Q _____

Say: Now, as you read this passage aloud, I'm going to mark some things that you say. We will go over them later.

---

2 = full-credit response
1 = part-credit response
0 = incorrect/not included

Retelling	Questioning
_____ x 10 = _____	

Oral Reading Accuracy
Number of words = 183
Each error = .55

# of errors	% score
1	99
2	99
3	98
4	98
5	97
6	97
7	96
8	96
9	95
10	95

Student Score _____ %

A Good-Looking Bear

"Dad, do I look good to you?" asked
Little Bear.

"You look good to me," said Papa Bear.

"But I look like a bear," said Little Bear.

"You DO look like a bear," said Papa.
"You ARE a bear!"

"I don't want to look like a bear.
I want to look good," said Little Bear.

"You do look good," said Papa.
"You are a good-looking bear."

Little Bear went to see Lion.

He asked, "Lion, do you like the way
you look?"

"I think I look good," said Lion.

"Do I look good to you?" asked Little Bear.

"You are a good-looking bear," said Lion.

"I want to look like you!" said Little Bear.

"But you are a bear, not a lion.
You can't look like me," said Lion.

"I think I can," said Little Bear.
"You will see, Lion."

Little Bear said to himself,
"It will be fun to look like Lion.
I think I will look good.
Lion will think I look good, too."

Little Bear fixed himself up.

"I think I look good now.
I look like Lion," he said.

Student Name _____

No One Should Have Six Cats!: Protocol
Level 1

2 = full-credit response
1 = part-credit response
0 = incorrect/not included

Retelling	Questioning

_____ x 10 = _____

Oral Reading Accuracy
Number of words = 118
Each error = .85

# of errors	% score
1	99
2	98
3	97
4	97
5	96
6	95
7	94
8	93
9	92
10	92

Student Score _____ %

Say: I'm going to ask you to read part of a story about David, a boy who has six cats. In this part of the story, David tells about a hard choice he has to make. Then he tells about one of his six cats. This cat is named Herkie, and David found him in an alley.

Sample background questions: Do you know any cats? . . . What do cats like to do? . . . What do you call a cat's foot?

Say: Read this part of the story silently. I will ask you to tell me what you have read, and then I will ask you some questions about the story.

(Student reads silently.)

Say: Tell me everything you can about the selection. (As student retells, for each numbered point that the student includes, write **2** or **1** by the **R** for a full or part-credit response. After the student has told all he/she remembers, ask only the questions needed to bring out any points omitted, and write **2** or **1** by the **Q** next to any point the student tells after being prompted by the question.)

1. **David has six cats.**
   What pets does David have?
   R _____
   Q _____

2. **His mother says no one should have six cats.**
   What does David's mother say about the cats?
   R _____
   Q _____

3. **Cat number one is Herkie.**
   What is the name of cat number one?
   R _____
   Q _____

4. **When David found him, Herkie had a hurt paw.**
   How was Herkie when David found him?
   R _____
   Q _____

5. **Now Herkie's paw is better,** or **Now Herkie can run and play and climb trees.**
   How is Herkie now?
   R _____
   Q _____

Say: Now, as you read this passage aloud, I'm going to mark some things that you say. We will go over them later.

No One Should Have Six Cats!

We have six cats at my house.
But soon that will change.

This morning my mom told me,
"No one should have six cats, David!"

I can tell that Mom thinks
I should give one cat away.
But which one?
I love them all.

Herkie is cat number one.
I found him in an alley one day.
He had a hurt paw.
He looked so sad and lonely.

Nobody knew where Herkie lived.
And nobody wanted him.

What could I do?
I had no choice.
I let him live with us.

Now Herkie's paw is all better.
He can run and play and climb trees.

He and I are good friends.
I just can't give my Herkie away.

Student Name _____

Ronald Morgan Goes to Bat: Protocol
Level 2

Say: I'm going to ask you to read part of a story about children playing baseball.

Sample background questions: Have you ever played baseball? . . . What are some things people do when they play baseball? . . . What do you try to do when you go to bat?

Say: Read this part of the story silently. I will ask you to tell me what you have read, and then I will ask you some questions about the story.

(Student reads silently.)

Say: Tell me everything you can about the selection. (As student retells, for each numbered point that the student includes, write **2** or **1** by the **R** for a full or part-credit response. After the student has told all he/she remembers, ask only the questions needed to bring out any points omitted, and write **2** or **1** by the **Q** next to any point the student tells after being prompted by the question.)

1. **Mr. Spano said everyone could play baseball.**　　　　　　**R** _____
   What did Mr. Spano say on the first day of baseball?　　　**Q** _____

2. **Tom said that Ronald Morgan can't hit or catch, or can't do anything.**　　　　　　　　　　　　　　　　　　**R** _____
   What did Tom say about Ronald?　　　　　　　　　　　**Q** _____

3. **Ronald put on a shirt that said GO TEAM GO.**　　　　　**R** _____
   What did Ronald's shirt look like?　　　　　　　　　　**Q** _____

4. **Mr. Spano told them to try hard and to keep their eye on the ball.**　　　　　　　　　　　　　　　　　　　　**R** _____
   What advice did Mr. Spano give the team?　　　　　　　**Q** _____

5. **When Michael hit the ball, Ronald cheered for him.**　　**R** _____
   What did Ronald do when Michael hit the ball?　　　　　**Q** _____

Say: Now, as you read this passage aloud, I'm going to mark some things that you say. We will go over them later.

---

2 = full-credit response
1 = part-credit response
0 = incorrect/not included

Retelling	Questioning

_____ x 10 = _____

Oral Reading Accuracy
Number of words = 113
Each error = .88

# of errors	% score
1	99
2	98
3	97
4	96
5	96
6	95
7	94
8	93
9	92
10	91

Student Score _____ %

Ronald Morgan Goes to Bat

Baseball started today. Mr. Spano said everyone could play.

"Even me?" I asked.

And Tom said, "You're letting Ronald Morgan play? He can't hit, he can't catch. He can't do anything."

Mr. Spano looked at me. "Everyone," he said.

"Yahoo!" I yelled.

I pulled on my red and white shirt, the one that says GO TEAM GO, and ran outside to the field.

"Two things," Mr. Spano told us. "Try hard, and keep your eye on the ball."

Then it was time to practice. Michael was up first. He smacked the ball with the bat. The ball flew across the field.

"Good," said Mr. Spano.

"Great, Slugger!" I yelled. "We'll win every game."

The Titanic: Protocol
Level 3

Say: I'm going to ask you to read a true story about a famous passenger ship called the *Titanic*. In this part of the story, the *Titanic* is on its first trip across the ocean.

Sample background questions: What do you think it would be like to go across the ocean on a ship? . . . What could be dangerous about it?

Say: Read this part of the story silently. I will ask you to tell me what you have read, and then I will ask you some questions about the story.

(Student reads silently.)

Say: Tell me everything you can about the selection. (As student retells, for each numbered point that the student includes, write **2** or **1** by the **R** for a full or part-credit response. After the student has told all he/she remembers, ask only the questions needed to bring out any points omitted, and write **2** or **1** by the **Q** next to any point the student tells after being prompted by the question.)

1. **The *Titanic* is off the coast of Canada in icy waters.**   **R** _____
   Where is the Titanic?   **Q** _____

2. **Most of the passengers are sleeping.**   **R** _____
   What are most of the Titanic's passengers doing?   **Q** _____

3. **The lookout watches for danger from the crow's nest.**   **R** _____
   What is the lookout's job?   **Q** _____

4. **The lookout sees a mountain of ice directly ahead.**   **R** _____
   What does the lookout see?   **Q** _____

5. **A seaman below tries to turn the ship away, but it is too late.**   **R** _____
   What happens after the lookout rings the alarm?   **Q** _____

Say: Now, as you read this passage aloud, I'm going to mark some things that you say. We will go over them later.

2 = full-credit response
1 = part-credit response
0 = incorrect/not included

Retelling	Questioning

_____ x 10 = _____

Oral Reading Accuracy
Number of words = 135
Each error = .74

# of errors	% score
1	99
2	99
3	98
4	97
5	96
6	96
7	95
8	94
9	93
10	93

Student Score _____ %

The *Titanic*

It is April 14, 1912. The *Titanic* is in icy waters off the coast of Canada.

It is almost midnight. The ship is quiet. The sea is smooth as glass. The air is biting cold.

The passengers have had a good dinner. Some of them are still up playing cards. Most are asleep in their rooms.

It is a good night to be inside. But the lookout must watch for danger. He is high above the ship in the crow's-nest. He stares into the darkness.

Suddenly the lookout sees a dark shape. It is a mountain of ice! And the *Titanic* is heading right into it! The lookout rings an alarm. He calls, "Iceberg straight ahead!"

A seaman is below, steering the ship. He tries to turn the ship away. But it is too late.

The Case of the Missing Roller Skates: Protocol
Level 4

2 = full-credit response
1 = part-credit response
0 = incorrect/not included

Retelling	Questioning

_____ x 10 = _____

Oral Reading Accuracy
Number of words = 153
Each error = .65

# of errors	% score
1	99
2	99
3	98
4	97
5	97
6	96
7	95
8	95
9	94
10	94

Student Score _____ %

Say: I'm going to ask you to read part of a story about a boy named Encyclopedia Brown. He is a detective. He solves mysteries for the kids in his neighborhood.

Sample background questions: Do you know what a detective is? . . . What does a detective do when working on a case?

Say: Read this part of the story silently. I will ask you to tell me what you have read, and then I will ask you some questions about the story.

(Student reads silently.)

Say: Tell me everything you can about the selection. (As student retells, for each numbered point that the student includes, write **2** or **1** by the **R** for a full or part-credit response. After the student has told all he/she remembers, ask only the questions needed to bring out any points omitted, and write **2** or **1** by the **Q** next to any point the student tells after being prompted by the question.)

1. **A pair of roller skates disappeared from the waiting room of a dentist's office.**
   What disappeared from the dentist's office?
   R _____
   Q _____

2. **Encyclopedia Brown was in the dentist's chair.**
   Where was Encyclopedia Brown when the crime took place?
   R _____
   Q _____

3. **Encyclopedia was having a tooth pulled.**
   What was Encyclopedia doing at the dentist?
   R _____
   Q _____

4. **Encyclopedia put the tooth in his pocket,** or **saved the tooth to give to a friend.**
   What did Encyclopedia do with the tooth?
   R _____
   Q _____

5. **When he went back out to the waiting room, he saw that the skates were gone.**
   When did Encyclopedia discover that the skates were gone?
   R _____
   Q _____

Say: Now, as you read this passage aloud, I'm going to mark some things that you say. We will go over them later.

The Case of the Missing Roller Skates

Between nine and nine-thirty on Tuesday morning Sally Kimball's roller skates disappeared from the waiting room in Dr. Vivian Wilson's office.

And where was Encyclopedia Brown, boy detective? He was not ten feet away from the scene of the crime. He was sitting in a chair, with his eyes shut and his mouth wide open!

In a way, he had an excuse.

Dr. Wilson was pulling one of Encyclopedia's teeth.

"There!" said Dr. Wilson. He said it cheerfully, as if he were handing Encyclopedia an ice cream cone instead of a tooth.

"Ugh!" said Encyclopedia.

Dr. Wilson said, "All right. Hop down from the chair."

Encyclopedia hopped down and put the tooth in his pocket. He was going to give it to Charlie Stewart, who collected teeth and kept them in a flowered cookie jar.

Encyclopedia went into the waiting room. The chair on which he had left Sally's roller skates was empty!

Student Name _____

To Space & Back: Protocol
Level 5

Say: I'm going to ask you to read a selection from a book by Sally Ride, who was the first American woman to travel in space.

Sample background questions: What are people who travel in space called? . . . What do you know about astronauts?

Say: In this selection the author tells what it is like to be weightless in space.

Say: Read this part of the story silently. I will ask you to tell me what you have read, and then I will ask you some questions about the story.

(Student reads silently.)

Say: Tell me everything you can about the selection. (As student retells, for each numbered point that the student includes, write **2** or **1** by the **R** for a full or part-credit response. After the student has told all he/she remembers, ask only the questions needed to bring out any points omitted, and write **2** or **1** by the **Q** next to any point the student tells after being prompted by the question.)

1. **When you are weightless, you can float in the air without effort or slither around like a seal.**
   What kinds of wonderful things can you do when you   R _____
   are weightless?   Q _____

2. **You feel the same upside down as right-side up in space because gravity is not pulling the blood toward your head or because there is no gravity in space.**
   Why do people in space feel the same upside down as   R _____
   right-side up?   Q _____

3. **When you are weightless, your heartbeat stays the same; swallowing and digesting food are the same; and your eyes, ears, nose, and taste buds work the same. (Note:** Give full credit for any two similarities mentioned.)   R _____
   What are two things that don't change when you are weightless? Q _____

4. **Because more fluid stays in their faces, astronauts in space have puffy cheeks.**   R _____
   Why do astronauts in space have puffy cheeks?   Q _____

5. **Astronauts in space are an inch taller because their spines are not compressed by gravity.**   R _____
   What causes astronauts to be an inch taller while they are in orbit? Q _____

Say: Now, as you read this passage aloud, I'm going to mark some things that you say. We will go over them later.

2 = full-credit response
1 = part-credit response
0 = incorrect/not included

Retelling	Questioning

_____ x 10 = _____

Oral Reading Accuracy Number of words = 217 Each error = .46	
# of errors	% score
1	99
2	99
3	99
4	98
5	98
6	97
7	97
8	96
9	96
10–11	95
Student Score _____ **%**	

To Space & Back

The best part of being in space is being weightless. It feels wonderful to be able to float without effort; to slither up, down, and around the inside of the shuttle just like a seal; to be upside down as often as I'm right-side up and have it make no difference. On Earth being upside down feels different because gravity is pulling the blood toward my head. In space I feel exactly the same whether my head is toward the floor or toward the ceiling.

When I'm weightless, some things don't change. My heart beats at about the same rate as it does on Earth. I can still swallow and digest food. My eyes, ears, nose, and taste buds work fine; I see, hear, smell, and taste things just as I do at home.

I *look* a little different, though—all astronauts do. Since the fluid in our bodies is not pulled toward our feet as it is on Earth, more of this fluid stays in our faces and upper bodies. This makes our faces a little fatter and gives us puffy-looking cheeks. We are also about an inch taller while in orbit because in weightlessness our spines are not compressed. Unfortunately (for me, anyway), we shrink back to normal height when we return to Earth.

Long Claws: Protocol
Level 6

2 = full-credit response
1 = part-credit response
0 = incorrect/not included

Retelling	Questioning

_____ x 10 = _____

Oral Reading Accuracy
Number of words = 251
Each error = .40

# of errors	% score
1	99
2	99
3	99
4	98
5	98
6	98
7	97
8	97
9	96
10	96
Student Score _____ %	

Say: I'm going to ask you to read part of a story about a boy named Pitohok and a girl named Upik who live in the Arctic.

Sample background questions: Where is the Arctic? . . . What do you think it would be like to live in the Arctic?

Say: In this part of the story, Pitohok and Upik's family runs out of food during a blizzard. Because they are desperate, they let the children go look for a caribou, or deer, that their grandfather had shot but couldn't carry home. After traveling many days, Pitohok and Upik spot an owl that leads them to the caribou. Pitohok tries to carry the caribou home on his back. Later, their troubles become worse when they must escape from a huge grizzly bear, which they call an *akla*.

Say: Read this part of the story silently. I will ask you to tell me what you have read, and then I will ask you some questions about the story.

(Student reads silently.)

Say: Tell me everything you can about the selection. (As student retells, for each numbered point that the student includes, write **2** or **1** by the **R** for a full or part-credit response. After the student has told all he/she remembers, ask only the questions needed to bring out any points omitted, and write **2** or **1** by the **Q** next to any point the student tells after being prompted by the question.)

1. **Upik and Pitohok have been running.**
   Why are Upik and Pitohok so tired? (**Note:** It is acceptable but not necessary for the student to mention that they were running from a bear.)   R _____
   Q _____

2. **Pitohok was carrying a caribou.**   R _____
   What was Pitohok carrying?   Q _____

3. **Pitohok couldn't see through the fog.**   R _____
   Why didn't Pitohok know which way to go?   Q _____

4. **An owl appeared out of the fog.**   R _____
   What happened when Upik asked for help?   Q _____

5. **The owl stared at Upik and hovered, seeming to signal her.**   R _____
   What did the owl do?   Q _____

Say: Now, as you read this passage aloud, I'm going to mark some things that you say. We will go over them later.

Long Claws

"I hope we are far enough away from him," Pitohok gasped. "I can walk no farther."

He sank to his knees and let the heavy weight of the caribou sag down until it rested on the wind-cleared stones. He lay against it, his chest heaving as he tried to catch his breath. Although the air was stinging cold, Upik had to kneel and wipe the frost-white sweat from her brother's face.

"He's gone." Upik sighed, glad to rest the heavy rifle in the snow. She looked around in the still-thick fog. "Which way do we go now?"

Pitohok peered over his shoulder and felt cold sweat trickling down his spine. He could see no sign of the sun. Everything was hidden by a wall of fog.

"I . . . I don't know," he admitted. "I was trying so hard to get away from the *akla* that now . . . we're lost!"

Pitohok struggled painfully onto his knees and looked in all directions. He saw nothing but gray ice fog that drifted in phantom swirls along the frozen river.

"Oh, I wish someone would help us," Upik whispered aloud, and as if in answer to her words, the snowy owl came toward her, winging low out of the fog. Upik saw the owl turn its head as though it had seen the bear, then stare at her with its huge golden-yellow eyes. Suddenly the owl changed its wingbeat, hovering as if by magic at the very edge of the smokelike mists. It seemed to signal Upik.

The Importance of Pigeons in World War II: Protocol
Level 7

Say: I'm going to ask you to read part of an article about carrier pigeons in World War II.

Sample background questions: Do you know what a carrier pigeon or homing pigeon is? . . . Can you imagine how they might help soldiers communicate with one another during a war?

Say: During World War II, in the 1940s, carrier pigeons were used for communications. They were able to carry vital messages when there was no other way to communicate.

Say: Read this part of the story silently. I will ask you to tell me what you have read, and then I will ask you some questions about the story.

(Student reads silently.)

Say: Tell me everything you can about the selection. (As student retells, for each numbered point that the student includes, write **2** or **1** by the **R** for a full or part-credit response. After the student has told all he/she remembers, ask only the questions needed to bring out any points omitted, and write **2** or **1** by the **Q** next to any point the student tells after being prompted by the question.)

1. **Pigeons were used to carry messages between different groups of troops in World War II.**
   What were pigeons used for in World War II?
   R _____
   Q _____

2. **Pigeons carried messages behind enemy lines, in Normandy, in Europe, and in the South Pacific. (Note:** Give full credit if student mentions any two of these places.)
   What are some of the places where pigeons carried messages during the war?
   R _____
   Q _____

3. **To make sure at least one of the pigeons would get through with the message, two pigeons were often sent out carrying the same message.**
   Why were two pigeons often sent out with the same message?
   R _____
   Q _____

4. **There was a special award created to honor pigeons with outstanding records.** What was the Dickin Medal?
   R _____
   Q _____

5. **The first pigeon hero to win a medal saved a bomber crew which had crashed at sea.**
   How did the pigeon hero Winkie win the medal?
   R _____
   Q _____

Say: Now, as you read this passage aloud, I'm going to mark some things that you say. We will go over them later.

---

2 = full-credit response
1 = part-credit response
0 = incorrect/not included

Retelling	Questioning

_____ x 10 = _____

Oral Reading Accuracy
Number of words = 208
Each error = .48

# of errors	% score
1	99
2	99
3	99
4	98
5	98
6	97
7	97
8	96
9	96
10–11	95
Student Score _____ %

The Importance of Pigeons in World War II

By the time of World War II it was thought that the pigeon would be out of date as a messenger. Why not? Radio and telephones connected the troops everywhere. But the hard-flying pigeons still were needed. They were out there flying through the combat zones. When a call went out early in the war, America's pigeon owners responded with fifty-four thousand birds.

Paratroopers dropped behind enemy lines with pigeon boxes strapped to their backs. Pigeons accompanied the Normandy invasion, served with our armed forces in Europe, and landed with the Marines on South Pacific islands. The messages they carried often were sent in duplicate; if one bird failed to get through, the other usually made it back to the home loft, sometimes flying five hundred miles and averaging up to seventy miles an hour.

In Great Britain there was even a special medal created to honor pigeons that made outstanding records. It was known as the Dickin Medal. The first bird to receive this medal was a pigeon named Winkie. Winkie, along with a bomber crew, had the misfortune to crash at sea. The crew released Winkie, and of course he flew directly home. The message Winkie carried told the rescuers where to find the lost crew.

Look Back at the Sea: Protocol
Level 8

Say: I'm going to ask you to read part of a story about a girl who finds herself lost at sea after taking a nap on a float.

Sample background questions: Have you ever fallen asleep in the sun by accident? . . . Have you ever wondered what it would be like to be lost at sea?

Say: Clara is on vacation at the beach. While swimming near the beach on a float, she falls asleep in the sun. When she wakes up, she finds herself far away from shore and can barely see land.

Say: Read this part of the story silently. I will ask you to tell me what you have read, and then I will ask you some questions about the story.

(Student reads silently.)

Say: Tell me everything you can about the story. (As student retells, for each numbered point that the student includes, write **2** or **1** by the **R** for a full or part-credit response. After the student has told all he/she remembers, ask only the questions needed to bring out any points omitted, and write **2** or **1** by the **Q** next to any point the student tells after being prompted by the question.)

1. **When she woke up, Clara had no idea how long she had been on the float.**
   How long had Clara been on the float?
   R _____
   Q _____

2. **In the rough seas, the float tipped over and Clara was thrown into the sea.**
   What happened when the float tipped over?
   R _____
   Q _____

3. **Clara swam after the float to try to get it back, but she couldn't reach it, and swallowed lots of water.**
   What happened to Clara when she swam after the float?
   R _____
   Q _____

4. **Clara almost got the float, but it drifted away on the waves.**
   Did Clara reach the float?
   R _____
   Q _____

5. **Clara was scared because she could no longer see the float.**
   What made Clara so afraid?
   R _____
   Q _____

Say: Now, as you read this passage aloud, I'm going to mark some things that you say. We will go over them later.

2 = full-credit response
1 = part-credit response
0 = incorrect/not included

Retelling	Questioning

_____ x 10 = _____

Oral Reading Accuracy
Number of words = 215
Each error = .46

# of errors	% score
1	99
2	99
3	99
4	98
5	98
6	97
7	97
8	96
9	96
10–11	95

Student Score _____ %

Look Back at the Sea

Clara had no idea how long she had been on the float—all her life, it seemed. The part of her life spent on dry land—walking, sleeping, eating, doing normal things—seemed like a brief, vague dream. This was hard cold reality.

A wave slapped against the float, and Clara suddenly felt it tipping over. She screamed and clutched the float tighter, but her scream was cut short. The float flipped over and Clara was thrown into the sea.

Her head went under water, and she came up choking. She slung her wet hair from her face and looked around. The float was drifting away.

Clara swam after it. She reached out. The current pulled the float just beyond her grasp. She struggled through the waves, her eyes on the float, gasping for breath, swallowing salt water.

Her fingers touched the corner of the float and she fumbled to hold it. The float slipped away on the crest of a wave. She touched it again. It was gone. It was as if a playful hand were jerking the float out of her reach.

Clara began to swim. Another wave rose and she sank into the trough between waves. The float was out of sight. Clara was gripped with a terrible fear.

Student Name_____

A House for Cat: Protocol

Preprimer/Primer Level

Retelling	Questioning

_____ x 10 = _____

Oral Reading Accuracy
Number of words = 102
Each error = .98

# of errors	% score
1	99
2	98
3	97
4	96
5	95
6	94
7	93
8	92
9	91
10	90

Student Score _____ %

Say: I'm going to ask you to read part of a story about a cat who is looking for a place to live.

Sample background questions: Where do cats usually live? . . . What would make a good house for a cat? . . . What do cats like to eat?

Say: Read this part of the story silently. I will ask you to tell me what you have read, and then I will ask you some questions about the story.

(Student reads silently.)

Say: Tell me everything you can about the selection. (As student retells, for each numbered point that the student includes, write **2** or **1** by the **R** for a full or part-credit response. After the student has told all he/she remembers, ask only the questions needed to bring out any points omitted, and write **2** or **1** by the **Q** next to any point the student tells after being prompted by the question.)

1. **Cat needed a house.**
   What did Cat need?
   R _____
   Q _____

2. **First, Dog told Cat to go up to a tree.**
   What was the first place Dog told Cat to go?
   R _____
   Q _____

3. **Cat didn't like it because there were too many birds.**
   Why didn't Cat like the tree?
   R _____
   Q _____

4. **Next, Dog told Cat to go in the water.**
   What was the next place Dog told Cat to go?
   R _____
   Q _____

5. **Cat didn't like it because there were too many fish.**
   Why didn't Cat like the water?
   R _____
   Q _____

Say: Now, as you read this passage aloud, I'm going to mark some things that you say. We will go over them later.

A House for Cat

"I need a house," Cat said to Dog.

"You can go up in a tree," said Dog.

So Cat went up in a tree. But she did not like it.

"Too many birds," she said.

"This is not a good house for me."

Cat went back to Dog.

"I need a house with no birds," said Cat.

"There are no birds in the water," said Dog.

"You will like it in the water."

So Cat went in the water.

There were no birds.

But she did not like it.

"Too many fish!" she said.

"This is not a good house for me."

If You Give a Moose a Muffin: Protocol
Level 1

2 = full-credit response
1 = part-credit response
0 = incorrect/not included

Retelling	Questioning

_____ x 10 = _____

Say: I'm going to ask you to read part of a story about what happens when a moose visits a little boy and eats a muffin.

Sample background questions: What is a moose? . . . Can a moose really talk? . . . What might happen next after you give a moose a muffin?

Say: Read this part of the story silently. I will ask you to tell me what you have read, and then I will ask you some questions about the story.

(Student reads silently.)

Say: Tell me everything you can about the selection. (As student retells, for each numbered point that the student includes, write **2** or **1** by the **R** for a full or part-credit response. After the student has told all he/she remembers, ask only the questions needed to bring out any points omitted, and write **2** or **1** by the **Q** next to any point the student tells after being prompted by the question.)

1. **If you give a moose a muffin, he'll want jam to go with it.**
   What is the first thing a moose will want if you give him a muffin?
   R _____
   Q _____

2. **Then he'll want more muffins.**
   What will he want when he's finished?
   R _____
   Q _____

3. **You'll have to go to the store to get more muffin mix.**
   What will you have to do before you can make more muffins?
   R _____
   Q _____

4. **The moose will borrow a sweater so he can go to the store with you.**
   What will the moose borrow from you? Why?
   R _____
   Q _____

5. **First he'll sew a loose button on the sweater.**
   What will the moose do when he puts the sweater on?
   R _____
   Q _____

Say: Now, as you read this passage aloud, I'm going to mark some things that you say. We will go over them later.

Oral Reading Accuracy
Number of words = 108
Each error = .93

# of errors	% score
1	99
2	98
3	97
4	96
5	95
6	94
7	94
8	93
9	92
10	91

Student Score _____ %

If You Give a Moose a Muffin

If you give a moose a muffin, he'll want some jam to go with it.

So you'll bring out some of your mother's homemade blackberry jam.

When he's finished eating the muffin, he'll want another. And another. And another.

When they're all gone, he'll ask you to make more.

You'll have to go to the store to get some muffin mix.

He'll want to go with you.

When he opens the door and feels how chilly it is, he'll ask to borrow a sweater.

When he puts the sweater on, he'll notice one of the buttons is loose.

He'll ask for a needle and thread.

He'll start sewing.

Student Name _____

Arthur's Pet Business: Protocol
Level 2

2 = full-credit response
1 = part-credit response
0 = incorrect/not included

Retelling	Questioning

_____ x 10 = _____

Oral Reading Accuracy	
Number of words = 102	
Each error = .98	
# of errors	% score
1	99
2	98
3	97
4	96
5	95
6	94
7	93
8	92
9	91
10	90

Student Score _____ %

Note: You may want to preview the word *responsibility* with children.

Say: I'm going to ask you to read part of a story about a boy who wants a puppy. The boy's name is Arthur. D.W. is his sister.

Sample background questions: Why might someone want a puppy? . . . Do you think it is hard or easy to take care of a pet? . . . What does it mean to be responsible?

Say: Read this part of the story silently. I will ask you to tell me what you have read, and then I will ask you some questions about the story.

(Student reads silently.)

Say: Tell me everything you can about the selection. (As student retells, for each numbered point that the student includes, write **2** or **1** by the **R** for a full or part-credit response. After the student has told all he/she remembers, ask only the questions needed to bring out any points omitted, and write **2** or **1** by the **Q** next to any point the student tells after being prompted by the question.)

1. **Arthur wanted a puppy.**
   What did Arthur want?
   R _____
   Q _____

2. **Mother said, "We'll think about it."**
   What did Mother say?
   R _____
   Q _____

3. **D.W. thought that meant no.**
   What did D.W. think, "We'll think about it" meant?
   R _____
   Q _____

4. **Mother and Father said Arthur could have a puppy if he could take care of it.**
   What did Mother and Father finally decide?
   R _____
   Q _____

5. **First he had to show them he was responsible.**
   What did Arthur have to do before he could have a puppy?
   R _____
   Q _____

Say: Now, as you read this passage aloud, I'm going to mark some things that you say. We will go over them later.

Arthur's Pet Business

That night at dinner, Father asked, "What's new?"

"Arthur wants a puppy," said D. W.

"Blabbermouth!" said Arthur.

"A puppy is a big responsibility," said Father.

"I can take care of it," said Arthur.

"We'll think about it," Mother said.

"That means no," explained D.W.

After dinner Mother and Father did the dishes.

"Can you hear what they're saying?" asked Arthur.

"They're worried about the new carpet," whispered D.W.

Suddenly the door opened.

"We've decided you may have a puppy if you can take care of it," said Father.

"Wow!" said Arthur.

"But," said Mother, "first you need to show us you're responsible."

Student Name_____

Pompeii . . . Buried Alive!: Protocol
Level 3

2 = full-credit response
1 = part-credit response
0 = incorrect/not included

Retelling	Questioning

_____ x 10 = _____

Oral Reading Accuracy Number of words = 177 Each error = .57	
# of errors	% score
1	99
2	99
3	98
4	98
5	97
6	97
7	96
8	96
9	95
10	94
Student Score _____ %	

Note: You may want to preview the words *Pompeii* and *Vesuvius* with students.

Say: I am going to ask you to read part of a true story about a volcano and an ancient town named Pompeii.

Sample background questions: What is a volcano? . . . When is it dangerous to be near a volcano? . . . What happens when a volcano erupts?

Say: Read this part of the story silently. I will ask you to tell me what you have read, and then I will ask you some questions about the story.

(Student reads silently.)

Say: Tell me everything you can about the selection. (As student retells, for each numbered point that the student includes, write **2** or **1** by the **R** for a full or part-credit response. After the student has told all he/she remembers, ask only the questions needed to bring out any points omitted, and write **2** or **1** by the **Q** next to any point the student tells after being prompted by the question.)

1. **Next to the town of Pompeii was a mountain called Vesuvius.** **R** _____
   What was next to the town of Pompeii? **Q** _____

2. **The people of Pompeii liked the mountain because it was a good place to grow grapes and to raise sheep, and because it looked so peaceful. (Note:** Give full credit if the student mentions any two of these three reasons.) **R** _____
   Why did the people of Pompeii like the mountain? **Q** _____

3. **The mountain was really a dangerous volcano.** **R** _____
   What was wrong with the mountain? **Q** _____

4. **The gas was pushing the melted rock up through the mountain.** **R** _____
   What was happening under the mountain? **Q** _____

5. **The melted rock was about to blast through the top of the mountain.** **R** _____
   What was about to happen? **Q** _____

Say: Now, as you read this passage aloud, I'm going to mark some things that you say. We will go over them later.

Pompeii . . . Buried Alive!

Once there was a town named Pompeii. Near the town there was a mountain named Vesuvius.

The people in Pompeii liked living by the mountain. It was a good place to grow grapes. It was a good place to raise sheep. And—it looked so peaceful!

But the mountain was really a dangerous volcano. It was like a sleeping giant. If the giant woke up, it could destroy the town. Did the people know about the danger? No, they did not!

A volcano is a special kind of mountain. It has a hole at the top.

One day—almost two thousand years ago—something was happening under Vesuvius. Way down deep it was very, very hot. It was so hot that rock was melting. As the rock melted, a gas was made. The gas was trying to escape.

The gas and the melted rock were mixed together. The mixture was hot and bubbly. The gas was pushing the melted rock up through Vesuvius. The melted rock was about to blast right out the hole at the top!

The Case of the Disgusting Sneakers: Protocol
Level 4

2 = full-credit response
1 = part-credit response
0 = incorrect/not included

Retelling	Questioning

_____ x 10 = _____

Oral Reading Accuracy
Number of words = 141
Each error = .71

# of errors	% score
1	99
2	99
3	98
4	97
5	97
6	96
7	95
8	94
9	93
10	93

Student Score	_____ %

Note: You may want to preview the name *Phoebe* and the word *somersaulting* with students.

Say: I'm going to ask you to read part of a story about a boy named Encyclopedia Brown. He likes to imagine he is a detective. His friend Sally works with him to solve cases for kids in the neighborhood.

Sample background questions: Do you know what a detective is? . . . What does a detective do when working on a case?

Say: Read this part of the story silently. I will ask you to tell me what you have read, and then I will ask you some questions about the story.

(Student reads silently.)

Say: Tell me everything you can about the selection. (As student retells, for each numbered point that the student includes, write **2** or **1** by the **R** for a full or part-credit response. After the student has told all he/she remembers, ask only the questions needed to bring out any points omitted, and write **2** or **1** by the **Q** next to any point the student tells after being prompted by the question.)

1. **It was the day of the Disgusting Sneaker Contest.**
   What event was happening on the day of the story?

   R _____
   Q _____

2. **Phoebe, last year's champion, came to see Encyclopedia Brown.**
   Who came to see Encyclopedia?

   R _____
   Q _____

3. **She wore the same pair of sneakers all year.**
   How did Phoebe prepare for the contest?

   R _____
   Q _____

4. **Some girl swiped her right sneaker.**
   Why did Phoebe want to hire Encyclopedia?

   R _____
   Q _____

5. **She had left her sneakers out in the garage.**
   Where had she left her disgusting sneakers?

   R _____
   Q _____

Say: Now, as you read this passage aloud, I'm going to mark some things that you say. We will go over them later.

The Case of the Disgusting Sneakers

On the day of the Disgusting Sneaker Contest, Phoebe Eastwood, last year's champion, walked into the Brown Detective Agency. She had on shoes.

Encyclopedia immediately knew something was afoot.

All year Phoebe had prepared for the defense of her title by wearing the same pair of sneakers. She had them in really disgusting shape.

"I want to hire you," she said, laying twenty-five cents on the gas can beside Encyclopedia. "Some girl swiped my right sneaker."

Bad as her left sneaker was, her right sneaker was worse. It had two large holes in front. Her toes poked through like stunned tadpoles.

"I kept the sneakers outside the garage," Phoebe said. "Mom never allows them in the house. She says the smell would make an elephant faint."

All at once Encyclopedia wished he were somewhere else, like somersaulting down a ski jump.

Wolves: Protocol
Level 5

Say: I'm going to ask you to read part of a selection about wolves.

Sample background questions: What do you know about wolves? . . . One of the words in this story is *domesticated*. If a pet dog is a domestic animal, what do you think *domesticated* means?

Say: Read this part of the story silently. I will ask you to tell me what you have read, and then I will ask you some questions about the story.

(Student reads silently.)

Say: Tell me everything you can about the selection. (As student retells, for each numbered point that the student includes, write **2** or **1** by the **R** for a full or part-credit response. After the student has told all he/she remembers, ask only the questions needed to bring out any points omitted, and write **2** or **1** by the **Q** next to any point the student tells after being prompted by the question.)

1. **Wolves are like dogs and lions.**
   What two animals are wolves like?
   R _____
   Q _____

2. **Dogs are descended from domesticated wolves.**
   How are dogs related to wolves?
   R _____
   Q _____

3. **Like dogs, wolves are loyal, they are friendly, they are intelligent, and they are playful.** (**Note:** Give full credit if the student mentions any three of these four reasons.)
   Can you name three ways in which wolves are like dogs?
   R _____
   Q _____

4. **Like lions, wolves are good hunters that work in groups to catch prey.**
   How are wolves like lions?
   R _____
   Q _____

5. **The author thinks it's strange that people like dogs and lions, but don't like wolves.**
   What does the author think is strange?
   R _____
   Q _____

Say: Now, as you read this passage aloud, I'm going to mark some things that you say. We will go over them later.

2 = full-credit response
1 = part-credit response
0 = incorrect/not included

Retelling	Questioning

_____ x 10 = _____

Oral Reading Accuracy	
Number of words = 160	
Each error = .63	
# of errors	% score
1	99
2	99
3	98
4	98
5	97
6	96
7	96
8	95
9	94
10	94
Student Score _____ %	

Wolves

In many ways, wolves are like dogs and lions; yet wolves have a bad reputation, unlike dogs and lions. Dogs are our "best friends," but all the dogs in the world are descended from wolves that were domesticated more than ten thousand years ago. And most of the things people like about dogs are also true about wolves.

Like dogs, wolves are very loyal to other wolves in their family. Wolves raised by people become loyal to those people as well. Dogs are friendly and intelligent, and these traits too come from wolves. Wolves in a pack are playful with each other. They are among the most intelligent animals in nature.

Like lions, wolves are marvelous hunters that work together in groups to catch their prey. Yet lions are called the "kings of the jungle," while wolves are described in many nursery tales as "sly and cowardly." It seems strange that people love dogs and admire lions but dislike wolves.

Student Name_____

The Pinballs: Protocol
Level 6

2 = full-credit response
1 = part-credit response
0 = incorrect/not included

Retelling	Questioning

_____ x 10 = _____

Oral Reading Accuracy Number of words = 173 Each error = .58	
# of errors	% score
1	99
2	99
3	98
4	98
5	97
6	97
7	96
8	95
9	95
10	94

Student Score _____ %

Say: I'm going to ask you to read part of a story about a girl and two boys who are sent to live in a foster home.

Sample background questions: What is a foster home? . . . Who takes care of children in a foster home?

Say: In this part of the story, Carlie, Harvey, and Thomas J arrive at their new foster home. The three children are from different families and they don't know each other. They spend a difficult day trying to get used to each other.

Say: Read this part of the story silently. I will ask you to tell me what you have read, and then I will ask you some questions about the story.

(Student reads silently.)

Say: Tell me everything you can about the selection. (As student retells, for each numbered point that the student includes, write **2** or **1** by the **R** for a full or part-credit response. After the student has told all he/she remembers, ask only the questions needed to bring out any points omitted, and write **2** or **1** by the **Q** next to any point the student tells after being prompted by the question.)

1. **Carlie had never had her own room before.**
   Why was the new home strange to Carlie?
   R _____
   Q _____

2. **She looked in the mirror and practiced her new smile.**
   What did she do in the room?
   R _____
   Q _____

3. **The new smile would hide her crooked lower teeth.**
   Why did she want a new smile?
   R _____
   Q _____

4. **She realized Thomas J was behind her.**
   Who was behind her?
   R _____
   Q _____

5. **He had found her earring and wanted to return it.**
   Why was Thomas J there?
   R _____
   Q _____

Say: Now, as you read this passage aloud, I'm going to mark some things that you say. We will go over them later.

The Pinballs

Carlie entered her room slowly. It was the first time she had slept in a room by herself. At one time in her life she had slept with a cousin, her stepfather's two daughters and a half sister, all in one bed. She had spent her nights saying "Move over, will you?" and "Who do you think you are—Miss America?"

She walked slowly over to the dresser and looked at herself in the mirror. She had developed a way of smiling that hid her crooked lower teeth. She smiled at herself now, making sure she still had the technique.

Suddenly she heard a noise behind her. She swirled around. She didn't like anybody watching her when she was looking at herself. When she saw it was Thomas J, she could have stung him. "What are you staring at?"

"Nothing. I just wanted to tell you I found your earring." He came in with a small pleased smile. He was thin and walked as carefully as an old person. He held out the earring.

Student Name _____

Wolf Pack: Protocol

Level 7

Say: I'm going to ask you to read a selection from a book called *Wolf Pack.* The author explains that wolves live in a family group called a pack. Each wolf knows its position, or rank, in the pack.

Sample background questions: What do you know about the behavior of wolves? . . . What might it mean for a wolf to have a certain position in a pack?

Say: In this selection, the author discusses some of the ways that wolves of different ranks behave.

Say: Read this part of the story silently. I will ask you to tell me what you have read, and then I will ask you some questions about the selection.

(Student reads silently.)

Say: Tell me everything you can about the selection. (As student retells, for each numbered point that the student includes, write **2** or **1** by the **R** for a full or part-credit response. After the student has told all he/she remembers, ask only the questions needed to bring out any points omitted, and write **2** or **1** by the **Q** next to any point the student tells after being prompted by the question.)

2 = full-credit response
1 = part-credit response
0 = incorrect/not included

Retelling	Questioning

_____ x 10 = _____

Oral Reading Accuracy
Number of words = 256
Each error = .39

# of errors	% score
1	99
2	99
3	99
4	98
5	98
6	98
7	97
8	97
9–11	96
12–14	95
Student Score _____ %	

1. **The alpha male and the alpha female are the leaders of the pack,** or **they are the most important wolves in the pack.** What are the alpha male and the alpha female?   R _____   Q _____

2. **The lowest-ranking wolves tuck their tails between their legs to show that they know they are not as important as the other wolves,** or **to show respect to the other wolves.** Why do the lowest-ranking wolves in the pack tuck their tails between their legs?   R _____   Q _____

3. **Wolves show that they are of lower rank by holding their ears back and flattening their fur.** In what way do wolves show that they are of lower rank with their ears and fur?   R _____   Q _____

4. **When a lower-ranking wolf approaches a higher-ranking one, it drops its tail, flattens its ears and fur, and keeps its body low,** or **it licks the muzzle of the higher-ranking wolf. (NOTE:** Give full credit for any of these examples.) When a lower-ranking wolf approaches a higher-ranking one, what does it do?   R _____   Q _____

5. **Wolves show feelings of friendship and respect toward their leaders through certain kinds of behavior. (NOTE:** Students may use the term *active submission,* but this is not required.) How do wolves show their feelings of friendship and respect toward their leaders?   R _____   Q _____

Say: Now, as you read this passage aloud, I'm going to mark some things that you say. We will go over them later.

Wolf Pack

In any pack, the wolf carrying its tail high like a hairy banner will almost always be the alpha male. The alpha female also holds her tail high, although usually not as high as that of her mate. Wolves occupying positions below the pack leaders keep their tails correspondingly low, especially in any confrontation with the alpha pair. The lowest-ranking members of the pack tuck their tails between their legs to express their inferiority to the wolves above them in the hierarchy.

The positions of other body parts are also used as a means of communicating status in the pack. An alpha wolf usually keeps its ears standing up, while low-ranking pack members lay their ears back. They also keep their fur flat, in contrast to the fluffed-out fur of the pack leaders.

There are some occasions in the life of the pack that call for more specific expressions of the relationships among the pack members. When a low-ranking wolf approaches one of the pack leaders, it keeps its body low to the ground, with its fur and ears flattened. From this position, it reaches up with its muzzle and gently licks or nips the muzzle of the alpha wolf.

Sometimes all the pack members gather around the alpha male and greet him in this manner, often when he returns to the pack after being away for a while.

Scientists call this behavior *active submission* and see it as a method whereby the pack members express friendly feelings toward their leaders and respect for their authority.

The Fuller Brush Man: Protocol
Level 8

2 = full-credit response
1 = part-credit response
0 = incorrect/not included

Retelling	Questioning
_____ x 10 = _____	

Oral Reading Accuracy
Number of words = 274
Each error = .36

# of errors	% score
1	99
2	99
3	99
4	99
5	98
6	98
7	97
8–9	97
10–12	96
13–15	95

Student Score _____ %

Say: I'm going to ask you to read part of a story about a high school student named Donald. Donald has something that he feels he must do, but he can't bring himself to do it.

Sample background questions: Why is it sometimes so hard for people to do what they feel they must do? . . . How is avoiding a problem likely to make a person feel?

Say: Donald has an after-school job as a Fuller brush man. He drives to people's homes and tries to sell them brushes and other household items. But a more important problem is always on his mind.

Say: Read this part of the story silently. I will ask you to tell me what you have read, and then I will ask you some questions about the story.

(Student reads silently.)

Say: Tell me everything you can about the selection. (As student retells, for each numbered point that the student includes, write **2** or **1** by the **R** for a full or part-credit response. After the student has told all he/she remembers, ask only the questions needed to bring out any points omitted, and write **2** or **1** by the **Q** next to any point the student tells after being prompted by the question.)

1. **Donald has been selling brushes all day but does not want to go home and see his mother.** Why does Donald spend long hours selling brushes?   R _____   Q _____

2. **Donald gives his customers free samples so that they will listen to his sales pitch,** or **so that they will feel they should buy something.** Why does Donald give free samples to his customers?   R _____   Q _____

3. **Donald's mother seems to be ill—she has stopped driving, they have a housekeeper, she goes to sleep early, she can't talk, and probably wouldn't recognize him.** What are two clues that tell you that something is wrong with Donald's mother?   R _____   Q _____

4. **Donald wants to avoid seeing their housekeeper because she will insist that he go talk to his mother.** Why does Donald want to avoid seeing their housekeeper?   R _____   Q _____

5. **Donald feels angry, frightened, upset,** or **worried about his mother's illness. (Note:** Give credit for other reasonable conclusions.) How do you think Donald feels about his mother's illness?   R _____   Q _____

Say: Now, as you read this passage aloud, I'm going to mark some things that you say. We will go over them later.

The Fuller Brush Man

Donald leaned into the car trunk to find the box holding the give-aways. He had to pay for each letter opener, shoehorn, and vegetable brush, money out of his own commission, but it was worth it. Why else would people listen to his sales spiel if it wasn't because they felt indebted the second they reached for a sample?

What a mess, he thought, getting grease on his hand. Ever since Mom stopped driving. Ever since she . . . Well, there was no use dwelling on that. When he had time he'd try to get rid of some of the junk. He dropped a dozen plastic shoehorns into his sample case, snapped the lock, and glanced at his watch.

Man, he was hungry. He'd been working steadily since right after school, four hours. All he'd eaten was a doughnut from the breadbox at home, running out the door with Ava running after him to get a glass of milk first.

He'd sold enough brushes to call it quits for the day, but maybe he'd work another hour. If he went home now, even though it would mean a real meal, not McDonald's, Ava would be there. Their newest house-keeper, she'd sit there at the kitchen table, arms folded, watching him, and she'd go into her usual song and dance.

"Go in to your mother. Just for a minute. Say hello. Say something."

"Later."

"Now. She'll be asleep later."

"Why? She can't talk. She probably doesn't even know who I am. What difference does it make?"

"Donnie, Donnie. You love her. I know you do. Do it for you, if not for her."

"Leave me alone."

Student Name_____

Halmoni and the Picnic: Protocol
Level 3

Retelling	Questioning

_____ x 10 = _____

Oral Reading Accuracy	
Number of words = 162	
Each error = .62	
# of errors	% score
1	99
2	99
3	98
4	98
5	97
6	96
7	96
8	95
9	94
10	94
Student Score _____ %	

Say: I'm going to ask you to read part of a story about a little girl and her grandmother. Halmoni, which means *grandmother* in Korean, has just moved from Korea to America.

Sample background questions: How might you feel if you moved to a new place? . . . How would you feel if you couldn't speak the language in a new place?

Note: You might want to preview *Korea* and the names *Yunmi* and *Halmoni.*

Say: Read this part of the story silently. I will ask you to tell me what you have read, and then I will ask you some questions about the story.

(Student reads silently.)

Say: Tell me everything you can about the selection. (As student retells, for each numbered point that the student includes, write **2** or **1** by the **R** for a full or part-credit response. After the student has told all he/she remembers, ask only the questions needed to bring out any points omitted, and write **2** or **1** by the **Q** next to any point the student tells after being prompted by the question.)

1. **Halmoni found America too different from Korea.**
   Why was Yunmi sad for her grandmother?
   R _____
   Q _____

2. **Every morning she gave Yunmi's friends bags of fruit.**
   What did Halmoni give to Yunmi's friends?
   R _____
   Q _____

3. **Yunmi wanted Halmoni to say hello to her friends in English.**
   What did Yunmi want Halmoni to do?
   R _____
   Q _____

4. **Halmoni wouldn't say hello because she didn't think her English was good enough.**
   Why wouldn't Halmoni say hello to Yunmi's friends?
   R _____
   Q _____

5. **Halmoni gave the bags of fruit to the girls, but she just nodded at them.**
   What did Halmoni do when the girls arrived?
   R _____
   Q _____

Say: Now, as you read this passage aloud, I'm going to mark some things that you say. We will go over them later.

Halmoni and the Picnic

Yunmi was sad for her grandmother, who found America too different from Korea.

"Halmoni," she said, "my friends like the bags of fruit you give them each morning."

"I am glad. It is always nice to share with friends," said Halmoni.

"Will you please say hello to my friends in English this morning? They will be so surprised to hear you talk to them. I know you can. Please, Halmoni?"

Halmoni replied, "No, I have only been here for two months. English words are still too difficult for my old tongue. I will sound funny. I will give them this fruit; that is my way of saying hello to them. Besides, you do enough talking for the both of us!"

"Yunmi, Yunmi, wait for me!" they heard Anna Marie shout from behind them.

Then Helen came running up from a side street. "Hi, Anna Marie! Hi, Yunmi!"

They said hello to Halmoni. Halmoni nodded and gave one brown bag to each girl.

Pride in the City: Protocol
Level 4

2 = full-credit response
1 = part-credit response
0 = incorrect/not included

Retelling	Questioning

_____ x 10 = _____

Oral Reading Accuracy
Number of words = 114
Each error = .88

# of errors	% score
1	99
2	98
3	97
4	97
5	96
6	95
7	94
8	93
9	92
10	91

Student Score _____ %

Say: I'm going to ask you to read a selection about a group called City Year.

Sample background questions: What do you know about living in a big city? . . . What can people do to make cities better places to live? . . . What do you know about community service projects?

Say: Read this part of the story silently. I will ask you to tell me what you have read, and then I will ask you some questions about the story.

(Student reads silently.)

Say: Tell me everything you can about the selection. (As student retells, for each numbered point that the student includes, write **2** or **1** by the **R** for a full or part-credit response. After the student has told all he/she remembers, ask only the questions needed to bring out any points omitted, and write **2** or **1** by the **Q** next to any point the student tells after being prompted by the question.)

1. **American cities have problems like overcrowding, pollution, and too much garbage. (Note:** Give full credit if the student mentions any two of these three problems.)
   What kinds of problems do American cities have?
   R _____
   Q _____

2. **City Year members are trying to change some of the problems.**
   What are the members of City Year trying to do?
   R _____
   Q _____

3. **City Year members are young people between the ages of seventeen and twenty-three, and they are from all different backgrounds.**
   Who are the members of City Year?
   R _____
   Q _____

4. **They take pride in making their cities better places to live.**
   What are the City Year members proud of?
   R _____
   Q _____

5. **They build houses for the homeless, teach in schools, plant gardens, clean up parks and playgrounds, and help senior citizens. (Note:** Give full credit if the student mentions any three of these five services.)
   What kinds of jobs do City Year members do?
   R _____
   Q _____

Say: Now, as you read this passage aloud, I'm going to mark some things that you say. We will go over them later.

Pride in the City

Many American cities suffer from overcrowding, pollution, and too much garbage. But the young people of City Year are working to change all that.

City Year members are between seventeen and twenty-three years old and are from all different backgrounds. They take pride in working to make their cities better places to live.

City Year members work at full-time jobs in community-service projects such as building houses for the homeless, teaching in schools, planting gardens, cleaning up parks and playgrounds, and helping senior citizens. It's hard work. But City Year members know at the end of each day that they have helped put a little pride back into the communities they serve.

Me, Mop, and the Moondance Kid: Protocol
Level 5

2 = full-credit response
1 = part-credit response
0 = incorrect/not included

Retelling	Questioning

_____ x 10 = _____

Oral Reading Accuracy Number of words = 172 Each error = .58	
# of errors	% score
1	99
2	99
3	98
4	98
5	97
6	97
7	96
8	95
9	95
10	94

Student Score _____ %

Say: I'm going to ask you to read part of a story about a baseball game. A boy named T.J. is telling the story.

Sample background questions: Have you ever played baseball?... What are some things that people do when they play baseball?... What does an outfielder do?

Say: In this part of the story, the Elks are playing the Pumas in a very important game. The Elks are losing and the Pumas are up to bat. T.J. is playing right field. His father, who used to be a professional baseball player, is watching the game.

Say: Read this part of the story silently. I will ask you to tell me what you have read, and then I will ask you some questions about the story.

(Student reads silently.)

Say: Tell me everything you can about the selection. (As student retells, for each numbered point that the student includes, write **2** or **1** by the **R** for a full or part-credit response. After the student has told all he/she remembers, ask only the questions needed to bring out any points omitted, and write **2** or **1** by the **Q** next to any point the student tells after being prompted by the question.)

1. **The batter hit the first pitch.**   R _____
   What happened when the team's best batter was at bat?   Q _____

2. **The ball was heading toward T.J. or the boy telling the story.**   R _____
   Where was the ball heading?   Q _____

3. **T.J. missed the ball.**   R _____
   What happened when T.J. tried to catch the ball?   Q _____

4. **T.J.'s teammates threw down their mitts in anger.**   R _____
   What did T.J.'s teammates do when he missed the ball?   Q _____

5. **T.J.'s dad shook his head.**   R _____
   What did T.J.'s dad do when T.J. missed the ball?   Q _____

Say: Now, as you read this passage aloud, I'm going to mark some things that you say. We will go over them later.

Me, Mop, and the Moondance Kid

Mike loaded the bases by walking the next batter. Then their best hitter got up. He swung at the first pitch.

I could hear the crack of the bat and saw the ball coming right out to me. It looked like it was growing bigger as it came.

I went running in for it. I knew I was going to catch it. It came down and down. I was banging my glove with my fist. I was all ready to catch it.

It was a little higher than I thought.

I went back two steps and reached up as far as I could. The ball flew just over my glove. It bounced over the fence for an automatic double.

Everybody in the infield was throwing their gloves down and looking at me. Everybody.

Even from where I was standing, way in the outfield, all by myself, I could see Dad shaking his head. I knew what he was thinking. He was wondering how come he had such a lousy kid playing ball.

Tales Mummies Tell: Protocol
Level 6

2 = full-credit response
1 = part-credit response
0 = incorrect/not included

Retelling	Questioning

_____ x 10 = _____

Oral Reading Accuracy
Number of words = 215
Each error = .47

# of errors	% score
1	99
2	99
3	99
4	98
5	98
6	97
7	97
8	96
9	96
10–11	95

Student Score _____ %

Say: I'm going to ask you to read a selection about a mysterious mummy in a museum in England.

Sample background question: What do you know about mummies?. . . Why are people interested in mummies?

Say: Read this part of the story silently. I will ask you to tell me what you have read, and then I will ask you some questions about the story.

(Student reads silently.)

Say: Tell me everything you can about the selection. (As student retells, for each numbered point that the student includes, write **2** or **1** by the **R** for a full or part-credit response. After the student has told all he/she remembers, ask only the questions needed to bring out any points omitted, and write **2** or **1** by the **Q** next to any point the student tells after being prompted by the question.)

1. **Autopsies are not often done on mummies because mummies are so rare.**
   Why are autopsies rarely done on mummies?
   R _____
   Q _____

2. **An autopsy might be done on a mummy a museum does not want to display.**
   What kind of mummy might have an autopsy performed on it?
   R _____
   Q _____

3. **A museum in England had a mummy it did not want to display.**
   Why was there a mummy available for autopsy?
   R _____
   Q _____

4. **A team of scientists studied the wrappings and body in detail.**
   What did the scientists do with the mummy?
   R _____
   Q _____

5. **X-rays showed that the lower part of the mummy's legs were missing, and that there was a rounded object next to the leg bones.**
   What two strange things did X-rays show about this mummy?
   R _____
   Q _____

Say: Now, as you read this passage aloud, I'm going to mark some things that you say. We will go over them later.

Tales Mummies Tell

Museums have a limited number of mummies. Every time one is unwrapped, the number grows smaller, and so autopsies are not often performed. But sometimes a museum has a mummy that is not important to its collection. This is a mummy it does not want to display and a mummy about which almost nothing is known. As it happened, the Manchester Museum in England had just such a mummy. Its wrappings were in poor condition and no one knew what period it dated from, where it was found, or who the dead person was. The mummy was known only by its museum number, 1770. This was the mummy the museum made available to a team of scientists who wanted to use modern techniques to study the wrappings and body in detail.

It was also a mummy with a mystery. X-rays taken years earlier had shown the mummy was that of a young person. The lower parts of the legs were missing, and close to the leg bones was a rounded object. The X-rays did not reveal what it was, but its shape suggested a baby's head. Was this the mummy of a mother and child? Had the mother died shortly after giving birth? Those were questions the scientists wondered about as they began their work.

Sarah Bishop: Protocol

Level 7

2 = full-credit response
1 = part-credit response
0 = incorrect/not included

Retelling	Questioning

_____ x 10 = _____

Oral Reading Accuracy
Number of words = 230
Each error = .43

# of errors	% score
1	99
2	99
3	99
4	98
5	98
6	97
7	97
8	97
9–10	96
11–12	95

Student Score _____ %

Say: I'm going to ask you to read part of a story about a woman named Sarah Bishop, who lived by a lake called Long Pond during the Revolutionary War, and about the Indian family who came to visit her.

Sample background questions: What would it feel like to live alone in a cave? . . . Can you imagine what it would be like if it took your nearest neighbors a whole day to get to your house?

Say: Sarah Bishop lives by herself near a lake full of big trout, where Helen Longknife and her family come to fish in the summer. Helen pays Sarah a visit, to introduce her family and help her prepare for winter.

Say: Read this part of the story silently. I will ask you to tell me what you have read, and then I will ask you some questions about the story.

(Student reads silently.)

Say: Tell me everything you can about the selection. (As student retells, for each numbered point that the student includes, write **2** or **1** by the **R** for a full or part-credit response. After the student has told all he/she remembers, ask only the questions needed to bring out any points omitted, and write **2** or **1** by the **Q** next to any point the student tells after being prompted by the question.)

1. **A family came to visit the narrator, Sarah.**
   Who came to visit Sarah?

   R _____
   Q _____

2. **The Indian woman introduced her family to Sarah.**
   (**Note:** Students may specify the names of the family members and say that the baby was not yet named, but these points are not required.) What did the Indian woman do when she came to the door?

   R _____
   Q _____

3. **Sarah invited them to come in; they sat around the fire.**
   What did Sarah and the visitors do after Mrs. Longknife introduced herself and her family?

   R _____
   Q _____

4. **The Longknives told about coming to the lake every summer to fish for trout.** Why did the family come to the lake in the summertime?

   R _____
   Q _____

5. **Helen and her family lived a day's journey away, over the ridge.** Where did Helen and her family live?

   R _____
   Q _____

Say: Now, as you read this passage aloud, I'm going to mark some things that you say. We will go over them later.

Sarah Bishop

The last day of the wind, visitors came—a young man and his wife, with a baby strapped to her back and a child holding her hand. At first sight I took her to be an Indian, with her high cheekbones and coppery skin, but then I saw that she had blue eyes and was only part Indian. She spoke with an accent, but I understood her.

"My name is Helen," she said. "And this is my husband, John Longknife. My little girl is named Bertha. The baby has no name yet. We are waiting for a better moon. Then we will give her a name."

The young man seemed ill at ease. I took it that stopping by for a visit was his wife's idea. I had things to do, but I opened the door and invited them in.

We sat around the fire. Mrs. Longknife took off her shoes and warmed her feet; her husband kept his shoes on.

"We come in the summertime and fish in the lake," the woman said. "We fished here last summer. We caught more than a hundred trout. That was before you came."

I asked her where she lived.

She pointed north. "Over the ridge, a day's journey in the summer, longer in the winter," she said. "My grandfather lived here at nearby Waccabuc, which is the Indian name for Long Pond. . . ."

Hot Air Balloons: Protocol
Level 8

2 = full-credit response
1 = part-credit response
0 = incorrect/not included

Retelling	Questioning

_____ x 10 = _____

Oral Reading Accuracy
Number of words = 185
Each error = .54

# of errors	% score
1	99
2	99
3	98
4	98
5	97
6	97
7	96
8	96
9	95
10	95

Student Score _____ %

Say: I'm going to ask you to read part of an article about the invention of the hot air balloon.

Sample background questions: Do you know what a hot air balloon is? How long do you think people have been trying to fly balloons?

Say: About two hundred years ago Joseph and Etienne Montgolfier started experimenting with smoke-filled balloons in France.

Say: Read this part of the article silently. I will ask you to tell me what you have read, and then I will ask you some questions about the article.

(Student reads silently.)

Say: Tell me everything you can about the selection. (As student retells, for each numbered point that the student includes, write **2** or **1** by the **R** for a full or part-credit response. After the student has told all he/she remembers, ask only the questions needed to bring out any points omitted, and write **2** or **1** by the **Q** next to any point the student tells after being prompted by the question.)

1. **Historical evidence shows that balloons probably existed thousands of years ago in Peru and China. (Note:** It is not necessary for students to mention Peru or China.) About how long ago did the earliest balloons probably exist? R _____ Q _____

2. **The experiments of Joseph and Etienne Montgolfier took place about two centuries ago.** About how long ago did the experiments of Joseph and Etienne Montgolfier take place? R _____ Q _____

3. **The bits of paper rising in their chimney inspired the Montgolfier brothers to make paper spheres.** How did the bits of scrap paper rising in their chimney inspire the Montgolfier brothers? R _____ Q _____

4. **The Montgolfiers secretly made and flew an assortment of smoke-filled paper balloons.** What did the brothers secretly do after their initial experiment with paper spheres in the fireplace? R _____ Q _____

5. **The brothers decided to show their balloons to the public when they were sure that a bigger balloon bag filled with smoke from a large fire could float.** Why did they feel ready to bring ballooning to the attention of the public in 1782? R _____ Q _____

Say: Now, as you read this passage aloud, I'm going to mark some things that you say. We will go over them later.

Hot Air Balloons

Ancient Peruvian artifacts, old Chinese tales, and other historic evidence give hints that balloons, or at least small objects resembling balloons, probably existed thousands of years ago. However, the written history of ballooning dates back only two centuries to the experiments of two French brothers named Joseph and Etienne Montgolfier. The Montgolfiers were intrigued by the bits of scrap paper that soared up their chimney along with the smoke from their fireplace. Assuming that the smoke caused the paper to rise, they began making lightweight paper spheres, open at the mouth. Then they held the small balloons over a smoking fire until the spheres were filled with enough smoke to rise toward the ceiling.

Delighted with their discovery, the brothers secretly made and flew an assortment of small, smoke-filled paper balloons. They became enthralled with the possibilities of ballooning and visualized many ways that balloons might be put to use.

Finally they decided to bring ballooning to public attention. By the end of 1782, they were satisfied that a bigger balloon bag filled with smoke from a large enough fire could be made to float.

IRI Summary

Student _____ **Date** _____

School _____ **Teacher** _____

Grade _____ **Examiner** _____

☐ **Form A**   ☐ **Form B**   ☐ **Form C**

Observations/Notes _____

Passage Level	Comprehension Score (%)	Oral Reading Accuracy (%)	Comments

Summary of Reading Levels (List the passage level.)

Independent _____ Instructional _____

Frustration _____ Listening _____

Overall Comments/Observations

Interest/Motivation _____

Understanding of passages _____

Reading strategies _____

Reading fluency _____

General comments _____

Miscue Summary (optional)

Student _____   **Date** _____

List of Miscues
(Draw a line between passages; use extra sheets as needed.)

Passage number	Text said:	Student said:	Did the student self-correct?	Did the miscue make sense?	Was the miscue grammatically correct?

Miscue Diagnostic Checklist
(A = Adequate performance. L = Limited performance.)

_____ Consonants

_____ Digraphs

_____ Vowels

_____ Prefixes and suffixes

_____ Use of context

_____ Use of self-correcting strategies

_____ Flexible use of decoding strategies

_____ Use of punctuation

_____ Use of grammatical structure

_____ Phrasing in thought units

_____ Appropriate rate

Timed Fluency Test

Administer the Timed Fluency Test to all students who are candidates for intervention according to their scores on a standardized achievement test and teacher observation (see the criteria described on page T37, Selecting Students).

Oral reading fluency refers to the speed and accuracy with which students are able to read words aloud. It is one aspect of a student's overall reading performance. Fluency is determined by counting the total number of words in the one-minute unit read and subtracting the incorrect words.

Incorrect words are as follows:

(a) mispronunciations

(b) substitutions

(c) omissions

(d) words not read within three seconds (If a student is struggling to pronounce a word or hesitates for three seconds, tell the student the word and count it as an error.)

Materials   The passages provided for the Timed Fluency Test are from books at the end of this level of *SOAR TO SUCCESS*. Choose one that you think will be appropriate for the student. You will need:

- A Teacher's Copy of the passage to mark for each student.

- A Student Copy of the passage for students to read. If you are testing a number of students, photocopy the passage and attach it to card stock or a file folder to make it durable.

- A clock or watch with a second hand.

Administering the Timed Fluency Test

- Say to the student: "I want you to read this text aloud with expression. As you read, I will mark some of the things you say."

- Write down the student's starting time. At the end of one minute, draw a heavy line after the last word read. If the student is in the middle of a sentence, have him/her continue to the end.

- As the student reads, write in his/her misreadings.

    said
    Example: ~~silly~~

If a student self-corrects a misreading, write SC above it.

    said SC
    Example: ~~silly~~

- Retelling: After the student reads to the end of the sentence, ask him/her to retell what was read. Make a note as to whether it was generally accurate or inaccurate.

- Figure the Score: Write the total number of words read. (The numbers in the margin by the passage give the cumulative number of words at the end of each line.) Count the incorrect words and subtract them to determine the Words Correct Per Minute (WCPM).

Level of Fluency	Beginning of Year: WCPM	Middle of Year: WCPM	End of Year: WCPM	Use the recommendation below to plan instruction:
Expected Progress	106–126	118–143	128–151	The student can go into *SOAR TO SUCCESS* without additional support.
Below Expected Progress	77–105	93–117	100–127	• Administer the *Houghton Mifflin Phonics/Decoding Screening Test*. • Compile the results on page R170; enter this fluency rate on page R171. • Refer to the chart on page R164.
Seriously Below Expected Progress	0–76	0–92	0–99	• Administer the *Houghton Mifflin Phonics/Decoding Screening Test*. • Compile the results on page R170; enter this fluency rate on page R171. • Refer to the chart on page R164.

Table uses data adapted from Hasbrouck, Jan E. and Tindal, Gerald. "Curriculum-Based Oral Reading Fluency Norms for Students in Grades 2 Through 5." Teaching Exceptional Children, Spring, 1992, p. 41.

Student Name _____   **Date** _____

From An Even Break *Book 16, Level 8*

	No. Words
Frisk was four feet five inches tall, and skinny. He had large ears and a dimpled chin.	17
Springing from his head was an unruly mass of red hair. His eyes were bright blue, he was	35
speckled all over with freckles, and he had a high-pitched voice. Sometimes, much to his	50
embarrassment, he squeaked when he got excited.	57
Frisk and Shelly lived in a four-room apartment in downtown Wilma. The apartment was	71
located above Billy Compton's hardware store. If you could find the town, it was a cinch	87
finding the store. Wilma had only one street.	95
As small towns go, Wilma was the kind of place where everyone pretty much knew	110
everyone else. Usually that was a good thing, but sometimes it wasn't. Familiarity breeds	124
gossip, and depending on who you were and what you had been up to lately, maybe you	141
wouldn't want to know everyone. Yet the folks from Wilma were a forgiving crowd.	155

Retelling:

☐ Acceptable (told most information from the passage)

☐ Not acceptable (told less than 50% of the information)

Start Time _____ Stop Time _____

Words Per Minute _____

Minus Incorrect Words — _____

Words Correct Per Minute (WCPM) _____

Level of Fluency	Beginning of Year: WCPM	Middle of Year: WCPM	End of Year: WCPM	Use the recommendation below to plan instruction:
Expected Progress	106–126	118–143	128–151	The student can go into *SOAR TO SUCCESS* without additional support.
Below Expected Progress	77–105	93–117	100–127	• Administer the *Phonics/Decoding Screening Test*. • Compile the results on page R170; enter this fluency rate on page R171. • Refer to the chart on page R164.
Seriously Below Expected Progress	0–76	0–92	0–99	• Administer the *Phonics/Decoding Screening Test*. • Compile the results on page R170; enter this fluency rate on page R171. • Refer to the chart on page R164.

From *An Even Break*
Book 16, Level 8

Frisk was four feet five inches tall, and skinny. He had large ears and a dimpled chin. Springing from his head was an unruly mass of red hair. His eyes were bright blue, he was speckled all over with freckles, and he had a high-pitched voice. Sometimes, much to his embarrassment, he squeaked when he got excited.

Frisk and Shelly lived in a four-room apartment in downtown Wilma. The apartment was located above Billy Compton's hardware store. If you could find the town, it was a cinch finding the store. Wilma had only one street.

As small towns go, Wilma was the kind of place where everyone pretty much knew everyone else. Usually that was a good thing, but sometimes it wasn't. Familiarity breeds gossip, and depending on who you were and what you had been up to lately, maybe you wouldn't want to know everyone. Yet the folks from Wilma were a forgiving crowd.

Student Name _____   **Date** _____

From El Duque   *Book 17, Level 8*

	No. Words
He stood on the pitcher's mound at Yankee Stadium as thousands of fans cheered his name.	16
"Du-que! Du-que! Du-que!"	19
Although he hadn't yet thrown his first pitch, Orlando "El Duque" Hernandez was already	33
a star. Now, standing in the center of the most famous baseball stadium in the world, he took	51
a moment to let it all soak in. He gazed around the crowd with an expression of disbelief.	69
People he had never seen before were rooting for him because they knew he had risked his	86
life in order to be there. And now it was clear that he had finally made it.	103
"Du-que! Du-que! Du-que!"	106
"Strike one!" yelled the umpire as El Duque delivered his first major league pitch. The	121
crowd's cheers grew even louder.	126
"Strike two!" the umpire shouted.	131
El Duque took a deep breath and glanced around the stadium. Cuban flags dangled from	146
the upper decks as fans stood on their feet, clapping and hollering for a strikeout.	161

Retelling:

☐ Acceptable (told most information from the passage)

☐ Not acceptable (told less than 50% of the information)

Start Time _____ Stop Time _____

Words Per Minute _____

Minus Incorrect Words — _____

Words Correct Per Minute (WCPM) _____

Level of Fluency	Beginning of Year: WCPM	Middle of Year: WCPM	End of Year: WCPM	Use the recommendation below to plan instruction:
Expected Progress	106–126	118–143	128–151	The student can go into *SOAR TO SUCCESS* without additional support.
Below Expected Progress	77–105	93–117	100–127	• Administer the *Phonics/Decoding Screening Test*. • Compile the results on page R170; enter this fluency rate on page R171. • Refer to the chart on page R164.
Seriously Below Expected Progress	0–76	0–92	0–99	• Administer the *Phonics/Decoding Screening Test*. • Compile the results on page R170; enter this fluency rate on page R171. • Refer to the chart on page R164.

From *El Duque*
Book 17, Level 8

He stood on the pitcher's mound at Yankee Stadium as thousands of fans cheered his name.

"Du-que! Du-que! Du-que!"

Although he hadn't yet thrown his first pitch, Orlando "El Duque" Hernandez was already a star. Now, standing in the center of the most famous baseball stadium in the world, he took a moment to let it all soak in. He gazed around the crowd with an expression of disbelief. People he had never seen before were rooting for him because they knew he had risked his life in order to be there. And now it was clear that he had finally made it.

"Du-que! Du-que! Du-que!"

"Strike one!" yelled the umpire as El Duque delivered his first major league pitch. The crowd's cheers grew even louder.

"Strike two!" the umpire shouted.

El Duque took a deep breath and glanced around the stadium. Cuban flags dangled from the upper decks as fans stood on their feet, clapping and hollering for a strikeout.

Student Name _____   **Date** _____

From Marisol and Magdalena: The Sound of Our Sisterhood *Book 18, Level 8*

	No. Words
Do you know what it's like to be in a room full of people, but to feel completely alone?	19
Outside of the noise and the talking and the eating — just apart from it, watching it all?	36
That's how I felt tonight in the Rosarios' kitchen.	45
I've known the Rosario family since I was a little baby. I've been over to their house a	63
million times. But tonight it was like noticing it all for the first time. Noticing not just what	81
everything looked like, but how it all felt. When I stopped to think about it, I realized how	99
happy it all made me — these same things, these same people, that I have seen over and over	117
again, my whole life long.	122
The Rosarios' kitchen is bright yellow. The wall by the stove is stained brown with oil that	139
splatters from the stove. It's one of those kitchens that's like a magnet; whenever friends come	155
over, everyone ends up in the kitchen.	162

Retelling:

☐ Acceptable (told most information from the passage)

☐ Not acceptable (told less than 50% of the information)

Start Time _____ Stop Time _____

Words Per Minute _____

Minus Incorrect Words — _____

Words Correct Per Minute (WCPM) _____

Level of Fluency	Beginning of Year: WCPM	Middle of Year: WCPM	End of Year: WCPM	Use the recommendation below to plan instruction:
Expected Progress	106–126	118–143	128–151	The student can go into *SOAR TO SUCCESS* without additional support.
Below Expected Progress	77–105	93–117	100–127	• Administer the *Phonics/Decoding Screening Test.* • Compile the results on page R170; enter this fluency rate on page R171. • Refer to the chart on page R164.
Seriously Below Expected Progress	0–76	0–92	0–99	• Administer the *Phonics/Decoding Screening Test.* • Compile the results on page R170; enter this fluency rate on page R171. • Refer to the chart on page R164.

From *Marisol and Magdalena: The Sound of Our Sisterhood*
Book 18, Level 8

Do you know what it's like to be in a room full of people, but to feel completely alone? Outside of the noise and the talking and the eating — just apart from it, watching it all? That's how I felt tonight in the Rosarios' kitchen.

I've known the Rosario family since I was a little baby. I've been over to their house a million times. But tonight it was like noticing it all for the first time. Noticing not just what everything looked like, but how it all felt. When I stopped to think about it, I realized how happy it all made me — these same things, these same people, that I have seen over and over again, my whole life long.

The Rosarios' kitchen is bright yellow. The wall by the stove is stained brown with oil that splatters from the stove. It's one of those kitchens that's like a magnet; whenever friends come over, everyone ends up in the kitchen.

Administering, Scoring, and Analyzing the Houghton Mifflin Phonics/Decoding Screening Test

Directions for Administration and Scoring

What Is the Screening Test?

The Houghton Mifflin Phonics/Decoding Screening Test assesses the phonics and phonics-related skills that have a high rate of application in beginning decoding. Each task presents a number of lists of letters and words for the student to identify or decode. Pseudowords, or made-up words, are included since the student must use decoding skills to correctly pronounce these words and cannot have memorized them. These assessments are best used to plan instruction for students who lack basic decoding skills and to develop instructional groups. They may be administered after instruction to assess progress.

Why Administer the Screening Test?

A student's ability to use knowledge of sound/letter correspondences (phonics) to decode words determines, in large measure, his or her ability to read individual words. A detailed assessment of a student's phonics skills points to areas in which the student is likely to benefit most from systematic, explicit phonics instruction. Also, knowing the skills that the student does possess will help in selecting reading tasks that offer the most effective reinforcement of those skills.

How Do I Administer the Screening Test and How Long Will It Take?

- Individually administered

- 15–25 minutes

What Materials Do I Need to Administer the Screening Test?

- Protocol and Analysis—Recording Sheets 1–6 (pp. R170–R176; duplicate one copy for each student. Permission is granted for reproducing these pages.)

- Student Copy, pages 1–4 (pp. R176–R179; duplicate one set and mount each page on card stock or in a manila folder. Permission is granted for reproducing these pages.)

- Lined paper and pencil for each student

- One blank sheet of paper

What Procedures Do I Use to Administer the Screening Test?

Instructions for administering each of the tasks on the *Houghton Mifflin Phonics/Decoding Screening Test* are included on the Protocol and Analysis Sheets. Students read from the Student Copy. To focus the student's attention on the part of the test being given, cover the other parts with a piece of paper. The Protocol and Analysis Sheet shows the same material that appears on the Student Copy, but it is arranged so that you may easily record the student's responses.

How Do I Score the Screening Test?

After administering the *Houghton Mifflin Phonics/Decoding Screening Test*, transfer the student's scores to the Phonics/Decoding Summary Sheet. Use the next section to analyze the results for each student and plan instruction.

Analyzing the Screening Test

Use the following guidelines to analyze each student's performance and plan instruction.

1. Use Protocol and Analysis Sheet 1 (page R170) to tally tasks the student could perform.

2. Study the sample case study on pages R165–R169 to help you learn to use this process.

3. Locate your student's pattern of phonics/decoding behaviors in the table on page R164. Use the suggestions provided to plan instruction. Note your plans on Protocol and Analysis Sheet 2 (page R171).

4. Retest and revise your plans as needed.

Phonics/Decoding Behaviors	Suggested Instruction	Comments
A. Decodes well but has poor fluency: • Scores at least 80% on phonics/decoding tasks in isolation but • Scores Below Expected Progress on the Timed Fluency Test.	• Start the student in *SOAR TO SUCCESS.* • Use Making Words Lessons. • During *SOAR* lessons, teacher and student model CLARIFY/PHONICS frequently. • Provide additional rereading of independent-level texts to build fluency during Revisiting (replacing Group Conferences).	• Student needs to focus on a decoding strategy to use the phonics he or she knows.
B. Can decode simple words but has very poor fluency: • Scores at least 80% on each of the phonics/decoding tasks (through Task F), including pseudowords up to the multi-syllabic portion, but —does not achieve 80% score on the multisyllabic portion (Tasks G and H) or • Scores 80% on each of the phonics/decoding tasks through Task C but —does not achieve 80% score on one or more vowel tasks, typically, the long vowels and diphthongs (Tasks D and F), and —does not achieve 80% score on the multisyllabic portion (Tasks G and H) • Scores Seriously Below Expected Progress on the Timed Fluency Test.	• Examine Protocol and Analysis Sheet for the student's patterns of performance and start phonics intervention where the student first scores below 80%. • Start the student in *SOAR TO SUCCESS* • Use Decoding Longer Words and Making Words Lessons. • During *SOAR* lessons, teacher and students model CLARIFY/PHONICS frequently. • Provide additional rereading of independent-level texts to build fluency during Revisiting (replacing Group Conferences).	• Monitor student progress frequently by retesting with Phonics/Decoding Tasks and and by using the *SOAR TO SUCCESS* Oral Reading Checks.
C. Cannot decode simple words and has very poor fluency: • Does not do well on the Phonics/Decoding Tasks and • Scores Seriously Below Expected Progress on the Timed Fluency Test. This student has no phonics/decoding skills or strategies.	• Begin with *Houghton Mifflin Phonics Intervention.* • Begin *SOAR TO SUCCESS* when student is able to score 80% on the phonics task and at least better than Seriously Below Expected Progress on the Timed Fluency Test.	• The number of older struggling readers in this category is usually quite small. • Move into *SOAR TO SUCCESS* as quickly as possible.

Case Study: Mark Lester

Houghton Mifflin Phonics/Decoding Screening Test
Protocol and Analysis Sheet

Name Mark Lester   **Grade** 5   **Date** 11/20

Phonics/Decoding Summary Sheet

Alphabet Skills

26 /26	(21)	**Task 1.**	Letter names—uppercase
26 /26	(21)	**Task 2.**	Letter names—lowercase
23 /23	(18)	**Task 3.**	Consonant sounds
5 /5	(4)	**Task 4.**	Long-vowel sounds
5 /5	(4)	**Task 5.**	Short-vowel sounds

Task 6. Reading and Decoding Skills

10 /10	(8)	**A.**	Short vowels in CVC words
9 /10	(8)	**B.**	Short vowels, digraphs, and -tch trigraph
20 /20	(16)	**C.**	Short vowels and consonant blends
10 /10	(8)	**D.**	Long vowels
10 /10	(8)	**E.**	r- and l-controlled vowels
10 /10	(8)	**F.**	Vowel diphthongs

Multisyllabic Words:

24 /24	(19)	**G.**	Two-syllable words
3 /8	(6)	**H.**	Multisyllabic words

Task 7. Spelling Skills

5 /5	(4)	**A.**	Initial consonants
5 /5	(4)	**B.**	Final consonants
5 /5	(4)	**C.**	CVC words
5 /5	(4)	**D.**	Long-vowel words

Components/Observations

Knows all basic decoding elements.

Gave /p/ for ph in pseudo word (probably not a problem; will provide review).

Can apply basic decoding skills to reading CVC words.

Has difficulty applying decoding skills to multisyllabic words.

R170 *Houghton Mifflin Phonics/Decoding Screening Test:* **Recording Sheet 1**

Directions

Study the protocol sheets and comments on Mark Lester to help you learn to analyze the *Houghton Mifflin Phonics/ Decoding Screening Test.*

Background on Mark Lester

- Eleven-year-old fifth grader

- Reading approximately second-grade level

- Has been selected for *SOAR TO SUCCESS*

Analysis and Discussion

- Mark knows all letter names and sounds in isolation.

- He missed the *ph* digraph. This is probably not a problem but may require a quick review.

- Mark applies basic decoding skills to VCV words but has difficulty applying skills to multisyllabic words.

- Mark uses basic decoding skills to spell words.

Note of Timed Fluency Test Score

- Mark's score of 76 Words Correct Per Minute (WCPM) shows that he is Seriously Below Expected Progress on the Timed Fluency Test, which is an indication that he has very poor fluency and needs additional phonics support.

- Mark's retelling of the text in the Timed Fluency Test indicated that his comprehension was affected by his inability to decode.

Analysis and Comment

- Mark's difficulty in applying skills to multisyllabic words is likely to be affecting his fluency, accounting for his very low rate on the Timed Fluency Test. His inability to decode multisyllabic words and lack of fluency are likely to be influencing his comprehension, which would account for his low comprehension score on standardized achievement tests.

Protocol and Analysis Sheet page 2

Name *Mark Lester*

Timed Fluency Test: WCPM _____ *76* _____

    ☐ Expected Progress
    ☐ Below Expected Progress
    ☑ Seriously Below Expected Progress

Instructional Needs

Skills to review: *Quick review of ph = /f/*

Skills to teach: *Focus on application of all decoding skills to multisyllabic words. Use Decoding Longer Words lessons on Optional Day. Does not need Making Words because he already knows basic skills. Place heavy emphasis on CLARIFY/PHONICS: THINK ABOUT WORDS during SOAR lesson.*

    ☐ Needs regular SOAR TO SUCCESS lessons only
    ☑ Needs regular SOAR TO SUCCESS lessons plus additional decoding support
    ☐ Needs Phonics Intervention

Houghton Mifflin Phonics/Decoding Screening Test: **Recording Sheet 2**   **R171**

- Mark's major need is to learn to apply decoding skills to multisyllabic words (see Multisyllabic Words Task, p. R175). Use the Decoding Longer Words lessons and more emphasis on CLARIFY/PHONICS during *SOAR TO SUCCESS* lessons.

TASK 1. Letter names—Uppercase

MATERIALS: Student Materials, p. R176

Say to the student: *Tell me the names of thes...*
cannot name three or more consecutive letter...
ones you do know.

	D	A	N	S	X
	T	Y	E	C	O
<u>26</u>/26	K	U	G	B	F

correct

TASK 2. Letter Names—Lowercase

MATERIALS: Student Materials, p. R176...

Say to the student: *Tell me the names of these...*
cannot name three or more consecutive letter...
ones you do know.

	d	a	n	s	x
	t	y	e	c	o
<u>26</u>/26	k	u	g	b	f

correct

TASK 3. Consonant Sounds

MATERIALS: Student Materials, p. R176...

Say to the student: *Look at these letters. Tell...*
she knows of another sound for the letters *g...*
this form. If it is incorrect, write the sound th...
given, circle the letter. If the student cannot s...
ters, **say:** *Look at all of the letters and tell me ...*

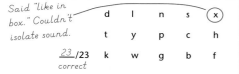

Said "like in box." Couldn't isolate sound.

	d	l	n	s	(x)
	t	y	p	c	h
<u>23</u>/23	k	w	g	b	f

correct

TASK 4. Vowel Sounds

MATERIALS: Student Materials, p. R176

Say to the student: *Tell me the sounds of each letter.* If the student names the letter, count it as the long-vowel sound. Then **ask:** *Can you tell me the other sound for the letter?* The student should name the short-vowel sound.

e <u>l</u> <u>s</u> i <u>l</u> <u>s</u> a <u>l</u> <u>s</u> o <u>l</u> <u>s</u> u <u>l</u> <u>s</u>

l = long sound   s = short sound

Record "l" on the first line for the long sound (letter name) and "s" for the short sound on the second line. If the student makes an error, record the error over the letter.

<u>5</u>/5 Long-vowel sounds (count the number of *l*'s above)

<u>5</u>/5 Short-vowel sounds (count the number of *s*'s above)

TASK 5. Reading and Decoding

MATERIALS: Student Materials, p. R177–179

For items A through G, students must read both real and pseudowords (made-up words). For the first line of real words, **tell the student:** *I want you to read these words.* If the student cannot read two or more of the real words, do not administer the line of pseudowords. Go to the next set of items. Before asking the student to read the line of pseudowords, **say:** *Now I want you to read some made-up words. Do not try to make them sound like real words.*

A. Short vowels in CVC words

<u>5</u>/5	sip	cat	let	but	hog	(real)
<u>5</u>/5	vop	fut	dit	keb	laz	(pseudo)

B. Short vowels, digraphs, and *-tch* trigraph

<u>5</u>/5	when	chop	rich	shut	match	(real)
<u>4</u>/5	wheck	shorm	thax	~~phitch~~ *pitch*	chud	(pseudo)

C. Consonant blends with short vowels

<u>5</u>/5	stop	trap	quit	spell	plan	(real)
<u>5</u>/5	stig	brab	qued	snop	dran	(pseudo)
<u>5</u>/5	clip	fast	sank	limp	held	(real)
<u>5</u>/5	frep	nast	wunk	kimp	jelt	(pseudo)

Points to Note

• Mark has no real problems with these tasks.

Analysis and Comments

• Mark's inability to isolate the sound for *x* (Task 3) is not a problem. He was able to give it within the context of a word.

• On Task 5-B, Mark was unable to give the correct sound for the *ph* digraph in a pseudoword. This information is the basis for a quick review of this skill.

Analysis and Comments

- Mark is able to apply basic decoding skills to VCV words and two-syllable words. When he gives both pronunciations for pseudowords, this shows that he has good understanding of decoding strategies and the applications of phonics.

D. Long-vowel spellings

_5_/5   tape   key   lute   paid   feet   (real)

_5_/5   loe   bine   joad   vay   soat   (pseudo)

E. Variant spellings and diphthongs

_5_/5   few   down   toy   hawk   coin   (real)

_5_/5   voot   rew   fout   zoy   bawk   (pseudo)

(**Note:** Student can pronounce *oo* in *voot* as in *moon* or *book*.)

F. *r*- and *l*-controlled vowels

_5_/5   bark   horn   chirp   term   cold   (real)

_5_/5   ferm   dall   gorf   murd   char   (pseudo)

G. Two-syllable words

Administer these items if the student is able to read most of the single-syllable real and pseudowords in the previous items. **Say to the student:** *Now I want you to read down the first column of words. Each of the real words in this column has two syllables.* Point to the first column. If the student can read at least three out of eight of the words in this column, **say:** *Now I want you to read some made-up words.* Point to the second column. Repeat the same procedure for the third column. **Note:** The following made-up words can be pronounced in two ways: *sunop* (*su-nop* or *sun-op*); *wopam* (*wo-pam* or *wop-am*); *potife* (*po-tife* or *pot-ife*); *zuride* (*zu-ride* or *zur-ide*); and *zubo* (*zu-bo* or *zub-o*). If words are read correctly, do not make any marks.

_3_/3	Closed	kidnap	pugnad	quilbrap
_3_/3	Silent *e*	compete	slifnate	prubkine
_3_/3	Open, closed	depend	sunop — wopam	*gave both pronunc.*
_3_/3	Closed or open, open	zero	zubo	yodu
_3_/3	Open, silent *e*	locate	potife *pō-tīf*	zuride *zū-rīd*
_3_/3	Consonant -*le*	stable	grickle	morkle
_3_/3	r-controlled	further	tirper	pharbid
_3_/3	Vowel team	outlaw	doipnow	loymaud

H. Multisyllabic Words

Administer these items only if the student is able to read six of the eight items in Task G. **Say to the student:** *Now I want you to read down the first column of words. Each of the real words in this column has more than two syllables.* Point to the first column. If the student can read at least three of the 4 words in this column, **say:** *Now I want you to read some made-up words.* Point to the second column. If the words are read correctly, make no marks. If words are read incorrectly, record the student's response above the word. Expected pronunciations for the pseudowords are given below the word.

<u>1</u>/2 (Closed, unaccented, closed)   *cär-ə-van*
caravan   petimel
                 (pet i mel) or (pe tim el)

<u>0</u>/2 (r-controlled, unaccented, silent e)   *mar mald*   *dorl-ish-an*
marmalade   dorlishane
                 (dor li shane)

<u>2</u>/2 (Open, closed, closed)   momentum   bolansun
                 (bo lan sun) or (bol an sun)

<u>0</u>/2 (Closed, unaccented, vowel team)   *vel vēe ten*   *mat loo pen*
velveteen   matlopeen
                 (mat lo peen) or (mat lop een)

TASK 6. Spelling

A. Give the student a pencil and a sheet of lined paper. **Tell the student:** *Number your paper from 1 through 5. Listen to each of the words I read and write the first sound you hear.* Write the student's responses over the words.

<u>5</u>/5   1. fit   2. map   3. pen   4. kid   5. hand

B. **Tell the student:** *Number 1 through 5. Listen to each of the words I read, and write the last sound you hear.*

<u>5</u>/5   1. rub   2. fled   3. leg   4. sell   5. less

C. **Tell the student:** *Number 1 through 10. Listen to each of the words I read, and write the whole word.*

<u>5</u>/5   1. fork   2. yarn   3. sip   4. shop   5. tub

<u>5</u>/5   6. coin   7. float   8. steep   5. drive   10. spoon

Houghton Mifflin Phonics/Decoding Screening Test: **Recording Sheet 6**   R175

Points to Note

• The tasks on this page involve both reading and spelling.

Analysis and Comments

• Mark does not appear to know how to apply the decoding skills he uses in VCV words and two-syllable words to longer words in context. This supports the decision to use the Decoding Longer Words lessons (see page R180).

• As far as spelling is concerned, Mark is able to use basic decoding skills of beginning consonants, ending consonants, short medial vowels, and long vowels to spell one-syllable words.

Houghton Mifflin Phonics/Decoding Screening Test

Protocol and Analysis Sheet

Name _____ **Grade** _____ **Date** _____

Phonics/Decoding Summary Sheet

Alphabet Skills

___/26	(21)	**Task 1.**	Letter names—uppercase
___/26	(21)	**Task 2.**	Letter names—lowercase
___/23	(18)	**Task 3.**	Consonant sounds
___/5	(4)	**Task 4.**	Long-vowel sounds
___/5	(4)	**Task 5.**	Short-vowel sounds

Task 6. Reading and Decoding Skills

___/10	(8)	**A.**	Short vowels in CVC words
___/10	(8)	**B.**	Short vowels, digraphs, and *-tch* trigraph
___/20	(16)	**C.**	Short vowels and consonant blends
___/10	(8)	**D.**	Long vowels
___/10	(8)	**E.**	r- and l-controlled vowels
___/10	(8)	**F.**	Vowel diphthongs

Multisyllabic Words:

___/24	(19)	**G.**	Two-syllable words
___/8	(6)	**H.**	Multisyllabic words

Task 7. Spelling Skills

___/5	(4)	**A.**	Initial consonants
___/5	(4)	**B.**	Final consonants
___/5	(4)	**C.**	CVC words
___/5	(4)	**D.**	Long-vowel words

Components/Observations

Protocol and Analysis Sheet page 2

Name _____

Timed Fluency Test: WCPM _____

    ☐ Expected Progress

    ☐ Below Expected Progress

    ☐ Seriously Below Expected Progress

Instructional Needs

Skills to review: _____

_____

_____

_____

_____

Skills to teach: _____

_____

_____

_____

_____

☐ Needs regular SOAR TO SUCCESS lessons only

☐ Needs regular SOAR TO SUCCESS lessons plus additional decoding support

☐ Needs Phonics Intervention

TASK 1. Letter names—Uppercase

MATERIALS: Student Materials, p. R176

Say to the student: *Tell me the names of these letters.* Circle all incorrect responses. If the student cannot name three or more consecutive letters, **say:** *Look at all of the letters and tell me which ones you do know.*

D A N S X Z J L H

T Y E C O M R P W

___/26 K U G B F Q V I

TASK 2. Letter Names—Lowercase

MATERIALS: Student Materials, p. R176

Say to the student: *Tell me the names of these letters.* Circle all incorrect responses. If the student cannot name three or more consecutive letters, **say:** *Look at all of the letters and tell me which ones you do know.*

d a n s x z i l h

t y e c o m r p w

___/26 k u g b f q v i

TASK 3. Consonant Sounds

MATERIALS: Student Materials, p. R176

Say to the student: *Look at these letters. Tell me the sound each letter stands for.* Ask if he or she knows of another sound for the letters *g* and *c*. If the sound given is correct, do not mark this form. If it is incorrect, write the sound the student gives above each letter. If no sound is given, circle the letter. If the student cannot say the sound for three or more consecutive letters, **say:** *Look at all of the letters and tell me which sounds you do know.*

d l n s x z j

t y p c h m r

___/23 k w g b f q v

TASK 4.   Vowel Sounds

MATERIALS: Student Materials, p. R176

Say to the student: *Tell me the sounds of each letter.* If the student names the letter, count it as the long-vowel sound. Then **ask:** *Can you tell me the other sound for the letter?* The student should name the short-vowel sound.

e_____ _____   i_____ _____   a_____ _____   o_____ _____   u_____ _____

l = long sound   s = short sound

Record "l" on the first line for the long sound (letter name) and "s" for the short sound on the second line. If the student makes an error, record the error over the letter.

____/5 Long-vowel sounds (count the number of *l*'s above)

____/5 Short-vowel sounds (count the number of *s*'s above)

TASK 5.   Reading and Decoding

MATERIALS: Student Materials, p. R177–179

For items A through G, students must read both real and pseudowords (made-up words). For the first line of real words, **tell the student:** *I want you to read these words.* If the student cannot read two or more of the real words, do not administer the line of pseudowords. Go to the next set of items. Before asking the student to read the line of pseudowords, **say:** *Now I want you to read some made-up words. Do not try to make them sound like real words.*

A.   Short vowels in CVC words

____/5	sip	cat	let	but	hog	(real)
____/5	vop	fut	dit	keb	laz	(pseudo)

B.   Short vowels, digraphs, and -*tch* trigraph

____/5	when	chop	rich	shut	match	(real)
____/5	wheck	shorm	thax	phitch	chud	(pseudo)

C.   Consonant blends with short vowels

____/5	stop	trap	quit	spell	plan	(real)
____/5	stig	brab	qued	snop	dran	(pseudo)
____/5	clip	fast	sank	limp	held	(real)
____/5	frep	nast	wunk	kimp	jelt	(pseudo)

D. Long-vowel spellings

___/5   tape   key   lute   paid   feet   (real)

___/5   loe   bine   joad   vay   soat   (pseudo)

E. Variant spellings and diphthongs

___/5   few   down   toy   hawk   coin   (real)

___/5   voot   rew   fout   zoy   bawk   (pseudo)

(**Note:** Student can pronounce *oo* in *voot* as in *moon* or *book*.)

F. *r*- and *l*-controlled vowels

___/5   bark   horn   chirp   term   cold   (real)

___/5   ferm   dall   gorf   murd   char   (pseudo)

G. Two-syllable words

Administer these items if the student is able to read most of the single-syllable real and pseudowords in the previous items. **Say to the student:** *Now I want you to read down the first column of words. Each of the real words in this column has two syllables.* Point to the first column. If the student can read at least three out of eight of the words in this column, **say:** *Now I want you to read some made-up words.* Point to the second column. Repeat the same procedure for the third column. **Note:** The following made-up words can be pronounced in two ways: *sunop* (*su-nop* or *sun-op*); *wopam* (*wo-pam* or *wop-am*); *potife* (*po-tife* or *pot-ife*); *zuride* (*zu-ride* or *zur-ide*); and *zubo* (*zu-bo* or *zub-o*). If words are read correctly, do not make any marks.

___/3	Closed	kidnap	pugnad	quilbrap
___/3	Silent *e*	compete	slifnate	prubkine
___/3	Open, closed	depend	sunop	wopam
___/3	Closed or open, open	zero	zubo	yodu
___/3	Open, silent *e*	locate	potife	zuride
___/3	Consonant-*le*	stable	grickle	morkle
___/3	r-controlled	further	tirper	pharbid
___/3	Vowel team	outlaw	doipnow	loymaud

H. Multisyllabic Words

Administer these items only if the student is able to read six of the eight items in Task G. **Say to the student:** *Now I want you to read down the first column of words. Each of the real words in this column has more than two syllables.* Point to the first column. If the student can read at least three of the 4 words in this column, **say:** *Now I want you to read some made-up words.* Point to the second column. If the words are read correctly, make no marks. If words are read incorrectly, record the student's response above the word. Expected pronunciations for the pseudowords are given below the word.

____/2 (Closed, unaccented, closed)   caravan   petimel
                                                          (pet i mel) or (pe tim el)

____/2 (r-controlled, unaccented, silent e) marmalade   dorlishane
                                                          (dor li shane)

____/2 (Open, closed, closed)   momentum   bolansun
                                                          (bo lan sun) or (bol an sun)

____/2 (Closed, unaccented, vowel team) velveteen   matlopeen
                                                          (mat lo peen) or (mat lop een)

TASK 6. Spelling

A. Give the student a pencil and a sheet of lined paper. **Tell the student:** *Number your paper from 1 through 5. Listen to each of the words I read and write the first sound you hear.* Write the student's responses over the words.

    ____/5   1. fit   2. map   3. pen   4. kid   5. hand

B. **Tell the student:** *Number 1 through 5. Listen to each of the words I read, and write the last sound you hear.*

    ____/5   1. rub   2. fled   3. leg   4. sell   5. less

C. **Tell the student:** *Number 1 through 10. Listen to each of the words I read, and write the whole word.*

    ____/5   1. fork   2. yarn   3. sip   4. shop   5. tub

    ____/5   6. coin   7. float   8. steep   5. drive   10. spoon

Houghton Mifflin Phonics/Decoding Screening Test

1.
D	A	N	S	X	Z	J	L	H
T	Y	E	C	O	M	R	P	W
K	U	G	B	F	Q	V	I	

2.
d	a	n	s	x	z	j	l	h
t	y	e	c	o	m	r	p	w
k	u	g	b	f	q	v	i	

3.
d	l	n	s	x	z	j
t	y	p	c	h	m	r
k	w	g	b	f	q	v

4.
e	i	a	o	u

5. Reading and Decoding

A.

sip	cat	let	bog	hog
vop	fut	dit	keb	laz

B.

when	chop	rich	shut	match
wheck	shom	thax	phitch	chud

C.

stop	trap	quit	spell	plan
stig	brab	qued	snop	dran
chip	fast	sank	limp	held
frep	nast	wunk	kimp	jelt

D.

tape	key	lute	paid	feet
loe	bine	joad	vay	soat

E.

bark	horn	chirp	term	cold
ferm	dall	gorf	murd	char

F.

few	down	toy	hawk	coin
voot	rew	fout	zoy	bawk

G.

kidnap	pugnad	quibrap
compete	slifnate	prubkine
depend	sunop	wopan
zero	zubo	yodu
locate	potife	zuride
stable	grickle	morkle
further	tirper	pharbid
outlaw	doipnoe	loymaud

H.

caravan	petimel
marmalade	dorlishane
momentum	bolansun
velveteen	matlopeen

Optional Lessons

· ·

Optional Lessons provide an extra day's instruction for each of the 18 books. Each lesson has the following components:

Summarizing

Students use their completed graphic organizers to summarize the *SOAR TO SUCCESS* book they have just read. Summarizing activities are scaffolded across the 18 Optional Lessons, progressing from strong teacher support to student independence.

During this part of the lesson, remind students of the Summarize Strategy:

- When I summarize, I tell in my own words the important things I have read.

Discuss ways to decide what is important; for example:

- For *SOAR TO SUCCESS* books, refer to the graphic organizers to get a basis for the summary.
- Identify a main idea or problem.
- Eliminate unnecessary information and details.
- Group things that are alike, using a general term that describes a category of things or a set of actions.
- Eliminate repeated words.

Decoding Longer Words Lesson

Explicit instruction is provided for an organized sequence of skills. Students learn how to apply their basic phonics skills to decode longer words, using the CLARIFY/PHONICS: Think About Words strategy. Lessons teach syllabication, compound words, base words, inflected forms, prefixes, and suffixes.

Each lesson includes blackline masters for two pages, including material that supports the instruction as well as practice. Provide students with copies of those blackline masters, which appear on pages R200–R235.

Making Words Activity

Each Optional Lesson concludes with Making Words, an active, hands-on manipulative teaching strategy to help students use letter-sound relationships and word patterns.

- See pages T64–T66 in Section 8, Helping Students with Decoding Problems, for the procedure for Making Words.

- You can make prefix and/or suffix cards so that students can expand the word to reflect the Decoding Longer Words skills. Those affixes are shown in parentheses in the chart of contents on the next page.

Book	Summarizing	Decoding Longer Words Lesson	Making Words: Book Word
1. A Beauty of a Plan	Oral Summary	CLARIFY/PHONICS: Break Words into Chunks	architect
2. The Lost Expedition		Chunking Words Using Pattern VC•CV	*Endurance*
3. Owl		Chunking Words Using Patterns V•CV, VC•V	covered
4. The Babe & I	Group-Written Summary	Syllables: Consonant-*le*	wrinkled
5. Journey Home		Words of More Than Two Syllables	directions
6. Cal Ripken, Jr.		Base Words with Endings -s, -es, -ed, -ing	searching
7. Mountains		Base Words with Endings That Compare	reminder
8. Jesse Jackson		Base Words with Prefixes re-, pre-	organized (re)
9. Lakota Hoop Dance		Base Words with Negative Prefixes un-, dis-, mis-, in-, il-, im-, ir-	related (un)
10. Tunnels, Tracks, and Trains		Base Words with Suffixes -y, -ly	complete (ly)
11. Gloria Estefan		Base Words with Suffixes -l, -less, -ful	playing play (ful)
12. Benjamin Banneker		Base Words with Suffixes -ous, -able	question (able)
13. Lightning		Base Words with Suffixes -ment, -ness, -ion	brightness
14. Sports Lab	Independent Summary	CLARIFY/PHONICS: Break Words into Chunks	entirely
15. Lisa Leslie		Base Words, Endings, Suffixes	undefeated
16. An Even Break		Prefixes, Base Words, Endings, Suffixes	desirable (un)
17. El Duque		Prefixes, Base Words, Suffixes	decreased
18. Marisol and Magdalena		CLARIFY/PHONICS: Break Words into Chunks	unforgettable

A Beauty of a Plan
Optional Lesson, Book 1

Summary:

Sheila and Michael have finished their shop project. Now Sheila must pick a new project for them to work on. However, Sheila's grandmother wants Sheila to study something that would be of use at the family's beauty salon. They make a bet. Sheila has three weeks to put her shop knowledge to use at the salon. If she succeeds, Grandma will do the sweeping for a month. If she fails, she will drop shop class. Sheila redesigns the salon, and, with the help of the students in her shop class, builds cabinets and partitions. Her sister, Jackie, gets Grandma out of the salon so the students can install everything. When she returns, Grandma surveys the work, then gets a broom and begins to sweep.

Making Words

Letter Cards: a e i c c h r t t
Book Word: architect (page 12)

- Take two letters and make *at.*
- Add one letter to make *ate.*
- Change one letter to make *are.*
- Rearrange the letters to make *ear.*
- Add one letter to make *hear.*
- Add one letter to make *heart.*
- Rearrange the letters to make *earth.*
- Rearrange the letters and add one to make *threat.*
- Now use all your letters to make a word from the book, *architect.*

Sorts

- words that rhyme
- words with *ea* combinations
- words with *ear* combinations
- words with *th*

Summarizing

Using the completed graphic organizer, model summarizing the first section of the book orally. Have a volunteer use the graphic organizer to add to the summary. Have the last part summarized orally. Have students use the graphic organizer to orally summarize the book to each other.

Decoding Longer Words
Clarify/Phonics: Break Words into Chunks

Teach/Model Tell students that unfamiliar-looking words may be made of known word parts, or chunks. Common chunks include (a) compounds, smaller words combined into a larger one; (b) syllables, one or more letters with just one vowel sound; and (c) base words with endings, with prefixes, and with suffixes. Have students read the five questions in the five sections of the chart. Use the first example word after each of the five questions to model breaking a word into chunks:

> MODEL If the longer word is a compound word, I'll find two smaller words in it. In the first example, **some** and **what** combine to make the word **somewhat**.

> The letter **a** at the beginning of a word might be a separate syllable pronounced **uh**, as in **around**, **amaze**, and **along**.

> A base word is a word that stands alone. If I see an ending such as **-er**, it might be added to a base word I know: **old** plus **-er** makes **older**.

> A prefix is added before a base word to change the base word's meaning. A common prefix is **mis-**. The prefix **mis-** plus the base word **place** makes **misplace**.

> A suffix is added after a base word to change the base word's meaning. A common suffix is **-able**. The base word **depend** plus the suffix **-able** makes **dependable**.

Have students take turns similarly modeling the breaking apart of each of the remaining examples in the chart. Prompt them to note base-word spelling changes in the words **rebelled**, **happiest**, **believing**, and **happiness**.

Review students' answers to the questions under the chart. Guide them in verbalizing what they have learned about categories of chunks.

Connect to strategy CLARIFY/PHONICS Have students review the steps of the CLARIFY/PHONICS strategy (Poster 3). Write this sentence on the board and read it aloud, skipping the word **deductions**. Model using the strategy, as shown below:

> **When people pay taxes, what deductions can they make?**

> MODEL I know every word in the sentence except this one (underline **deductions**). I look for chunks and see the prefix **de-** at the beginning; I see **-tion** at the end and the ending **-s**. I say **de/duc/tions**. I've heard of tax deductions. It makes sense.

Practice A Partners complete items 1–8. Students take turns saying each longer word.

Practice B Read the directions, and go over item 1 with the group if necessary. Students complete the items on their own. Afterward, discuss the meanings of the phrases.

Apply/Comprehension Check

Students work independently. For the Apply items, have students tell how they used the CLARIFY/PHONICS strategy to figure out each word of two or more syllables, as well as any other words in the text. Discuss responses to the Comprehension Check.

Making Words

Use the activity to the left. See pp. T64–T66 to review the procedure.

Lost Expedition
Optional Lesson, Book 2

Summary:

In the early 20th century, Ernest Shackleton wanted to be the first man to cross Antarctica on foot. He and his crew sailed south on the *Endurance* to South Georgia Island. They sailed on in December, but soon after, the ship became trapped in the ice. The men built warmer living quarters and waited for the spring thaw. The ship was crushed by the ice, but the crew were able to salvage supplies and possessions. Shackleton and his men dragged lifeboats across the ice and set sail. When they reached Elephant Island, Shackleton and a small group continued on to South Georgia Island. It took four months, but Shackleton returned and rescued his crew.

Making Words

Letter Cards: a e e u c d n n r
Book Word: endurance (page 5)

- Take three letters to make *car.*
- Add a letter to make *care.*
- Change a letter to make *cure.*
- Add a letter to make *cured.*
- Rearrange the letters to make *crude.*
- Rearrange letters and add one to make *reduce.*
- Rearrange letters and change one to make *endure.*
- Now use all your letters to make a word from the book, *endurance.*

Sorts

- words that rhyme
- words with a prefix
- words ending in *e*
- words with two or more chunks

Summarizing

Using the completed graphic organizer, model summarizing the first section of the book orally. Have a volunteer use the graphic organizer to add to the summary. Have the last part summarized orally. Have students use the graphic organizer to orally summarize the book to each other.

Decoding Longer Words
Chunking Words Using VC•CV Patterns

Teach/Model Tell students that a syllable is a sound chunk that contains just one vowel sound. The syllables of longer words can be pronounced as separate chunks. To break a word into syllables, readers look for consonants and vowels. If there are two consonants between vowels, the first syllable often ends with the first consonant.

Have students pronounce each syllable in the chart.

Use the first word, **temper**, to model breaking a word into syllables.

> MODEL The **m** and **p** in this word are consonants between vowels. I chunk after the first consonant, **m**, and pronounce the first syllable: **tem**. Then I say the second syllable, **per**. Taken together: **temper**.

Have students take turns similarly modeling the chunking of **person**, **concert**, **persist**, and **common**.

You may point out to students that two like consonants can be pronounced as one sound: They hear only one **m** sound in **common**.

Review students' answers to the questions under the chart.

Connect to strategy CLARIFY/PHONICS Have students review the steps of the CLARIFY/PHONICS strategy (Poster 3). Write this sentence on the board and read it aloud, skipping the word **confide**. Model using the strategy, as shown below:

> **A true friend is someone you can confide in and trust.**

> MODEL I know every word in the sentence except this one (underline **confide**). I see two consonants between vowels, so I'll break the first syllable after the first consonant, **n**. I say the syllables separately and then together: **con**, **fide**, **confide**. The sentence talks about trusting a friend, so **confide** probably means "to tell something privately."

Practice A Partners complete items 1–7. Students then take turns saying each syllable and word aloud.

Practice B Read the directions, and go over item 1 with the group if necessary. Students complete the remaining items on their own. Afterward, discuss the meanings of the phrases.

Apply/Comprehension Check

Students work independently. For the Apply items, have students tell how they used the CLARIFY/PHONICS strategy to figure out each two-syllable word, as well as any other words in the text. Discuss responses to the Comprehension Check.

Making Words

Use the activity to the left. See pp. T64–T66 to review the procedure.

Owl
Optional Lesson, Book 3

Summary:

Owls eat insects, birds, fish, and mice. Parent owls catch food and bring it home to their babies. Most owls raise four to six young each year. Owls build nests in trees, barns, and other buildings. They live everywhere, from the Arctic to the rainforest. The snowy owl lives in the north and lays its eggs on the ground. It is white, so it can hide in the snow. Burrowing owls live in underground tunnels. Owls are active only at night, so when the sun rises, an owl returns to its nest to wait for another sunset.

Making Words

Letter Cards: e e o c d r v
Book Word: covered (page 12)

- Take two letters to make *do.*
- Add a letter to make *doe.*
- Add a letter to make *dove.*
  I dove into the water.
- Change a letter to make *cove.*
- Change a letter to make *rove.*
- Add a letter to make *rover.*
- Change a letter to make *cover.*
- Now use all your letters to make a word from the book, *covered.*

Sorts

- words that rhyme
- words with *er*
- words with two syllables

Summarizing

Using the completed graphic organizer, model summarizing the first section of the book orally. Have a volunteer use the graphic organizer to add to the summary. Have the last part summarized orally. Have students use the graphic organizer to orally summarize the book to each other.

Decoding Longer Words
Chunking Words Using Patterns V•CV, VC•V

Teach/Model Tell students that the syllables of longer words can be pronounced as separate chunks. To break a word into syllables, readers look for patterns of consonants and vowels. If there is just one consonant between vowels, the first syllable may be open, ending with the first vowel. Or the first syllable may be *closed*, ending with the consonant.

Have students pronounce each first syllable in the chart. Explain that the letters and symbols between slanted lines show sounds. A bar shows a long vowel, a curve shows a short vowel, and an upside-down, backward **e** shows a schwa. (A schwa is an unstressed vowel sound, somewhat in between a short **i** and a short **u**.)

Use the first word, promise, to model breaking a word into syllables.

> MODEL The consonant **m** is between the vowels **o** and **i**. I try breaking the first syllable after the **o** and saying a long **o**, **PRO-mise**, but that doesn't sound like a word I know. If I break after the consonant, I get a word I recognize: PROM-ise.

Have students take turns similarly modeling the chunking of the remaining listed words.

Review students' answers to the questions under the chart. Guide them in verbalizing what they have learned about chunking words with one consonant between vowels.

Connect to strategy CLARIFY/PHONICS Have students review the steps of the CLARIFY/PHONICS strategy (Poster 3). Write this sentence on the board and read it aloud, skipping the word **humid**. Model using the strategy, as shown below:

> **It's hard to move fast on hot and humid days.**

> MODEL I know every word in the sentence except this one (underline **humid**). I see one consonant between vowels, so I'll try breaking the first syllable after the first vowel, **u**. I'll try a long vowel sound first: **HYOO-mid**. Yes, I recognize the word. Humid air feels wet and sticky, so humid makes sense in the sentence.

Practice A Partners complete items 1–8. Students then take turns saying each syllable and word aloud.

Practice B Read the directions, and go over item 1 with the group if necessary. Students complete the remaining items on their own. Afterward, discuss the meanings of the phrases.

Apply/Comprehension Check

Students work independently. For the Apply items, have students tell how they used the CLARIFY/PHONICS strategy to figure out each VCV word, as well as any other words in the text. Discuss responses to the Comprehension Check.

Making Words

Use the activity to the left. See pp. T64–T66 to review the procedure.

The Babe & I
Optional Lesson, Book 4

Summary:

During the Great Depression, money was scarce for many families. In this story, a boy got nothing but a dime for his birthday. After his father had left for work, the boy saw him selling apples in the street. The boy's friend Jacob suggested they make money by selling newspapers at Yankee Stadium, so that the boy could help, too. The boy did well. He gave the money he earned to his mother. She told him to keep his new job a secret, but his father found out. The boy agreed to keep his father's secret about selling apples. After Babe Ruth bought a paper and gave the boy five dollars, he and Jacob watched the game. The boy realized that he and his father worked together as a team, just as the Babe and the Yankees did.

Making Words

Letter Cards: i e d l k n r w
Book Word: wrinkled (page 9)

- Take three letters to make *kid.*
- Change a letter to make *lid.*
- Change a letter to make *lie.*
- Add a letter to make *line.*
- Change a letter to make *link.*
- Change a letter to make *wink.*
- Add the ending *ed* to make *winked.*
- Now use all your letters to make a word from the book, *wrinkled.*

Sorts

- words that rhyme
- words ending in *ed*
- words beginning with *l*
- word with more than two chunks

Summarizing

Using the completed graphic organizer, model summarizing the first section of the book orally; then write your summary on chart paper. Have a volunteer use the graphic organizer to add to the summary. Write it on chart paper. Follow this procedure to summarize the last part of the book.

Decoding Longer Words
Syllables: Consonant-*le*

Teach/Model Tell students that longer words can be pronounced by breaking them into chunks. To break a word into syllables, readers look for patterns of consonants and vowels. One common pattern is an ending syllable of **Consonant-le**. The letters **l-e** are chunked with the consonant that comes before them.

Have students read the second column of the chart and name the consonant in the **Consonant-le** pattern.

Use the first word, **bubble**, to model breaking a word into syllables.

> MODEL I see a **Consonant-le** at the end of this word, so I break the syllable before the consonant, which is **b**. That leaves a first syllable that I say separately: **bub**. Putting the syllables together, I say **bubble**.

Have students take turns similarly modeling the chunking of the remaining listed words.

Review students' answers to the questions under the chart, and help them to verbalize the generalization for chunking a word that ends with **Consonant-le**.

Connect to strategy CLARIFY/PHONICS Have students review the steps of the CLARIFY/PHONICS strategy (Poster 3). Write this sentence on the board and read it aloud, skipping the word **stifle**. Model using the strategy, as shown below:

> **She clapped a hand to her mouth to stifle a cry.**

> MODEL I know every word in the sentence except this one (underline **stifle**). I see a **Consonant-le** at the end, so I break the syllable before the consonant, **f**. The first syllable ends with a vowel, **i**, so I'll try a long **i** sound: **STY-fle**. **Stifle** sounds familiar to me. To stifle something means to stop it from happening, and that makes sense in the sentence.

Practice A Partners complete items 1–8. Students then take turns saying each syllable and word aloud.

Practice B Read the directions, and go over item 1 with the group if necessary. Students complete the remaining items on their own. Afterward, discuss the meanings of the phrases.

Apply/Comprehension Check

Students work independently. For the Apply items, have students tell how they used the CLARIFY/PHONICS strategy to figure out each **Consonant-le** word, as well as any other words in the text. Discuss responses to the Comprehension Check.

Making Words

Use the activity to the left. See pp. T64–T66 to review the procedure.

Journey Home
Optional Lesson, Book 5

Summary:

Mai's mother, Lin, is a Vietnamese orphan who was raised in America. Together they travel to Vietnam, where Lin hopes to find her birth family. Mai wants to bring her mother's special kite, but Lin says no. In Saigon, they visit the People's Hall of Records, looking for a photo that matches one of Lin as a child. They visit many orphanages, with no success. On the waterfront, they see a merchant with kites just like Lin's. He gives them the name of the kite-maker. The kite-maker recognizes the photo. He tells Lin her birth name, and explains that he rescued her when her parents were killed in the war.

Making Words

Letter Cards: e i i o c d n r s t
Book Word: directions (page 12)

- Take three letters to make *rid.*
- Add a letter to make *ride.*
- Change a letter and make *side.*
- Change a letter and make *tide.*
- Change a letter and make *tire.*
- Change a letter and make *dire.*
- Add two letters to make *direct.*
- Add the suffix *ion* to make *direction.*
- Add the ending *s* to make a word from the book, *directions.*

Sorts

- words that rhyme
- words with *ion* endings
- words with a long *I*
- word with two or more syllables

Summarizing

Using the completed graphic organizer, model summarizing the first section of the book orally; then write your summary on chart paper. Have a volunteer use the graphic organizer to add to the summary. Write it on chart paper. Follow this procedure to summarize the last part of the book.

Decoding Longer Words
Words of More Than Two Syllables

Teach/Model Tell students that the syllables of longer words can be pronounced as separate chunks. To break a word into syllables, readers look for patterns of consonants and vowels. The same patterns found in two-syllable words are in words of more than two syllables. As words get longer, syllable stress becomes more important. Stress is the amount of emphasis given to each syllable.

Have students read the second column of the chart and spell the stressed syllable.

Use the first word, **determine**, to model breaking a word into syllables.

> MODEL I see a consonant, **t**, between two vowels. I'll first try breaking before the consonant, making the first syllable **de**. Then I see two consonants, **r** and **m**, between vowels, so I can break between the consonants to get **ter** and **mine**. I'll try different stresses: **/DEE/ter/mine/, /dih/TER/mine/, /dih/TER/min/**. The last try sounds right: The word is **determine**.

Have students take turns similarly modeling the chunking of the remaining listed words. Emphasize using oral language to guide decisions about syllable stress.

Review students' answers to the questions under the chart.

Connect to strategy CLARIFY/PHONICS Have students review the steps of the CLARIFY/PHONICS strategy (Poster 3). Write this sentence on the board and read it aloud, skipping the word **habitat**. Model using the strategy, as shown below:

> **Clearing forests may reduce an animal's habitat.**

> MODEL I know every word in the sentence except this one (underline **habitat**). I see a consonant **b** between vowels and a consonant **t** between vowels, so I can try ending each syllable with a vowel or a consonant. I'll try different pronunciations: **/HAY/by/tat/, /HAY/bit/at/, /HAB/ih/tat/**. Yes, I recognize the word **habitat**, which names an animal's living space. That makes sense in the sentence.

Practice A Partners complete items 1–8. Students then take turns saying each syllable and word aloud.

Practice B Read the directions, and go over item 1 with the group if necessary. Students complete the remaining items on their own. Afterward, discuss the meanings of the phrases.

Apply/Comprehension Check

Students work independently. For the Apply items, have students tell how they used the CLARIFY/PHONICS strategy to figure out each three-syllable word, as well as any other words in the text. Discuss responses to the Comprehension Check.

Making Words

Use the activity to the left. See pp. T64–T66 to review the procedure.

Cal Ripken, Jr.
Optional Lesson, Book 6

Summary:

Cal Ripken, Jr.'s father was a professional baseball coach, and Cal and his brothers and sister grew up playing sports. After high school, Cal was drafted by the Baltimore Orioles. Soon he was a success in the minor leagues. He was named Rookie of the Year and Most Valuable Player. He moved up to the majors, married, and had a son and a daughter. For a while in 1987, Cal's brother Billy played for the Orioles, and their father was the manager. Cal continued to play every game. In 1995 he tied, and then beat, Lou Gehrig's record for most consecutive games played. He was given Gehrig's nickname, the Iron Man of baseball. On September 20, 1998, Cal took himself out of the lineup. He had played in 2,632 consecutive games.

Making Words

Letter Cards: a e i c g h n r s
Book Word: searching (page 17)

- Take three letters to make *air.*
- Add a letter to make *hair.*
- Change one to make *hare.*
- Rearrange the letters and change one to make *arch.*
- Rearrange letters and add one to make *reach.*
- Rearrange letters and add one to make *search.*
- Add the ending *ing* to make *searching.*

Sorts

- words with *ea*
- words that sound the same
- words with *ch*
- words with two chunks

Summarizing

Using the completed graphic organizer, model summarizing the first section of the book orally; then write your summary on chart paper. Have a volunteer use the graphic organizer to add to the summary. Write it on chart paper. Follow this procedure to summarize the last part of the book.

Decoding Longer Words
Base Words with Endings

Teach/Model Tell students that endings are commonly added to base words. (Base words can stand alone.) The endings may change the way a base word is spelled. Readers should look for endings and try to identify the base word in order to pronounce and understand the longer word.

Have students read the three column headings in the chart and name the four different endings (called inflected endings, or inflections): **-s**, **-es**, **-ed**, **-ing**.

Use the first row to model building a word:

> MODEL The base word is **adventure**. When the ending **-s** is added, the word is **adventures**. The base word does not change its spelling.

Have students take turns similarly modeling the addition of endings to build longer words. Prompt them to note spelling changes in **strawberries**, **permitted**, **staring**, and **starring**.

Review students' answers to the questions under the chart. Guide students in verbalizing generalizations about base words with endings.

Connect to strategy CLARIFY/PHONICS Have students review the steps of the CLARIFY/PHONICS strategy (Poster 3). Write this sentence on the board and read it aloud, skipping the word **supplies**. Model using the strategy, as shown below:

> **Before the storm, many stores ran out of supplies.**

> MODEL I know every word in the sentence except this one (underline **supplies**). When I look for known chunks, I see an ending, **-es**. Often, a **y** changes to **i** before that ending, so the base word might be spelled with a final **y**: **s-u-p-p-l-y**. That's a base word I know: **supply**. The sentence is about stores running out of supplies—that makes sense.

Practice A Partners complete items 1–8. Students then take turns saying each base word and longer word.

Practice B Read the directions, and go over item 1 with the group if necessary. Students complete the remaining items on their own. Afterward, have students tell how they knew which word in the phrase has an ending and how they identified the base word.

Apply/Comprehension Check

Students work independently. For the Apply items, have students tell how they used the CLARIFY/PHONICS strategy to figure out the words with endings, as well as any other words in the text. Discuss responses to the Comprehension Check.

Making Words

Use the activity to the left. See pp. T64–T66 to review the procedure.

Mountains
Optional Lesson, Book 7

Summary:

Most mountains are part of long chains or ranges. Mountains are formed in different ways. Mountain ranges arise where two plates of the earth's crust meet. Two plates pushing against each other or pulling away from each other can also form mountains. Hot magma under the surface can force the rock above it up into a mountain, or it can break through the surface and then cool, forming a mountain. As soon as they are formed, mountains begin to be worn away by wind, water, and temperature changes. Mountains can affect the weather around them. Often the climate is very rainy on one side of a mountain range and very dry on the other. As you go higher up a mountain, the temperature gets colder, the air gets thinner, and fewer plants and animals live there.

Making Words

Letter Cards: e e i d m n r r
Book Word: reminder (page 5)

- Take three letters to make *rim*.
- Change a letter to make *dim*.
- Add a letter to make *dime*.
- Change a letter to make *dine*.
- Change a letter to make *mine*.
- Change a letter to make *mind*.
- Add the prefix *re* to make *remind*.
- Add the ending *er* to make *reminder*.

Sorts

- words that rhyme
- words with a prefix
- word with two chunks
- word with three chunks

Summarizing

Using the completed graphic organizer, model summarizing the first section of the book orally; then write your summary on chart paper. Have a volunteer use the graphic organizer to add to the summary. Write it on chart paper. Follow this procedure to summarize the last part of the book.

Decoding Longer Words
Base Words with Endings that Compare

Teach/Model Tell students that endings are commonly added to base words. The endings -er and -est can signal comparisons. These endings may change the way a base word is spelled. Readers should look for these endings because they are separate chunks, and try to identify the base word in order to pronounce and understand the longer word.

Have students read the three column headings in the chart and spell the two endings that compare.

Use the first row to model building a word:

> MODEL The base word is **small**. When the ending **-er** is added, the word is **smaller**. When the ending **-est** is added, the word is **smallest**. The base word does not change its spelling.

Have students take turns similarly modeling the addition of endings to build longer words. Prompt them to note the spelling changes in the remaining words.

Review students' answers to the questions under the chart. Guide students in verbalizing what they have learned about base words with endings that compare.

Connect to strategy CLARIFY/PHONICS Have students review the steps of the CLARIFY/PHONICS strategy (Poster 3). Write this sentence on the board and read it aloud, skipping the word **purer**. Model using the strategy, as shown below:

> **Is spring water purer than tap water?**

> MODEL I know every word in the sentence except this one (underline **purer**). When I look for known chunks, I see **e-r** at the end. It might be an ending that compares, so I look for a base word. I don't recognize the word spelled **p-u-r**, but maybe a final **e** was dropped. The spelling **p-u-r-e** gives me a word I know: **pure**. The sentence is asking about which water is purer—that makes sense.

Practice A Partners complete items 1–8. Students then take turns saying each base word and longer word.

Practice B Read the directions, and go over item 1 with the group if necessary. Students complete the remaining items on their own. Afterward, have students tell how they knew which word in the phrase has an ending that compares and how they identified the base word.

Apply/Comprehension Check

Students work independently. For the Apply items, have students tell how they used the CLARIFY/PHONICS strategy to figure out the words with endings that compare, as well as any other words in the text. Discuss responses to the Comprehension Check.

Making Words

Use the activity to the left. See pp. T64–T66 to review the procedure.

Jesse Jackson
Optional Lesson, Book 8

Summary:

Jackson was born in South Carolina at a time when many laws forced blacks and whites to live separately. At the University of Illinois, Jackson played football, but he couldn't become quarterback because he was black. He transferred to a mostly black college in North Carolina and became a student activist. Later, he became a minister and joined the S.C.L.C., which was led by Dr. Martin Luther King, Jr. In Chicago, Jackson organized groups to march in Alabama in support of voting rights, and started Operation Breadbasket. When Dr. King was shot, Jackson called for nonviolence. He started groups called PUSH and PUSH-Excel. He also established the Rainbow Coalition and ran for U.S. President.

Making Words

Letter Cards: a e i o d g n r z (re)
Book Word: organized (page 16)

- Take two letters to make *no*.
- Add a letter to make *nod*.
- Add a letter to make *rod*.
- Add a letter to make *road*.
- Add a letter and change one to make *groan*.
- Rearrange the letters to make *organ*.
- Add a three-letter suffix to make *organize*.
- Add a letter to make a word from the book, *organized*.
- Add the prefix *re* to the word to make *reorganized*.

Sorts
- words that rhyme
- words with a long *o*
- words with a suffix
- words with two or more chunks
- words with an *r* controlled vowel

Summarizing

Using the completed graphic organizer, model summarizing the first section of the book orally; then write your summary on chart paper. Have a volunteer use the graphic organizer to add to the summary. Write it on chart paper. Follow this procedure to summarize the last part of the book.

Decoding Longer Words
Base Words with Prefixes re-, pre-

Teach/Model Tell students that unfamiliar-looking words may be made of known word parts, or chunks. Prefixes are common chunks appearing at the beginning of words. Sometimes the prefixes **re-** and **pre-** come before base words and can help readers figure out pronunciation and meaning.

Have students read the four column headings in the chart.

Use the first prefix **re-** to model building a word and thinking about meaning:

> MODEL The letters **r-e** are added to the base word told to make the longer word **retold**. Something that is retold is told again. The prefix **re-** can mean "again."

Have students take turns similarly modeling the prefix **re-** in **repay** and the prefix **pre-** in **pretest**. Prompt as needed.

Review students' answers to the questions under the chart.

Connect to strategy CLARIFY/PHONICS Have students review the steps of the CLARIFY/PHONICS strategy (Poster 3). Write this sentence on the board and read it aloud, skipping the word **retrain**. Model using the strategy, as shown below:

> **It took time to retrain everyone on the new computers.**

> MODEL I know every word in the sentence except this one (underline **retrain**). When I look for known chunks, I see a prefix, **re-**, and a base word, **train**. In this context, **train** probably means "teach." So **retrain** means "teach again" or "train again." That makes sense in the sentence.

Practice A Partners complete items 1–8. Students then take turns saying each phrase aloud, giving an example or a description, and noting how knowledge of the prefixes and base words helped them figure out meaning.

Practice B Read the directions, and go over item 1 with the group if necessary. Students complete the remaining items on their own. Afterward, discuss sentence meanings.

Apply/Comprehension Check

Students work independently. For the Apply items, have students tell how they used the CLARIFY/PHONICS strategy to figure out each prefixed word, as well as any other words in the text. Discuss responses to the Comprehension Check.

Making Words

Use the activity to the left. See pp. T64–T66 to review the procedure.

Lakota Hoop Dancer
Optional Lesson, Book 9
Summary:

Homeland and tradition are important to Kevin Locke, and to his hoop dancing. Hoop dancing has been performed for generations on the Lakota reservation. Extended families live together on the reservation and share Lakota traditions. Kevin wants to keep the Lakota traditions alive. He has learned three Lakota dialects, he takes his children along when he performs, he collects flute music and stories, and he and his family attend powwows. Kevin creates his hoops and regalia as a personal statement. When he dances, Kevin makes the hoops look like the sun and moon, flowers, eagles, and other shapes.

Making Words

Letter Cards: a e e d l r t (un)
Book Word: related (page 9)

- Take three letters to make *eat.*
- Rearrange the letters to make *tea.*
- Rearrange the letters to make *ate.*
- Add a letter to make *date.*
- Change a letter to make *rate.*
- Change a letter to make *late.*
- Add the prefix *re* to make *related.*
- Add the suffix *ed* to make a word from the book, *related.*
- Add the prefix *un* to make the opposite of related, *unrelated.*

Sorts

- words that rhyme
- word with a long *a*
- words with prefixes
- words with two or more chunks

Summarizing

Using the completed graphic organizer, model summarizing the first section of the book orally; then write your summary on chart paper. Have a volunteer use the graphic organizer to add to the summary. Write it on chart paper. Follow this procedure to summarize the last part of the book.

Decoding Longer Words
Base Words with Negative Prefixes un-, dis-, mis-, in-, il-, im-, ir-

Teach/Model Tell students that unfamiliar-looking words may be made of known word parts, or chunks. Prefixes are common chunks appearing at the beginning of words. Negative prefixes change the meaning of the base word in negative, or opposite, ways. Common negative prefixes are **un-**, **dis-**, **mis-**, and **in-** (also spelled **il-**, **im-**, and **ir-**). Knowing about negative prefixes can help readers figure out pronunciation and meaning of longer words.

Have students read the four column headings in the chart.

Use the first prefix **un-** to model building a word and thinking about meaning:

> MODEL The letters **u-n** are added to the base word **able** to make the longer word **unable**. If you are unable to do something, you are not able to do it. The prefix **un-** can mean "not."

Have students take turns similarly modeling the building of negatively prefixed words using the examples in the chart. Prompt as needed.

Review students' answers to the questions under the chart.

Connect to strategy CLARIFY/PHONICS Have students review the steps of the CLARIFY/PHONICS strategy (Poster 3). Write this sentence on the board and read it aloud, skipping the word **displeased**. Model using the strategy, as shown below:

> **The man's frown showed that he was displeased.**

> MODEL I know every word in the sentence except this one (underline **displeased**). When I look for known chunks, I see a prefix, **dis-** before a word I know, **pleased**. Since **dis-** is a negative prefix, the word **displeased** may mean "not pleased." That makes sense, since someone with a frowning face is not at all pleased.

Practice A Partners complete items 1–8. Students then take turns saying each phrase aloud, telling what it means, and noting how knowledge of the prefixes and base words helped them figure out meaning. For items 6–8, have students tell how they knew which word has a negative prefix.

Practice B Read the directions, and go over item 1 with the group if necessary. Students complete the remaining items on their own. Afterward, discuss sentence meanings.

Apply/Comprehension Check

Students work independently. For the Apply items, have students tell how they used the CLARIFY/PHONICS strategy to figure out each prefixed word, as well as any other words in the text. Discuss responses to the Comprehension Check.

Making Words

Use the activity to the left. See pp. T64–T66 to review the procedure.

Tunnels, Tracks, and Trains

Optional Lesson, Book 10

Summary:

A new subway is being built in Los Angeles. It will take 20 years to complete. The first section will run under the downtown area. Workers begin to dig, but stop when they find valuable artifacts. Archaeologists have to search the area for more artifacts before digging can continue. Meanwhile, workers drain the lake in MacArthur Park and dig a big hole where the lake used to be. The hole is reinforced with concrete walls. Then a boring machine is brought into the hole to drill a tunnel. As the tunnel gets longer, trains carry the dirt out and huge fans suck fresh air in. Meanwhile, crews dig up downtown streets at night when there is less traffic. They put a cover over the hole so cars can drive on it during the day. Other crews build the stations that architects designed, and put up art that was created for the stations. Finally, the first train rolls through the tunnel.

Making Words

Letter Cards: e e o c l m p t (ly)
Book Word: complete (page 4)

- Take two letters to make *to.*
- Add a letter to make *top.*
- Change a letter to make *cop.*
- Add a letter to make *cope.*
- Change a letter to make *come.*
- Add a letter to make *comet.*
- Add two letters to make *compete.*
- Add a letter to make a word from the book, *complete.*
- Add the suffix *ly* to make *completely.*

Sorts

- words that rhyme
- word with a long *o*
- word with a suffix
- words with two or more chunks

Summarizing

Using the completed graphic organizer, model summarizing the first section of the book orally; then write your summary on chart paper. Have a volunteer use the graphic organizer to add to the summary. Write it on chart paper. Follow this procedure to summarize the last part of the book.

Decoding Longer Words
Base Words with Suffixes -y, -ly

Teach/Model Tell students that unfamiliar-looking words may be made of known word parts, or chunks. Suffixes are common chunks added to the end of words. The suffixes **-y** and **-ly** may be added alone or together. They change the way a word can be used in a sentence and may change the way a base word is spelled. Readers should look for these suffixes and try to identify the base word in order to pronounce and understand the longer word.

Have students read the three column headings in the chart.

Use the first row to model building a word:

> MODEL The base word is **sun**. When the suffix **-y** is added, the word is **sunny**, which means "filled with sunlight." When the suffix **-y** is added, the base word changes its spelling. The final **n** of sun is doubled.

Have students take turns similarly modeling the building of suffixed words using the examples in the chart. Prompt them to note any spelling changes.

Review students' answers to the questions under the chart.

Connect to strategy CLARIFY/PHONICS Have students review the steps of the CLARIFY/PHONICS strategy (Poster 3). Write this sentence on the board and read it aloud, skipping the word **shakily**. Model using the strategy, as shown below:

> **The old car moved shakily up the hill.**

> MODEL I know every word in the sentence except this one (underline **shakily**). I look for chunks and see **-ly** at the end. Almost no base words end in **i**, so **y** was probably changed to **i**. That leaves **s-h-a-k-y**. The final y might be a suffix too. I don't recognize the base word spelled s-h-a-k, but maybe a final **e** was dropped. The spelling **s-h-a-k-e** gives me a word I know: **shake**. The word **shake** plus **-y** plus **-ly** forms **shakily**. An old car moves shakily, or "in a way that shakes." That makes sense.

Practice A Partners complete items 1–8. Students then take turns saying each base word and suffixed word. They also say each phrase aloud, give an example or a description, and tell how knowledge of base words and suffixes helped them figure out meaning. For items 5–7, have students tell how they knew which word was suffixed.

Practice B Read the directions, and go over item 1 with the group if necessary. Students complete the remaining items on their own. Afterward, have students tell how they identified each base word. Discuss sentence meanings.

Apply/Comprehension Check

Students work independently. For the Apply items, have students tell how they used the CLARIFY/PHONICS strategy to figure out the words with suffixes **-y** and **-ly**, as well as any other words in the text. Discuss responses to the Comprehension Check.

Making Words

Use the activity to the left. See pp. T64–T66 to review the procedure.

Gloria Estefan
Optional Lesson, Book 11

Summary:

Gloria Fajardo was born in Havana, Cuba, but her family soon moved to the United States. Her father joined the U.S. Army, and the family moved from army base to army base. Gloria always considered Miami her home, even though she often felt like an outsider because she was Latina. As a teenager, she joined the band The Miami Sound Machine. After she was graduated from college, Gloria married fellow band member Emilio Estefan. The band signed a contract with CBS Records. They became very popular with Spanish-speaking people, and eventually crossed over to English-speaking audiences as well. In 1990, Gloria was seriously injured in a bus accident. Through hard work and determination, she recovered in only a few months and resumed her career.

Making Words

Letter Cards: a i g l n p y (ful)
Book Word: playing (page 21)

- Take two letters to make *in.*
- Add one letter to make *pin.*
- Change a letter to make *pan.*
- Add a letter to make *pain.*
- Rearrange the letters and change one to make *plan.*
- Change a letter to make *play.*
- Add an ending to make a word from the book, *playing.*
- Change the ending to the suffix *ful* to make *playful.*

Sorts

- words that rhyme
- words with a suffix
- words with *pl*
- words with two chunks

Summarizing

Using the completed graphic organizer, model summarizing the first section of the book orally; then write your summary on chart paper. Have a volunteer use the graphic organizer to add to the summary. Write it on chart paper. Follow this procedure to summarize the last part of the book.

Decoding Longer Words
Base Words with Suffixes -less, -ful

Teach/Model Tell students that unfamiliar-looking words may be made of known word parts, or chunks. Suffixes are common chunks added to the end of words. The suffixes **-less** and **-ful** change the meaning of a base word and may change the way a base word is spelled. Readers should look for these suffixes and try to identify the base word in order to pronounce and understand the longer word.

Have students read the four column headings in the chart.

Use the first row to model building a word:

> MODEL The suffix **-less** means "without." When added to the end of the base word **hope**, it forms the longer word **hopeless**, which means "without hope." There is no spelling change in the base word. When the suffix **-less** is added to the base word **penny**, it forms the longer word **penniless**, meaning "without a penny, or poor." The final **y** of the base word changes to **i** in the longer word.

Have students take turns similarly modeling the building of suffixed words using the examples in the chart. Prompt them to note any spelling changes.

Review students' answers to the questions under the chart.

Connect to strategy CLARIFY/PHONICS Have students review the steps of the CLARIFY/PHONICS strategy (Poster 3). Write this sentence on the board and read it aloud, skipping the word **restful**. Model using the strategy, as shown below:

> **Did you have a restful night's sleep?**

> MODEL I know every word in the sentence except this one (underline **restful**). I look for chunks and see **-ful** at the end. That is often a suffix, so I look for a base word and find **rest**. Putting the chunks together, I say **restful**. A restful night's sleep is probably "full of rest."

Practice A Partners complete items 1–8. Students then take turns saying each base word and suffixed word. They also say each phrase aloud, give an example or a description, and tell how knowledge of base words and suffixes helped them figure out meaning.

Practice B Read the directions, and go over item 1 with the group if necessary. Students complete the remaining items on their own. Afterward, have students tell how they identified each base word. Discuss sentence meanings.

Apply/Comprehension Check

Students work independently. For the Apply items, have students tell how they used the CLARIFY/PHONICS strategy to figure out each suffixed word, as well as any other words in the text. Discuss responses to the Comprehension Check.

Making Words

Use the activity to the left. See pp. T64–T66 to review the procedure.

Benjamin Banneker
Optional Lesson, Book 12

Summary:

In 1736, six-year-old Benjamin counted everything he saw as he worked in his grandmother's tobacco fields. His parents sent him to a Quaker school, where he learned arithmetic, geography, and spelling. After school, he worked on his family's farm. When Benjamin was 20, he borrowed a friend's gold watch and took it apart, studying each piece. Then he spent two years making his own clock out of wood. When his father died, Benjamin took over the family farm. When he was 52, Benjamin helped a friend's son study surveying and astronomy. Benjamin learned them, too. When Washington, D.C. was being planned, Benjamin was selected to help survey the site. While he was there, he met President George Washington. Benjamin became so good at astronomy that he wrote an almanac. It was successful, and he continued to publish almanacs for several years.

Making Words

Letter Cards: e i o u q s t (able)
Book Word: question (page 35)

- Take two letters to make *it.*
- Add a letter to make *sit.*
- Add a letter to make *suit.*
- Change a letter to make *quit.*
- Change the vowel and add a letter to make *quest.*
- Add the ending *ion* to make a word from your book *question.*
- Add the suffix *able* to make *question-able.*

Sorts

- words that rhyme
- words with *qu*
- word with a suffix
- words with two or more chunks

Summarizing

Using the completed graphic organizer, model summarizing the first section of the book orally; then write your summary on chart paper. Have a volunteer use the graphic organizer to add to the summary. Write it on chart paper. Follow this procedure to summarize the last part of the book.

Decoding Longer Words
Base Words with Suffixes -ous, -able

Teach/Model Tell students that unfamiliar-looking words may be made of known word parts, or chunks. Suffixes are common chunks added to the end of words. The suffixes **-ous** and **-able** change the meaning of a base word and may change the way a base word is spelled. Readers should look for these suffixes and try to identify the base word in order to pronounce and understand the longer word.

Have students read the four column headings in the chart.

Use the first row to model building a word:

> MODEL The suffix **-ous** means "having." When added to the end of the base word danger, it forms the longer word **dangerous**, which means "having danger." There is no spelling change in the base word. When the suffix **-ous** is added to the base word **fame**, it forms the longer word **famous**, meaning "having fame." The final **e** of the base word is dropped in the longer word.

Have students take turns similarly modeling the building of suffixed words using the examples in the chart. Prompt them to note any spelling changes.

Review students' answers to the questions under the chart.

Connect to strategy CLARIFY/PHONICS Have students review the steps of the CLARIFY/PHONICS strategy (Poster 3). Write this sentence on the board and read it aloud, skipping the word **forgettable**. Model using the strategy, as shown below:

> **The plot of the movie was pointless and forgettable.**

> MODEL I know every word in the sentence except this one (underline **forgettable**). I look for chunks and see **-able** at the end. That is often a suffix, so I look for a base word and find **forget**, with a doubled final **t**. Putting the chunks together, I say **forgettable**. A forgettable plot is a story line that is easy to forget.

Practice A Partners complete items 1–8. Students then take turns saying each base word and suffixed word. They also say each phrase aloud, give an example or a description, and tell how knowledge of base words and suffixes helped them figure out meaning.

Practice B Read the directions, and go over item 1 with the group if necessary. Students complete the remaining items on their own. Afterward, have students tell how they identified each base word. Discuss sentence meanings.

Apply/Comprehension Check

Students work independently. For the Apply items, have students tell how they used the CLARIFY/PHONICS strategy to figure out each suffixed word, as well as any other words in the text. Discuss responses to the Comprehension Check.

Making Words

Use the activity to the left. See pp. T64–T66 to review the procedure.

Lightning
Optional Lesson, Book 13

Summary:

Lightning is a large electrical spark. It is caused when electrons move through the air so fast that the air glows. Lightning can travel from clouds to the ground because electrons in clouds are attracted to positive charges in the ground. It can also travel from cloud to cloud, within clouds, or from the ground to a cloud. Most lightning has four parts. Thunder is caused when lightning heats the air so much that it expands explosively. Most lightning comes from large clouds called thunderheads that form on warm, sunny days. Most thunderstorms occur near the equator because the warm, moist air there helps thunderheads form. If you are outside when a thunderstorm starts, you should find a safe place right away.

Making Words

Letter Cards: i e b g h n r s s t
Book Word: brightness (page 18)

- Take three letters to make *sag.*
- Add a letter to make *sang.*
- Change a letter to make *sing.*
- Rearrange the letters to make *sign.*
- Change a letter to make *sigh.*
- Add a letter to make *sight.*
- Change a letter to make *right.*
- Add a letter to make *bright.*
- Add the suffix *ness* to make a word from the book, *brightness.*

Sorts

- words that rhyme
- words with *gh*
- word with a suffix

Summarizing

Using the completed graphic organizer, model summarizing the first section of the book orally; then write your summary on chart paper. Have a volunteer use the graphic organizer to add to the summary. Write it on chart paper. Follow this procedure to summarize the last part of the book.

Decoding Longer Words
Base Words with Suffixes -ment, -ness, -ion

Teach/Model Tell students that unfamiliar-looking words may be made of known word parts, or chunks. Suffixes are common chunks added to the end of words. The suffixes **-ment**, **-ness**, and **-ion** change the the way a word can be used in a sentence and may change the way a base word is spelled. Readers should look for these suffixes and try to identify the base word in order to pronounce and understand the longer word.

Have students read the three column headings in the chart.

Use the first row to model building a word:

> MODEL The base word is **treat**. When the suffix **-ment** is added, the word is **treatment**, which means "the treating of someone or something."

Have students take turns similarly modeling the building of suffixed words, using the examples in the chart. Prompt them to note any spelling changes.

Review students' answers to the questions under the chart.

Connect to strategy CLARIFY/PHONICS Have students review the steps of the CLARIFY/PHONICS strategy (Poster 3). Write this sentence on the board and read it aloud, skipping the word **selection**. Model using the strategy, as shown below:

> **There are so many items on this menu, it's hard to make a selection.**

> MODEL I know every word in the sentence except this one (underline **selection**). I look for chunks and see **-ion** at the end. That might be a suffix added to a base word. Yes, I do recognize a base word: **select**. When you select something, you choose it. So a selection is a choice. That makes sense.

Practice A Partners complete items 1–8. Students then take turns saying each base word and suffixed word. They also say each phrase aloud, give an example or a description, and tell how knowledge of base words and suffixes helped them figure out meaning.

Practice B Read the directions, and go over item 1 with the group if necessary. Students complete the remaining items on their own. Afterward, have students tell how they identified each base word. Discuss sentence meanings.

Apply/Comprehension Check

Students work independently. For the Apply items, have students tell how they used the CLARIFY/PHONICS strategy to figure out the words with the target suffixes as well as any other words in the text. Discuss responses to the Comprehension Check.

Making Words

Use the activity to the left. See pp. T64–T66 to review the procedure.

Sports Lab
Optional Lesson, Book 14

Summary:

Modern advances in science, such as equipment made of new materials, and computers to analyze motion, improve athletes' performances. Science can tell us how the way a ball spins affects its path through the air. Psychology brings us techniques like visualization, meditation, and biofeedback to improve performance. At the U.S. Olympic Committee Training Center, scientists and trainers help athletes improve their performances. Medical techniques like cross-training, MRI, and arthroscopic surgery increase performance and reduce recovery time from injuries. On the other hand, some athletes misuse science by abusing drugs like steroids.

Making Words

Letter Cards: e e i l n r t y
Book Word: entirely (page 14)

- Take three letters to make *yet.*
- Change a letter to make *net.*
- Change a letter to make *let.*
- Change a letter to make *lit.*
- Rearrange letters and add one to make *tile.*
- Change a letter to make *tire.*
- Add the prefix *en* to make *entire.*
- Add the ending *ly* to make a word from the book, *entirely.*

Sorts

- words that rhyme
- words with a short *e*
- words with a long *i*
- word with an *ly* ending

Summarizing

Using the completed graphic organizer, have students write summaries of the first section; then have volunteers share what they have written, and discuss them briefly. Then have students write summaries of the remaining sections of the book independently. Have students share their summaries and discuss ways to improve them.

Decoding Longer Words
CLARIFY/PHONICS: Break Words into Chunks

Teach/Model Tell students that unfamiliar-looking words may be made of known word parts, or chunks. Common chunks include (a) compounds, smaller words combined into a larger one; (b) syllables, one or more letters with just one vowel sound; and (c) base words with endings, with prefixes, and with suffixes.

Have students read the list under the first column heading, "Kinds of Chunks."

Use the first longer word to model breaking a word into chunks:

> MODEL I see two smaller words, **snow** and **storm**, which combine to make the compound word **snowstorm**.

Have students take turns similarly modeling the breaking apart of the longer words in the chart. Prompt them to note base-word spelling changes in the words **permitted**, **littlest**, and **happily**.

Review students' answers to the questions under the chart. Guide them in naming the different kinds of chunks to look and listen for (prefixes, base words, suffixes, endings, syllables).

Connect to strategy CLARIFY/PHONICS Have students review the steps of the CLARIFY/PHONICS strategy (Poster 3). Write this sentence on the board and read it aloud, skipping the word **unfavorable**. Model using the strategy, as shown below:

> **We liked the movie, even though the reviews were unfavorable.**

> MODEL I know every word in the sentence except this one (underline **unfavorable**). I look for chunks and see a prefix, **un-**, at the beginning, and a suffix, **-able**, at the end. That leaves **f-a-v-o-r**, which might be a base word. Since it has one consonant, **v**, in the middle, I can try saying it with a long a vowel sound in the first syllable: **FAY-vor**. Putting it all together: **unfavorable**. Movie reviews that are unfavorable do not favor, or approve, the movie. That makes sense in this sentence.

Practice A Partners complete items 1–8. Students then take turns saying each chunk and word aloud.

Practice B Read the directions, and go over item 1 with the group if necessary. Students complete the remaining items on their own. Afterward, discuss the meanings of the phrases.

Apply/Comprehension Check

Students work independently. For the Apply items, have students tell how they used the CLARIFY/PHONICS strategy to figure out each word of three or more syllables, as well as any other words in the text. Discuss responses to the Comprehension Check.

Making Words

Use the activity to the left. See pp. T64–T66 to review the procedure.

Lisa Leslie
Optional Lesson, Book 15

Summary:

Lisa Leslie was twelve when she played basketball for the first time. She soon joined her junior-high basketball team, and later her high school girls' basketball team. She also made the starting lineup of the Olympic Festival junior team. Lisa had to take the SAT three times, but she was finally accepted to USC. In her junior year, she played for the U.S. National Team and was named Best Female Athlete of the Year. After graduation, Lisa joined an Italian professional team in order to keep playing basketball. She was part of the U.S. team that won a gold medal in the 1996 Olympics. When the WNBA was formed, Lisa joined the Los Angeles Sparks.

Making Words

Letter Cards: a e e e u d d f n t
Book Word: undefeated (page 15)

- Take three letters to make *dad.*
- Add a letter to make *dead.*
- Change a letter to make *deed.*
- Change a letter to make *feed.*
- Change a letter to make *feet.*
- Change a letter to make *feat.*
- Add the prefix *de* to make *defeat.*
- Add the ending *ed* to make *defeated.*
- Add the prefix *un* to make a word from the book, *undefeated.*

Sorts

- words that rhyme
- words with a prefix
- words with *ee*
- words with *ea*
- words with two or more chunks

Summarizing

Using the completed graphic organizer, have students write summaries of the first section; then have volunteers share what they have written, and discuss them briefly. Then have students write summaries of the remaining sections of the book independently. Have students share their summaries and discuss ways to improve them.

Decoding Longer Words
Base Words, Endings, and Suffixes

Teach/Model Tell students that unfamiliar-looking words may be made of known word parts, or chunks. By looking at the end of a word, readers may find one or more known chunks attached to a known base word. Readers should look for these endings and try to identify the base word in order to pronounce and understand the longer word.

Have students read the four column headings and say each listed ending or suffix.

Use the first row to model building a word:

> MODEL The base word is **interest**. When the ending **-ing** is added, the word is interesting. When the suffix **-ly** is added, the word becomes **interestingly**.

Have students take turns similarly modeling the addition of more than one suffix to build longer words. Prompt them to note the spelling change when the suffixes **-able** and **-ly** are combined into **-ably**.

Review students' answers to the questions under the chart.

Connect to strategy CLARIFY/PHONICS Have students review the steps of the CLARIFY/PHONICS strategy (Poster 3). Write this sentence on the board and read it aloud, skipping the word **sparingly**. Model using the strategy, as shown below:

> **Apply the cleaner sparingly and wipe with a damp rag.**

> MODEL I know every word in the sentence except this one (underline **sparingly**). I see two chunks at the end: **-ing** and **-ly**. That leaves **s-p-a-r**, which might be a base word. It looks like **spar**, but the final **r** was not doubled before the ending **-ing**. So this might be a base word in which a final **e** was dropped: **s-p-a-r-e**. That spells **spare**. Yes, directions might tell me to apply the cleaner "in a spare way," or sparingly.

Practice A Partners complete items 1–8. Students then take turns saying each longer word.

Practice B Read the directions, and go over item 1 with the group if necessary. Students complete the remaining items on their own. Afterward, discuss the meanings of the phrases.

Apply/Comprehension Check

Students work independently. For the Apply items, have students tell how they used the CLARIFY/PHONICS strategy to figure out each word made of a base word and one or more ending chunks, as well as any other words in the text. Discuss responses to the Comprehension Check.

Making Words

Use the activity to the left. See pp. T64–T66 to review the procedure.

An Even Break
Optional Lesson, Book 16

Summary:

In the small town of Wilma, twelve-year-old Frisk and his mother Shelly didn't have the money for the things they wanted. Frisk got a job managing a pool room—surprisingly, since he was too young to play there. The regulars picked on him because he was so young. Dan Breedon, the best pool player in town, taught Frisk to play. Frisk tried to set Dan up with his mom, and arranged for them to meet up at the movies. At the end of the summer was the big pool tournament. One of the contestants turned out to be a girl, Beverly Ferris. Dan and Beverly made it to the finals. But Dan was called away, and he asked Frisk to play for him. Frisk won, earning the respect of the regulars and money for a bike.

Making Words

Letter Cards: a e e i b d l r s
Book Word: desirable (page 14)

- Take three letters to make *bed.*
- Change one letter to make *red.*
- Add one letter to make *read.*
  I like to read the newspaper.
- Add a letter to make *reads.*
- Change one letter to make *reeds.*
- Rearrange letters and add one to make *desire.*
- Take a letter away and add the suffix *able* to make a word from the book, *desirable.*
- Add the prefix *un* to make a new word, *undesirable.*

Sorts

- words that rhyme
- words that sound the same
- word with a prefix
- word with a suffix

Summarizing

Using the completed graphic organizer, have students write summaries of the first section; then have volunteers share what they have written, and discuss them briefly. Then have students write summaries of the remaining sections of the book independently. Have students share their summaries and discuss ways to improve them.

Decoding Longer Words
Prefixes, Base Words, Endings, and Suffixes

Teach/Model Tell students that unfamiliar-looking words may be made of known word parts, or chunks. By looking for known chunks attached to the beginning and the end of a word, readers may find a known base word. Readers should look for prefixes, base words, endings, and suffixes in order to pronounce and understand the longer word.

Have students read the five column headings.

Use the first row to model building a word:

> MODEL The prefix **dis-** is added to the base word agree to make **disagree**. The ending **-ing** is added to make **disagreeing**.

Have students take turns similarly modeling the addition of one chunk at a time to build longer words. Prompt them to note the base-word spelling changes in **unhappiest** and **immovable**.

Review students' answers to the questions under the chart.

Connect to strategy CLARIFY/PHONICS Have students review the steps of the CLARIFY/PHONICS strategy (Poster 3). Write this sentence on the board and read it aloud, skipping the word **unquestionable**. Model using the strategy, as shown below:

> **My dog gives me unquestionable love and loyalty.**
>
> MODEL I know every word in the sentence except this one (underline **unquestionable**). I see the negative prefix un- at the beginning and the suffix **-able** at the end. That leaves **question**, which is a base word I know. Putting the chunks together, I get **unquestionable**. That must mean "not able to be questioned." That makes sense, since a dog's love and loyalty can't be questioned or doubted.

Practice A Partners complete items 1–8. Students then take turns saying each longer word.

Practice B Read the directions, and go over item 1 with the group if necessary. Students complete the remaining items on their own. Afterward, discuss the meanings of the phrases.

Apply/Comprehension Check

Students work independently. For the Apply items, have students tell how they used the CLARIFY/PHONICS strategy to figure out each word made of a prefix, base word, and an ending chunk, as well as any other words in the text. Discuss responses to the Comprehension Check.

Making Words

Use the activity to the left. See pp. T64–T66 to review the procedure.

El Duque
Optional Lesson, Book 17

Summary:

Orlando Hernandez was raised in Cuba by his single mother. He became a baseball star and got the nickname "El Duque." After his brother Livian defected to the United States, Cuban officials made life hard for El Duque. When he realized he would never be able to play baseball again, he decided to defect, too. He and several companions escaped to Costa Rica. He signed with an American baseball team, came to the U.S., and was reunited with Livian. He soon moved from the minor leagues to the majors, as a starting pitcher for the Yankees. With his help, the Yankees won the World Series. His family was permitted to come to the U.S. to celebrate.

Making Words

Letter Cards: a e e e c d d r s
Book Word: decreased (page 56)

- Take three letters to make *car*.
- Add a letter to make *care*.
- Change a letter to make *case*.
- Change a letter to make *ease*.
- Add a letter to make *cease*.
- Add a letter to make *crease*.
- Add the ending *ed* to make *creased*.
- Add the suffix *de* to make a word from the book, *decreased*.

Sorts

- words that rhyme
- words with *ea*
- words ending with *ed*

Summarizing

Using the completed graphic organizer, have students write summaries of the first section; then have volunteers share what they have written, and discuss them briefly. Then have students write summaries of the remaining sections of the book independently. Have students share their summaries and discuss ways to improve them.

Decoding Longer Words
Prefixes, Base Words, and Suffixes

Teach/Model Tell students that unfamiliar-looking words may be made of known word parts, or chunks. By looking for known chunks attached to the beginning and the end of a word, readers may find a known base word. Readers should look for prefixes, base words, and suffixes in order to pronounce and understand the longer word.

Have students read the four column headings.

Use the first row to model building a word and thinking about meaning:

> MODEL The prefix **re-** is added to the base word assign to make **reassign**. The suffix **-ment** is added to make **reassignment**. Since **re-** means "again," a **reassignment** may be something that is assigned again, like a new job.

Have students take turns similarly modeling the addition of one chunk at a time to build longer words. Prompt them to give ideas about the meaning of the longer word.

Review students' answers to the questions under the chart.

Connect to strategy CLARIFY/PHONICS Have students review the steps of the CLARIFY/PHONICS strategy (Poster 3). Write this sentence on the board and read it aloud, skipping the word **uneventful**. Model using the strategy, as shown below:

> **Everyone predicted disaster, but the day turned out to be uneventful.**

> MODEL I know every word in the sentence except this one (underline **uneventful**). I see the negative prefix **un-** at the beginning and the suffix **-ful** at the end. That leaves **event**, which is a base word I know. Putting the chunks together, I get **uneventful**. A day that turns out to be uneventful is probably one in which not many events happened. That makes sense in the sentence.

Practice A Partners complete items 1–8. Students then take turns reading each sentence aloud.

Practice B Read the directions, and go over item 1 with the group if necessary. Students complete the remaining items on their own. Afterward, discuss the meanings of the phrases.

Apply/Comprehension Check

Students work independently. For the Apply items, have students tell how they used the CLARIFY/PHONICS strategy to figure out each word with more than one affix, as well as any other words in the text. Discuss responses to the Comprehension Check.

Making Words

Use the activity to the left. See pp. T64–T66 to review the procedure.

Marisol and Magdalena
Optional Lesson, Book 18

Summary:

Marisol had to leave her best friend, Magda, and her home in New York when she moved to Panama to live with her grandmother. She decided to look for her father, Lucho, there. Marisol arrived in Panama and was picked up by her *abuela*. She was homesick already. Marisol met a new friend, Ana, and developed a crush on a boy at school named Rubén. Marisol and Ana searched for Lucho, but didn't find him. Marisol learned about her Panamanian heritage and made new friends. But she also kept in touch with her best friend from home.

Making Words

Letter Cards: a e e o u b f g l n r t t
Book Word: unforgettable (page 2)

- Take three letters to make *bat*.
- Change a letter to make *rat*.
- Add a letter to make *rate*.
- Add a letter to make *grate*.
- Rearrange to make *great*.
- Rearrange letters and add one to make *target*.
- Change two letters to make *forget*.
- Double a letter and add the suffix *able* to make *forgettable*.
- Add the prefix *un* to make a word from the book, *unforgettable*.

Sorts

- words that rhyme
- words that are animal names
- words that sound the same
- word with a prefix
- words with a suffix
- words with two or more chunks

Summarizing

Using the completed graphic organizer, have students write summaries of the first section; then have volunteers share what they have written, and discuss them briefly. Then have students write summaries of the remaining sections of the book independently. Have students share their summaries and discuss ways to improve them.

Decoding Longer Words
CLARIFY/PHONICS: Break Words into Chunks

Teach/Model Tell students that long, unfamiliar-looking words may be made of known word parts, or chunks. The chunk called a base word may be split into smaller chunks called syllables. Added word parts such as prefixes, endings, and suffixes are other chunks. Finding and thinking about all these kinds of chunks help readers pronounce and understand longer words.

Have students read the two column headings. Review the kinds of chunks listed by having students give examples of each.

Use the first longer word to model breaking a word into chunks:

> MODEL I see the letters **c-o-n**, which spell a common syllable, **con**. The next chunk could be the open syllable **s-i**, with a long i sound; or a closed syllable pronounced **sid**. I try both: **con/SY/der**, **con/SID/er**. The second one sounds right. I've heard the word **consider**; when you consider something, you think about it.

Have students take turns similarly modeling the breaking apart of the longer words in the chart. Prompt them to note the base word, **consider**, around which each of the remaining longer words is built.

Review students' answers to the questions under the chart.

Connect to strategy CLARIFY/PHONICS Have students review the steps of the CLARIFY/PHONICS strategy (Poster 3). Write this sentence on the board and read it aloud, skipping the words **digestible** and **indigestion**. Model using the strategy, as shown below:

> **If the meal is not digestible, you may get indigestion.**

> MODEL I know every word in the sentence except these two (underline **digestible** and **indigestion**). I see the same chunk in each, which is spelled **d-i-g-e-s-t**. Breaking that into syllables, I say **di/gest**. I know the word **digest**. When you digest food, your body turns it into energy. But when food is not digestible, or able to be digested, then you may get indigestion–the state in which food is not digested, and your stomach hurts. Now the sentence makes sense.

Practice A Partners complete items 1–8. Students then take turns saying each chunk and word aloud.

Practice B Read the directions, and go over item 1 with the group if necessary. Students complete the remaining items on their own. Afterward, have students read each sentence aloud.

Apply/Comprehension Check

Students work independently. For the Apply items, have students tell how they used the CLARIFY/PHONICS strategy to figure out which longer words were built from the same base word, as well as any other words in the text. Discuss responses to the Comprehension Check.

Making Words

Use the activity to the left. See pp. T64–T66 to review the procedure.

Clarify/Phonics: Break Words into Chunks

When you use CLARIFY/PHONICS to figure out a long word, ask yourself . . .

Is this a compound word made of smaller words?

somewhat (some + what)
whatever (what + ever)
evergreen (ever + green)

What syllables do I see and hear?
(A syllable is a chunk that has just one vowel sound.)

Syllables commonly found at the beginning of words:	Syllables commonly found at the end of of words:
a as in *around, amaze, along* **be** as in *belong, believe, between* **re** as in *remain, report, respect* **de** as in *decide, depend, deliver*	**tion** as in *caption, nation, portion* **ture** as in *picture, nature, feature*

Do I see a base word with an ending -s, -es, -ed, -ing, -er, -est ?
(There may be a spelling change in the base word.)

older (old + er)   *happiest (happy + est)*
rebelled (rebel + ed)   *believing (believe + ing)*

Do I see a prefix added before a base word?

misplace (mis + place)   *undecided (un + decided)*
disrespect (dis + respect)

Do I see a suffix added to the end of a base word? (There may be a spelling change in the base word.)

dependable (depend + able)   *happiness (happy + ness)*
respectful (respect + ful)

1. Can a syllable also be a prefix? _____ Why do you think that?

   _____

2. What kinds of chunks can you find in the word *dependable*?

   _____

3. What is a compound word?

   _____

Practice A

Read each word. Write the separate chunks you find. Be ready to say the word.

1. however _____
2. refusing _____
3. lectured _____
4. detention _____

5. disbelieving _____
6. unamused _____
7. hardhearted _____
8. capturing _____

Practice B

Read each phrase. Say the underlined word to yourself. Circle the answer that shows the best way to break the word into chunks.

1. train stations	stati/ons	sta/tion + s
2. to disagree on a point	dis + a/gree	di/sag/ree
3. heavy rainstorms	rain + storm + s	rains/torm + s
4. amazing sights	am/az + ing	a/maze + ing
5. the unhappiest child	un +happ +iest	un + happy + est
6. a fractured arm	frac/ture + ed	fra/ctured
7. respectable people	re/spect + able	re/spec + table

Apply

Read the text. Then list the five words of two or more syllables. Be ready to show how you would use CLARIFY/PHONICS to say each word and figure out its meaning.

> **Our school's basketball team has been undefeated all year. Our skillful passing and great speed make us unbeatable!**

_____

_____

Comprehension Check

1. What must a team do to be undefeated? _____

_____

2. What makes this team unbeatable? _____

Chunking Words Using VC•CV Patterns

Syllables	Words
per	temper
cert	person
son	concert
con	persist
tem	common
sist	
com	
on	

1. What is the first syllable of each listed word?

   _____ _____ _____ _____ _____

2. What are the two consonants in the middle of each word?

   _____ _____ _____ _____ _____

3. Which of those two consonants do you hear as one sound? _____

Practice A

Write the first syllable of each word. Be ready to say the whole word.

1. picnic   _____

2. surround   _____

3. splendid   _____

4. absorb   _____

5. entire   _____

6. compose   _____

7. format   _____

Practice B

Read each phrase. Underline the word that has two consonants between vowels. Write the word and draw a line between the syllables. Be ready to tell how you figured out how to say the word.

1. to consume food _____

2. to argue and shout _____

3. wise advice _____

4. elbow joint _____

5. to capture a moment _____

6. an old custom _____

7. as stubborn as a mule _____

Apply

Read the text. Then list the five words of more than one syllable. Draw a line between the syllables. Be ready to show how you would use CLARIFY/PHONICS to figure out how to say each word.

> **The members of the dance group performed. Their costumes shimmered in the light. They leaped and twirled to the beat of drums. We all admired their strength and skill.**

_____

_____

Comprehension Check

1. Who danced?

_____

2. How can you tell that the writer liked the show?

_____

Owl

Chunking Words Using Patterns V•CV, VC•V

Word	First Syllable
promise	prom /prŏm/
promote	pro /prə/
vacant	va /vā/
valid	val /văl/
finish	fin /fĭn/
final	fi /fī/

1. In which listed words does the first syllable end with a vowel?

_____

2. In which listed words does the first syllable end with a consonant?

_____

3. Which listed words have a long vowel sound in the first syllable?

_____

4. When you see a single consonant between vowels, where might the first syllable end?

_____

Practice A

Write the first syllable of each word. Be ready to say the whole word.

1. nature _____

2. pilot _____

3. river _____

4. punish _____

5. polite _____

6. deny _____

7. amaze _____

8. habit _____

Owl

Practice B

Read each phrase. Underline the word that has one consonant between vowels. Write the word and draw a line between the syllables. Be ready to tell how you figured out how to say the word.

1. candy flavors _____

2. humane treatment _____

3. a tidy room _____

4. a rapid step _____

5. credit card _____

6. recent times _____

7. news reports _____

8. remote control _____

Apply

Read the text. Then list the five words of more than one syllable. Draw a line between the syllables. Be ready to show how you would use CLARIFY/PHONICS to figure out how to say each word.

> **The house mouse is well named. It lives with humans in their homes and depends on them for food. The house mouse is not a native rodent. It traveled here on ships in the past.**

_____

_____

Comprehension Check

1. How can you tell that the house mouse needs people?

_____

2. What kind of animal is a house mouse?

_____

Syllables•Consonant-le

Word	Second Syllable
bubble	ble
trouble	ble
giggle	gle
beagle	gle
middle	dle
idle	dle
whistle	tle

1. Which listed words have a first syllable that ends with a consonant?

_____

2. Which listed words have a first syllable that ends with a vowel?

_____

Practice A

Write the first syllable of each word. Be ready to say the whole word.

1. hurdle _____

2. thimble _____

3. couple _____

4. sparkle _____

5. cable _____

6. dazzle _____

7. nestle _____

8. noodle _____

Practice B

Read each phrase. Underline the word with Consonant-*le*. Write the word and draw a line between the syllables. Be ready to tell how you figured out how to say the word.

1. to scramble eggs _____

2. to muffle sounds _____

3. to scribble a note _____

4. cries that startle _____

5. the royal castle _____

6. needle and thread _____

7. an eagle's nest _____

8. to play a bugle _____

Apply

Read the text. Then list the five words with Consonant-*le*. Draw a line between the syllables. Be ready to show how you would use CLARIFY/PHONICS to figure out how to say each word.

> **Uncle Fred has a black poodle named Midnight. Midnight trembles with fear at the sight of water. That is odd, since the breed was once known as a water dog. It gets its name from a word meaning "puddle." Midnight doesn't know that he's supposed to enjoy swimming. He hides under the table if he even hears the word *bath*.**

_____

_____

Comprehension Check

1. What kind of dog does Uncle Fred have?

_____

2. What does Midnight do when he sees water or hears the word *bath*?

_____

Words of More Than Two Syllables

Word	Syllables and Stress
determine	de/ter/mine
disaster	dis/as/ter
terrible	ter/ri/ble
carpenter	car/pen/ter
terrific	ter/rif/ic

1. In which listed words is the second syllable stressed?

_____

2. In which listed words is the first syllable stressed?

_____

Practice A

Say each word aloud syllable by syllable. Then say it as a word.

1. continue

2. energy

3. volunteer

4. formula

5. difficult

6. colony

7. terminal

8. syllable

Practice B

Read each phrase. Underline the word that has three syllables. Write the word and draw lines between the syllables. Be ready to tell how you figured out how to say the word.

1. with sincere gratitude _____

2. a probable event _____

3. a tiny particle _____

4. horrible masks _____

5. capital city _____

6. to consider a change _____

7. tornado damage _____

8. to entertain a crowd _____

Apply

Read the text. Then list the five words of three syllables. Draw lines between the syllables. Be ready to show how you would use CLARIFY/PHONICS to figure out how to say each word.

> If you play a sport, then you know how important confidence can be. If you feel strong and capable, then you are likely to play well. Skill is not always enough. You must have a positive attitude, too.

_____

_____

Comprehension Check

1. What is a positive attitude?

_____

2. What is true of a capable player?

_____

Base Words with Endings -s, -es, -ed, -ing

Base Word	Ending	Longer Word
adventure	-s	adventures
possess	-es	possesses
strawberry	-es	strawberries
permit	-ed	permitted
stare	-ing	staring
star	-ing	starring

1. In which longer word has a *y* changed to *i* before an ending?

_____

2. In which longer words has a final consonant doubled before an ending?

_____

3. In which longer word has an e been dropped before an ending?

_____

Practice A

Write the base word in each of these longer words. Be ready to say the longer word.

1. centuries _____

2. hopping _____

3. limited _____

4. committed _____

5. scrambling _____

6. denied _____

7. eyeglasses _____

8. outlines _____

Practice B

Read each phrase. Underline the word with the ending. Write the base word. Be ready
to tell how you figured out how to find the base word.

1. to collect pennies _____

2. playground recesses _____

3. a ragged dress _____

4. amazing adventure _____

5. daring rescue _____

6. deserved a reward _____

7. teaches a class _____

8. busy cities _____

Apply

Read the text. Then list the five words with endings. Write the base word for each. Be
ready to show how you would use CLARIFY/PHONICS to say each word and figure out
its meaning.

> **A new TV show is beginning. It is supposed to be entertaining. The network is hoping
> that families will watch it together.**

_____

_____

Comprehension Check

1. What is the purpose of the new TV show?

_____

2. If a brother, sister, and parent are watching the TV show together, who is watching it?

_____

Base Words with Endings That Compare

Base Word	Ending	Longer Word
small	-er, -est	smaller, smallest
thin	-er, -est	thinner, thinnest
little	-er, -est	littler, littlest
tiny	-er, -est	tinier, tiniest

1. In which longer words has a *y* changed to *i* before an ending?

_____

2. In which longer words has a final consonant doubled before an ending?

_____

3. In which longer words has an *e* been dropped before an ending?

_____

Practice A

Write the base word in each of these longer words. Be ready to say the longer word.

1. silliest _____

2. paler _____

3. taller _____

4. redder _____

5. gentler _____

6. angrier _____

7. yellowest _____

8. rarest _____

Name _____

Practice B

Read each phrase. Underline the word with the ending that compares. Write the base word. Be ready to tell how you figured out how to find the base word.

1. a steadier table　　　　　_____

2. the whitest clothes　　　 _____

3. the hungriest animal　　 _____

4. bluer skies　　　　　　 _____

5. a longer letter　　　　　_____

6. simplest and most honest _____

7. survival of the fittest　　_____

8. an emptier theater　　　 _____

Apply

Read the text. Then list the five words with endings that compare. Write the base word for each. Be ready to show how you would use CLARIFY/PHONICS to say each word and figure out its meaning.

> We ran six blocks through the wildest rainstorm we'd ever seen. We splashed through puddles that were larger than some ponds. I had never been wetter. When we got home, we looked in the mirror. "Have you ever seen a sorrier sight?" asked my brother. We looked as if buckets of water had been poured over us. I began to shiver. Even though I was already soaked, my one wish was for a shower—the hottest one I could get.

_____

_____

Comprehension Check

1. What kind of rainstorm was it?

_____

2. What might go wrong with the shower that the narrator wants to take?

_____

Base Words with Prefixes re-, pre-

Prefix (Meaning)	Base Word	Longer Word	Meaning
re ("again")	told	retold	"told again"
re ("back")	pay	repay	"pay back"
pre ("before")	test	pretest	"test before"

1. What is the first chunk in *retold?* _____ in *repay?* _____ in *pretest?* _____

2. What does the prefix *re-* mean in repay? _____

3. What does the prefix *re-* mean in retold? _____

4. What is one meaning for the prefix *pre-*? _____

Practice A

Underline the prefixed word in each phrase. Write the prefix and the base word. Be ready to say each phrase and give an example or a description.

1. prepaid bills _____

2. spelling retest _____

3. to preheat the oven _____

4. to regain health _____

5. to prearrange a meeting _____

6. to rearrange shelves _____

7. to rejoin the game _____

8. ball on the rebound _____

Practice B

Read each sentence. Underline the word with the prefix *re-* or *pre-*. Circle the prefix.
Then write the prefixed word after its meaning below. Be ready to tell what you know
about breaking words that begin with prefixes into chunks.

1. We'll recover the chair with purple fabric.

2. There are no writings from prehistory.

3. The student rewrote the story.

4. Airlines perform preflight checks.

5. Some dealers sell preowned cars.

6. Drivers were redirected to the new road.

Meaning	**Prefixed Word**
7. "owned before; used"	_____
8. "before flying"	_____
9. "wrote again"	_____
10. "changed the course; directed again"	_____
11. "cover again"	_____
12. "time before written history"	_____

Apply

Read the text. Then list the five prefixed words. Circle each prefix. Be ready to show
how you would use CLARIFY/PHONICS to say each word and figure out its meaning.

> **Our seventh-grade class helped the local preschool raise money. We filled and refilled
> huge bins with soda cans. Then we brought the cans to a recycling center for refunds.
> We'll use the money to rebuild the children's playground.**

_____

Comprehension Check

1. What was done to the huge bins?

_____

2. Was there already a playground at the preschool? _____ How do you know that?

_____

Base Words with Negative Prefixes un-, dis-, mis-, in-, il-, im-, ir-

Prefix (Meaning)	Base Word	Longer Word	Meaning
un("not")	able	unable	"not able"
un ("opposite of")	buckle	unbuckle	"opposite of buckle"
dis ("opposite of")	connect	disconnect	"opposite of connect"
mis ("wrongly")	place	misplace	"place wrongly"
in ("not")	correct	incorrect	"not correct"
il ("not")	legal	illegal	"not legal"
im ("not")	perfect	imperfect	"not perfect"
ir ("not")	regular	irregular	"not regular"

1. What are some common meanings of negative prefixes?

   _____

2. How are *unbuckle* and *disconnect* alike in meaning?

   _____

3. The second letter of the prefix *in-* sometimes changes when added to different base words.

   What other forms of the prefix *in-* are listed in the chart? _____

4. What is the first chunk in all of the longer words? _____

Practice A

Read each phrase. Underline the word with the negative prefix. Write the prefix and
the base word. Be ready to say each phrase and tell what it means.

   1. to mismatch socks   _____

   2. untold stories   _____

   3. an incomplete answer   _____

   4. immature behavior   _____

   5. irresponsible actions   _____

   6. to disobey the instructor _____

   7. interesting and unusual   _____

   8. unsure about the information _____

Practice B

Read each sentence. Underline the word with the negative prefix. Circle the prefix. Then write the prefixed word after its meaning below.

1. I misunderstood what the speaker said.

2. A dishonest person cannot be trusted.

3. People get angry when they're treated unfairly.

4. Check your paper for misspelled words.

5. It is impolite to talk while chewing.

6. Everything was jumbled and disorganized.

7. Are any of these bills unpaid?

8. Our plans are still indefinite.

Meanings	Prefixed Word	Meanings	Prefixed Word
a. "not in a fair way"	_____	**e.** "not polite; rude"	_____
b. "not clear or definite"	_____	**f.** "not paid"	_____
c. "spelled wrongly"	_____	**g.** "not honest"	_____
d. "opposite of organized; arranged wrongly"	_____	**h.** "understood wrongly"	_____

Apply

Read the text. Then list the five prefixed words. Circle each prefix. Be ready to show how you would use CLARIFY/PHONICS to say each word and figure out its meaning.

"I think the sign misdirected us," said Tom. "Maybe we shouldn't have taken this unmarked trail."

Brian studied the map. "I disagree," he said. "If we keep going north, we should find the campsite. This trail is better than the indirect route."

"If you say so," said Tom, but his voice sounded uncertain.

_____

Check Comprehension

1. Does Brian want to take the direct route? _____ Why or why not?

_____

2. How can you tell that Tom is not sure that Brian is right?

_____

Base Words with Suffixes -y, -ly

Base Word + Suffix(es)	Longer Word	Meaning
sun + -y	sunny	"filled with sunlight"
happy + -ly	happily	"in a happy way"
honest + -y	honesty	"the quality of being honest"
honest + -ly	honestly	"in a way that is honest"
noise + -y	noisy	"filled with noise"
noise + -y + -ly	noisily	"in a way that is filled with noise"

Meaning Note: The suffix -y changes the way a word can be used in a sentence. The suffix -ly changes a word into one that describes how something is done.

1. Which three longer words would fit in the blank in this sentence? "We talked _____."

    _____

2. What is the base word in *happily*? How has the spelling of the base word changed?

    _____

3. What is the base word in *sunny*? How has the spelling of the base word changed?

    _____

4. What is the base word in *noisy*? How has the spelling of the base word changed?

    _____

5. What two suffixes are added to *noise* to make *noisily*? _____

6. In all the longer words, what is the last chunk? _____

Practice A

Read each phrase. Underline the word with the suffix -y or -ly or -ily. Write the base word. Be ready to say each phrase and give an example or a description.

1. speaking softly _____
2. spinning dizzily _____
3. a runny nose _____
4. poking about nosily _____

5. a shady bench in the city _____
6. a healthy body _____
7. to reply politely _____
8. to tiptoe sneakily _____

Practice B

Read each sentence. Underline the word with the suffix *-y* or *-ly* or *-ily*. Write each of those suffixed words under Longer Word in the chart. Fill out the chart with the base words and suffixes.

Longer Word	Base Word +Suffix(es)
(1) _____	_____
(2) _____	_____
(3) _____	_____
(4) _____	_____
(5) _____	_____
(6) _____	_____
(7) _____	_____
(8) _____	_____

1. Did you have any difficulty with the homework?

2. The girl has very wavy hair.

3. The bear's belly was completely full.

4. The silly show finally ended.

5. Try not to leave muddy tracks.

6. The lions roared mightily.

7. The birds chirped cheerily.

8. Let's not decide too hastily.

Apply

Read the text. Then list the five words with suffixes *-y* or *-ly* or *-ily*. Write the base word for each. Be ready to show how you would use CLARIFY/PHONICS to say each word and figure out its meaning.

> **The trip home from Grandmother's usually takes an hour. But on that terribly icy night, the drive took ten hours. Luckily, the family arrived home safely.**

_____

Check Comprehension

1. Why did the drive home take ten hours?

_____

2. What happened at the end of the ten hours?

_____

Base Words with Suffixes -less, -ful

Suffix (Meaning)	Base Word	Longer Word	Meaning
-less ("without")	hope penny	hopeless penniless	"without hope" "without a penny; poor"
-ful ("full of, having")	hope plenty	hopeful plentiful	"full of hope" "having plenty"
-ful ("an amount that fills")	hand	handful	"an amount that fills a hand"

1. Which suffix means "full of" or "having"? _____

2. What does the suffix -ful mean in the word handful?

   _____

3. In which suffixed words has the spelling of the base word changed? What is the spelling change?

   _____

4. What does the suffix -less mean? _____

5. What is the last chunk of each longer word? _____

Practice A

Read each phrase. Underline the word with the suffix -less or -ful. Write the base
word. Be ready to say each phrase and give an example or a description.

1. a careful job   _____

2. a carful of people   _____

3. a careless driver   _____

4. fearful cries   _____

5. a beautiful smile   _____

6. a cordless phone   _____

7. apples by the basketful _____

8. a pitiful whine   _____

Practice B

Read each sentence. Underline the word with the suffix *-less* or *-ful*. Write each of those suffixed words under Longer Word in the chart. Fill out the chart with the base words and suffixes.

Longer Word	Base Word + Suffix
(1) _____	_____
(2) _____	_____
(3) _____	_____
(4) _____	_____
(5) _____	_____
(6) _____	_____
(7) _____	_____
(8) _____	_____

1. Add a teaspoonful of salt.

2. Which dog is nearly hairless?

3. Kittens are usually playful.

4. Some germs are harmful.

5. Is that a harmless snake?

6. This broken hammer is useless.

7. Thank you for the useful advice.

8. The story was too fanciful to believe.

Apply

Read the text. Then list the five words with suffixes *-ful* or *-less*. Write the base word for each. Be ready to show how you would use CLARIFY/PHONICS to say each word and figure out its meaning.

> **Would you like a night of peaceful sleep? Then get rid of your old, painful mattress and stretch out on a Cozy Comfort mattress instead. Your body will feel weightless. You'll wake up feeling refreshed and cheerful. With a Cozy Comfort mattress, you'll say good-by to sleepless nights forever.**

_____

Comprehension Check

1. Why would you want to get rid of a painful mattress?

_____

2. How might a "weightless body" feel?

_____

Base Words with Suffixes -ous, -able

Suffix (Meaning)	Base Word	Longer Word	Meaning
-ous ("having")	danger	dangerous	"having danger"
	fame	famous	"having fame"
-able ("having")	wash	washable	"having the ability to be washed"
	value	valuable	"having value"
	rely	reliable	"having the ability to be relied on"

1. What meaning is shared by the suffixes -ous and -able?

   _____

2. What is the base word in *famous*? How has the spelling of the base word changed?

   _____

3. What is the base word in *valuable*? How has the spelling of the base word changed?

   _____

4. What is the base word in *reliable*? How has the spelling of the base word changed?

   _____

5. What is the last chunk of each longer word? _____

Practice A

Read each phrase. Underline the word with the suffix -ous or -able. Write the base word. Be ready to say each phrase and give an example or a description.

1. a reasonable plan   _____

2. an adventurous explorer   _____

3. a dependable worker   _____

4. joyous shouts   _____

5. stretchable fabric   _____

6. glorious sunshine   _____

7. humorous stories   _____

8. an excitable dog   _____

Name _____

Practice B

Read each sentence. Underline the word with the suffix -ous or -able. Write each of those suffixed words under Longer Word in the chart. Fill out the chart with the base words and suffixes.

Longer Word	Base Word + Suffix
(1) _____	_____
(2) _____	_____
(3) _____	_____
(4) _____	_____
(5) _____	_____
(6) _____	_____
(7) _____	_____
(8) _____	_____

1. These vitamins are chewable.

2. A rattlesnake is poisonous.

3. What makes a friend likable?

4. Your story is questionable.

5. Sometimes, the weather is changeable.

6. The movie got a favorable review.

7. The boy was envious of his friend's success.

8. The courageous travelers pushed on.

Apply

Read the text. Then list the five words with suffixes -able or -ous. Write the word to which the suffix has been added. Be ready to show how you would use CLARIFY/PHONICS to say each word and figure out its meaning.

> **"Every puzzle is solvable," says the detective in this story. The detective figures out a mysterious message that no one thinks is decodable. The ending of this story is not predictable. But it is still believable.**

_____

_____

Comprehension Check

1. How can you tell that the detective thinks that the problem can be figured out?

_____

2. Why is the message described as mysterious?

_____

Base Words with Suffixes -ment, -ness, -ion

Base Word + Suffix	Longer Word	Meaning
treat + -ment	treatment	"the treating of someone or something"
pay + -ment	payment	"the act of paying"
fit + -ness	fitness	"the state of being fit"
ugly + -ness	ugliness	"the state of being ugly"
direct + -ion	direction	"the act of directing"
complete + -ion	completion	"the act of completing"

Meaning Note: The suffixes -ment, -ness, and -ion change the way a word can be used in a sentence. Each suffixed word becomes the name of a person, place, or thing.

1. Which longer words have no spelling change in the base word?

   _____

2. In which longer word has the final e of the base word been dropped before the suffix?

   _____

3. In which longer word has the final y of the base word been changed to i before the suffix?

   _____

4. What is the last chunk of each longer word? _____

Practice A

Read each phrase. Underline the word with the suffix -ment, -ness, or -ion. Write the base word. Be ready to say each phrase and give an example or a description.

1. the teacher's instruction   _____

2. giggles of silliness   _____

3. unfair punishment   _____

4. noise and confusion   _____

5. a true prediction   _____

6. the vastness of space   _____

7. with perfect neatness   _____

8. a loud argument   _____

Practice B

Read each sentence. Underline the word with the suffix *-ment*, *-ness*, or *-ion*. Write each of those suffixed words under Longer Word in the chart. Fill out the chart with the base words and suffixes.

Longer Word	Base Word + Suffix
(1) _____	_____
(2) _____	_____
(3) _____	_____
(4) _____	_____
(5) _____	_____
(6) _____	_____
(7) _____	_____
(8) _____	_____

1. Our feet left an impression in the wet sand.

2. Complete darkness followed the sunset.

3. Teachers study child development.

4. Is this a time for hard work or for laziness?

5. We pay taxes to the government.

6. Everyone needs a high school education.

7. Praise and encouragement help people.

8. Thank you for your kindness.

Apply

Read the text. Then list the five words with the suffixes *-ment*, *-ness*, or *-ion*. Write the word to which the suffix has been added. Be ready to show how you would use CLARIFY/ PHONICS to say each word and figure out its meaning.

> My friends and I are in agreement that dizziness brings great enjoyment. That is why we try to visit the amusement park at Wallis Lake as often as we can. It's fun to look at people's expressions when they get off the spinning rides.

_____

_____

Comprehension Check

1. Do the friends like to go on spinning rides? _____ How can you tell?

_____

2. Where do the friends look to see a rider's expression?

_____

Clarify/Phonics: Break Words into Chunks

Kinds of Chunks	Examples	Longer Words
Words that form compounds	snow + storm	snowstorm
	blue + berry	blueberry
Base words with endings	interrupt + ing	interrupting
	permit + ed	permitted
	success + es	successes
	little + est	littlest
Base words with prefixes	un + cover	uncover
	mis + state	misstate
	im + permanent	impermanent
Base words with suffixes	interrupt + ion	interruption
	happy + ly	happily
	state + ment	statement
	success + ful	successful
Syllables	in/ter/rupt	interrupt
	per/ma/nent	permanent
	de/liv/er	deliver

1. Which longer words have two base words?

   _____

   What are these words called?

   _____

2. Write one longer word that has a base word and an ending.

   _____

3. Write one longer word that has a base word and a suffix.

   _____

4. Which longer words in the chart have base words with spelling changes in them?

   _____

Name _____

Sports Lab

Practice A

Read each word. Write the separate chunks you find. Be ready to say the word.

1. permitting _____
2. uninterrupted _____
3. unhappiness _____
4. blueberries _____
5. misstatement _____
6. unsuccessfully _____
7. thunderstorms _____
8. deliveries _____

Practice B

Read each phrase. Say the underlined word to yourself. Circle the answer that shows the word broken into chunks in the best way.

1. a <u>satisfied</u> smile ———— sat/is/fy(i) + ed   sa/ti/s/fied
2. a <u>masterpiece</u> of art ———— mas/ter + piece   mas + ter/pie/ce
3. <u>unspoiled</u> land ———— un/spo/il + ed   un + spoil + ed
4. <u>detectable</u> clues ———— det/ec/ta/ble   de/tect + able
5. an <u>impossible</u> dream ———— im + pos/si/ble   im/possi/ble
6. many <u>advertisements</u> ———— ad/ver/ti/se/ment + s   ad/ver/tise + ment + s
7. Sunday <u>newspaper</u> ———— new/spap + er   news + pa/per
8. <u>misunderstood</u> words ———— mis + under + stood   mi/sun/ders/tood

Apply

Read the text. Then list the five words of three or more syllables. Be ready to show how you would use CLARIFY/PHONICS to say each word and figure out its meaning.

> **Our class had an animated discussion about movies. Some of us think that the most entertaining movies have lots of fast action. It's true that action movies are big moneymakers. But others in our class think that a movie is not worthwhile unless it tells a believable story.**

_____

Comprehension Check

1. Why are some movies called moneymakers?

_____

2. For some students in this class, what is more important than action in a movie?

_____

Base Words, Endings, and Suffixes

Base Word	Ending	Suffix(es)	Longer Word
interest	-ing	-ly	interestingly
hope		-ful, -ly	hopefully
hope		-less, -ly	hopelessly
fear		-less, -ness	fearlessness
reason		-able, -ly	reasonably
agree		-able, -ness	agreeableness

1. What ending is in the longer word *interestingly*? _____

2. What suffixes are in the longer word *reasonably*? _____

3. Two of the longer words have opposite meanings. What are the words?

_____

Practice A

Write the base word in each of these longer words. Be ready to say the longer word.

1. agreeably _____

2. spotlessness _____

3. fearfully _____

4. daringly _____

5. winningly _____

6. pointlessness _____

7. reasonableness _____

8. fearlessly _____

Practice B

Read each phrase. Underline the word with more than one ending or suffix. Write the base word and the word parts at its end. Be ready to tell how you figured out how to find the base word.

1. amazingly calm _____

2. smiling cheerfully _____

3. beautifully done _____

4. a reliably working car _____

5. strolling aimlessly _____

6. the changeableness of weather _____

7. the uselessness of broken tools _____

8. fittingly spoken words _____

Apply

Read the text. Then list the five words that have more than one word part added at the end. Write the base word for each. Be ready to show how you would use CLARIFY/PHONICS to say each word and figure out its meaning.

> **Ed started the cleanup willingly, but he grew bored. Instead of carefully covering the paint cans, he thoughtlessly tossed the lids out. Predictably, the paint dried up, and Ed saw the problem caused by carelessness.**

_____

_____

Comprehension Check

1. What problem was caused by Ed's carelessness?

_____

2. How was Ed acting when he tossed the lids out?

_____

Prefixes, Base Words, Endings, and Suffixes

Prefix	Base Word	Ending	Suffix	Longer Word
dis	agree	-ing		disagreeing
mis	treat	-ed		mistreated
un	happy	-est		unhappiest
in	complete		-ly	incompletely
im	move		-able	immovable
re	pay		-ment	repayment

1. In which longer words has the spelling of the base word changed?

_____

What are the spelling changes?

_____

2. How many word parts make up each longer word? _____

Practice A

Write the base word in each of these longer words. Be ready to say the longer word.

1. disagreement _____

2. disconnected _____

3. impatiently _____

4. resupplied _____

5. mistrusting _____

6. unreasonable _____

7. indefinitely _____

8. unfairest _____

Practice B

Read each phrase. Underline the word that has a prefix and a suffix or ending. Write the prefix, the base word, and the ending or suffix. Be ready to tell how you figured out how to find the base word.

1. rewriting the story _____

2. disobeyed the rules _____

3. asked impolitely _____

4. an unreliable computer _____

5. a misleading clue _____

6. the rearrangement of plans _____

7. to save from mistreatment _____

8. an incomparable champion _____

Apply

Read the text. Then list the five words that have a prefix and a suffix or ending. Write the base word for each. Be ready to show how you would use CLARIFY/PHONICS to say each word and figure out its meaning.

"This meat is unchewable," said Tina.

"Yes, I admit I cooked it incorrectly." said Arno. "I misjudged the cooking time and grilled the meat for about an hour too long."

"It tastes like rubber," said Tina unhappily. "Let's do some rethinking of our dinner plans," she added.

_____

_____

Comprehension Check

1. Why does Tina say that the meat is unchewable?

_____

2. How can you tell that Arno did not judge the cooking time well?

_____

Prefixes, Base Words, and Suffixes

Prefix (Meaning)	Base Word	Suffix(es)	Longer Word
re ("again")	assign	ment	reassignment
un ("not")	attain	able	unattainable
in ("not")	exact	ly	inexactly
	care	ful, ness	carefulness
	danger	ous, ly	dangerously
	nerve	ous, ness	nervousness

1. When something is *attainable*, it can be attained, or reached. What is true of something that is *unattainable*?

   _____

2. Which longer word means "not in an exact way"? _____

3. What suffix is found in both *dangerously* and *nervousness*? _____

Practice A

Think about the base word in each of the underlined words. Complete the sentence by writing the base word. Be ready to read the sentence aloud.

1. When something is <u>unimaginable</u>, it is hard to _____.

2. The team members shouted <u>victoriously</u> because they were thrilled with their _____.

3. Some bad actions are simply <u>inexcusable</u>; there is just no _____ for them.

4. If an animal is <u>retrainable</u>; someone will have to _____ it again.

5. <u>Adventurousness</u> is a feeling that makes people look for _____.

6. Some storms are <u>unpredictable</u>; no one can _____ when they will occur.

7. If something has great <u>usefulness</u>, you will find you can _____ it in many ways.

8. When the problem of <u>unemployment</u> has been solved, businesses will want to

   _____ everyone who wants to work.

Practice B

Read each phrase. Underline the word with more than one affix. (An affix is a prefix or a suffix.) Write the base word and the affixes. Be ready to tell how you figured out how to find the base word.

1. uncontrollable laughter _____

2. to make a repayment _____

3. an indefinable feeling _____

4. written humorously _____

5. an unavoidable accident _____

6. the infamous thief _____

7. helpfulness and concern _____

8. recyclable plastic bottles _____

Apply

Read the text. Then list the five words with more than one affix. Write the base word for each. Be ready to show how you would use CLARIFY/PHONICS to say each word and figure out its meaning.

> **When an unusually fine gift mysteriously appeared on my doorstep, I knew it could only be from you. My gratitude is indescribable. Thank you for your unsurpassable thoughtfulness.**

_____

_____

Comprehension Check

1. What is "indescribable gratitude"?

_____

2. What phrase does the writer use to mean "kindness that cannot be outdone"?

_____

Clarify/Phonics: Break Words into Chunks

Long Word	Chunks (Syllables, Base Words, Endings, Prefixes, Suffixes)
consider	con sid er
considered	con sid er ed
reconsider	re con sid er
considerate	con sid er ate
consideration	con sid er a tion
inconsiderate	in con sid er ate
inconsiderately	in con sid er ate ly
inconsideration	in con sid er a tion

1. The letters _tion_ make a syllable usually pronounced /shun/. The letters _ion_ are a suffix that change the way a word is used in a sentence. To what words in the chart has the suffix _-ion_ been added?

   _____

2. What do you do when you reconsider a plan? _____

3. If _considerate_ means "polite and kind," how does someone act who acts inconsiderately?

   _____

Practice A

Break each of these words into chunks. Be ready to say the longer word.

1. fortune   _____

2. misfortune   _____

3. fortunate   _____

4. unfortunate   _____

5. unfortunately   _____

6. pronounce   _____

7. mispronouncing   _____

8. pronouncements   _____

Practice B

Think about the chunks and meaning of each underlined word. Complete the sentence by writing a different form of the underlined word, one that fits in the blank. Be ready to read the sentence aloud.

1. The vase had a tiny chip; without that <u>imperfection</u>, the vase would have been

   _____ fine.

2. The artist was known as a <u>perfectionist</u> because she tried to paint a _____

   picture every time.

3. The customer was <u>satisfied</u> when she read the product label: "Our product will

   _____ you, or we'll refund your money."

4. The diners' frowns of <u>dissatisfaction</u> showed they were clearly not _____ with

   the meal.

5. The neighbors looked <u>envyingly</u> at the new car and did not hide their _____

   from its owner.

6. The job was an <u>unenviable</u> task, and nobody _____ the person who had to do it.

7. After <u>misplacing</u> the keys for the second time, the homeowner _____ an extra

   set under a rock.

8. Something that is <u>irreplaceable</u> cannot be _____.

Apply

Read the text. Then list the five words that are built from the same base word. Write the base word too. Be ready to show how you would use CLARIFY/PHONICS to say each word and figure out its meaning.

> The books in this series present the continuing adventures of a schoolboy detective. He is continually facing danger and using his wits to solve problems. Each book is a continuation of the one before. The suspense keeps readers continuously turning pages. Many readers would be discontented if the author ever discontinued these books.

_____

_____

Comprehension Check

1. Are the events in one book connected to the events in the next? _____ Why do you think that?

   _____

2. Has the author stopped writing the books of this series? _____ Why do you think that?

   _____

Left page (R200)

Name _____

| | A Beauty of a Plan |

Clarify/Phonics: Break Words into Chunks

When you use CLARIFY/PHONICS to figure out a long word, ask yourself . . .

Is this a compound word made of smaller words?
somewhat (some + what)
whatever (what + ever)
evergreen (ever + green)

What syllables do I see and hear?
(A syllable is a chunk that has just one vowel sound.)

Syllables commonly found at the beginning of words:
a as in around, amaze, along
be as in belong, believe, between
re as in remain, report, respect
de as in decide, depend, deliver

Syllables commonly found at the end of of words:
tion as in caption, nation, portion
ture as in picture, nature, feature

Do I see a base word with an ending -s, -es, -ed, -ing, -er, -est ?
(There may be a spelling change in the base word.)
older (old + er)   happiest (happy + est)
rebelled (rebel + ed)   believing (believe + ing)

Do I see a prefix added before a base word?
misplace (mis + place)   undecided (un + decided)
disrespect (dis + respect)

Do I see a suffix added to the end of a base word? (There may be a spelling change in the base word.)
dependable (depend + able)   happiness (happy + ness)
respectful (respect + ful)

1. Can a syllable also be a prefix? _____Yes_____ Why do you think that?
Each prefix in the chart—mis, dis, and un—has one vowel sound, so it is one syllable.

2. What kinds of chunks can you find in the word dependable?
the syllables de and pend, and the suffix able

3. What is a compound word?
a longer word made up of smaller ones

Right page (R201)

Name _____

| | A Beauty of a Plan |

Practice A

Read each word. Write the separate chunks you find. Be ready to say the word.
Accept variations that can be justified.

1. however   how + ever
2. refusing   re/fuse + ing
3. lectured   lec/ture + ed
4. detention   de/ten/tion
5. disbelieving   dis + be/lieve + ing
6. unamused   un + a/muse + ed
7. hardhearted   hard + heart + ed
8. capturing   cap/ture + ing

Practice B

Read each phrase. Say the underlined word to yourself. Circle the answer that shows the best way to break the word into chunks.

1. train stations — stati/ons — (sta/tion + s)
2. to disagree on a point — (dis + a/gree) — di/sag/ree
3. heavy rainstorms — (rain/storm + s) — rains/torm + s
4. amazing sights — am/az + ing — (a/maze + ing)
5. the unhappiest child — un +happ +iest — (un + happy + est)
6. a fractured arm — (fra/cture + ed) — fra/ctured
7. respectable people — (re/spect + able) — re/spec + table

Apply

Read the text. Then list the five words of two or more syllables. Be ready to show how you would use CLARIFY/PHONICS to say each word and figure out its meaning.

> Our school's basketball team has been undefeated all year. Our skillful passing and great speed make us unbeatable!

basketball, undefeated, skillful, passing, unbeatable

Comprehension Check

1. What must a team do to be undefeated? The team must win every game. They can't let another team defeat them.

2. What makes this team unbeatable? skillful passing and great speed

Chunking Words Using VC•CV Patterns

Syllables	Words
per	temper
cert	person
son	concert
con	persist
tem	common
sist	
com	
on	

1. What is the first syllable of each listed word?

tem _____ per _____ con _____ per _____ com _____

2. What are the two consonants in the middle of each word?

mp _____ rs _____ nc _____ rs _____ mm _____

3. Which of those two consonants do you hear as one sound? _____

Practice A

Write the first syllable of each word. Be ready to say the whole word.

1. picnic   pic _____
2. surround   sur _____
3. splendid   splen _____
4. absorb   ab _____
5. entire   en _____
6. compose   com _____
7. format   for _____

Practice B

Read each phrase. Underline the word that has two consonants between vowels. Write the word and draw a line between the syllables. Be ready to tell how you figured out how to say the word.

1. to consume food   con/sume
2. to argue and shout   ar/gue
3. wise advice   ad/vice
4. elbow joint   el/bow
5. to capture a moment   cap/ture
6. an old custom   cus/tom
7. as stubborn as a mule   stub/born

Apply

Read the text. Then list the five words of more than one syllable. Draw a line between the syllables. Be ready to show how you would use CLARIFY/PHONICS to figure out how to say each word.

**The members of the dance group performed. Their costumes shimmered in the light.
They leaped and twirled to the beat of drums. We all admired their strength and skill.**

mem/bers, per/formed, cos/tumes, shim/mered, ad/mired

Comprehension Check

1. Who danced?

   members of the dance group

2. How can you tell that the writer liked the show?

   The writer admired the dancers' strength and skill.

Chunking Words Using Patterns V•CV, VC•V

Word	First Syllable
promise	prom /prŏm/
promote	pro /prə/
vacant	va /vā/
valid	val /văl/
finish	fin /fĭn/
final	fi /fī/

1. In which listed words does the first syllable end with a vowel?

promote, vacant, final

2. In which listed words does the first syllable end with a consonant?

promise, valid, finish

3. Which listed words have a long vowel sound in the first syllable?

vacant, final

4. When you see a single consonant between vowels, where might the first syllable end?

It might end after the vowel or after the consonant.

Practice A

Write the first syllable of each word. Be ready to say the whole word.

1. nature — na
2. pilot — pi
3. river — riv
4. punish — pun
5. polite — po
6. deny — de
7. amaze — a
8. habit — hab

Owl

Owl

Practice B

Read each phrase. Underline the word that has one consonant between vowels. Write the word and draw a line between the syllables. Be ready to tell how you figured out how to say the word.

1. candy flavors — fla/vors
2. humane treatment — hu/mane
3. a tidy room — ti/dy
4. a rapid step — rap/id
5. credit card — cred/it
6. recent times — re/cent
7. news reports — re/ports
8. remote control — re/mote

Apply

Read the text. Then list the five words of more than one syllable. Draw a line between the syllables. Be ready to show how you would use CLARIFY/PHONICS to figure out how to say each word.

> The house mouse is well named. It lives with humans in their homes and depends on them for food. The house mouse is not a native rodent. It traveled here on ships in the past.

hu/mans, de/pends, na/tive, ro/dent, trav/eled

Comprehension Check

1. How can you tell that the house mouse needs people?

Sample: It depends on humans for homes and food.

2. What kind of animal is a house mouse?

It is a rodent.

Name _____

Syllables•Consonant-le

The Babe & I

Word	Second Syllable
bubble	ble
trouble	ble
giggle	gle
beagle	gle
middle	dle
idle	dle
whistle	tle

1. Which listed words have a first syllable that ends with a consonant?

bubble, giggle, middle, whistle

2. Which listed words have a first syllable that ends with a vowel?

trouble, beagle, idle

Practice A

Write the first syllable of each word. Be ready to say the whole word.

1. hurdle   hur
2. thimble   thim
3. couple   cou
4. sparkle   spar
5. cable   ca
6. dazzle   daz
7. nestle   nes
8. noodle   noo

Name _____

The Babe & I

Practice B

Read each phrase. Underline the word with Consonant-*le*. Write the word and draw a line between the syllables. Be ready to tell how you figured out how to say the word.

1. to scramble eggs   **scram/ble**
2. to muffle sounds   **muf/fle**
3. to scribble a note   **scrib/ble**
4. cries that startle   **star/tle**
5. the royal castle   **cas/tle**
6. needle and thread   **need/le**
7. an eagle's nest   **ea/gle**'s
8. to play a bugle   **bu/gle**

Apply

Read the text. Then list the five words with Consonant-*le*. Draw a line between the syllables. Be ready to show how you would use CLARIFY/PHONICS to figure out how to say each word.

> Uncle Fred has a black poodle named Midnight. Midnight trembles with fear at the sight of water. That is odd, since the breed was once known as a water dog. It gets its name from a word meaning "puddle." Midnight doesn't know that he's supposed to enjoy swimming. He hides under the table if he even hears the word *bath*.

Un/cle, poo/dle, trem/bles, pud/dle, ta/ble

Comprehension Check

1. What kind of dog does Uncle Fred have?

a poodle

2. What does Midnight do when he sees water or hears the word *bath*?

He trembles with fear or hides under the table.

Decoding Longer Words Facsimiles with Answers

Name _____

Words of More Than Two Syllables

Word	Syllables and Stress
determine	de/ter/mine
disaster	dis/as/ter
terrible	ter/ri/ble
carpenter	car/pen/ter
terrific	ter/rif/ic

1. In which listed words is the second syllable stressed?

   determine, disaster, terrific

2. In which listed words is the first syllable stressed?

   terrible, carpenter

Practice A

Say each word aloud syllable by syllable. Then say it as a word.

1. continue
2. energy
3. volunteer
4. formula
5. difficult
6. colony
7. terminal
8. syllable

Name _____

Practice B

Read each phrase. Underline the word that has three syllables. Write the word and draw lines between the syllables. Be ready to tell how you figured out how to say the word.

1. with sincere gratitude _____ grat/i/tude
2. a probable event _____ prob/a/ble
3. a tiny particle _____ par/ti/cle
4. horrible masks _____ hor/ri/ble
5. capital city _____ cap/i/tal
6. to consider a change _____ con/si/der
7. tornado damage _____ tor/na/do
8. to entertain a crowd _____ en/ter/tain

Apply

Read the text. Then list the five words of three syllables. Be ready to show how you would use CLARIFY/PHONICS to figure out how to say each word.

> **If you play a sport, then you know how important confidence can be. If you feel strong and capable, then you are likely to play well. Skill is not always enough. You must have a positive attitude, too.**

im/por/tant, con/fi/dence, ca/pa/ble, pos/i/tive, at/ti/tude

Comprehension Check

1. What is a positive attitude?

   It is a feeling of confidence. It is a feeling of being strong and capable.

2. What is true of a capable player?

   A capable player has skill. A capable player can play well.

_____

Name _____

Practice B

Read each phrase. Underline the word with the ending. Write the base word. Be ready to tell how you figured out how to find the base word.

1. to collect pennies — penny
2. playground recesses — recess
3. a ragged dress — rag
4. amazing adventure — amaze
5. daring rescue — dare
6. deserved a reward — deserve
7. teaches a class — teach
8. busy cities — city

Apply

Read the text. Then list the five words with endings. Write the base word for each. Be ready to show how you would use CLARIFY/PHONICS to say each word and figure out its meaning.

> A new TV show is beginning. It is supposed to be entertaining. The network is hoping that families will watch it together.

beginning, begin; supposed, suppose; entertaining, entertain; hoping, hope; families, family

Comprehension Check

1. What is the purpose of the new TV show?
Its purpose is to entertain.
2. If a brother, sister, and parent are watching the TV show together, who is watching it?
A family is watching.

Blackline Masters for Decoding Longer Words   R211

Name _____

Base Words with Endings -s, -es, -ed, -ing

Base Word	Ending	Longer Word
adventure	-s	adventures
possess	-es	possesses
strawberry	-es	strawberries
permit	-ed	permitted
stare	-ing	staring
star	-ing	starring

1. In which longer word has a y changed to i before an ending?
strawberry
2. In which longer words has a final consonant doubled before an ending?
permitted, starring
3. In which longer word has an e been dropped before an ending?
staring

Practice A

Write the base word in each of these longer words. Be ready to say the longer word.

1. centuries — century
2. hopping — hop
3. limited — limit
4. committed — commit
5. scrambling — scramble
6. denied — deny
7. eyeglasses — eyeglass
8. outlines — outline

R210   *Blackline Masters for Decoding Longer Words*

Decoding Longer Words Facsimiles with Answers   R241

Name _____

Mountains

Practice B

Read each phrase. Underline the word with the ending that compares. Write the base word. Be ready to tell how you figured out how to find the base word.

1. a <u>steadier</u> table   steady
2. the <u>whitest</u> clothes   white
3. the <u>hungriest</u> animal   hungry
4. <u>bluer</u> skies   blue
5. a <u>longer</u> letter   long
6. <u>simplest</u> and most honest   simple
7. survival of the <u>fittest</u>   fit
8. an <u>emptier</u> theater   empty

Apply

Read the text. Then list the five words with endings that compare. Write the base word for each. Be ready to show how you would use CLARIFY/PHONICS to say each word and figure out its meaning.

> We ran six blocks through the wildest rainstorm we'd ever seen. We splashed through puddles that were larger than some ponds. I had never been wetter. When we got home, we looked in the mirror. "Have you ever seen a sorrier sight?" asked my brother. We looked as if buckets of water had been poured over us. I began to shiver. Even though I was already soaked, my one wish was for a shower—the hottest one I could get.

wildest, wild; larger, large; wetter, wet; sorrier, sorry; hottest, hot

Comprehension Check

1. What kind of rainstorm was it?

the wildest one ever seen

2. What might go wrong with the shower that the narrator wants to take?

It might be too hot, or it might not be hot enough.

Name _____

Mountains

Base Words with Endings That Compare

Base Word	Ending	Longer Word
small	-er, -est	smaller, smallest
thin	-er, -est	thinner, thinnest
little	-er, -est	littler, littlest
tiny	-er, -est	tinier, tiniest

1. In which longer words has a *y* changed to *i* before an ending?

tinier, tiniest

2. In which longer words has a final consonant doubled before an ending?

thinner, thinnest

3. In which longer words has an *e* been dropped before an ending?

littler, littlest

Practice A

Write the base word in each of these longer words. Be ready to say the longer word.

1. silliest   silly
2. paler   pale
3. taller   tall
4. redder   red
5. gentler   gentle
6. angrier   angry
7. yellowest   yellow
8. rarest   rare

**Jesse Jackson:
I Am Somebody!**

Practice B

Read each sentence. Underline the word with the prefix *re-* or *pre-*. Circle the prefix. Then write the prefixed word after its meaning below. Be ready to tell what you know about breaking words that begin with prefixes into chunks.

1. We'll (re)cover the chair with purple fabric.

2. There are no writings from (pre)history.

3. The student (re)wrote the story.

4. Airlines perform (pre)flight checks.

5. Some dealers sell (pre)owned cars.

6. Drivers were (re)directed to the new road.

Meaning	Prefixed Word
7. "owned before; used"	preowned
8. "before flying"	preflight
9. "wrote again"	rewrote
10. "changed the course; directed again"	redirected
11. "cover again"	recover
12. "time before written history"	prehistory

Apply

Read the text. Then list the five prefixed words. Circle each prefix. Be ready to show how you would use CLARIFY/PHONICS to say each word and figure out its meaning.

> Our seventh-grade class helped the local preschool raise money. We filled and refilled huge bins with soda cans. Then we brought the cans to a recycling center for refunds. We'll use the money to rebuild the children's playground.

(pre)school; (re)filled; (re)cycling; (re)funds; (re)build

Comprehension Check

1. What was done to the huge bins?

   They were filled and refilled.

2. Was there already a playground at the preschool? _____ Yes _____ How do you know that?

   The class was going to rebuild it.

**Jesse Jackson:
I Am Somebody!**

Base Words with Prefixes re-, pre-

Prefix (Meaning)	Base Word	Longer Word	Meaning
re ("again")	told	retold	"told again"
re ("back")	pay	repay	"pay back"
pre ("before")	test	pretest	"test before"

1. What is the first chunk in *retold?* __re__ in *repay?* __re__ in *pretest?* __pre__

2. What does the prefix *re-* mean in repay? back

3. What does the prefix *re-* mean in retold? again

4. What is one meaning for the prefix *pre-?* before

Practice A

Underline the prefixed word in each phrase. Write the prefix and the base word. Be ready to say each phrase and give an example or a description.

1. prepaid bills — pre + paid

2. spelling retest — re + test

3. to preheat the oven — pre + heat

4. to regain health — re + gain

5. to prearrange a meeting — pre + arrange

6. to rearrange shelves — re + arrange

7. to rejoin the game — re + join

8. ball on the rebound — re + bound

Name _____

Base Words with Negative Prefixes un-, dis-, mis-, in-, il-, im-, ir-

Prefix (Meaning)	Base Word	Longer Word	Meaning
un("not")	able	unable	"not able"
un ("opposite of")	buckle	unbuckle	"opposite of buckle"
dis ("opposite of")	connect	disconnect	"opposite of connect"
mis ("wrongly")	place	misplace	"place wrongly"
in ("not")	correct	incorrect	"not correct"
il ("not")	legal	illegal	"not legal"
im ("not")	perfect	imperfect	"not perfect"
ir ("not")	regular	irregular	"not regular"

1. What are some common meanings of negative prefixes?

   "not," "opposite of," "wrongly"

2. How are *unbuckle* and *disconnect* alike in meaning?

   Both name things that are taken apart, the reverse or opposite of putting them together.

3. The second letter of the prefix *in-* sometimes changes when added to different base words.

   What other forms of the prefix *in-* are listed in the chart? _____ il-, im-, ir-

4. What is the first chunk in all of the longer words? _____ the prefix

Practice A

Read each phrase. Underline the word with the negative prefix. Write the prefix and the base word. Be ready to say each phrase and tell what it means.

1. to mismatch socks _____ mis + match

2. untold stories _____ un + told

3. an incomplete answer _____ in + complete

4. immature behavior _____ im + mature

5. irresponsible actions _____ ir + responsible

6. to disobey the instructor _____ dis + obey

7. interesting and unusual _____ un + usual

8. unsure about the information _____ un + sure

[Lakota Hoop Dancer]

Name _____

Practice B

Read each sentence. Underline the word with the negative prefix. Circle the prefix. Then write the prefixed word after its meaning below.

1. I (mis)understood what the speaker said.

2. A (dis)honest person cannot be trusted.

3. People get angry when they're treated (un)fairly.

4. Check your paper for (mis)spelled words.

5. It is (im)polite to talk while chewing.

6. Everything was jumbled and (dis)organized.

7. Are any of these bills (un)paid?

8. Our plans are still (in)definite.

Meanings	Prefixed Word
a. "not in a fair way"	unfairly
b. "not clear or definite"	indefinite
c. "spelled wrongly"	misspelled
d. "opposite of organized; arranged wrongly"	disorganized

Meanings	Prefixed Word
e. "not polite; rude"	impolite
f. "not paid"	unpaid
g. "not honest"	dishonest
h. "understood wrongly"	misunderstood

Apply

Read the text. Then list the five prefixed words. Circle each prefix. Be ready to show how you would use CLARIFY/PHONICS to say each word and figure out its meaning.

"I think the sign misdirected us," said Tom. "Maybe we shouldn't have taken this unmarked trail."

Brian studied the map. "I disagree," he said. "If we keep going north, we should find the campsite. This trail is better than the indirect route."

"If you say so," said Tom, but his voice sounded uncertain.

(mis)directed, (un)marked, (dis)agree, (in)direct, (un)certain

Check Comprehension

1. Does Brian want to take the direct route? _____ No _____ Why or why not?

   He wants to take the indirect route. He thinks it is better.

2. How can you tell that Tom is not sure that Brian is right?

   Tom's voice sounds uncertain.

[Lakota Hoop Dancer]

Name _____

Practice B

Read each sentence. Underline the word with the suffix -y or -ly. Write each of those suffixed words under Longer Word in the chart. Fill out the chart with the base words and suffixes.

Longer Word	Base Word +Suffix(es)
(1) difficulty	difficult + y
(2) wavy	wave + y
(3) completely	complete + ly
(4) finally	final + ly
(5) muddy	mud + y
(6) mightily	might + ily; also might+y+ly
(7) cheerily	cheer + ily; also cheer+y+ly
(8) hastily	haste + ily; also haste+y+ly

1. Did you have any difficulty with the homework?

2. The girl has very wavy hair.

3. The bear's belly was completely full.

4. The silly show finally ended.

5. Try not to leave muddy tracks.

6. The lions roared mightily.

7. The birds chirped cheerily.

8. Let's not decide too hastily.

Apply

Read the text. Then list the five words with suffixes -y or -ly or -ily. Write the base word for each. Be ready to show how you would use CLARIFY/PHONICS to say each word and figure out its meaning.

The trip home from Grandmother's usually takes an hour. But on that terribly icy night, the drive took ten hours. Luckily, the family arrived home safely.

usually, usual; terribly, terrible; icy, ice; luckily, luck; safely, safe

Check Comprehension

1. Why did the drive home take ten hours?
The road was terribly icy.

2. What happened at the end of the ten hours?
The family arrived home safely.

Blackline Masters for Decoding Longer Words   R219

Name _____

Base Words with Suffixes -y, -ly

Base Word + Suffix(es)	Longer Word	Meaning
sun + -y	sunny	"filled with sunlight"
happy + -ly	happily	"in a happy way"
honest + -y	honesty	"the quality of being honest"
honest + -ly	honestly	"in a way that is honest"
noise + -y	noisy	"filled with noise"
noise + -y + -ly	noisily	"in a way that is filled with noise"

Meaning Note: The suffix -y changes the way a word can be used in a sentence. The suffix -ly changes a word into one that describes how something is done.

1. Which three longer words would fit in the blank in this sentence? "We talked _____."
happily, honestly, noisily

2. What is the base word in *happily?* How has the spelling of the base word changed?
The *y* of *happy* changed to *i* before *-ly.*

3. What is the base word in *sunny?* How has the spelling of the base word changed?
The *n* of *sun* doubled before *-y.*

4. What is the base word in *noisy?* How has the spelling of the base word changed?
The final *e* of *noise* was dropped before the suffix *-y.*

5. What two suffixes are added to *noise* to make *noisily?* _____ -y and -ly

6. In all the longer words, what is the last chunk? _____ a suffix

Practice A

Read each phrase. Underline the word with the suffix -y or -ly or -ily. Write the base word. Be ready to say each phrase and give an example or a description.

1. speaking softly _____ soft
2. spinning dizzily _____ dizzy
3. a runny nose _____ run
4. poking about nosily _____ nose
   also accept nosy
5. a shady bench in the city _____ shade
6. a healthy body _____ health
7. to reply politely _____ polite
8. to tiptoe sneakily _____ sneak
   also accept sneaky

R218   *Blackline Masters for Decoding Longer Words*

Practice B

Read each sentence. Underline the word with the suffix *-less* or *-ful*. Write each of those suffixed words under Longer Word in the chart. Fill out the chart with the base words and suffixes.

Longer Word	Base Word + Suffix
(1) teaspoonful	teaspoon + ful
(2) hairless	hair + less
(3) playful	play + ful
(4) harmful	harm + ful
(5) harmless	harm + less
(6) useless	use + less
(7) useful	use + ful
(8) fanciful	fancy + ful

1. Add a <u>teaspoonful</u> of salt.
2. Which dog is nearly <u>hairless</u>?
3. Kittens are usually <u>playful</u>.
4. Some germs are <u>harmful</u>.
5. Is that a <u>harmless</u> snake?
6. This broken hammer is <u>useless</u>.
7. Thank you for the <u>useful</u> advice.
8. The story was too <u>fanciful</u> to believe.

Apply

Read the text. Then list the five words with suffixes *-ful* or *-less*. Write the base word for each. Be ready to show how you would use CLARIFY/PHONICS to say each word and figure out its meaning.

> Would you like a night of **peaceful** sleep? Then get rid of your old, **painful** mattress and stretch out on a Cozy Comfort mattress instead. Your body will feel **weightless**. You'll wake up feeling refreshed and **cheerful**. With a Cozy Comfort mattress, you'll say good-by to **sleepless** nights forever.

peaceful, peace; painful, pain; weightless, weight; cheerful, cheer; sleepless, sleep

Comprehension Check

1. Why would you want to get rid of a painful mattress?
Sample: You want to get rid of the pain it causes.

2. How might a "weightless body" feel?
Sample: It would feel as if it didn't have any weight.

Base Words with Suffixes -less, -ful

Suffix (Meaning)	Base Word	Longer Word	Meaning
-less ("without")	hope	hopeless	"without hope"
	penny	penniless	"without a penny; poor"
-ful ("full of," "having")	hope	hopeful	"full of hope"
	plenty	plentiful	"having plenty"
-ful ("an amount that fills")	hand	handful	"an amount that fills a hand"

1. Which suffix means "full of" or "having"? _____ -ful
2. What does the suffix -ful mean in the word *handful*?
"an amount that fills"
3. In which suffixed words has the spelling of the base word changed? What is the spelling change?
In *plentiful* and *penniless*, the *y* changed to *i* before the suffix.
4. What does the suffix -less mean? _____ without
5. What is the last chunk of each longer word? _____ a suffix

Practice A

Read each phrase. Underline the word with the suffix *-less* or *-ful*. Write the base word. Be ready to say each phrase and give an example or a description.

1. a <u>careful</u> job _____ care
2. a <u>carful</u> of people _____ car
3. a <u>careless</u> driver _____ care
4. <u>fearful</u> cries _____ fear
5. a <u>beautiful</u> smile _____ beauty
6. a <u>cordless</u> phone _____ cord
7. apples by the <u>basketful</u> _____ basket
8. a <u>pitiful</u> whine _____ pity

Name _____

Practice B

Read each sentence. Underline the word with the suffix -ous or -able. Write each of those suffixed words under Longer Word in the chart. Fill out the chart with the base words and suffixes.

Longer Word	Base Word + Suffix
(1) chewable	chew + able
(2) poisonous	poison + ous
(3) likable	like + able
(4) questionable	question + able
(5) changeable	change + able
(6) favorable	favor + able
(7) envious	envy + ous
(8) courageous	courage + ous

1. These vitamins are chewable.
2. A rattlesnake is poisonous.
3. What makes a friend likable?
4. Your story is questionable.
5. Sometimes, the weather is changeable.
6. The movie got a favorable review.
7. The boy was envious of his friend's success.
8. The courageous travelers pushed on.

Apply

Read the text. Then list the five words with suffixes -able or -ous. Write the word to which the suffix has been added. Be ready to show how you would use CLARIFY/PHONICS to say each word and figure out its meaning.

"Every puzzle is solvable," says the detective in this story. The detective figures out a mysterious message that no one thinks is decodable. The ending of this story is not predictable. But it is still believable.

solvable, solve; mysterious, mystery; decodable, decode; predictable, predict; believable, believe

Comprehension Check

1. How can you tell that the detective thinks that the problem can be figured out?
Sample: The detective says that every puzzle is solvable. That means it can be solved.
2. Why is the message described as mysterious?
Sample: It is like a mystery that no one knows the answer to. No one can decode it.

Blackline Masters for Decoding Longer Words **R223**

Name _____

Base Words with Suffixes -ous, -able

Suffix (Meaning)	Base Word	Longer Word	Meaning
-ous ("having")	danger	dangerous	"having danger"
	fame	famous	"having fame"
-able ("having")	wash	washable	"having the ability to be washed"
	value	valuable	"having value"
	rely	reliable	"having the ability to be relied on"

1. What meaning is shared by the suffixes -ous and -able?
They can both mean "having."

2. What is the base word in *famous*? How has the spelling of the base word changed?
The final *e* of *fame* has been dropped before the suffix.

3. What is the base word in *valuable*? How has the spelling of the base word changed?
The final *e* of *value* has been dropped before the suffix.

4. What is the base word in *reliable*? How has the spelling of the base word changed?
The final *y* of *rely* has changed to *i* before the suffix.

5. What is the last chunk of each longer word? ____ a suffix

Practice A

Read each phrase. Underline the word with the suffix -ous or -able. Write the base word. Be ready to say each phrase and give an example or a description.

1. a reasonable plan — reason
2. an adventurous explorer — adventure
3. a dependable worker — depend
4. joyous shouts — joy
5. stretchable fabric — stretch
6. glorious sunshine — glory
7. humorous stories — humor
8. an excitable dog — excite

R222 *Blackline Masters for Decoding Longer Words*

Decoding Longer Words Facsimiles with Answers

Name _____

Base Words with Suffixes -ment, -ness, -ion

Base Word + Suffix	Longer Word	Meaning
treat + -ment	treatment	"the treating of someone or something"
pay + -ment	payment	"the act of paying"
fit + -ness	fitness	"the state of being fit"
ugly + -ness	ugliness	"the state of being ugly"
direct + -ion	direction	"the act of directing"
complete + -ion	completion	"the act of completing"

Meaning Note: The suffixes -ment, -ness, and -ion change the way a word can be used in a sentence. Each suffixed word becomes the name of a person, place, or thing.

1. Which longer words have no spelling change in the base word?

    treatment, payment, fitness, direction

2. In which longer word has the final e of the base word been dropped before the suffix?

    completion

3. In which longer word has the final y of the base word been changed to i before the suffix?

    ugliness

4. What is the last chunk of each longer word? _____ the suffix

Practice A

Read each phrase. Underline the word with the suffix -ment, -ness, or -ion. Write the base word. Be ready to say each phrase and give an example or a description.

1. the teacher's instruction ____ instruct

2. giggles of silliness ____ silly

3. unfair punishment ____ punish

4. noise and confusion ____ confuse

5. a true prediction ____ predict

6. the vastness of space ____ vast

7. with perfect neatness ____ neat

8. a loud argument ____ argue

Name _____

Practice B

Read each sentence. Underline the word with the suffix -ment, -ness, or -ion. Write each of those suffixed words under Longer Word in the chart. Fill out the chart with the base words and suffixes.

	Longer Word	Base Word + Suffix
(1)	impression	impress + ion
(2)	darkness	dark + ness
(3)	development	develop + ment
(4)	laziness	lazy + ness
(5)	government	govern + ment
(6)	education	educate + ion
(7)	encouragement	encourage + ment
(8)	kindness	kind + ness

1. Our feet left an impression in the wet sand.

2. Complete darkness followed the sunset.

3. Teachers study child development.

4. Is this a time for hard work or for laziness?

5. We pay taxes to the government.

6. Everyone needs a high school education.

7. Praise and encouragement help people.

8. Thank you for your kindness.

Apply

Read the text. Then list the five words with the suffixes -ment, -ness, or -ion. Write the word to which the suffix has been added. Be ready to show how you would use CLARIFY/PHONICS to say each word and figure out its meaning.

> **My friends and I are in agreement that dizziness brings great enjoyment. That is why we try to visit the amusement park at Wallis Lake as often as we can. It's fun to look at people's expressions when they get off the spinning rides.**

agreement, agree; dizziness, dizzy; enjoyment, enjoy; amusement, amuse; expressions,

express

Comprehension Check

1. Do the friends like to go on spinning rides? ____ Yes ____ How can you tell?

    They think that dizziness brings great enjoyment.

2. Where do the friends look to see a rider's expression?

    They look at the person's face.

Name _____

Clarify/Phonics: Break Words into Chunks

Kinds of Chunks	Examples	Longer Words
Words that form compounds	snow + storm blue + berry	snowstorm blueberry
Base words with endings	interrupt + ing permit + ed success + es little + est	interrupting permitted successes littlest
Base words with prefixes	un + cover mis + state im + permanent	uncover misstate impermanent
Base words with suffixes	interrupt + ion happy + ly state + ment success + ful	interruption happily statement successful
Syllables	in/ter/rupt per/ma/nent de/liv/er	interrupt permanent deliver

1. Which longer words have two chunks and two base words?
snowstorm, blueberry
What are these words called?
compound words

2. Write one longer word that has a base word and an ending.
interrupting, permitted, successes, or littlest

3. Write one longer word that has a base word and a suffix.
interruption, happily, statement, or successful

4. Which longer words in the chart have base words with spelling changes in them?
permitted, littlest, happily

Name _____

Practice A Accept variations that can be justified.
Read each word. Write the separate chunks you find. Be ready to say the word.

1. permitting — per/mit + ing
2. uninterrupted — un + in/ter/rupt + ed
3. unhappiness — un + hap/py + ness
4. blueberries — blue + ber/ry + es
5. misstatement — mis + state + ment
6. unsuccessfully — un + suc/cess + ful + ly
7. thunderstorms — thun/der + storm + s
8. deliveries — de/liv/er + y + es

Practice B
Read each phrase. Say the underlined word to yourself. Circle the answer that shows the word broken into chunks in the best way.

1. a satisfied smile — (sat/is/fy(i) + ed) sa/tis/fied
2. a masterpiece of art — (mas/ter + piece) mas + ter/pie/ce
3. unspoiled land — un/spoi/il + ed (un + spoil + ed)
4. detectable clues — (de/tect + able) de/tec/ta/ble
5. an impossible dream — (im + pos/si/ble) im/possi/ble
6. many advertisements — ad/ver/tise/ment + s (ad/ver/tise + ment + s)
7. Sunday newspaper — new/spap + er (news + pa/per)
8. misunderstood words — (mis + under + stood) mi/sun/ders/tood

Apply
Read the text. Then list the five words of three or more syllables. Be ready to show how you would use CLARIFY/PHONICS to say each word and figure out its meaning.

> Our class had an animated discussion about movies. Some of us think that the most entertaining movies have lots of fast action. It's true that action movies are big moneymakers. But others in our class think that a movie is not worthwhile unless it tells a believable story.

animated, discussion, entertaining, moneymakers, believable

Comprehension Check

1. Why are some movies called moneymakers?
Sample: Lots of tickets are sold, so the movie makes money for the movie company.

2. For some students in this class, what is more important than action in a movie?
a believable story

Left Worksheet (R228)

Name _____

Base Words, Endings, and Suffixes

Base Word	Ending	Suffix(es)	Longer Word
interest	-ing	-ly	interestingly
hope		-ful, -ly	hopefully
hope		-less, -ly	hopelessly
fear		-less, -ness	fearlessness
reason		-able, -ly	reasonably
agree		-able, -ness	agreeableness

1. What ending is in the longer word *interestingly*? __-ing__

2. What suffixes are in the longer word *reasonably*? __-able, -ly__

3. Two of the longer words have opposite meanings. What are the words?
__hopefully and hopelessly__

Practice A

Write the base word in each of these longer words. Be ready to say the longer word.

1. agreeably __agree__
2. spotlessness __spot__
3. fearfully __fear__
4. daringly __dare__
5. winningly __win__
6. pointlessness __point__
7. reasonableness __reason__
8. fearlessly __fear__

Right Worksheet (R229)

Name _____

Practice B

Read each phrase. Underline the word with more than one ending or suffix. Write the base word and the word parts at its end. Be ready to tell how you figured out how to find the base word.

1. amazingly calm — amaze + ing, ly
2. smiling cheerfully — cheer + ful, ly
3. beautifully done — beauty + ful, ly
4. a reliably working car — rely + able, ly
5. strolling aimlessly — aim + less, ly
6. the changeableness of weather — change + able, ness
7. the uselessness of broken tools — use + less, ness
8. fittingly spoken words — fit + ing, ly

Apply

Read the text. Then list the five words that have more than one word part added at the end. Write the base word for each. Be ready to show how you would use CLARIFY/PHONICS to say each word and figure out its meaning.

> Ed started the cleanup willingly, but he grew bored. Instead of carefully covering the paint cans, he thoughtlessly tossed the lids out. Predictably, the paint dried up, and Ed saw the problem caused by carelessness.

willingly, will; carefully, care; thoughtlessly, thought; predictably, predict; carelessness, care

Comprehension Check

1. What problem was caused by Ed's carelessness?
The paint dried up because Ed didn't cover the cans.

2. How was Ed acting when he tossed the lids out?
He was acting thoughtlessly.

Prefixes, Base Words, Endings, and Suffixes

Prefix	Base Word	Ending	Suffix	Longer Word
dis	agree	-ing		disagreeing
mis	treat	-ed		mistreated
un	happy	-est	-ly	unhappiest
in	complete		-able	incompletely
im	move		-ment	immovable
re	pay			repayment

1. In which longer words has the spelling of the base word changed?

unhappiest, immovable

What are the spelling changes?

The *y* of *happy* changed to *i*; the final *e* of *move* was dropped.

2. How many word parts make up each longer word? _____ three

Practice A

Write the base word in each of these longer words. Be ready to say the longer word.

1. disagreement _____ agree
2. disconnected _____ connect
3. impatiently _____ patient
4. resupplied _____ supply
5. mistrusting _____ trust
6. unreasonable _____ reason
7. indefinitely _____ definite
8. unfairest _____ fair

Practice B

Read each phrase. Underline the word that has a prefix and a suffix or ending. Write the prefix, the base word, and the ending or suffix. Be ready to tell how you figured out how to find the base word.

1. rewriting the story _____ re + write + ing
2. disobeyed the rules _____ dis + obey + -ed
3. asked impolitely _____ im + polite, ly
4. an unreliable computer _____ un + rely + able
5. a misleading clue _____ mis + lead, ing
6. the rearrangement of plans _____ re + arrange, ment
7. to save from mistreatment _____ mis + treat + ment
8. an incomparable champion _____ in + compare + able

Apply

Read the text. Then list the five words that have a prefix and a suffix or ending. Write the base word for each. Be ready to show how you would use CLARIFY/PHONICS to say each word and figure out its meaning.

> **"This meat is unchewable," said Tina.**
> **"Yes, I admit I cooked it incorrectly," said Arno. "I misjudged the cooking time and grilled the meat for about an hour too long."**
> **"It tastes like rubber," said Tina unhappily. "Let's do some rethinking of our dinner plans," she added.**

unchewable, chew; misjudged, judge; incorrectly, correct; unhappily, happy; rethinking, think

Comprehension Check

1. Why does Tina say that the meat is unchewable?

Sample: She thinks that it tastes like rubber, so she can't chew it.

2. How can you tell that Arno did not judge the cooking time well?

Sample: He says that he misjudged the time.

Name _____   El Duque

Prefixes, Base Words, and Suffixes

Prefix (Meaning)	Base Word	Suffix(es)	Longer Word
re ("again")	assign	ment	reassignment
un ("not")	attain	able	unattainable
in ("not")	exact	ly	inexactly
	care	ful, ness	carefulness
	danger	ous, ly	dangerously
	nerve	ous, ness	nervousness

1. When something is *attainable*, it can be attained, or reached. What is true of something that is *unattainable*?

It cannot be attained or reached.

2. Which longer word means "not in an exact way"? inexactly

3. What suffix is found in both *dangerously* and *nervousness*? ous

Practice A

Think about the base word in each of the underlined words. Complete the sentence by writing the base word. Be ready to read the sentence aloud.

1. When something is unimaginable, it is hard to imagine .

2. The team members shouted victoriously because they were thrilled with their victory .

3. Some bad actions are simply inexcusable; there is just no excuse for them.

4. If an animal is retrainable; someone will have to train it again.

5. Adventurousness is a feeling that makes people look for adventure .

6. Some storms are unpredictable; no one can predict when they will occur.

7. If something has great usefulness, you will find you can use it in many ways.

8. When the problem of unemployment has been solved, businesses will want to employ everyone who wants to work.

Name _____   El Duque

Practice B

Read each phrase. Underline the word with more than one affix. (An affix is a prefix or a suffix.) Write the base word and the affixes. Be ready to tell how you figured out how to find the base word.

1. uncontrollable laughter — un + control + able

2. to make a repayment — re + pay + ment

3. an indefinable feeling — in + define + able

4. written humorously — humor + ous + ly

5. an unavoidable accident — un + avoid + able

6. the infamous thief — in + fame + ous

7. helpfulness and concern — help + ful + ness

8. recyclable plastic bottles — re + cycle + able

Apply

Read the text. Then list the five words with more than one affix. Write the base word for each. Be ready to show how you would use CLARIFY/PHONICS to say each word and figure out its meaning.

> When an unusually fine gift mysteriously appeared on my doorstep, I knew it could only be from you. My gratitude is indescribable. Thank you for your unsurpassable thoughtfulness.

unusually, usual; mysteriously, mystery; indescribable, describe; unsurpassable, surpass; thoughtfulness, thought

Comprehension Check

1. What is "indescribable gratitude"?

Sample: It is thanks that cannot be described in words.

2. What phrase does the writer use to mean "kindness that cannot be outdone"?

unsurpassable thoughtfulness

Marisol and Magdalena

Clarify/Phonics: Break Words into Chunks

Long Word	Chunks (Syllables, Base Words, Endings, Prefixes, Suffixes)
consider	con sid er
considered	con sid er ed
reconsider	re con sid er
considerate	con sid er ate
consideration	con sid er a tion
inconsiderate	in con sid er ate
inconsiderately	in con sid er ate ly
inconsideration	in con sid er a tion

1. The letters *tion* make a syllable usually pronounced /shun/. The letters *ion* are a suffix that change the way a word is used in a sentence. To what words in the chart has the suffix *-ion* been added?

   considerate, inconsiderate

2. What do you do when you reconsider a plan? _____ You consider it again.

3. If *considerate* means "polite and kind," how does someone act who acts inconsiderately?
   Sample: in a way that is impolite and unkind.

Practice A

Break each of these words into chunks. Be ready to say the longer word.
Accept variations that can be justified.

1. fortune _____ for tune
2. misfortune _____ mis for tune
3. fortunate _____ for tun(e) ate
4. unfortunate _____ un for tun(e) ate
5. unfortunately _____ un for tun(e) ate ly
6. pronounce _____ pro nounce
7. mispronouncing _____ mis pro nounc(e) ing
8. pronouncements _____ pro nounce ment s

Marisol and Magdalena

Practice B

Think about the chunks and meaning of each underlined word. Complete the sentence by writing a different form of the underlined word, one that fits in the blank. Be ready to read the sentence aloud.

1. The vase had a tiny chip; without that <u>imperfection</u>, the vase would have been _____ perfect _____ fine.
   perfectly

2. The artist was known as a <u>perfectionist</u> because she tried to paint a _____ perfect picture every time.

3. The customer was <u>satisfied</u> when she read the product label: "Our product will _____ satisfy _____ you, or we'll refund your money."

4. The diners' frowns of <u>dissatisfaction</u> showed they were clearly not _____ satisfied _____ with the meal.

5. The neighbors looked <u>envyingly</u> at the new car and did not hide their _____ envy _____ from its owner.

6. The job was an <u>unenviable</u> task, and nobody _____ envied _____ the person who had to do it.

7. After <u>misplacing</u> the keys for the second time, the homeowner _____ placed _____ an extra set under a rock.

8. Something that is <u>irreplaceable</u> cannot be _____ replaced _____.

Apply

Read the text. Then list the five words that are built from the same base word. Write the base word too. Be ready to show how you would use CLARIFY/PHONICS to say each word and figure out its meaning.

> The books in this series present the continuing adventures of a schoolboy detective. He is continually facing danger and using his wits to solve problems. Each book is a continuation of the one before. The suspense keeps readers continuously turning pages. Many readers would be discontented if the author ever discontinued these books.

continuing, continually, continuation, continuously, discontinued; base word—continue

Comprehension Check

1. Are the events in one book connected to the events in the next? __Yes__ Why do you think that?
   Each book is a continuation of the one before.

2. Has the author stopped writing the books of this series? __No__ Why do you think that?
   Sample: The author has not yet discontinued these books.

Acknowledgments

For each of the selections listed below, grateful acknowledgement is made for permission to reprint copyrighted material in the Oral Reading Checks.

From *A Band of Angels: A Story Inspired by the Jubilee Singers,* by Deborah Hopkinson. Text copyright © 1999 by Deborah Hopkinson. Reprinted by arrangement with Atheneum Books for Young Readers, Simon & Schuster Children's Publishing Division. All rights reserved.

From *An Even Break,* by Sid Hite. Copyright © 1995 by Sid Hite. Reprinted by arrangement with Henry Holt and Company, LLC.

From *Cal Ripken, Jr.: Play Ball!,* by Cal Ripken, Jr. and Mike Bryan, illustrated by Stan Silver. Text copyright © 1999 by Cal Ripken, Jr. Reprinted by arrangement with Penguin Putnam, Inc.

From *El Duque: The Story of Orlando Hernandez,* by Kenneth LaFreniere. Copyright © 1999 by Kenneth LaFreniere. Reprinted by arrangement with Random House Children's Books, a division of Random House, Inc.

From *Gloria Estefan: Cuban-American Singing Star,* by Fernando Gonzalez. Copyright © 1993 by Fernando Gonzalez. Reprinted by arrangement with The Millbrook Press, Inc.

From *Jesse Jackson: I Am Somebody!,* by Charnan Simon. Copyright © 1997 by Children's Press, a division of Grolier Publishing Co., Inc. Reprinted by arrangement with the publisher.

From *Journey Home,* by Lawrence McKay, Jr., illustrated by Dom & Keunhee Lee. Text copyright © 1998 by Lawrence McKay, Jr. Reprinted by arrangement with Lee and Low Books.

From *Lakota Hoop Dancer,* by Jacqueline Left Hand Bull and Suzanne Haldane, photographs by Suzanne Haldane. Text copyright © 1999 by Jacqueline Left Hand Bull and Suzanne Haldane. Reprinted by arrangement with Penguin Putnam, Inc.

From *Marisol and Magdalena: The Sound of Our Sisterhood,* by Veronica Chambers. Copyright © 1998 by Veronica Chambers. Reprinted by arrangement with Hyperion Books for Children.

From *Mountains,* by Seymour Simon. Copyright © 1999 by Seymour Simon. Reprinted by permission of William Morrow & Co.

From *On the Court with. . .Lisa Leslie,* by Matt Christopher. Copyright © 1998 by Matt Christopher. Reprinted by arrangement with Little, Brown & Company.

From *Owl,* by Rebecca Stefoff. Text copyright © 1998 by Rebecca Stefoff. Reprinted by arrangement with Benchmark Books, Marshall Cavendish Corporation.

From *Sports Lab: How Science Has Changed Sports,* by Robert Sheely, with Louis Bourgeois. Copyright © 1994 by Robert Sheely. Reprinted by arrangement with Silver Moon Press.

From *The Babe & I,* by David A. Adler. Text copyright © 1999 by David A. Adler. Reprinted by arrangement with Harcourt Inc.

From *Tunnels, Tracks, and Trains: Building a Subway,* by Joan Hewett, photographs by Richard Hewett. Text copyright © 1994 by Joan Hewett. Reprinted by permission of Penguin Putnam, Inc.

From *Ultimate Field Trip 3: Wading Into Marine Biology,* by Susan E. Goodman, photographs by Michael J. Doolittle. Text copyright © 1999 by Susan E. Goodman. Reprinted by arrangement with Atheneum Books for Young Readers, Simon & Schuster Children's Publishing Division. All rights reserved.

From *What Are You Figuring Now? A Story about Benjamin Banneker,* by Jeri Ferris, illustrated by Amy Johnson. Copyright © 1998 by Carolrhoda Books, Inc. Published by Carolrhoda Books, Inc., Minneapolis, Minnesota. Used by permission of the publisher. All rights reserved.

For each of the selections listed below, grateful acknowledgement is made for permission to reprint copyrighted material in the Informal Reading Inventory.

Excerpt from "The Amazing Pigeon," by George Laycock, from the November 1975 issue of *Boy's Life* magazine. Copyright © by George Laycock. Reprinted by permission of the author.

From *The Animal, the Vegetable & John D. Jones,* by Betsy Byars, illustrated by Ruth Sanderson. Copyright © 1982 by Betsy Byars. Reprinted by permission of Dell Publishing, a division of Random House, Inc.

From *Arthur's Pet Business,* by Marc Brown. Copyright © 1990 by Marc Brown. Reprinted by permission of Little, Brown & Company.

From *Encyclopedia Brown and the Case of the Disgusting Sneakers,* by Donald J. Sobol. Copyright © 1990 by Donald J. Sobol. Reprinted by permission of HarperCollins Publishers.

From *Encyclopedia Brown, Boy Detective,* by Donald J. Sobol. Copyright © 1963 by Donald J. Sobol. Reprinted by permission of Lodestar Books, an affiliate of Dutton Children's Books, a division of Penguin Putnam Inc.

From "The First Flights," excerpt adapted from pages 13–16 (under title "The First Flight") in *Hot Air Ballooning*, by Charles Coombs. Copyright © 1981 by Charles Coombs. Reprinted by permission of HarperCollins Publishers.

"The Fuller Brush Man" by Gloria D. Miklowitz, from *Visions*, by Donald R. Gallo, Editor. Copyright © 1987 by Gloria D. Miklowitz. Reprinted by permission of Dell Publishing, a division of Random House, Inc.

From *Halmoni and the Picnic*, by Sook Nyul Choi, illustrated by Karen M. Dugan. Copyright © 1993 by Sook Nyul Choi. Reprinted by permission of Houghton Mifflin Company. All rights reserved.

From *If You Give a Moose a Muffin*, by Laura Joffe Numeroff. Copyright © 1991 by Laura Numeroff. Reprinted by permission of HarperCollins Publishers.

From *Long Claws*, by James Houston. Copyright © 1981 by James Houston. Reprinted by permission of the author and Margaret K. McElderry Books, an imprint of Simon & Schuster Children's Publishing Division.

From *Me, Mop and the Moondance Kid*, by Walter Dean Myers. Copyright © 1988 by Walter Dean Myers. Reprinted by permission of Random House Children's Books, a division of Random House, Inc.

From *No One Should Have Six Cats!*, by Susan Mathias Smith. Copyright © 1982 by Susan Mathias Smith. Published by Follett Publishing Company, an imprint of Modern Curriculum Press, Pearson Learning. Reprinted by permission.

From *The Pinballs*, by Betsy Byars. Copyright © 1977 by Betsy Byars. Reprinted by permission of HarperCollins Publishers.

From *Pompeii . . . Buried Alive!*, by Edith Kunhardt. Copyright © 1987 by Edith Kunhardt. Reprinted by permission of Random House Children's Books, a division of Random House, Inc.

From *Ronald Morgan Goes to Bat*, by Patricia Reilly Giff, illustrated by Susan Natti. Copyright © 1988 by Patricia Reilly Giff. Reprinted by permission of Viking Penguin, a division of Penguin Putnam Inc.

From *Sarah Bishop*, by Scott O'Dell. Copyright © 1980 by Scott O'Dell. Reprinted by permission of Houghton Mifflin Company.

From *Tales Mummies Tell*, by Patricia Lauber. Copyright © 1985 by Patricia G. Lauber. Reprinted by permission of HarperCollins Publishers.

From *The Titanic: Lost and Found*, by Judy Donnelly. Copyright © 1987 by Judy Donnelly Gross. Reprinted by permission of Random House Children's Books, a division of Random House, Inc.

From *To Space and Back*, by Sally Ride and Susan Okie. Copyright © 1986 by Sally Ride and Susan Okie. Reprinted by permission of HarperCollins Publishers.

From *Wolf Pack*, by Sylvia Johnson and Alice Aamodt. Copyright © 1985 by Lerner Publications, Minneapolis, MN. Reprinted by permission of the publisher.

From *Wolves*, by Seymour Simon. Copyright © 1993 by Seymour Simon. Reprinted by permission of HarperCollins Publishers.

Houghton Mifflin Phonics/Decoding Screening Test is based on the "CORE Phonics Survey" pages 63–80 from CORE Assessing Reading: Multiple Measures for Kindergarten Through Eighth Grade, Arena Press, Novato, CA. Copyright © 1999 by Consortium On Reading Excellence, Inc. Reprinted by permission of Consortium On Reading Excellence, Inc.